WHITE ROAD

WHITE ROAD

A Russian Odyssey
1919 – 1923

OLGA ILYIN

A William Abrahams Book

HOLT, RINEHART AND WINSTON

New York

Published by Holt, Rinehart and Winston,
383 Madison Avenue, New York, New York 10017.
Published simultaneously in Canada by Holt, Rinehart and
Winston of Canada, Limited.

Library of Congress Cataloging in Publication Data
Ilyin, Olga.
White road.
1. Ilyin, Olga—Biography.   2. Soviet Union—
History—Revolution, 1917–1921—Personal narratives.
3. Authors, American—20th century—Biography.
I. Title.
PS3559.L9Z476 1984   813'.54 [B]   83-26692
ISBN: 0-03-000078-5

First Edition

Designer: Joy Taylor

Printed in the United States of America
1 3 5 7 9 10 8 6 4 2

ISBN 0-03-000078-5

To my husband and brothers,
and to all those who fought this losing but noble battle.

The two domains of darkness and of light
We equally must search into and fathom.

—*Eugene Baratynski*
1800—1844

AUTHOR'S NOTE

The persons, places, and events are true.
Certain names have been changed as a form
of protective disguise.

INTRODUCTION

WHEN MY FATHER first saw my mother at a formal St. Petersburg function in 1889 he said to himself that if she were as beautiful within as she was without, he would propose to her.

The following week fate conveniently arranged a second meeting at an informal evening tea dedicated to readings, some with piano accompaniments (this was called "melodeclamation"), by several young, unknown poets. One of these young poets was my father, Alexander Ogarin, as I chose to call him in my autobiographical novel, *Dawn of the Eighth Day*. To my father's happy astonishment, the lady poet of the group turned out to be Nadejda Shilov (whose last name I also changed), the very one with whom he was smitten. That evening he felt he was brilliant. As a matter of fact, he even provided his own piano accompaniment to the "melodeclamation."

I have no idea what poems were read or what subtleties were exchanged that evening, but they must have been effective, for the couple was engaged the following spring, soon after my father was graduated from Pravovedinie, the prestigious law school that was supposed to produce future diplomats. When he received his first position of Junior Court Assistant they were married.

My father had indeed found an extraordinarily beautiful woman with great sensitivity and inner depth. She, on the other hand, had escaped from a life of rigid court elegance that she had for a time liked and admired, but that had begun to stifle her. A poetess and a gifted painter, she needed the intellectual and artistic stimulation that she found in my father and his family, and in their country estate called Sinniy Bor.

My father was not planning a diplomatic career. What interested him were the reforms being carried out under the Zemstvo system. First introduced by Alexander II after the abolition of serfdom, this system strove, sometimes haltingly but with increasing success after 1905, to raise the educational and economic level of the peasantry.

For some Americans it has become customary to regard the social and economic contrasts of pre-revolutionary Russia as very nearly medieval, and to think of the Russian upper classes as being thoroughly blind to the plight of those below. The Revolution has put history's permanent seal on the fact that, at the beginning of World War I, the divisions in Russian society were very great. But these divisions were certainly no more startling than the ones that exist today in New York between Park Avenue and Harlem, or in San Francisco between Pacific Heights and Hunter's Point. As a matter of fact we, the younger generation, grew up in an atmosphere of constant idealistic work carried on all around us. New schools were going up, "peasant banks" and medical centers were opening.

Not all Russian aristocrats counseled their less fortunate countrymen to eat cake. There were undoubtedly many educated and economically comfortable people whose hands fell, as the Russian phrase goes, at the prospect of delving into a multitude of inherited problems. But there also were those who worked on these problems as best they could, and a few who devoted their lives to their resolution.

I certainly cannot claim to have been headed in this direction when I was very young. I was far too much engrossed in writing poetry and playing the piano. But I am very proud that my father and my whole family were some of those who worked, very much "within the system," but with great devotion and effectiveness, for social justice.

In my father's case the direct way to achieve this was to follow in the footsteps of his own father, who was "marshal of nobility" of the province of Tamborsk. This was an unpaid office that supervised and directed the various functions of the administration, urban and rural, with emphasis on the work of the Zemstvo. The office came to him earlier than he would have liked—he was still in his twenties when my grandfather died and he was immediately elected to take his place.

Since all his summers and times away from Petersburg had been spent in the family estate of Sinniy Bor, he had enough preparation for working with and for the peasants. He knew their chief needs and weaknesses; he also had the gift of entering into close contact with people, whoever they were. The villagers of Sinniy Bor constantly came to him for advice and help. In recognition of his dynamic concern for them, they even often invited him to take part in their business meetings (*skhody*).

Sinniy Bor was the favorite estate of the Ogarins, picturesque, unpretentious, located near the Volga, a beautiful two-hour troika drive from Tamborsk, and my mother immediately fell in love with it, with her new in-laws, with their enthusiasm for life, for poetry, for searching thought—also with the way they combined the ancestral traditions of hospitality and sociability and intense work.

She loved their stimulating friends. Regularly every summer, relatives and friends came for long visits to Sinniy Bor, some from Petersburg and Moscow, others from Rome and Vienna. Two guest houses had to be built in addition to the main house. ("Coming to Sinniy Bor for a refueling of the soul," one of them wrote in announcing his impending visit.) They came for intellectual stimulation, for rest, for long heart-to-heart talks, as much as for sheer summer pleasure. In its rather unassuming way, Sinniy Bor had everything: good riding horses, a river for swimming, marshes for duck hunting, croquet grounds, a tennis court, and even a soccer field. In the park, there was an old theater badly in need of restoration, where at least one gala play was produced each summer, directed by my father. The rehearsals alone were a thrill, the flirtations that developed around them, sheer delight. The theater also housed concerts of a peasant choir trained by my father's sister Katya, my favorite aunt. There were picnics in the forest, long walks on moonlit nights, rather complex philosophical games in the evening (at times these games wound up in tempestuous discussions that filled the house with belligerent voices; unfailingly, however, these arguments ended in laughter, embraces, and expressions of mutual admiration).

Beauty without, beauty within. I always felt that it was my family's faith in that *within*—in the divine spark in man, in some sacred meaning of life—that was the main thing pulling people to Sinniy Bor and binding them together. And it was this faith that helped my father struggle out from under the ruins of his life when my mother died suddenly of scarlet fever. He was only thirty-six.

He wanted to leave life behind, to enter a monastery, to go away somewhere forever, to die, to find any sort of oblivion. But once I heard him say, "Oblivion is a lie, a quitter's lie; and I am no quitter."

It was, then, his devotion to some sort of mysterious truth that made him survive and made the lives of us children, once we had passed this terrible crisis, unshadowed and full.

The genes of my Ogarin ancestors had combined to make me write poetry from the age of five. I shall be immodest enough to say that it was a considerable gift and my career in it was actually beginning to take shape when, still in my teens, war and revolution overtook me.

This gift should not have been lost. It should have survived all that I experienced. Even in exile I should have written poetry and published it in émigré magazines. But somehow, somewhere on that long White

Road that led me away from home I became not a poet, but a memoirist. Why? Because the memory of that life in Sinniy Bor was such a bright treasure. Because it had to be carried with me and preserved for my children. Also for all the wonderful friends whom I came to love together with this country, in the second long installment of my life.

So (while living through illnesses, depression, and the conduct of a dress-designing business in San Francisco) I became a memoirist, in English. What I have been recounting was the subject of my first family chronicle, *Dawn of the Eighth Day*. Rather than ask new readers to go in search of it—it was published in 1951 and has been out of print for several years—I shall summarize the historical events and personal experiences that constituted the last part of that book and that brought me to the night late in 1919, when *White Road* begins.

THE FIRST WORLD WAR started in Russia in August 1914 and ended in the March 1917 Revolution. This so-called Bloodless Revolution from the Top uncovered the staggering unpreparedness of the liberal humanitarians, mostly members of the Duma, who had engineered the coup and taken over the government. The well-meaning, democratically minded Provisional Government, which we all tried to support against the Communist Party, had tied its own hands by promises of nonviolence and found itself unable to enforce its own decrees and orders. The structure of a thousand-year-old empire swayed and crumbled under the onslaught of the Bolsheviks and their terrorist tactics. We, the intelligentsia, tried desperately and futilely to catch the shattered pieces and fit them into place, but then the bloody Red October Revolution fell upon us with its enslavement, fear, and general starvation.

In answer to Bolshevik terrorist actions, underground anti-Red groups began to form that winter, most of them headed by the military. One of them was an officers' organization in our native city. Igor Volotskoy, a cavalry lieutenant, whom I married in 1917, had been active in this underground, and thus I also became involved in clandestine activities. What a relief it was finally to be doing something constructive, preparing to fight back instead of folding up like a blunt penknife. I was acting as courier for Igor and as lookout when members of the group came to see him; I helped him to bury his weapons, which everyone had been ordered to surrender under threat of death. Yet I was still kept from any knowledge of the nature of the organization; only later did I learn that this underground was in touch with an anti-Communist movement in Southern Russia. I knew nothing about cossack colonel Ataman Semenov, who, with the help of Japan, later became a self-styled warlord in the Baikal region, and who, with seven or eight other officers, had overthrown the Communists in Eastern Siberia.

Meantime, in September 1917, the Czech Legions (a division of our former prisoners of war, who had come over to the Russian side in 1916 and fought with us against Germany) had also rebelled against the Soviets. According to their agreement with our former government, they were already halfway on their around-the-world journey to the French front through Siberia, their trains stretching at intervals from Central Russia to Vladivostok, when the Soviets attempted to block their way and disarm them. Fighting started right there aboard those trains and spread like wildfire along the railroad. The rear Czech trains were still west of the Volga River, and our underground kept close watch on their whereabouts.

As the distant rumbling of their guns became audible in Tamborsk, Igor and his group of officers went to join the advancing Russian detachment of one of our young war heroes, Colonel Kappel. For another couple of days we listened to their bombardment getting closer and closer; we watched the city empty of Red officials; and, one brilliant July morning, insane with joy, we met our men victoriously entering the city. Crowds of people, consumed by the craving to hold our city against the Reds, were stampeding to the Tamborsk Kremlin to join the newborn volunteer army. (Tamborsk was especially needed by the Reds, for the Eastern powder magazines and the gold reserves that had been evacuated from Moscow were both here.)

Every man and woman fought and worked frenziedly, sleeplessly. Many of my friends, young girls, were with the fighting units. I helped wherever I could, but I was expecting momentarily the birth of my first child. My father had tried to join the army, but at his age (he was fifty then) it embarrassed the younger people to have him under their command, and he was appointed head of the Department of Supplies.

Long funeral processions, some thirty or more coffins in a row, crept daily across town to the somber rhythm of Chopin's Funeral March. The Red bombardment was coming closer every day, planes starting fires all over the city. My son was only nine days old when the death blow came: Tamborsk had to be abandoned. Its surrender should have been expected sooner, yet it came suddenly. The havoc of our retreat began.

It was September, the time of rains and autumn night frosts. Our volunteer units in their tattered summer cotton khakis and worn-out boots, short of ammunition, penniless—Igor and my brothers, Dimitri and eighteen-year-old Alik, among them—were pushing eastward fighting off the Reds who were trying to close in on them from all sides. A great part of the population came snowballing after them down the only route that was still open. It led to Siberia. Siberia, as we learned, had by that time entirely freed itself from the Reds in a series of local uprisings.

I had not wanted to flee. I had wanted to remain with my father, who was staying at Tamborsk to face certain death. To leave him behind was as impossible for me as for him to leave his dying mother, his sister, and my brother Dimitri's wife, Sonya, with her babies. Should my father leave, the blow that would inevitably have fallen upon him as one of the most prominent men of the community would instead fall upon the women of the family. I had to stay with him. But Igor had seen my name on a list, together with that of my father, of people wanted by the Reds for execution. When orders came for our units to pull back—and these came suddenly in the middle of the night—Igor galloped from the front line (already on the outskirts of the city), saying that if I stayed behind, he would stay with me. I yielded. He put me on a peasant cart, and I was carried away by the tide of refugees who fled with our retreating army.

First the peasant cart, next a wagon for the wounded, then a Volga steamer, and finally a cattle car. In Siberia our volunteer units would reman, reorganize, and, with the help of our allies, rearm, and then attack the enemy with full force. Such were our hopes.

After we settled in Western Siberia, by some miracle these hopes began to materialize. A strange assortment of anti-Communist factions had assembled there. Each had done its share of heroic fighting, yet the only bond between them was their frenzied hatred of Bolshevism. They differed in everything else.

But then came November—sunny, windless, sparkling with abundant snow, a time for new hopes, new beginnings. The confusion, the struggle for power between the different anti-Communist elements came to an end. For some time our allies had been desperate to reopen an Eastern front against Germany. With their discreet assistance, clumsy at times, but welcome and necessary, the young White movement entered a new phase ("Whites" was what the Reds had nicknamed us). On November 16, 1918, Admiral Kolchak, one of our national war heroes, ex—commander in chief of the Black Sea Fleet, was proclaimed Supreme Ruler of the Democratic Siberian Government, with Omsk as our new capital. Admiral Kolchak became a symbol of our movement, the eye of our storm.

"I shall follow neither the road of reaction, nor that of partisanship . . . my objective is the creation of a powerful army and victory over the Bolsheviks . . . so that the Russian people may choose the form of government they wish." Such was Kolchak's pledge, around which the dynamics of building this new democratic government and the "Siberian People's Army" went into full swing.

My brother Dimitri had been appointed Chief Engineer of the Votkinsk Division; my brother Alik was undergoing training as a private in the infantry. Igor, with other cavalry officers who had fought at Tamborsk, was reorganizing their detachment into an old-style cavalry regiment—the Tamborsk Dragoons. This was in the Ob River region near Novonikolaevsk, now called Novosibirsk.

Our White offensive started in March 1919, just before the first thaws, and rolled on without stopping through the roadless time of river floods and into spring. By April, when I had moved to Omsk and was working as a translator of French, English, and American newspapers, we had already gone over five hundred versts into Russia proper and were only some eighty versts* from Tamborsk.

Then suddenly our offensive began to slow down. Had we overextended ourselves? Had the Red Army under Trotsky's ruthless grip achieved a force Admiral Kolchak had been unable to match?

Whatever it was, our first reverses started in June, our retreat later in summer. By October we were rolling back, having left behind the chaotic evacuation of Omsk and its fall.

But the fight was not over; there were still 5,000 square miles that we could hold, and would hold, we felt, until our last breath. At this point my story begins.

San Francisco
1984

*1 verst equals 0.663 miles.

PART ONE

Freezing to
the Tracks

1

WINTER WAS CREEPING over November snowdrifts toward Christmas 1919. Heavy storms had already built walls house-high along the Siberian roads, and when a north wind blew, birds froze in their flight. Yet the frosts here in Western Siberia were dry and often windless, the clear days many; at sunrise and sunset such radiance fell upon the endless reaches of steppe that even the scrolls of frost on the windows of our train turned into jewels.

By four o'clock, however, darkness would steal into the cars, rapidly gathering in the crowded compartments, thus cutting drastically into our supply of kerosene and candles. I have never forgotten one such late afternoon when Countess Cygnen came out into the corridor, her smoke-gray pompadour thrust high, to declare to me and my cousin Polya Kasimov that we had procrastinated long enough. Waning daylight fell on one side of Countess Cygnen's face, bringing into relief the chalky skin that fitted her strong bone structure like a wrinkled linen slipcover. Against the threadbare black velvet of her gown, the string of pearls on her bosom (her prospective fare to Europe) gleamed a creamy white.

"We must start the Christmas decorations at once!" she said.

The incongruity of this statement in our circumstances was like a photographic flash that drew out of confusion and held in its light all that belonged to the moment: the murky stretch of the car's corridor behind Countess Cygnen's imposing figure; the broad square of our wagon-lit window; beyond this window the shadowy lavender of snow that swept toward the horizon to drain the last flush of sunset; the immense emptiness of the steppe, in the middle of which our crowded Red Cross train had been stalled for over a week. We were ignorant of what was happening anywhere in the world outside of this train's narrow tube, except for the fact that the Reds were already on our heels.

We were standing in front of our adjoining compartments: Countess Cygnen, mother-in-law of the chief of the Siberian army Red Cross; my cousin Polya, the chief's administrative assistant and head nurse of the train, thin and delicate in her nurse's uniform; and I, with my fifteen-month-old baby, Bibik, simply a friend whom they had squeezed into this crowded Red Cross personnel car on the very last day before the surrender of the city of Omsk—Omsk, so recently the capital and stronghold of our "White" Siberian government, but now Red-occupied, a dark wound from which we averted our eyes.

At the start of the evacuation, the wife of a staff general of the Siberian army, a pretty redhead, a poetess of sorts, had promised me a small compartment in her husband's private car. However, when I arrived at the station on the eve of our scheduled departure, when the Reds were already at the outskirts of the city, I found the train overcrowded and my compartment occupied by some wounded young officers.

"You understand how terrible I feel," the red-headed poetess had said tearfully, "but leaving these officers behind means certain death for them, while women with children still have a chance."

I understood. I also knew that something else would come to my aid. It had been my repeated experience that when you said to life calmly and firmly (but very firmly!), "I trust you, do what you must," life had an uncanny way of responding to your need. And indeed, that same week this very Red Cross train had pulled into Omsk, and my cousin Polya had found me and shared her compartment with me, my baby, and our family *bonna*, Panna Krylocka.

Polya, now on the way to make the rounds of her patients, slipped into a rough army-issue coat while I stood by, holding my child on my left and making futile movements with my right arm to indicate my eagerness to help her. "When you are in no position to assist someone, to open a door or pick up something another has dropped, at least shuffle your feet," our elders used to admonish us.

This was the pre-twilight hour, my favorite time of day, when I always came out in the corridor to watch the swiftly changing colors of the landscape. If there was not enough coal for our train to move on, there evidently was enough left to heat the cars. It was the hour when the radiators began to hiss, when we knew we would really be warm for a short time, and when the pressure of all that had happened to us in the last two years and all that was still to happen would magically recede. There were even moments when the serenity of the dying day outside would transmute the hopelessness of our predicament into daydreams about all that was no longer possible.

And yet, how much was still possible! Although the First Cavalry was probably now covering our retreat, I hoped that when the army took its next stand, Igor and I would meet again. When I had seen him off to the front six weeks ago in the fierce October wind of the Omsk station he had said, "Now that I know you are leaving soon with the General Staff train, my mind is at rest. The farther east they evacuate you, the safer it will be." He had stood there in that relaxed cavalry slouch of his, one hand tucked into his revolver belt, his stance more or less offsetting the anxiety I sensed in him. "Just be sure," he had said with a forceful warmth that turned his light brown eyes into luminous amber, "just be sure that if I'm alive and whole, I shall find you, wherever you are." I knew that he would; he always had.

Unfortunately, I hadn't gone with that other train. Instead, here we were cut off from everything, only a few hundred versts east of Omsk, with the Reds apparently at our backs.

A clinking of utensils came from the car's kitchen, a murmur of voices from behind the doors of different compartments crowded with the families of the medical personnel. From the "salon," the office and family domain of the chief of the army Red Cross, Yuri Molsov, there often burst the outcries of his three children, engaged in their perpetual card game, referred to by their grandmother, Countess Cygnen, as "*Pique Dame*," by them as "Drunks."

"It is evident now," she was saying, "that at the rate we are moving, we can't get to Vladivostok before Christmas, not even to Lake Baikal, let alone the United States. So we might as well reconcile ourselves to having our Christmas tree right here, on the train." This last pronouncement she made in the same lofty tone in which, during her morning sessions with her grandchildren, she told them inspiring stories about the heroic deeds of great men. "We simply must give the children something to do. They are turning into little savages!" At this she opened her pale eyes wide, which she always did when she wished to fix some important point in your mind and did not trust your ability to perceive all its implications.

Did we younger women realize, her sharp stare was asking, how great was her responsibility to her poor sick daughter who was wasting away in a Swiss sanitarium, agonizing over the fate of her husband and children, who were by now God alone knew where, God alone knew whether alive or not?

I felt I must quickly say something. "One thing is certain, there'll be no shortage of Christmas trees in the taiga [Siberian forest] when we get into it."

Preparing to go, Polya had slipped a woolen scarf over her white nurse's coif and was tucking in wisps of her prematurely silver hair.

"Should we ever get that far," she said lightly, as if blowing away a bit of fluff, and, taking Bibik's hand, she gave it a few little comical good-bye shakes.

The bit of fluff floated, just as intended, past Countess Cygnen. Her son-in-law Yuri Molsov, "The Chief," as we called him behind his back, assured us that there was nothing to worry about. It was just a matter of getting some coal for the train. The city of Novonikolaevsk, where most of our retreating army was concentrating, was only eighty versts away, a two-hour rail journey. This was not the first time we had been stalled, and he had always managed to get us moving. Countess Cygnen's confidence in her adored Yuri was complete. Besides, people whose sight is adjusted to the scanning of broad horizons often become blind to what is right in front of them. I myself was one of these.

THE NEXT NIGHT when the Chief urgently left by sleigh for the flag station close by to get in touch with the Red Cross headquarters at Novonikolaevsk, the Countess seized on the opportunity. Right after supper, while he was away, we would all assemble in the "salon," she declared, and use his desk to make paper chains. She would supply us with gold paper and glue and read aloud to us from Pushkin's fairy tales. How she managed to stock up on such unprocurables, a volume of Pushkin especially, was incomprehensible.

"We owe this to the children, and it would mean a great deal to have you with us, Nita," she said, addressing me with the nickname used by family and friends.

I was looking forward to joining them. I was happy to find myself among old family friends, after a whole year spent with Panna in the town of Kurgan, and later in Omsk, at the homes of Siberian peasant-merchants with whom the army had quartered us. I could not miss this reading session. But I also intended to have a walk along the ties that night, by myself. Ever since the train had stalled I had wanted to take this walk, but something always interfered.

I longed to be alone. During the fifteen months since our uprising on the Volga, a year of heroic fighting and its outcome—our catastrophic retreat to Siberia—we had lived piled on top of each other, crowded always and everywhere; in houses, in the streets, at work. I had to have a few minutes of solitude to unravel the tangled threads of my life and bring them into some sensible pattern. "See here," I was going to say to myself, "today, as any day now, may easily be your last. Does this mean anything to you? Are you ready?"

I was sitting on Cousin Polya's berth. Neither she nor the woman doctor in the berth above was ever there. I had just finished changing the baby for the night, now kissed him and rose to go. "Do you mind if I take a short walk, Panna?" I asked, my voice apologetically groping in the inscrutable depths of Panna Krylocka's psychology.

All that Panna had been waiting for was to take Bibik from me. The chores of the day were done, and had they not been, they would eventually be done by her, not by me, something she knew too well.

She sat there on the opposite berth, folding the baby's clean clothes, which she washed daily in melted snow. A makeshift lamp, wick floating in oil, set in an inactive electric bracket on the wall, scooped her face out of the shadow. It highlighted the narrow strip of her forehead from which the dark hair was brushed into a bun on top of her head, flickered on the chain of safety pins that dangled down the front of her blouse. It was the same familiar stepladder of pins, only shorter now, that in our former life at home used to outrage my aesthetic sense, but the sight of which threw me into ecstasy when, in the course of my flight, cut off from all my family, I unexpectedly ran into her in a crowd of refugees. Panna, alone and lost just as I was! We fell into each other's arms then, our hearts brimming over with love.

Now, without looking at me, she reached for Bibik, stood him on her lap, said, "Whoops!" and tossed him high in the air. He gave a shriek of delight and she pressed him to herself, her eyes melting in bliss.

"I say, Panna . . . the Chief is away, the train can't start unannounced as it did last time, so . . ."

"Walk all you want, who's stopping you?" she suddenly boomed in the deep voice she used when she no longer could stand me. Then, switching to a playful singsong, as though speaking on Bibik's part, "Go wherever you wish, Mama, walk as long as you please. We'll get along fine without you."

I might have learned by this time that the vagueness by which I meant to indicate the fluidity of my plans, my readiness to change them if she so wished, was a strong irritant to her forceful, direct nature. However, now that my politeness had been rudely rejected, I was back on firm ground.

I slipped into my coat, torn beyond repair. The caracal fur and the lining showed strips of white wadding inside; to mend it no longer seemed worth the effort. My gloves, huge white canvas gloves with blue wristlets, distributed by the American Red Cross, their tremendous size a puzzle to us all, stuck out of the pocket. They served to cover a roll of Siberian money that lay beneath, "Kolchak" money. Igor, my husband, who, as most officers of the White army, had not been getting any salary for months, had suddenly received some in September and sent it to me from the front. This was the last time I had heard from him: September. "Spend it all quickly, Nita. Buy all you need for the winter," he had scribbled in a note. He was really saying, "It will be worthless soon." But you could still purchase all kinds of delicious food with it at the stations: fish or meat pies, *pelmeny*, which the Siberians froze in winter by the thousands; roast partridge, grouse, creamy bricks of frozen butter, and huge white cubes of frozen milk.

These stations presented a typical Siberian picture: peasant women in great, swaggering coats of Samoyed-dog fur, holding earthenware bowls wrapped in snow-white homespun towels. Their square, strong-boned faces were encircled in the heavy halo of tremendous upturned collars; their hard, incurious eyes peered from under square foreheads. The sturdy richness of their country was in the firm, satisfied fold of their lips; the impenetrable thicket of their forests stared from the stubborn opaqueness of their eyes. In the distance stood their tethered teams of broad, carpeted sleighs, small horses, hardy and vigorous as themselves; behind them the yellow station buildings, and farther behind the un-broken expanses of snowy steppe.

As I pulled my woolen beret over my ears, the vision of these stations loomed before me as something never to be reached again. We had left the last one a week ago, and it was probably cut off by the Reds by now.

I slid my door open a crack and peered into the semidark corridor to make certain that there was no one there to stop me from going out. It was empty.

THE FROSTY AIR hit my face, ran a pure icy trail up my nostrils, and flooded my lungs. The snow on the steps was a frozen bulge, and I caught hold of the railing; the cold touch of steel through the canvas glove burned my hand.

Before me, enormous and dark, lay the silence of the Siberian steppe. The sky hung low; no moon, no stars. And no wind. Just below the railroad grade there ran a sleigh track; alongside it a line of reed tops rising from a gully showed a ghostly gray above the snow. There was no other sound in the immeasurable quiet, only their dry, half-audible rustling.

Our car was one of the last ones in the train. I walked briskly to the rear, to have a glimpse of what was behind us.

Earth and sky merged into one limitless gray. Only in one spot to the west, the horizon was marked by a dark stubble of forest. We had crossed through it just before our train ran out of fuel. I knew that the Reds could be in this forest by now; that it was infested by Red partisans; that Igor with his regiment and my brother Dimitri with his artillery unit might be there in this forest, covering the retreat. But of this I did not dare to think.

I walked swiftly in the direction of the engine, my footfalls printing a clear crunch-crunch on the snowy path worn hard during the time we had stood here. The train was long. The windows were frosted almost to the middle, the light inside dim, but in one of them, above the semicircle of hoarfrost, loomed the bearded face of a soldier with a bandaged head. In another window was the profile of a young nurse in white headdress, her face raised toward a patient in the upper bunk, her chin and nostril lit by the candle she held. From one of the cars came the thudding of horses' hooves and the smell of manure; the next one was an open platform laden with sleighs stacked one over the other, their shafts stretching skyward like frozen arms. Every train had stocked up on horses and sleighs against an emergency.

"Siberia, I'm in the middle of Siberia," I told myself.

I had already spent over a year there, but it seemed to me that I had never until now been left face to face with it. It had been dimmed by my own personal Siberia, by all that had brought me here; by the failure of the anti-Red uprising in our native city, Tamborsk, that one September night had torn me so suddenly from the luminous circle of my home—torn me from my father, who had stayed behind to face certain death. And I had left him! Forced to, indeed; but still I had left him.

With crowds of other refugees I had been dragged across thousands of miles in the wake of our retreating insurrectional units. Now over some dirt road, lying supine in a peasant cart, holding on hard to my newborn baby in his quilted taffeta blanket; now in a wagon for the wounded, a bleeding teenager volunteer thrown across my knees; now sprawling on the floor of some rickety, bullet-riddled steamer down the Volga; now attacked by lice in an army train car. And thus until one dark October morning, when I found myself no longer going anywhere but sitting on the boarded floor of the fish dealer Ivanov's empty attic in the provincial town of Kurgan, penniless, all but baggageless, and very ill. Igor and both my brothers were somewhere behind us with our volunteer forces, the "White Guard," and there was no communication with them as yet.

A benumbed mind, bungled chores, clashes with Panna were my Siberia. The devastating needlessness of all I could do and be, my utter practical ineptness ("Yes, Panna, don't worry, I'll salt the soup. How much salt should I put in? A cupful?" And Panna's outraged response) became the substance of this new incarnation of mine.

Instead of the stimulating, gifted people in my family with whom I had always identified myself in serene ignorance of what I really amounted to without them, I was confronted with our bearded landlord and his square-jawed wife.

Yet all of this had only been a blurred background for the nights when, awakened by my baby, I would haul my aching body upright from the heap of straw on which I slept and grope my way toward him in darkness (no matches, no candles, everything used for our military units; no electricity in the attic). It was then that the vision of my father facing the firing squad would erupt from its daytime hiding place and turn me cold.

Soon, however, the shape of things changed. Our volunteer units had begun to retrain, to reorganize, filling with local volunteers. Daily through my attic window, with Bibik in my arms, I had watched them drill, marching over the first brilliant October snow, a Siberian song coming muffled but vigorous through the double panes:

> The stretcher, stretcher's not a plain one,
> Of muskets, muskets it is made.
> And all across the muskets
> Our sabers have been laid.

The cheerful, decisive rhythm to which the soldiers' felt boots trampled the snow, and its sharp contrast to the mournful, minor-key melody, echoed both the wild hopes and the anguish within us all.

Hazily I knew from my Tamborsk refugee friends, who were more free than I, entangled as I was with the baby, to communicate with the world outside, that a furious struggle had been going on between the different anti-Communist factions that had assembled in Siberia: Socialists, monarchists, the military, the Czechs, the Siberian separatists. Thus it was until mid-November, when a new Democratic Siberian Government was formed, headed by a man with a heroic war record and a blameless reputation, Admiral Alexander Kolchak. Spirits rose. A new era began.

A few sporadic successes on the front, and then, by early spring, our explosive all-out offensive.

By that time Siberia as such had simply ceased to exist for me: it had turned into a base of support for our hopes of stopping the Reds, of returning home. Home! February . . . March . . . one major city after another taken back. In April our army was deep into European Russia. The enormous burst of energy, the pride of our victories had magically washed away all our political differences, all the factional bickerings. By Easter we had been approaching Tamborsk. My dreams, against all reason, of soon going home and finding everyone there alive and safe, had turned this land of exile into a staging area for our final jump to Moscow.

If the offensive had slightly slowed down in May, this was of course to be expected in war. Meanwhile, we were still in high key. By June, however, all those dreams had been shattered for me by a new blow: my younger brother Alik was mortally wounded on the battlefield and officially pronounced dead.

I WAS NEARING the engine when the cab door creaked and the stodgy shape of a man lumbered down the steps. Another man, slender and nimble, with loosely dangling earflaps, jumped down after him, swinging a lantern and saying something in a jolly young voice. Then he squatted on the snow, holding the light for the older man, who had crawled under the car and was crouching by the wheels.

It seemed rude to pass by without saying a word, so I asked, "Well, how goes everything? Freezing to the tracks, aren't we?"

The younger one wagged his head and the earflaps swung like dog's ears. "Sure are. Looks like we're about to kiss the Red cheek."

"Do you think they are near?"

"How can you tell? No more communication with the station." And he jerked his head backward.

"There is that station ahead. Can't they provide some fuel for us?"

The young man wiped his nose with the back of his sleeve. "Where are they going to get the fuel from? You can't supply them *all* with fuel, can you?" He waved toward the east.

"And who is supposed to get you this fuel?" the older man growled, thrusting his face out from between the wheels. "Why should the railroad people get any fuel for you, if all they want is to let the Reds through? D'ya know how many trains they have already derailed and wrecked?"

The railroad people, whatever they might say to us Whites, were Red sympathizers. No doubt these men were too. "Well, let them, let the Reds through," I said defiantly. "When they kiss the Red cheek, as you say, they'll find out what is what. But it will be too late."

The gloomy one had just reappeared from under the car, snow on his kneecaps and sleeves. "Why d'ya talk like this to us, lady? To me and this fellow?" he barked out.

I said aggressively, "I'm saying this because so many people have no idea of what it is to be under the Reds."

"So tell it to them," he growled, "not to us, Izhevsk men."

Suddenly taken aback, feeling as when in darkness one searches the ascending stairs only to find them plunging downward, I muttered something about being sorry. "I had no idea you were Izhevsk men! Everyone knows . . . my older brother has been working closely with your division and he said that if everyone else were like you people . . ."

These divisions of the Izhevsk and Votkinsk munition plants were two of the best, most honored White units, and the Communists' direst enemies: simple factory hands who had risen against the Reds on their own, fought savagely, and would never give up the fight.

"Yes, if-if-if . . . ," the jolly one said and wagged his head in clownish dejection.

THE FOOTPATH ENDED by the engine door, and I was going to skirt the engine and then walk straight along the ties. There I would be really alone. But when, having twice sunk knee-deep into a snowdrift, I finally came out on the tracks, I stopped there stunned.

I don't know why I was taken so unawares by what I saw. I should have known. Hadn't I heard people talk about it, and hadn't the young fellow with whom I had just spoken said, "You can't supply them *all* with fuel?" How on earth had I managed not to grasp his meaning?

Now the horizon was open before me on all sides. Here the steppe, a dim gray, slightly lighter than the sky, sloped upward, and upon it, like an enormous black snake cut into disjointed pieces, lay a winding line of standing trains, stretching for versts into the darkness. Their windows blinked a feeble yellow; their taillights glowed like tiny, red-hot eyes. The total immobility of these trains locked in an ocean of snow, with their cargo of agonized human beings, kept me standing there spellbound, staring. Occasionally a muffled, drawn-out whistle, like the howl of a trapped animal, erupted from one of the engines and helplessly died in the void.

We needed fuel for some eighty versts only, they said, but all those eighty versts must be blocked by trains frozen to the tracks.

2

I HAD SAID to myself as I walked along the ties, "Don't think of Igor, not about him; you can't afford to." And something in me had obeyed this command, at least for the duration of the walk. But later that night, when I returned to my compartment after the Christmas decorating, nothing remained of my detached mood of an hour before.

"Torn into shreds . . . will be torn into shreds . . . ," I thought as I walked down the dimly lit corridor. Oh, this was nothing new; everything had already been torn to shreds—Russia, our lives—but while there was hope of seeing Igor, these shreds could still be held together. Not without him. Here it was November 25, and not a word from him or about him for over six weeks.

Our oil lamp flickered as I entered the compartment. I slid the door shut and began to take off my felt boots, holding on to the edge of the doctor's berth. She was not there yet, nor was Polya, who always worked late into the night. Polya's nightgown of frayed Chinese silk lay folded with geometrical precision at the head of her bunk, the old morocco *nécessaire* beside it.

Panna was breathing heavily—an audible reminder of what, years ago, our family doctor had described as a heart condition. Trying not to wake her, I climbed onto the upper shelf and began to take the pins out of my hair, inwardly repeating the same words, "will be torn, torn, torn into shreds," as if feeding them to some monster within me which must be diverted from gnawing at my heart.

I had always felt that there was some greater, higher reason for my comparatively tranquil state of mind than simply mental torpor. Over and over again through these last years, this confidence had proven to be a sort of magnetic center that attracted helpful life forces. They came to my rescue at the most hopeless moments. "Never give way to depression," were the words of my father's last note to me, written in prison when he already knew that they would shoot him that night. "Always rejoice in the ever creative Spirit of life and let it work its miracles."

But, I thought, pulling the rough army blanket up to my chin and turning decisively on my side, whatever awaited me tomorrow should be accepted by me tomorrow, not tonight. If I felt unable to tear my thoughts away from Igor, then I must make myself think only of the best, the happiest moments we had had together, a private device I had evolved in my bouts with depression.

These happiest moments—Igor's rare leaves from the front after our wedding in early June 1917, shortly after the first revolution—were like little islands in a rapidly rising stream on which he and I had stood together, holding tight to each other, jumping from one island to the next while they crumbled away, one by one, behind us.

Our honeymoon at the country estate of Igor's parents, Bezdonniy Kliutch, "Bottomless Spring", would flash before me first. I would summon its early June freshness steeped in the scent of jasmine and acacia trees in full bloom, its sunshine woven through by thousands of twitterings, buzzings, and whirrings. Against the amber greens and jade greens of old trees crowded by the creek and the flickerings of butterflies' wings, I would see Igor.

I saw him now. There he stood, his hands in the pockets of his gold-braided burgundy hussar breeches, slightly slouching as behooved the cavalryman when dismounted, his bronze suntan accentuating his striking coloring: the gloss of his hair so dark that the reflections on it were bluish, the amber of his eyes fringed all around with dark lashes. His lazy and caressing smile lifted the left corner of his mouth and his left eyebrow into a teasing zigzag. "Why did you have to bring Marcus Aurelius with you? To chaperone us?" he asked, reaching for my hand, which held the dull-looking volume, one of the books I had brought to prepare my thesis.

It was early afternoon. We had been walking through the park and had stopped by the bridge over the creek. The clear, low-running stream sparkled and breathed of sun-warmed dampness, and in answer to his words I threw my arms around him, laughing and saying something nonsensical over his shoulder.

"Because," I finally said, "I thought we might have nothing to talk about! Why? Well"—and now I stepped away from him—"What sort of conversation might there be between us, since you've always tried to belittle everything that interested me most?"

"What, for instance?" he asked. "Bach, Nietzsche, Schopenhauer? Why, I even renamed my favorite colt Nietzsche to please you!"

"Yes, I know. And the stablemen already call him 'Nichevo,' and resent it!"

But before we were married he would provoke me by maintaining that horses, sports, and all forms of enjoyment—some quite distasteful to me, such as gambling or drinking—were in no way inferior to music or philosophy. It was just a matter of who enjoyed what. I was aware that he was teasing me, and that since he always read everything he could put his hands on, he must know quite a bit more about Marcus Aurelius or Nietzsche or Schopenhauer than I. I even had good reason to suspect by now that he had consumed not only Marcus Aurelius, but all the half-dozen reference books that I had brought and not even opened. Yet this teasing was annoying to me.

"You have always made a point of emphasizing your own differences from my family and what we stand for," I said.

"But it's you who started that." He slipped his arm around me, and we walked across the sun-baked planks of the bridge. The odor of moist earth and water weeds was delicious. "You worship your family, and this makes me burst with jealousy." He spoke in a slow drawl, especially marked when his speech sprang from that ever-present pool of hidden amusement. "They're all so talented, intellectual, idealistic; where do I come in? I had to present myself as a drastic contrast to them, as a sort of débauché, in order to amount to anything at all in your eyes. And I certainly almost killed myself trying."

It was Igor's gift to ridicule himself with the same ruthless but good-natured insight with which he would ridicule others. "But I can be myself now. You can't get away from me anymore," and he held me tightly.

I could still hear him say it. I could feel his embrace, the strength of his arm through the flimsiness of my marquisette dress. I could still see us approaching the house over the hot reddish sand of the acacia walk, dappled with sun and shadows.

This moment by the creek always came to my mind first, as if it held the essence of our happiness and all its potential. Such also was the evening when we rode on horseback to the village of Tchermy, the estate of a late great-aunt of Igor, close to Bezdonniy. The heirs were living in London. The estate was to be sold, and it occurred to us that we might buy it.

The manor house was a colonnaded Empire building with an endless number of pompous salons, a ballroom, a music room, a library, all badly in need of repair. Igor and I had received a share of our inheritance from our families and we quickly calculated that our money put together would just about cover the cost of the purchase. Never mind the repairs.

This was June 1917. Kerensky was in power. The structure of a tremendous empire was cracking and shuddering under the impact of Communist propaganda. The army was demoralized, the front collapsing, cities seething with Bolshevik demonstrations, and riotous fights breaking out on every corner. There had been many cases of violence out in the country, too, but on the whole the shrewd peasant masses were still lying low, waiting to see who would get the upper hand.

A proclamation requisitioning land from landowners was expected any day. Nevertheless, there were districts in Russia where life had hardly changed. Everything had seemed peaceful in the estates of both our families. The old servants who stayed at Bezdonniy Kliutch all year round, with little to divert them except quarreling, fell upon us as upon a choice entertainment. Farmhands and peasants from the village came to congratulate us; they used the back entrance and as a matter of course expected to be treated by the housekeeper, Marfa, to tea or wine and *pirozhki*, baked daily for just such well-wishers. Once in a while some neighborhood landowners arrived with a ringing of troika bells and with gifts, staying only long enough not to intrude upon our bliss, and avoiding talk of the political situation. All of this had created a sense of security and permanence on the surface of our life.

As to life's inner region: shaken by war and the reality of death, my mind had been permeated by the awareness that there was neither permanence nor security here, on this outer plane anyway, revolution or no revolution. Thus, the realization of the impending disaster did not stand in the way of my desire to acquire this estate any more than it would have in normal circumstances. In fact, in normal circumstances, the foolishness of such an enterprise would have been clearer to us both, while now: "Certainly, let's buy it," Igor said. "What's the difference? If we own it for a short time only, we still will have had something, while having money in the bank that is already losing value, we have nothing."

But of course we could never have bought Tchermy anyway. One had just to imagine my Aunt Katya, who despised any kind of superfluities, let alone luxuries, Aunt Katya who had been constantly tormented by the fact that she owned more than did so many others. She would think: "Now that Nita is married to this handsome, spur-jingling youngster, there is no telling how she may change." Her voice heavy with reproach, she would ask me, "What will your father say to this? Do you realize that he hardly ever spends anything on himself so that he can help the greatest number of people?" And I saw Father, his eyes sending questioning sparks from under a concentrated frown, saw myself immediately throwing my arms around his neck, laughing and saying, "Oh, but, Father, these are foolish daydreams, simply silly talk! If this would worry you, then of course we should never . . . !"

Then Grand-maman Noire, Babushka, directing her ear trumpet toward me, an amused grin puckering her lips. "What's all this I hear? A delusion of grandeur, is it?"

Something similar, but slightly more ponderous would probably have come from Igor's family.

The sun was just setting when we came to Tchermy. Its crimson spears slanted through tall windows into rooms filled with Jacobean and eighteenth-century French furniture, splashing themselves over the intricately designed parquets, the work of the local peasants, famous all over Russia for this (particularly since they had been called upon to make the floors of the Winter Palace). All this magnificence breathed forlornly and yet so hopefully of decaying papers and aging wood. This was the house where Igor's great-grandparents used to entertain in style: where young Count Leo Tolstoy was said to have courted one of the Molsov girls; where the famous mathematician Lobachevsky fell in love with one of the daughters of the house, later to marry her. A group of poets, among them my great-grandfather, used to gather here and read their latest verses. Their spirits were still here, those gifted souls.

The old park—the place for me to think and dream and write! What a background for all those brilliant friends whom we would gather here, people we knew or would know, who had eyes to see and ears to hear all those elusive, nebulous things without which life was a house built on sand.

We ran from room to room, calling to each other from different ends of the house, meeting again and throwing ourselves into each other's arms, arguing about which one of our children would have which room, and whether our boys would have a French or English tutor, or both.

When we were on our way to Bezdonniy, the air was beginning to darken, but a strip of sunset burned in the west. The sky above was that weightless blue, as only in earliest June, the stars in it a moist silver. We rode at a walk along a winding river, the scarlet of sunset burnishing the water. All one could hear in the enormous fragrant stillness was the sound of our horses' hooves stepping over the springy road.

"You know, Igor," I said, turning in my sidesaddle, "when all of this has passed, and if we are still alive, we shall say: even if the life we have been planning never comes to be, still . . ."

"Yes, I know," Igor answered.

"What is it you know?"

"What you were going to say."

"What was I going to say?"

"That we still had it all tonight. Just the same, I would rather it came true."

"So would I! But if it doesn't . . . perhaps even years of a happy life at Tchermy could not give us more than we have had here tonight in these few hours. I have come to my own terms with time, you know. The passage of time used to terrify me so . . . the fact that it folds up like an accordion while death hides behind it. But now I have learned that one can break out of the bounds of time. Oh, yes, I mean it! It *is* possible! So I'm no longer afraid of it at all."

"Nor of death?" There was a mixture of archness and sadness in his voice.

"Nor of death. It will be difficult to tell. But you will understand!"

"You don't need to explain anything." He was no longer arch. "Because if you say it is possible to transcend time and death—isn't this what you were saying?—then I believe you, even if I don't understand how it can be done. I believe you and this is enough for me."

"Igor, but how can you believe without understanding?"

"Because I love you. It is only through love that one understands anything good, don't you think?" He reached for my hand, riding crop and all, and held it to his lips for a long moment.

BACK IN the Red Cross train, I lay there on my bunk looking at the spasmodic flicker of the oil lamp, the car's leatherette ceiling so low over me that I could touch it with my hand; yet Igor was still riding beside me, his silhouette in the saddle dark against the crimson of the horizon.

Only two years ago. And now, this present self of mine was probing into what I had said to him then, asking whether my convictions had stood the test of these two tragic years. Had I really made peace with death? With the horrible death of my father? Of Alik? Of my uncle and cousins? With my own, which was approaching?

But I had! I had! At least this was what I felt so far.

POLYA HAD just entered the compartment. Although she had walked almost noiselessly, Panna must have awakened. I heard her stir and sit up.

"Forgive me, Panna Krylocka, have I disturbed you? Were you resting?" Polya asked in a semiwhisper. Panna lifted her face from the little checkered handbag that contained all her belongings and served as her pillow. "Not at all. I just lay down for a moment to change my position," she replied, a winning smile in her voice.

Panna's relationship with Polya was quite a decorous one. Panna's ancestors, generations of Polish knights and serf owners, used to pomp and circumstance, were strongly represented in Panna and still demanded their due in social graces and amenities. The more so because of the many cruel frustrations Panna had encountered in her young days.

"Did you sleep well, Panna Krylocka?" Polya would usually ask her in the morning, and Panna, who always slept curled up in a knot at the foot of Bibik's berth so as not to deprive him of space, would respond with grave courtesy: "Thank you, I slept very well. And you?"

Polya's clear and delicate manner of speaking, the elegant orderliness in which she kept her berth, the set of silver brushes, the carefully folded Chinese gown, the diamond *chiffre* of a lady-in-waiting that she had managed to save at the time of her flight from Petrograd and carried in her only suitcase—all this evoked in Panna the ancestral castle, the gleaming parquets over which her proud forebears had once glided and curtsied. But the same question from me seemed starkly to reveal to her the disparity between word and fact, and the same ancestors, clad in heavy armor, would ride out at me on snorting chargers. For a decorous relationship is based on mutual independence, on a freedom from one another. This freedom Panna and I did not have.

We were tied together by everything—by the past and now even by such future as there was. Our ties went back eighteen years to the day when Panna had first appeared in our house, with this very same checkered handbag in her hands and with the reticent smile of a newly engaged governess who enters a close-knit, noisy family. The grip of these ties became stronger in the lee of the passionate devotion Panna developed for my parents and for my brother Alik. It was Alik, still a baby then, who became her god. And when a year ago she and I, each of us cast out alone upon Siberia, had by chance run into each other in Ufa, and when with luminous eyes she had taken Bibik from me, gazing at him with the same tender worship with which she used to look at Alik, she became my family and my chief prop. How could I have managed, ill as I was during most of the winter, but for her? It was she—even with her heart condition—who had cooked and washed, carried heavy buckets, and hacked at frozen firewood, while I for weeks and weeks had sat through my fever with Bibik constantly in my arms, with nowhere to put him except on the heap of straw in the icy draft over the floor.

But now we were bound once and for all by that moment last June when, stuffing Igor's letter hastily into my skirt, wanting at least to spare Panna the dreadful details about Alik, saying only that he had been wounded and was missing, I stood on my knees before her and said, putting Bibik into her numbed arms: "He will at least partly take Alik's place for you. He will always be with you, I promise. I promise it to you, Panna."

3

MY FATHER was coming out of his study with a briefcase under his arm, walking with his precipitous stride, all that should be and would be done registered in the forward thrust of his shoulders. We ran into each other in the doorway between the main green drawing room and the white ballroom, the *zala*. He wore his green tie with the gray dots. As he saw me he stopped abruptly, peered with anguish into my face, and cried, "What is the matter with your eye, Nita? Did you hurt yourself?" I was going to answer with humorous calm, the way I always used to counter his fits of worry over my health, that nothing was the matter with my eye, and say something teasing to make him laugh.

But instead I stood there paralyzed, shattered by the piercing clarity with which I saw him, every line on his face, his greenish eyes, the dark hair whitened at the temples; by the boiling current of concern that poured from his gaze. It's real *this* time, I was saying to myself, it's not a dream. Or else I couldn't have seen every dot on his necktie and how his eyes reflect the green. Now I know that it was all a lie, a false rumor! He had not been executed. He had escaped! To make sure that I was right, I looked around the zala for the two pianos, and they were there. The row of oil portraits on the walls was there also. But just then what seemed like blows of a hammer crashed right over my head, and I realized that the faces on the portraits were blurred, unfamiliar, and things began to take a terrifying turn. With a start I opened my eyes.

The quick lift from the pit of sleep made my heart beat with shallow, sickening speed. The hammering continued, echoing metallically through the empty corridor and down my emptied legs. Someone was pounding at the door of our car. I sat up abruptly, heard Polya moving below. A match flickered, she held it to the lamp. But my father's eyes were still peering into mine.

Wary murmurs and stirrings arose in the car. Instinctively my hand went groping for my hairpins under my folded coat. It is only through a dream that you can measure the force of your love and pain, I thought, as I twisted my slippery hair into a knot on my neck. And yet, but for the outside noise that woke me I never would have known I had this dream. It was too deep within me, too far from my surface mind. But then my thoughts broke off, smashed by the thunder of new blows, this time dealt on one of the car windows.

Polya's voice said coolly, pleasantly, like a fresh whiff of mint in the darkness, "They certainly seem to be impatient, whoever they are."

"Who do you think this is, Polya?"

"Soldiers, I think," she said, letting go the shade and holding her watch to the quivering, now elongated petal of light, its reflection pulsing on the silver sheath of her hair. "Yes, it's morning. Almost six!"

Some sort of commotion was afoot in the next compartment— Countess Cygnen either hushing or waking the children. Then the Chief's voice in the corridor, "What the hell?" and his long, boisterous strides advanced upon the noise. I leaned over the edge of my bunk to look at Panna. "Don't wake Bibik," I said in an authoritative tone. "In case of trouble I'll take him myself."

Panna, who always slept all buttoned up with not a hair out of place, was already sitting erect. She was watching Polya, a film of bewilderment dimming her face; but the sound of my words, like the dab of a cold sponge, immediately washed this bewilderment away. "Nobody's waking him except you by your shouting."

Polya opened our sliding door a crack, just wide enough to squeeze her slender form sideways through it. "I'll see what it's all about." She pulled the door shut behind her; the pounding started again.

I climbed down from my bunk and began hurriedly to straighten my skirt and twisted stockings. You'll never forget this, I was saying to myself, you'll never forget this sense of the approaching enemy. Not fear, quite a different savage feeling, at which you rejoice, because it is instead of fear and better than fear, a feeling from which your hands don't tremble, your blood doesn't chill, but gets thick and hot. Barbarism? Atavism? No matter what, it helps in times like these.

Slipping into my coat I said casually, "It may be nothing at all, Panna. Perhaps someone simply wants to see the Chief," and I pushed the door into the corridor half-open. But she, sensing that what I really meant was that anyone, she in particular, was welcome to lean with all her fears and worries upon my inflexible courage, cried, "Shut out that gale!" For the only worry she had, as icy air tore into the compartment (they must have just opened the outside door), was that Bibik would catch cold. So she fiercely slid the door closed right in front of me. Anger flushed my face. I was going to pull the door open again, but it stuck. "What have you done to it? It has locked itself!" I cried, giving frantic jerks to the handle, all the while thinking, This may be your last hour, this may be the Reds, and you are busy quarreling with her.

People were coming out of their compartments with questioning murmurs. The Chief's harsh, "Who is there?" boomed from the other end of the car. Muffled shouting came in answer from outside. Then the door slammed and someone entered. A rustle of bewildered gasps flew through the corridor and at once stopped short. The low, frost-roughened voice of a man spoke against the silence.

Not the Reds! Not yet. My knees were suddenly weak with relief. With a last effort I gave the door another frantic pull. This time it opened.

The first thing I saw was Countess Cygnen's back barring my doorway; in the light of a candle that someone held aloft, there loomed the shadows of the others, all congealed in listening attitudes, their topcoats thrown over their shoulders, their backs and profiles obscuring my view of someone around whom they all had clustered. I pushed my way across the threshold and stopped.

It was Igor.

He stood there in his military sheepskin jacket, his fur cap in one hand, the other smoothing his hair. He was speaking to the Chief, while his glance darted from face to face, probably seeking me. The flickering light brought into relief the dark stroke of his brows, the sheen of his eyes, the shadowy stubble of his cheeks. Then he saw me. The way between us was blocked, and he indicated to me with a sharp thrust of his hand to stay where I was, that he would join me in my compartment; and for a moment the corner of his mouth began to pull upward in an uncontrollable smile of relief.

"I came for my family," I heard him say to the Chief. "I am taking them with me to Novonikolaevsk at once to put them on an eastbound train tomorrow. All I can give them to get ready is twenty minutes." His voice was hoarse, not quite his own; but the familiar drawl that I had not heard for so long shook me. "And your whole train should also pack up and take to sleighs immediately."

The formal military manner in which he spoke in the stupefied silence was firm and matter-of-fact, a sort of metal platter to support the weight of his news. "Once in Novonikolaevsk you will be safe, our whole army is there." Still speaking, he began to edge his way toward me, but the Chief barred his way:

"What about the railway junction behind us?"

"At the last station on my way here, I was told that communications with it were cut off at three o'clock this morning, which probably means that the Reds might catch a few hours' rest there. Still, I wouldn't count on it."

I didn't care. The only reality for me was that Igor was alive and whole, and that he was taking us with him. Then he said something about an outpost, he had sent a couple of men as an outpost on the track behind us; also that he had brought two extra teams and several extra topcoats with him. I didn't know what outposts were or what the Chief was thanking Igor for. All I knew was that the people who were blocking his way toward me began to talk all at once.

"But how in God's name can we pack up all our patients?" someone cried. "There won't be enough teams, even with the extra ones you have brought."

"And who of the sick will volunteer to stay behind? Not one!"

Now Igor was making his way toward me and I stepped back to my compartment to let him enter. At the same time Polya, already dressed in coat and woolen scarf, was slipping out the door. "Great of you, Igor," she said, touching him briefly on the sleeve. It was amazing how a cobwebby voice, a light gesture, could transmit so much, imprint themselves so strongly on the memory against the chaotic onrush of impressions.

He came in, and with him there also came the smells of leather, frost, and thawing sheepskin; and that something else, powerful, electrifying, that made all things and problems change their texture and sharpen their outlines.

He put his arms around me and let out a huge sigh. "Oh, Lord! I was about to lose hope of ever finding you. I never dreamed your train was the last in line! An hour ago I was certain that you had been trapped by the Reds."

The strong pressure of his arms, the tough feel of his shoulders in the rough clothing, the gold-edged shoulder board that scratched my cheek, and in contrast the warmth and mellowness of his manner—it was the same after each long separation: a startling shock of recognition, a linking together of the disjointed pieces of my married life. However, we were not yet alone, not yet by ourselves. We were still tension, hurry, business. But when Igor told me that we should have the whole evening together in Novonikolaevsk and perhaps the next morning too, hurry and business turned into a magic bridge toward that spot of light.

The wick was burning at its lowest, our black shadows hovering on the walls, grotesquely repeating Igor's movements as he threw off his jacket and shook hands with Panna. "At last," she cried, as if Igor's arrival was exactly what she had been waiting for. Then he crouched beside his son. This was the moment I had dreamed about so much, a dream so imbued by the heartache of unattainability, that I could hardly recognize it for what it was.

Bibik had just awakened and was staring at his father, his eyes earnest and shining in the unsteady light. "Why, he's magnificent! He's enormous!" Igor took Bibik's hand and shook it with comic politeness; then, sensing that more was expected of him, kissed it rather sheepishly. "I'm afraid to touch him. I'm filthy. Can he walk? Talk?"

"Oh, Igor, he is only fifteen months! But he understands everything!"

"Too bad if he does," Igor grinned.

And Panna, proudly taking Bibik into her arms, said, "We surely often understand more than certain grown-ups we know."

But Igor was in a hurry. He had to talk with the Chief, to see that his drivers were fed and given some food and vodka to warm up, to do something about his "outposts." We would be following him to Novonikolaevsk all day without a stop, so we should eat all we could to last us until evening. Tomorrow he hoped to put us on an eastbound train. General Kostin, his regimental commander, was to make arrangements that day for some Allied train to take the families of the regiment along.

"The Czechs have seized control of the railway and are commandeering the engines of our trains, you know, but letting the Allied trains go through."

"Yes, yes, I know."

"But General Kostin has friends at the French mission, so I hope he will have it all arranged for you to leave tomorrow, by the time we get to Novonikolaevsk."

A great confusion had risen in the car. People were calling to one another, ordering the children to get out of their way, the children filling in the gaps with the wild elation of the released. Lanterns flashed to and fro in the darkness outside. I could hear the trampling of horses' hooves down wooden ramps as they were being led out of the cattle cars for hitching. Train personnel were evacuating the patients.

All this had happened before. It had happened fifteen months ago in the last hour before the fall of Tamborsk, when Igor came to make me leave immediately with our volunteer units. The same stubble of beard was on his cheeks; his eyes, after four days and nights of sleeplessness and hand-to-hand fighting, were sunken as they were now. This same darkness—only then it was September midnight—was outside, and he had given me the same few minutes to get ready. But that moment had torn me away from my father, who had refused to flee and leave his dying mother, his sisters, his daughter-in-law; it had uprooted me from my soil. I could still feel the tugging and tearing of those roots within me. Then it had been the end of everything. How different now: a new beginning!

Soon I heard Igor and the Chief reenter our car. They spoke in undertones, but as they stepped close to my door, I could hear every word.

"We shall probably have to take our new stand farther east," Igor was saying. "The Trans-Baikal region is much more tenable . . . Yes, about two thousand versts from here."

The Chief emitted something between a groan and a snort. "Eichk! Which means that the difficulties with Ataman Semenov will only increase. What sort of understanding can there ever be between him and Admiral Kolchak?"

"Once we get to Semenov's territory our army will take over, I'm sure," Igor was saying. "We still have a strong nucleus—General Kappel's army, the Izhevsk and Votkinsk divisions, our First Cavalry. There are even some indications that Semenov will cede the right of way to Admiral Kolchak of his own accord."

AS I GAVE Bibik his bottle, Igor came in. Hastily biting into our sandwiches, we talked in snatches. I couldn't understand how he had found us, and he said that until a few days ago his regiment had been engaged in rear-guard action, but then orders came for them to fall back full speed to Novonikolaevsk. Once there, he found out that our train was stalled, as were all other transport trains, and in danger of being cut off at any moment.

"You can imagine the shock! I had hoped that you were somewhere beyond Lake Baikal. Luckily the regiment was to have a twenty-four-hour rest, so I took several men who volunteered to go with me, and we led our horses on leash behind the sleighs." He lit his cigarette, held the match to Bibik to blow out, and snapped the cigarette case into his face, sending him into ecstasy. "We started out at four in the afternoon and drove all night."

"When did you sleep?"

"Oh, I slept in the sleigh. My men did, too. We took turns driving." They had followed the railway tracks alongside the unbroken line of standing trains, constantly stopping to ask the whereabouts of our train; but no one knew anything. "We scared people stiff, you know, telling them to shake themselves out of their trains, to take to sleighs or to their feet. The Trakt is just as jammed as the road alongside the railway line, but my drivers know some rarely traveled shortcuts and I have a fine pair of horses for you and a good sleigh. Listen, if Kostin . . ."

As if I cared what road and what sleigh, as long as we were to follow him! "If General Kostin doesn't succeed in getting you on board an Allied train you may have to go in freight cars, and it will be a long and uncomfortable trip."

"Oh, Igor, just as long as we get off," I said, swallowing the last of my sandwich and shaking the crumbs from my skirt for the Reds to sweep away.

"But at least you won't be alone. All the regimental families will be traveling together. You'll probably see some of them tonight. Masha Kostin, Alenka Gottel, even your Margarita, they're all there already, at Novonikolaevsk! Well, we've got to go. I'll pull in my outposts. Are you ready?"

Then, getting on his jacket, he added that this being November 26, the day of the patron of all warriors, Saint George, there would be a celebration of sorts at General Kostin's headquarters.

"A celebration? In the midst of this debacle? Celebrating what, exactly, Igor?"

"It just so happens that the staff is billeted in a very nice house, and, after all, this is the first forty-eight hours' rest for the regiment in months." As he buckled on his revolver, he interrupted himself. "My outposts will be back in five minutes. You have to be in the sleigh by then."

INTO MY SUITCASE I tossed a couple of towels, my only change of underwear, and a blouse of Japanese silk that I had made for myself just before leaving. The rest were Bibik's things. The canvas bag with my remaining jewelry hung on a string around my neck. Two bracelets, which I never took off, dangled on my left wrist; I also wore my mother's emerald ring. I owned nothing else except a packet of Alik's letters from the front, my old dog-eared Bible, and a notebook in which, during the last months in Omsk, I had been keeping a diary and writing a sort of family chronicle. These few things were my treasured link with some other, rapidly disappearing self of mine.

I knew too well what was awaiting us. The hard realist in me, the twin of the dreamer, knew that, once unleashed, the forces of destruction and hatred became the conquerors of the world. But whenever my fingers touched these things—these letters of Alik, which were pure poetry, this Bible, whose margins had been streaked all over with my pencil marks, this notebook, into which I had poured all I had of searching thoughts—I felt, even now in the midst of this dizzying upheaval, that I had brushed against some magic strings; and for an instant their music, tranquil and cooling, washed through me.

> Know that one's inner soul one never dares
> Into an earthly accent render.

I snapped the suitcase shut and slipped into my coat.

"Ready?" Igor came in. Panna was still folding her yesterday's wash into little bundles, securing each with a safety pin, when he suddenly flew at her in his squadron commander's voice.

"If you are not able to pack up three old rags in all this time, then throw them away. I haven't come here to have you and my men stuck with the Reds."

But Panna, immediately promoting herself above Igor in rank, replied with stern dignity, "It was easy to throw things away when we had houses full of them." And she calmly finished her task.

4

OUR DRIVER, Private Doushin, had a broad, weatherbeaten face to which clung an expression of humorous endurance. He was perched on the box seat of our sleigh, behind a pair of sturdy Siberian bays; the bulk of his back and huge cap of rabbit fur were right in front of me, screening the view and the riders ahead. Only at a turn in the road would the silhouettes of Igor and his troopers and their mounts come into sight through the foggy darkness of morning.

But he was there. How on earth could he still stay in his saddle after two days and nights of riding, and a whole day yet ahead of him? Again he had saved me; he had saved our whole train without giving a thought to himself. He was here! We were in motion again, rapidly increasing the distance between ourselves and the Reds, and it was wonderful to breathe the morning air, to have fine snow blow into our faces.

All was not lost as yet. We were to take a new stand in eastern Siberia: we could still hold it clear from the Reds, and if our army were to reorganize somewhere behind Lake Baikal, Igor and I still might spend the remaining winter months together. I wasn't trying to cheer myself with false hopes. I was simply being true to my God-oriented optimism.

I wore the same kind of coat—*dokha*—as our driver, a huge bulk of coarse samoyed-dog skins, fur inside, the coat's shaggy collar reaching the top of my head. Every traveler in Siberia had to wear such a dokha over his winter coat so as not to perish from the cold. Panna Krylocka was probably the first and last exception. In an outburst of repulsion, turning away from the orderly who held them in readiness for her, she had rejected both dokha and felt boots, calling them breeding grounds for insects, and was now driving in her light coat, leather shoes, and a knitted head scarf.

"But Panna," I cried, "you'll freeze to death!"

Silence.

Bibik was asleep on my lap in the warm tent built by the flaps of the dokha and the sheepskin lap robe that covered our knees. The bulk of the fur collar prevented me from seeing him. I would once in a while slip off my white American glove with the blue wristlet to touch his face and check whether he was getting enough air. His face was warm and silky, and he breathed evenly. Panna must have dozed off also. It was dark, but the darkness was acquiring an early-morning transparency, and I could see her head leaning against the corner of the high-backed sleigh, slightly swaying at the jolts in the road, her lips relaxed in a grave pout.

The desert of the steppe was broken only rarely by a cluster of snow-capped houses and barns of a farm—*zaimka*—with lights feebly squinting in some windows. Here and there a group of straw stacks, or the tracery of a few bare, frost-glazed trees, or the wings of a windmill, a broad, frozen X, would swim into relief out of the rapidly blanching grayness. The Siberian landscape was very much like that in our parts of European Russia, and at intervals in my disjointed thoughts, I could see myself arriving in Sinniy Bor with Alik. I saw everyone already gathered at the house waiting for us. Fires roared in the rooms; someone was playing the piano; someone else was singing; the voices of our elders, debating something thrilling, thought-provoking, were flying at each other in the drawing room, mingling with the music, with splashes of laughter. The fragrance of Sinniy Bor's special hors d'oeuvre—mushrooms in sour cream—was already wafting from the pantry, blending with the odor of pine needles. And almost visible to me were the iridescent threads that stretched in this house from room to room, from voice to voice, binding us all, family, friends, old servants, into a magic oneness. Magic—because these threads seemed to go beyond the confines of this house and our personal existence.

This was perhaps the first time since our flight that my memory was able to skip over the frightful years between, and return to Sinniy Bor as it had been before the war and the revolution, when I was still in my teens. For until now someone within me, calm and decisive, had been covering my eyes, warning me not to look back yet. But now I was back there, inside and outside the house, simultaneously with them all and yet alone, running down the frozen jasmine walk toward the church enclosure. This was the first thing I always did on arrival at Sinniy Bor. There I knelt in the dusk by my mother's grave, where the purity of silence had been repeating to me year after year, in her firm, tender voice, that *true* life could not die. What each of us had to do was to find it for himself. And I was promising myself with all the naïveté of youth to find this true life, find it at any cost.

A STREAK of yellow had just appeared in the east. Through narrowed eyelids and frosted lashes I watched it widen, turn coral, etching the leaden clouds that hung low over the horizon into schools of gold-scaled fish. Soon the sun began to climb over the steppe. I thought of Igor, of this evening we would have together, come what may tomorrow; and of the ease and freedom so oddly attached to homelessness, to futurelessness, to owning nothing, counting on nothing, and wanting so little. Yet how nice, just the same, to own the Japanese silk blouse that I had made for myself and into which I could change for tonight's regimental reunion.

And I began to think of the old friends whom I would see that night, of meeting some of Igor's comrades in arms whom I hadn't met as yet, his best friend Lorinov especially.

Then my thoughts leaped to the girl to whom Igor had referred as "my" Margarita.

MARGARITA . . . It was daylight now, but a cutting wind was rising, gradually sweeping the luminous clouds of a moment ago into one gray mass, hiding the sun. My breath, as it condensed on the fur of my upturned collar, froze into icicles that scratched my face. Again, I drifted toward the past . . . two years ago, and I was back in the white zala in Tamborsk. Alik's choir was lined up in a semicircle between the two grand pianos, the singers mostly his friends: girls with bows in their hair; the boys just ready for college; and in the center of this crescent, the pretty soprano, Margarita Tabakov. Two Gretchen braids of the palest gold hung down her back. Her huge blue eyes, slightly drawn down at the corners, gave her a half-frightened, half-prayerful expression. Those eyes were riveted on Alik's raised arm. . . .

Then, this past June, Margarita sobbing in my arms on the steps of the Cossack Cathedral in Omsk.

It had been late morning of a weekday. I had just entered the cathedral. The mass was over, the place filling with the mellow bleakness that engulfs an empty church once the music is over and the candles are extinguished. I walked to one of the darkest corners and stood there waiting for the funeral service for Alik to begin. The official letter that had come two days before had said *not* "wounded and missing," but "killed and left on the field of battle." Igor too had written that the field where Alik had been mortally wounded was so soggy that the men who carried him began to sink, and they had to leave him there, bleeding to death and unconscious. The place was then occupied by the Reds. But when the ground was almost immediately recaptured by our side, Alik's body was no longer to be found. The Reds had thrown the dead and wounded into the River Tanyp nearby.

Someone told me that I must hold a funeral service for Alik in absentia, and publish a death notice in a newspaper. I did as told, flinging the treasure of Alik's name into the endless stream of other names framed in black, for so many unknowing eyes to slide over. But to Panna I lied. The truth—rather, what at the time had been given to me as the truth—I had no strength to tell her. I said to her that Alik was wounded and missing, that he might have been taken prisoner and be recovering in some Soviet hospital. In fact, this was exactly what "rumor" brought us later.

We lived at the outskirts of the city. Panna would not see the newspaper. Under the conditions in which we refugees lived at the time, I hardly expected anyone who knew my family either to see the notice in the paper or to call on us, much less attend the service. So as I stood in that dark corner of the church, it was perhaps only from myself and from the emptiness around that I was hiding. Panna had stayed with the baby.

But they came, they came, those friends whom I had hardly seen since our exodus from Tamborsk, mostly older ones, for the younger were either at the front or at work, friends whom I had hardly seen because of the enormous distances in gray, wooden Omsk, because of the lack of time, of strength, because of lack of transportation fare, of shoes, of everything. Yet still they came. One by one they filed into the church, bedraggled figures, unrecognizable.

Madame Tongovsky, once stout but breezy, now a shadow of herself. Her husband had been executed at the same time as my father and thrown in the same grave. She came in, shuffling her feet in boatlike shoes. Alenka Gottel, a gracefully swaying reed before, was a broken one now, her dark hair a dusty gray. She had lost two of her sons: Misha killed in the battle of Tamborsk, Vova executed. Her daughter-in-law Tanya had died of typhus. There had been twelve of the Gottel clan two years ago; only three remained now. Thus it was with most of our Tamborsk families.

They had grouped themselves together ahead of me and were seeking me with their eyes. Then, as the candles were being passed around, they saw me and I felt ashamed of hiding from them and their sympathy, ashamed of my selfish fear that they couldn't understand the depth of my grief and who and what had been lost with Alik. For to them he was just a promising, talented boy. To me, he was a mysterious incarnation of all that lived above life.

I stood there, watching the drops of hot wax drip down from the candle flame to my hand, trying desperately to reach toward my luminous faith in joy. Through the weight of pain that crushed me, I repeated to myself that Alik had been prepared to step over to a new level of life, that my own knowledge of this other level was rooted in irrefutable experience. That Alik had never really belonged here, that this life alone was not worthy of being lived by him. Yet all the while another voice in me was crying out that there would be no more Alik. Not here. Never. And I was praying for Aunt Katya out there, in that pit of Soviet darkness, to die before she learned about Alik's death.

They all approached me when the service was over. They hugged me. They asked, tears for their own dead raining down their wrinkles, whether I had heard anything about my relatives in Soviet territory: my two aunts, my brother Dimitri's family, or about Igor's parents, who had both been arrested in Tamborsk and had disappeared since. Out of a stony throat I thanked them for coming. "No, no rumors," and then I said that I had to see the priest, so they wouldn't feel that they had to do anything about me. But a while later, when I stepped into the glare of the June day, a girl whose face I hadn't time to see threw herself upon my neck, sobbing and clinging to me. I knew who she was only because of the long Gretchen braids that hung down her back.

Her words fragmented by explosive sobs, she told me that Alik had been just a friend to her, but that the very thought of him, the hope that she would see him again someday, had helped her live through this frightful year of loss after loss. Just a few minutes before, in the office where she was working, she had picked up the newspaper, seen Alik's name framed in black, and, dropping everything, rushed out hatless and ran all the way to the cathedral.

I had been given the day off from my job at the General Staff, where I was a translator of English and French newspaper articles dealing with the Civil War in Russia. Margarita had to hurry back to her office but walked a few blocks with me. The June sun beat hot on the asphalt and brick of the main business streets, their sidewalks crowded; and Margarita held on to my elbow with her fingers, icy in spite of the heat, pouring out to me between spasms of tears all that must have accumulated in her during that year.

"First it was my older brother in Tamborsk—you know, you remember it! Shot because of some antique saber that hung over his desk . . . then my fiancé . . . then another boy who also . . . and how many of Alik's choir! More than half of them killed! And now . . . Alik!"

She seemed unaware of my hardly knowing who she was, for I didn't so much as remember her last name, whereas for her my presence at Alik's rehearsals two years ago back at Tamborsk must have integrated me into the most precious part of her youth. I had always attended the postrehearsal gatherings around the tea table, starting some discussion, improvising intellectual games.

Although only a few years older than these classmates of Alik, I, a married woman, a poet whose work had been published, must have belonged to a different generation in her eyes. As she walked with me from the cathedral that day, I felt she was falling back on me as upon a long-lost parent. She clung hard to me again before we parted. Might she come to see me on her way home from work? She lived with her father, the doctor; her mother and sisters were cut off at Tamborsk. "And Papa comes home so late from the hospital. . . ." Then I walked on alone through the business section of Omsk.

ONCE A PROVINCIAL town quietly breathing dust, Omsk had sprung almost overnight into fame. It had become the capital of western anti-Communist Siberia, the seat of the Supreme Ruler—the Knight Without Fear and Reproach (who was really no ruler at all)—Admiral Kolchak.

It was, since November 1918, a spot of historical importance, mentioned in every newspaper in the world, invaded by thousands of newcomers, crowded with cars of every foreign make. Smart uniforms of the Allied missions (alas, not those of Allied troops) mingled here with those of our own army and with the shabbily dressed refugees. French, English, American, Japanese, and Italian officers and soldiers paraded here, not to speak of our onetime prisoners of war, the Czechs, who sauntered about en masse. They were great heroes indeed, without whose armed units we could not possibly have started fighting the Reds. But they had fought their battle only in order to clear their way home, and to get home was what they were ripe for by that time. Although officially still fighting, they nevertheless had withdrawn from the front lines after the Armistice. Athletically built, their heads held high, they stalked the streets with an air of leisurely superiority, sweeping the Siberian women off their feet and making the men clench their fists.

The Czechs' attitude notwithstanding, Omsk was still teeming with life in early June, with the pride of recent victories. Although our army had withdrawn slightly from freshly occupied territories, it was still deep into European Russia. There was a bubbling animation, a purposefulness in the way people rushed about, in the din of their voices, and as I threaded my way among them I had the feeling of cutting a glacial trail through the sizzling summer day.

Then my mind leaped forward to another time at the same cathedral. By then the trees were gold, the sky a cool August blue. This was on Transfiguration Day, four months ago. Igor and I were sitting on the lower steps of the cathedral stairs. He had arrived less than a week before, sent to Omsk on temporary duty, and had to return to the front the very next day. That morning was so hard to live through that we both had quite suddenly decided to go to Confession and Communion.

After Confession, and after standing at church for over an hour, we came outside to take a rest from the long service while waiting for Communion time. Igor had picked up a pebble from the ground and was twirling it in his hands, knees apart, elbows propped on them. The trees around were just beginning to shed; bits of golden husks lay on the pavement; the sun-drenched air was imperturbably serene, living a life of its own. My eyes followed the people who ascended the stairs: bearded Siberian men who wore waistcoats over bright Russian shirts; women in gay holiday attire; the bedraggled figures of refugees with tired, intellectual faces.

We were silent. But I didn't want to be silent. I wanted to say something to Igor that he could take back with him to the front tomorrow, for he had just come away from heavy fighting and had to return the next day. The First Cavalry was covering our slow retreat in a section of the Ural Mountains, getting the whole impact of enemy pressure under rapidly deteriorating conditions. The supply of ammunition was decreasing by the hour; the Allies, disappointed in the whole venture, were no longer furnishing any war materiel and had recalled their troops. Crowds of refugees from newly abandoned territory clogged the railway, the roads, the towns. The local peasantry, most of it monarchist, was getting gloomier, less cooperative, accusing the Whites from European Russia of having dethroned the Czar, and simultaneously beginning to drift toward the greatest of magnets—the winning side.

This was Igor's first chance since Christmas to have a leave, perhaps his last one too, and how he must have looked forward to it! He probably thought when he was on his way that it had been two months since Alik was killed, and I should be over the worst of it by now. The courage to live, confidence in God, acceptance of suffering in His name were what I had always professed to be my faith. Anyway, Igor felt that his being with me would help me, and we should have a few precious days of rest together.

But he had brought Alik's knapsack with him. In it were Alik's diary and some letters, one addressed to me, which Alik had had no time to mail. Every line of it was poetry, poetry dark and tragic, yet made translucent by the gift that shone through it. And I was smitten anew with despair of what had been lost, not only by myself but by this life of ours.

I felt that I must transmute my mood into what Igor expected of me. For he had come in search of the simple bread and wine of life, of rest and love; and I, in my effort not to break down in his presence, had been walking around rigid, tongue-tied, the corners of my mouth too heavy to be lifted into a smile. It was only on the third morning of his leave that I awoke dismayed by the realization of what I was doing to him, to him who was soon going back to the front, perhaps to meet the same fate as Alik. And I was seized by a feverish urge to set things right immediately. But early on that very morning some officer appeared at our door, and said he must see Captain Volotskoy. After this man left, it was Igor who could hardly talk.

This officer, a Simbirsk Lancer from Igor's division, had arrived straight from the front and told Igor about the battle fought by his regiment during his absence. Three squadrons of the Tamborsk Dragoons under the command of Colonel Lorinov had been moving through a dense span of forest in the foothills of the Ural Mountains. As they came out into a large clearing, they found themselves face to face with the famous Steel Regiment of Red cavalry coming into the open from the other side. Without a moment's hesitation, Lorinov ordered his men to attack; he himself, charging the Red commander with bared saber, slashed him in half. There was a momentary panic among the Reds, but then a furious battle broke out. It was one of those battles that in other wars would have been written into the history of a regiment: a smashing White victory, the whole Steel Regiment either destroyed or put to flight by our three squadrons. But our losses were heavy: thirteen men and two officers of Igor's troop alone were killed. This had been three days before. And then, on the very next day, some adjacent White infantry unit allowed a Red breakthrough without offering any resistance. None! The heroic effort of the Tamborsk Dragoons had been for nothing, and had ended in retreat.

When this report came, only two more days remained before Igor was to return to the front. Since then we had hardly been able to talk. Again and again he repeated, "And I was not with them."

We actually forced ourselves to go to Confession and Communion. This meant attending a three-hour service and missing breakfast, a prospect unpleasant to me and insupportable to Igor, who hated any kind of self-imposed austerity. However, according to the traditions of our church and our families, we were to make our devotions at least once a year and had failed to do so since leaving home. But chiefly we had gone that day because we both, each in our own way, believed that if this outer world were run by the law of accident and human blunderings, the inner world of man might be ruled by a different code of laws, which could work the miracle of lifting our spirits.

Igor said, "You have done a lot more thinking about these things than I." He spoke slowly, as if dragging the words out of himself. "But when you are in the thick of violence and destruction, and when you see cruelty and deception win over and the best people perish, then there are moments when . . ." He turned to me and from his eyes surged that forceful truthfulness that was his very essence.

"I simply confess it to you, instead of having confessed it to the priest this morning," he put in with what was meant to be an ironic shrug, "that there are moments when all that has been ingrained in you—high moral principles, Christian ethics, and so forth—well, you simply stop understanding them. You begin to wonder whether . . ."

"To wonder what?"

"Whether such people as my closest comrades in arms Lorinov or Verin might not be right, after all; whether grabbing from life all you can, while you still can, might not be the most intelligent answer to life. The question of honor and devotion to the cause doesn't enter into this, you understand."

"But grabbing what?"

"Oh, anything which makes it easier: pleasure, excitement, oblivion. Anyway, to live full blast while it's still possible and blow one's brains out when you've had enough. When everything is going to the dogs, why deny yourself anything that might make life easier? Whatever helps one endure life must be right."

I knew that he was waiting for me to say no. He wanted this no from me because it lay at the very foundation of his being.

"Anything that you do to alleviate the burden is right," I said, "provided you are happy about it. I mean happy in the long run."

If I had uttered a hackneyed truth, I also felt how neatly my words hit at the very nucleus of the problem, dispelling whatever somber doubts had been pushing their way into the heart of a fighting man on his sixth year of a heroic struggle.

He took my hand and held it hard. Still, his speech had been so much out of character that I felt there was something else on his mind that he hesitated to put into words, and I suddenly knew what it was.

"Igor," I said, my hand clinging desperately to his, "I have been no help to you; but you know, you *know*, that it isn't for lack of love!"

"I know," he said, "but I had to hear you say it. I simply had to. Especially since we have only this one day left." And the overwhelming awareness that he was still here, with me, my horror of losing him, gathered into a huge sob in my throat that would strangle me at any moment, splintering the barrier of my grief, which stood between us.

I could not have explained exactly what had taken place within us later that morning as we walked home from the cathedral. It was not only our reestablished closeness. It was more than that. Our forthcoming separation, the destruction to which all our endeavors might be doomed, had seemingly been blown away by something indestructible that had arisen within us. For we suddenly felt lighthearted—gay! As if the August day had opened to make us part of its serenity.

Panna had baked a mushroom *pirog* for our lunch. If anyone knew how to invest a meal with festivity, it was Panna when she chose to do so. She poured tea for us, smiling tenderly, conversing with us, the "communed ones," *prichestniki*, as if we were important guests.

Later, when Igor had to leave for the General Headquarters, I took Bibik in my arms, intending to go for a walk with him. It was then that Margarita suddenly burst into our house.

"Nita! Nita!" She caught me by the arm and hung on, out of breath from running, her face flushed. "I have just met a man, a pilot . . . I was at the railway station seeing off a friend to the front . . . and met him. . . ." She had to regain her breath. "This pilot just recently defected from the Red side to ours. He had been wounded in June and was at a military hospital in Ufa, and in the same ward with him were several ex-Whites, prisoners, privates of course, and among them a boy quite young, he said, with ash-blond hair and the name was Ogariov, or Ogarin! No! You can't check on this now, this aviator has already left for the front. But he swore that—oh, but yes, yes, he described this Ogarin to me! He said that he had been severely wounded, terribly sick for some time, but later recovering. He said that they had a doctor in their ward who pretended to be a Red, but was snow-White inside, and that he was trying to save these prisoners and help them all he could . . . so he even brought some pencils and paper for this Ogarin, because the boy was an artist! An artist! Who else could it be, Nita? It must be Alik. It *couldn't* be anyone else!"

I stood there paralyzed, afraid to believe her; but, like someone at the bottom of a dark abyss, I saw a rope lowered to me. I caught at it avidly, desperately.

5

IT WAS NIGHT. There had hardly been any villages on the road. No stops, no food, no possibility of moving one's arms or legs. Darkness and fog lay over the steppe. The wind howled. Bibik, who had been amazingly quiet for almost ten hours, woke up hungry and miserable and began to struggle and cry. The milk in his bottle, though swaddled in blankets, was ice. From then on the minutes, filled with his wails, swelled into years, and the remaining twenty miles to Novonikolaevsk turned into unbearable torture.

By the time we reached the town I could hardly believe that anything else could ever be, except this nerve-racking struggle to keep Bibik quiet, to keep Panna quiet too—for his cries were being drowned out by hers. For the moment, I was to her the revolution, the Reds, the Civil War, the cause of Alik's tragedy. I was to her all those fools and criminals who had allowed it all to happen and were doing this to an innocent child.

As we drove into the suburban streets of Novonikolaevsk, lined by sturdy wooden homes with tall fences and locked driveway gates, we suddenly stopped by one house with a sign, Bakery, over the entrance. I was pressing my face against Bibik's, straining my arms to still his tossing, and was no longer able to understand why we had stopped or where I was.

"Perhaps"—this flashed through my mind as I walked across the threshold of the house—"perhaps this is what it's going to be like when we die." Out of the grip of darkness and cold, lashed by frantic screaming, we had just burst into the bliss of an enormous, light-flooded room, sparkling with cleanliness, breathing warmth and the fragrance of fresh baking. Life, like the beast in the fairy tale, had suddenly cast off its horny scales and stood before us in all its splendor. Bibik's shrieks dropped. Puzzled by the sudden change of environment, he was twisting his head right and left, staring at the bright electric bulbs, at the baking table loaded with food; at the people who crowded around it helping themselves to supper; at those who sat on their bundles or lay asleep all over the floor.

It appeared that the bakery owners were putting themselves out to feed every passing White refugee. They immediately brought some milk for Bibik. His cheeks were two saucerfuls of raspberry juice, his eyes the same shocking blue as his flannel shirt, now all wet around the neck. I fluffed his damp hair into ringlets, held the milk to his lips, and knew that this moment was happiness—a jewel, one that would sparkle for me through whatever darkness lay ahead.

Igor poured himself a glass of vodka, grabbed a couple of pirozhki, and said that he had to hurry back to his troop. It was imperative, he said, for his soldiers to feel that with their troop commander they came first, before his family. This was disappointing, but I felt it best to make light of it, so I laughed and quoted from a song, "Stenka Rasin":

> And behind he hears them growling,
> "He would swap us for a wench!"

"Exactly! I'll look after them and be back to take you to the party later. Anyway, it's getting too crowded here." He also said that the closer we kept to the General Headquarters the sooner we would know when and with what train we were to leave the next day. "I can't stand the thought of your staying here after the regiment leaves and going in cattle cars."

I knew too well that we could be stranded here and captured by the Reds; that for me, the wife of an officer, this could mean separation from my child, starvation, typhus, prison, if not worse. But a dazzling light glowed on this evening of ours together. "Igor, let's leave it to life," I said. "Let's not pull things out of God's hands by distrust."

"I've already left it to Kostin. Then, if he doesn't succeed, I'll see what I can do about it myself," he grinned. "After that, God won't mind my leaving it to Him."

Later, when Panna and I, dizzy with hunger, sat down at the laden table, the mistress of the house—a buxom, soft-spoken woman—came up and began to push toward us all the local delicacies—mushroom-stuffed pies, pelmeny, homemade sausage, crusty rolls baked in the Siberian way with a topping of sour cream—saying, in a caressing voice, that there was nothing she wouldn't do for the Whites. No matter what some others felt, she had never seen anything but good from the Whites. Business was booming, the officers were such polite gentlemen. She was from Kiev herself, but she loved it here.

Then, locking her hands under her chin, she began to speak in compassionate tones of the horrors that lay ahead of us refugees: Red partisans would certainly derail and attack our trains: "The Schetinkin bands especially are the ones who won't leave a soul alive, not even the babies." There were huge packs of wolves in the taiga, and how easy to freeze to death. "But just the same, you refugees are much better off than we, the Siberians. Sure you are! Because you've already lost everything, while we still have to go through it."

"Are you staying behind? Why?"

"Lord have mercy on us! You mean to leave all we have to the Reds? Just like that?" Her eyes bulged with horror. "If they take it all by force, then what can we do? But to leave everything to them of our own accord? Never! Besides, you can't tell—they promise that they won't touch us working people."

I said, buttering my bread with zest, "They'll touch everyone. Moreover, most of you in this town are also wealthy people—merchants, homeowners—aren't you?"

"Sure enough. There isn't a single poor family around here except for some drunkards perhaps, or some transient riffraff." And she went on to tell me of the wonderful life they had had here in Novonikolaevsk. When she first came here, twenty years ago, it was just a small village on the shore of the Ob River, but that was when the Trans-Siberian Railroad had just been built. "Look at it now! A big city!"

I knew a great deal about Novonikolaevsk from Igor, whose regiment had been trained near there during the winter, so I had a clear picture of the sort of town it was. Even if younger and booming, it was much like Kurgan and Omsk, and quite different in character from our Russian provincial towns. Here streets were straight, houses solid and square, with windows shuttered and doors locked with heavy bolts for the night; with basements deeply imbedded in the fertile Siberian soil and replete with stores of food. Most of the people in these western Siberian towns were peasants whose ancestors had migrated from Russia in search of land and become rich—peasants who had never known serfdom. They were sturdy, heavyset, with backs and heads that did not easily bend for anyone.

The Siberian intelligentsia—closely knit groups of idealistic, tireless culture-carriers, some of them descendants of political exiles of a century ago, such as the Decembrists and Polish nationalists—were just a thin sprinkling over a monolithic classless society of peasant-merchants, peasant-artisans, dairymen, cattlemen, grain dealers, and trappers. They wore waistcoats over their bright blouses, high boots, and watch chains across their stomachs. When you spoke to them they riveted their eyes on you, all the weight of their stubborn independence, of their rough-hewn integrity pressing upon you, resisting you. Unlike the Russian voices, sharply modulated, flowing, theirs were stiff and dull-toned. And unlike the Russian speech—fluid, rambling, and roundabout—theirs was brisk, thrifty, and to the point.

An odor of cleanliness, freshly waxed floors, and foody warmth permeated the interior of their homes, where order and rugged abundance prevailed. A stark God, who stood for no nonsense, looked down from shiny silver icons upon the motley homespun rugs, upon the mountainous edifices of down pillows on their beds, graduated from huge to microscopic. For some reason, it was not the handfuls of gold nuggets and semiprecious stones—for those could be picked up in the Urals almost for the bending—nor even the number of copper-bound trunks, bulging with sable, mink, and ermine—for almost every Siberian male could hit a squirrel in the eye at five hundred feet, and the taiga swarmed with wild life—but those down pillows in elaborate cases that symbolized the degree of the owner's wealth and prestige.

In winter the town prepared for bed by seven o'clock, and then a monotonous grumbling sound of the master's Bible-reading rose in the silent house. By five in the morning—which to us was the very middle of the night—fires were already beginning to crackle in the tile stoves, the place filling with the tantalizing aroma of baking pastry. And the day of hard work began long before sunrise.

There were times, however, when the dynamite of a party would blow this stolid pattern of life into bits. It was then that vodka, song, lovemaking, knifings, and tears of repentance would mingle into one savage whirlpool.

They must have loved their life, the people of these towns in which we refugees from Russia felt like aliens. They must have enjoyed their wealth, their work, their independence. It must have been hard for them to have European Russia invade their territory, upsetting their pattern of life, bringing with it war and mobilization. But the brief rule of communism that they had experienced had aroused such hatred in them that they accepted us. At least they had accepted us until this past fall, when they saw the Kolchak government begin to lose its grip on the situation.

There was the Siberia about which we had heard and read so much back in European Russia: the land of misery and gloom, of exiles and convicts, about whom we used to sing such plaintive, compassionate songs. And there was the Siberia of our present experience, immensely rich, independent, self-satisfied. Of course, all I had seen of it so far was only its western region to the taiga.

I HAD just one pair of shoes. They were old, high-heeled, but still shapely. Although felt boots had to be worn over warm socks, rather than over shoes, I simply had to wear high heels. I hated to be a disgrace to Igor, particularly in the eyes of those fellow officers of his whom I had not yet met. Foremost in my mind was his best friend since the beginning of the War, Serge Lorinov. He had been critically wounded just before the March Revolution, when my wedding was to have taken place. As a result, Igor, who was second in command of the troop, lost his leave, and our marriage had been postponed indefinitely. Thus the name of Lorinov and the specter of a dying man that loomed behind this name implanted themselves into the history of my life, interwoven into the desperate weltschmerz of those war years. Igor loved Lorinov, and I had agonized over his fate all through his torturing illness, establishing a sort of one-sided relationship with him.

I had just finished anchoring the uncontrollable mass of my hair at the back of my neck with my few remaining hairpins, when someone told me that Igor had arrived and was waiting for me in the hallway. As I hurried up to him, he smiled his slow, teasing smile. This morning in the dusky light, with the dark stubble on his cheeks, he had been entirely the Cavalry Captain. But now, waiting in the hall, he was simply himself, and I was struck anew by the vividness of his coloring, amber-brown eyes contrasted by the gloss of his sleek blue-black hair. As he put his arms around me, all that there was of my life, past and future, hopes and losses, was suddenly in some timeless world—one's only place of refuge. One's only true home.

6

GENERAL KOSTIN and the regimental staff were billeted in the upper flat of a two-story house that belonged to a wealthy merchant. As we climbed the cold inside staircase, we were met with torrents of music, muffled by the thick walls but stormy and jubilant, the kind only my cousin Paul Teolin could extract from a piano. Music, a party! In spite of constant exposure to a crowd, I had not been to a social gathering since our flight from home, nor had I heard any music except funeral marches. For a moment, part of me recoiled from this celebration, as from an indignity, an offense. I couldn't bear to hear the same familiar tunes that had been played and sung at home with that same Paul at the piano.

"We don't have to stay long, Igor, do we?" I asked, holding back.

"But where shall we go?" As usual he knew what I felt. "Anyway, we can't leave until we hear about tomorrow's plan." Then he frowned. "I have got to see you settled in some train before we march out."

The door opened, and I knew immediately that the spectacular male who stood there must be Lieutenant Verin, second in command of Igor's troop. Igor had mentioned him now and then: he was the son of a successful publisher and was once a member of the firm himself. "A true civilian intellectual," Igor had said, "now become a true officer." Verin was tall and spare; his features were firmly outlined, the dark stroke of his brows came low over his brilliant eyes. As he saw Igor, he exclaimed grandly, "Back, alive and whole!" And immediately turned to me with a deferential air, ready to be introduced.

"Lieutenant Vladimir Vladimirovich Verin," Igor said, in a perfunctory manner, "my wife, Olga Alexan'na"; and he at once asked if General Kostin was back and if some arrangements for the regiment's families had been made.

"Not yet. The general is still at it, gone to speak personally to the heads of the French Mission. We expect him any minute now." Lieutenant Verin spoke in a clipped Petersburg manner. "It would be unlike him to return empty-handed."

The hallway was crowded with felt boots and sheepskin jackets. A heap of military fur caps lay on a console by a gaudily framed mirror. My reflection therein I proudly avoided.

As Verin helped me out of my dilapidated coat, he spoke of some regimental matters, addressing himself to Igor—a manner possibly designed to make me feel like a faceless symbol of a woman. By the time he respectfully held the door draperies open for me, a state of mutual rejection had already established itself between us.

While only some twenty-five people were present in the large living room we entered, it looked as though every bit of space was filled with movement, furniture, conversation, music, cigarette smoke. The dim lighting of the room was intentional this time, for a red scarf was draped over the wall bracket. A few people clustered around the piano in the corner, others were grouped by a dying fire, glasses and cups in hand. Crimson reflections of the lamp, caught by several gilt-framed mirrors, lurked over their faces. In the adjoining dining room, also full of people, I glimpsed a table, as laden as the one in the bakery and crowded with bottles. The rooms were gaudy—crushed plush draperies and hideous paintings of galloping troikas and wolves in the snow. But my senses, starved by the bareness of our refugee life, were immediately intoxicated by this very gaudiness, uplifted by it, just as, in former days, they used to be uplifted by works of art. Good taste? But what, after all, was good taste? The question had time to focus itself in my mind and stop there unanswered, but I remembered it entwined with Paul Teolin's tempestuous rendition of his own version of "Dark Eyes." I saw his back at the piano, leaning low over the keyboard. My old friend Masha, née Hropin—now the wife of the regimental commander, General Kostin— stood by the piano. She wore her gray nurse's uniform, minus the veil, which accentuated the proud set of her head, on top of which a mass of brilliant yellow-gold hair was piled. At sight of us she threw up her arms and gave a wild scream. "Igor, you found them! At least one worry off our shoulders."

I was truly happy to be with her. Things between us had changed since our flight from Tamborsk. She and I had met once or twice at Omsk last autumn. We were both separated from our families, each with a brother wounded and missing, each utterly destitute with a baby boy in our arms and a husband at the front. Our former relationship—condescending on her side and serenely defiant on mine, based on competing in some sort of social vanity games—disappeared as if it had never existed. All at once we were sisters.

My cousin Paul had just turned and seen us. He jumped from the piano bench and, standing over the keys at an awkward angle, twisting his head back, burst into the march of Igor's former old-regime hussar regiment, singing the words in a special crackling, scratchy voice common to orchestra conductors. People converged on us from different sides of the room, many familiar faces of our Tamborsk acquaintances appearing among new ones.

So many contrasting impressions rushed at me at once, breaking against each other, that I did not know what I felt. The joy of seeing old friends, and the pain of missing those who should be among us and no longer were, were mixed with a sudden upsurge of hunger for life, called forth by the music, by the climate of the place. I was returning greetings and hugs—Madame Tongovsky's, Alenka Gottel's—uttering disjointed sentences: "I had no idea you were here too!" and "It's like an opera, isn't it? The characters meeting in another part of the forest in order to further the plot."

In the dining room, chairs scraped as they were pushed back, and a whole line of officers in campaign khaki left the table to move toward us. A few of my childhood friends were among them. These, together with Igor, had all taken part in the organization of our uprising and fought for Tamborsk. Igor began to introduce to me those whom I had not met.

Then Margarita rushed toward me. "You, Nita, you! We were so worried!" She threw her arms around my neck, and her touch told me that something wonderful had happened to her, that she was begging me to understand, to rejoice with her, perhaps to forgive. She had lost weight, and with her braids pinned around her head looked even prettier than before. I held her at arm's length, speaking to her with a sort of older-sister protective tenderness, my attention diverted by the officer who stood behind her beside Igor, prepared to be introduced to me. I could sense rather than see the blankness of his expression and the nonchalance of his stance. Was he another Verin? I thought, annoyed. Was stony formality a typical cavalry manner of meeting the wife of a fellow officer?

"Nita, may I present to you Colonel Serguey Yury'ch Lorinov," and the way Igor said this, using my nickname, made me feel that he was far from indifferent to the impression his wife was to make on his best friend.

Lorinov clicked his spurs, bowed briefly, and kissed my hand.

So this was the man whom I had seen in my imagination, tossing in delirium and agony, dying from wounds; for whom I had prayed with such fiery compassion. Here he stood now before me, very relaxed, at ease, looking as if he had never been in need of any prayers, mine especially. Nor did he look a bit like Verin. He was thin, of medium height, about twenty-six years old, his coloring lighter, his eyes a chilly rain-cloud gray. On one of them the eyelid came down a trifle lower than on the other, destroying the symmetry of his lean face just enough to command extra attention. In answer to some casual words of greeting, he gave me a foggy stare, and I had the impression that the fogginess was only a curtain drawn over the kind of eyes that saw too much and too sharply. Although the chances were that his attention was entirely absorbed by Margarita, it seemed to me that he was either prepared to dislike me, or that the first sight of Igor's wife and Margarita's friend was a disappointment to him; my avid interest in people immediately prompted me to remedy the situation by giving a little knock at this fogged windowpane, to see if anything would show through it. It was the same impulse that prompts one in childhood to play with a mirror by flashing sunlight into the face of a passerby; or to stick one's hand under running water and cause the spray to fly about. It was also an urge somehow to compensate for my shapeless blouse and worn-out shoes, this perhaps more for Igor's sake than my own; and I heard myself say to Lorinov, feigning deep earnestness, "You really shouldn't look at me so coldly, you know, not as if I were a total stranger to you. After all, I am the one whose marriage to your friend you once nearly prevented."

He blinked, the semblance of a smile drew two humorous creases down his cheeks. "An unforgivable gaffe on my part. I still regret it. I'm all against half-measures."

IGOR HAD finished his supper and sat beside me, slightly reclining, his arm stretched over the back of my chair, seemingly blissfully relaxed as he always was when we were together. However, each time we heard the door slam in the hallway, I could feel his arm suddenly tighten, in his readiness to rise.

I was always fascinated by Igor's ability to relax immediately and completely when he could, living the moment to the full (instead of letting his mind shuttle into past and future, as I did, comparing, wondering about life's impermanence, the ghostliness of time), and just as quickly, at the first alarm, to be charged with energy, ready for action.

But when one of the officers would call him away and he left me for some five or ten minutes, the black chasm of our impending separation would open before me and I would already be sliding into it. The mood of the place, dominated by close-knit martial masculinity, no matter how polished and self-contained in the presence of ladies, became painfully opaque when Igor was not with me. The sense of being excluded from what was Igor's world was intensified by the wild gaiety of the group of young people across the room, clustered around the fireplace, who seemed to be quite at home here. Lieutenant Verin was one of this group, its center a pretty, chestnut-haired girl with swinging gypsy earrings and a somewhat too resonant laugh.

"The old couple who live here," Masha Kostin said to me, "have been slaving to keep us fed, washing the dishes, cooking, and now they are asleep, both of them exhausted, but just listen to what these fools are planning!" She indicated the group by the fireplace. "They want to wake the old people up in order to get hold of a guitar that hangs on the wall of their bedroom. Why? Because they want Colonel Lorinov to sing gypsy songs for them, and he won't sing without the guitar."

"Oh, I'm all for it! I wish they would wake them. They can sleep sometime later," I said ruthlessly. "The only thing you ever told me about Lorinov, Igor, is how well he sings gypsy songs."

In fact, as I watched Lorinov, I remembered other things that Igor had told me about him at one time or another: "tinkers with some sort of inventions, wireless telegraphy . . . hard, arrogant, wild if anyone bars his way, but takes motherly care of his men . . . absolutely fearless, but pretends to be afraid of dogs. . . ." These contradictory ingredients had never come together to take the shape of a personality in my mind.

"You know, Igor, the idea I had of your Serge Lorinov had nothing in common with the real man. In fact, at the first moment I met them, he and Verin seemed to me very much alike."

"They're just as alike as night and day," Igor said. And added with a good-natured grin, "Of the same twenty-four-hour period, of course."

"Well, Lorinov is probably more high-strung, more aware—"

"Although he isn't looking our way," Igor replied, "he's aware enough to know that you are watching him."

"I'm not watching him," I heard myself lie, as if caught in some shameful act. "He's simply in front of me."

"So he's affecting Byronic airs. Why? Well, because he imagines himself to be totally imperturbable and hates to look like a fool in love."

"Which he is, just the same," Masha said. "And I don't blame him. That Margarita—what a lovely child! And just look at those two over there under the palm tree"—she indicated the girl with the earrings and Lieutenant Verin—"*des coups de foudre* all around. Met yesterday, in love today, gone tomorrow, and not even a solitary corner to kiss each other good-bye in."

I turned to have a better view of the girl. Her gypsy earrings dangled with every quick turn of her head, white teeth flashed, swirls of her laughter floated all over the room. Her skin had a glossy freshness, her manner a daring openness, and when she laughed she threw her head back as if she were letting the wind blow into her face. "Who is that girl?" I asked Masha.

"'Who's that girl?' she says," Masha mocked me. "Wasn't the writer Belov one of your closest family friends? This is Oksana, his niece. Remember that family, the ones whom the peasants massacred at the very outset of the revolution, still under Kerensky's reign? Yes, that was awful! They were the ones who had made a present of half their land to the peasants of the village, remember, Igor? And the only ones to be killed by them in the Tamborsk district."

Of course we both remembered. "The trouble was that they had always felt guilty with regard to the peasants, and told them so," Igor said, "so the peasants must have decided that the Belovs had a reason to feel guilty. Peasants never had any use for the repentant landowner type, you know."

"They were impractical idealists, all right, but bighearted and full of fun," Masha said. "And Oksana, although very unlike her parents, is also first class. No, no, she was away when this happened." And she called across the room to the girl. "Oksana! Come here! Imagine, Nita Ogarin—I mean, Nita Volotskoy—didn't recognize you!"

The girl couldn't hear her because Lieutenant Verin was telling some story to her group about General Janin, the head of the Allied Command with the Kolchak government, and as Masha caught Janin's name she began to clamor for everyone to listen to what she had to say about him and for Paul to stop playing. "Sh-sh-sh! Stop it, Paul!" She waved her cigarette holder vigorously at Paul, her face crinkled into comic annoyance. The music went on for another moment, then crashed to an infuriated stop.

When a little pool of silence formed around her, Masha started on her story about the article in the French newspaper that falsely ascribed some of our last year's victories, including the capture of the city of Perm, entirely to the Czech legions. "General Janin's report, no doubt—an effort on his part to embroil his own intrigues with General Syrovoy's unfortunate performance—"

And that started it. "Just to think that it's from such reports as Janin's and Syrovoy's that the world will be drawing its information about the White movement!" Oksana interrupted, her voice tight with anger. "I can imagine the memoirs he will write someday in self-justification!"

— 49 —

"*Les mémoires d'un âne!*" Paul shouted.

"May I say something?" Lieutenant Verin asked. "Shouldn't we try to be objective with regard to our Allies who did what they could for us at a time when England and France had been bled white? Intervention is the most thankless business, anyway. And hasn't the Kolchak government disappointed them on ever so many counts?"

"Thus spake Zarathustra," Igor murmured to me. I felt that he did not take the cerebrating Verin half as seriously as he did Verin, his comrade in arms.

After all, we knew too well what Verin was going to say: weak leadership on our side, disunity, party struggle; the spirit of anarchy—an aftermath of the Kerensky regime that had poisoned even the minds of some of our commanding officers—heroism in the front lines, and opportunism in the rear. We knew it all and didn't wish to hear any more of it.

"If that old ruin of a Clemenceau had not undermined our cause from the very first by refusing to recognize the Kolchak government, then we would have won!" Masha cried.

"They wanted a democratic government," someone else shouted angrily. "Well, Admiral Kolchak's was one!"

And now Oksana cried out, "Of course we have disappointed the Allies, but only after they dealt us this fatal blow of nonrecognition. The idiots assumed that we were fighting for the return of our possessions and privileges. In reality we have given up everything we had, to fight not only for Russia but for *them* also. Yes, for the whole world, its future. What about the Communist goal of world conquest? As if they had not made it as clear as campaign soup! Couldn't the Allies see it? Oh!" With a groan she buried her head in her hands.

In a few moments all the bitterness, frustration, and despair that had accumulated in us Whites began to erupt from all sides.

"Indulging in armistice festivities when Russia, who helped them win the war, is being destroyed, perishing!"

"Unable to see that they're digging their own graves!"

Paul banged down the piano lid. "The Allies have forgotten that their road to victory was paved by the . . . by the corpses of Russian soldiers! The Czechs at least fought valiantly for some time, and if it hadn't been for their leaders such as General Syrovoy—"

"And what about the French offer for us 'to talk it all over' with the Bolsheviks on the Princess Islands,* near Constantinople?" someone exclaimed angrily.

Colonel Lorinov, who until then had been leaning with crossed arms on the piano, straightened up and stood there as if ready to say something, provided he could make himself heard without too much effort.

"I don't blame the Allies for not understanding us," he said tersely. "It's impossible for the civilized world to understand this particular enemy—its savagery, its cunning, its deceptiveness. Not until this enemy makes a mess out of the personal lives of these same Allies." Again he turned to Margarita, his manner indicating that he was not going to involve himself any further in this discussion. Nor did I wish to listen any longer to anything but music, not during this short time of rest I had with Igor. This was what Igor wanted also. Taking his arm from the back of my chair, he spoke in a tone of finality that was almost fierce.

"So the Allies have left us, and we may deserve it. So we shall have to go it alone. And by God, we will do it. But now let's stop all of this and hear some singing." And he went toward Lorinov. Some of their closeness transmitted itself to me through the half-smiles with which they looked at each other while they talked; and I resolved I must, yes, by all means I must be included in this closeness, even if only for this one evening.

They seemed to have agreed upon something because Lorinov shrugged his shoulders as if to say, "as you wish," and Igor came up to Oksana and spoke to her briefly. Her face lit up quite suddenly and she cried, "Of course I will! I promised to, didn't I?" There was something extremely attractive in the spontaneity of her reactions, the quick changes in her expressions. "When, right *now*? Fine! Only if Colonel Lorinov swears that he will sing; or else I won't do it." Raising her arm and waving it over her head to call everyone's attention, she sprang up from her chair. "Wish me luck, everybody! I am on my way to the uncle's bedroom to borrow his guitar, so if you hear him scream for help . . ."

Someone heaved a broken sigh: "Eleven o'clock, and General Kostin not back yet!"

As a matter of fact, the guitar was by now indispensable, for in spite of the warmth of the house, slithering chills of worry were beginning to permeate the room.

LORINOV WAS sitting by the fireplace, one leg crossed over the other, his hands on the guitar, and he sang. He sang gypsy songs, and some old cavalry songs; and the meaning of the familiar words, often naïve, poorly rhymed, and discolored with use, rose from his voice, strikingly alive and penetrating. All conversation had stopped; people relaxed into their chairs. Lorinov had an ordinary baritone, but he possessed that same knack of telling a song as my brother Dimitri—only Dimitri never did it for anyone but the family, while Lorinov was obviously used to an admiring audience, and took its enjoyment in his stride. Almost without any change of intonation or facial expression, by sheer art of musical phrasing, by letting emotion press on the barrier of artistic restraint, he could suggest a groan of pain, a repressed sigh, creating a mood tender and pensive, which like a magnet drew out of life all its dearest memories, all its enchanting regrets.

Igor said to me under his breath, "The devil knows how he does it, and for once it looks to me as if he really lives what he is singing."

I said, "I hope he does! How the poor girl needs it. Even if only for this one evening. Just look at her—see those eyes!"

We both looked at Margarita. She felt our glance and turned toward us. How can this be, how can there still be such beauty in the midst of all this horror? her eyes were asking me. And how dare we enjoy all of this when those we love most—our brothers, all those others—will never— Or was it I perhaps who was asking myself these questions, while she was simply basking in a haze of almost frightened happiness?

"Encore, encore!" people called out as Lorinov paused between songs. "Let's have the 'Foggy Morning'!"

"'Two Guitars'!"

"No, first the hussar song!"

"'The Monotonous Sound of the Bell'!"

Lorinov went from one song to another while Paul, unable to restrain himself, began to embroider some pianissimo variations on the piano for each melody. No—all was not lost yet. No—Alik couldn't have died. Dimitri and I would still be reunited. "Oh, Igor," I said, between songs, "I simply have to tell Lorinov how good he is!"

"You don't have to; he knows it too well," Igor shrugged. But I had already jumped up from my chair, eager to pour out to Lorinov my admiration for his musicianship. I also felt a trifle uneasy about the silly, provocative manner in which I had spoken to him when we were introduced, instead of being open and friendly, and was hoping to set things straight.

"This is the first time in my life," I said, coming up to him, "the first time I realized that a gypsy song can be turned into a work of art!"

He rose, lowering the guitar. Just a second ago he had been gazing at Margarita with a fascinated, almost tender smile, but at my approach an impenetrable blankness descended over his face, making me feel a foolish intruder, as Igor must have known I would be. And now I must quickly explain my intrusion away. "I came to ask you to sing my favorite song."

Almost standing at attention, he made a little bow, raised the guitar, and began to strum the tune of "Autumn Winds." "Is that it?"

I laughed, astonished. "How did you know?"

"Isn't this Igor's favorite one?" And the humorous creases stretched down his cheeks.

Not that the tone of this question probed into my relationship with Igor, nor did it imply that the "we share it all" of husbands and wives was a ridiculous business; yet there was a suggestion of both in his manner, and I felt that the line I had taken with him at first was more to his liking than the warm sincerity with which I was addressing him now, and of which he was receiving a full measure from someone else.

I also sensed that, in spite of his fascination with Margarita, he was as aware of that terra incognita, Igor's wife, as I was of him. In fact, Margarita's clinging grasp on my arm and the ironically expectant countenance of Lorinov made me feel now that I was wanted by both—by him as a brief diversion to counterpart his idyllic romance, and by her as a sort of chaperone and confidante, and I was going to serve in all these capacities.

"It's nice to know that you understand the psychology of old married women so well, colonel," I said, letting rueful notes shade my voice. This must have sounded much more amusing to him than I could have hoped, because he suddenly broke into a grin.

"There are times when I wish I *could* understand it," he replied. His teeth were white and even, and, although neither his nor my words were much, I suddenly felt immensely pleased.

BUT IT WAS so silly of me, this urge to impress! From what neglected corner of my being had this play-starved child suddenly bolted forth, how could it still be alive in me? And why ask Lorinov to sing "Autumn Winds," the theme of Tchaikovsky's *October*, which brought back with it all the beauty of the Russian autumn, all the essence of our past, all its poetry, now trampled into blood and mire.

> Shadows of all that was loved and has perished,
> Voices now silent and faces once cherished. . . .

There were words in this song about first meetings and last ones that brought back my innumerable partings with Igor, of which this one might so easily be the last.

Most of the candles set in bottles had melted, their paraffin tears streaming down. Only a few coals glowed in the fireplace. A ghastly awareness of what lay ahead of us was beginning to engulf the place. If we were to stay on at Novonikolaevsk after the regiment had left, we would probably soon be cut off by the Reds. And all at once I resented the gaiety, the frivolity around me and in myself. I felt I had broken a mourning sacred to me, and I wished that the singing would stop, and Igor would take me back, so we could have at least these few remaining moments to ourselves.

LORINOV WAS tuning his guitar, his face inclined toward it, when the front door slammed, and some disruptive noises reached us from the entrance hall. Igor sat up. "This must be Kostin." Almost immediately General Kostin appeared on the threshold. I had not seen him for years. As people crowded around him, screening him from my view, I had only a glimpse of his heavyset figure, the thick eyebrows and short mustache, but my impression was that he had not changed at all. He was exactly the same as in my debutante days, when he had appeared at Tamborsk to shock everyone to attention by his dramatic vitality. It was this defiant overflow of life force that had made him what he was, and why many a girl—Masha Hropin among them—preferred him to other men. It was this same quality that had made him a hero of the war with Germany and now one of the outstanding figures of the White movement.

In his arrogant, step-out-of-my-way stride, which urged people to clear a passage for him, he crossed the room and stood by the piano, his fierce eyes sweeping his audience. The noise around him began to recede toward the corners of the room, where he blasted the residue of it with a thundering, "Ladies and gentlemen!"

"Ladies and gentlemen, but ladies especially! I shall make my announcement before paying my respects individually to those of you whom I have not had the honor of greeting yet." His voice came hoarse, as if sticking to the powerful muscles of his bovine neck. "I regret to have kept you waiting so long, when your fate has been hanging in the balance, but may I try your patience a trifle longer and ask Lieutenant Teolin" —he turned to Paul, who stood next to him—"that everyone's glass be filled before I inform you of the glorious outcome of my unsuccessful efforts.

"Every cloud has its silver lining, ladies and gentlemen," he went on. "The *clouds* are the representatives of our most valiant and admirable allies, who, to say the least, happen not to represent their own countries' best interests. . . . The silver lining" —he paused to take a glass of liqueur, which an orderly held on a tray before him—"the silver lining is that all the members of your families, gentlemen officers, will have to follow the regiment in sleighs. Yes, indeed, we are taking you all along with us. So here's to the brave Russian women, who will be crossing the Siberian wilderness in open sleighs, at fifty to seventy degrees below zero, just as the heroic wives of the Decembrists did a century ago—only they did it under less arduous conditions, and for quite different reasons. Hurray!"

WHEN IGOR brought me back to the bakery that night, the place was fast asleep, but where there had been plenty of room before to make one's way among the people who sat and lay on the floor, there was hardly any now. Crowds of refugees must have arrived since we left. It was dark except for the shaft of yellowish light which fell from a door in the far end of the room. As I slowly picked my way toward where I had left Panna and Bibik, I could hardly restrain the smile that was jerking at my lips. Not yet! The separation from Igor was postponed! Red reprisals, death had to wait. Igor and I could not be alone for a moment that night, but *soon*!

Now that I was threading a zigzag line among the sleeping figures on the floor, afraid to step on someone's leg or hand, I saw a shadow arm rise to wave at me, and the breaking whisper, unmistakably that of Countess Cygnen, made me stop. "Is that you, Nita?"

I crouched on the floor beside her. Although I had not given a thought to our train, to the Countess's family or even to Polya, I felt a sudden relief in finding her there. "How was it, Countess? Has everyone arrived safely?"

"Oh, Nita!" Her icy hand clutched mine. "I am here alone with my maid. I have no idea where the others are, not even Yuri. I am alone!" She spoke in a choking half-whisper. "He brought me to this place hoping to find your husband and get in touch with General Kostin through him, but missed him! Now he has gone to look for the General, I have no idea where. I lost the children also, Nita! Perhaps forever." She raised her head and in the semidarkness I saw the desperate sharpening of her gaze. "They have gone, gone!"

"Gone where? With whom? With Polya?"

"Oh, no! Gone for good, with some cousin of Yuri's on an American train that was to leave tonight. I can't speak of it now, don't ask me to! As to Polya . . . oh . . . I hate to tell you this, but at the last moment when there was not enough room in the sleighs for all the sick—yes, Nita, there was not, so that eight or ten of the dying patients had to stay behind, and Polya decided that she could not leave them."

"Oh, my lord! Did anyone else volunteer to stay with her?"

"Just one young nurse. Oh, Nita, Polya is a heroine! Naturally, Yuri would have stayed instead of her if he had not been in command. You can imagine the state he is in now!" Her head sank back on her pillow.

"But he must have sent someone for Polya and the rest from the flag station?"

"He has, but it may have been too late, and he is in agony! Perhaps this is why he did this crazy thing with his children, this unpardonable . . ." Unable to go on, she tore her hand out of mine and pressed it to her lips to steady their trembling. ". . . this cruel thing, so unlike him."

The shadowy figure of her maid, Glafira, who lay beside her, suddenly sat up. "I've been telling Madame," she began in an anxious whisper, "that we ought to be thankful to the Good Lord that the children have gone ahead. And as long as there was only one berth available for the four of them, including Niania . . ."

The Countess groaned, tumbling back on her pillow. "*Comme cette pauvre femme m'agace.*" Then she proceeded to tell me, making great efforts at composure, that indeed there had been only one berth available on the American train where the Chief's cousin was interpreter, a train that was to leave immediately. The cousin promised to take care of the children and to send them from Vladivostok via the United States to Paris, where their Uncle Alexey would meet them. "Oh, I suppose Yuri was right. He could not miss this chance—but oh, Nita, my dear," again she pressed her hand to her lips to stop their quivering, "I don't know for whom I agonize more: Yuri, the children, Polya, or for my poor daughter!" Then she asked me when and with what train we were leaving.

"No train would take us. We are to follow the regiment in sleighs," I said, ashamed of my luck, of my selfish joy, of my always having it better than anybody else. "But I am sure Igor can arrange for you and Glafira to come along with us. Then you wouldn't be alone."

"You mean without Yuri? Oh, no, no. Not without him!"

"But there would be your friends: Alenka, Madame Tongovsky. . . ."

A little later, as I was taking leave of her, she said, her eyes roaming over the dark ceiling, her voice weighed down with dejection: "Until the very nature of man changes and he is purified by spiritual knowledge, nothing can help him. This disruptive process will go on and on for thousands and millions of years to come."

Whenever she made some pronouncement, whether about the fate of the world, about her favorite theory of what is meant by the Second Coming, or about the necessity of making Christmas decorations, her words never vanished into nothingness, but stood firmly traced in the air for your memory to take along whether you felt like it or not.

PART
TWO

"Ponouzhaiy!"

("Move On!")

7

AS WE FOUND out later, the First Cavalry Division had received urgent orders to outdistance the flood of retreating units and to try at some point to stop the chaotic retreat. But these orders, probably misrouted, reached the division when most retreating troops were already deep into the taiga. The Great Siberian Highway—the *Sibirsky Trakt*—was only wide enough in winter for two sleighs to pass, and by now was packed solid with traffic; so that the task given the First Cavalry was unfulfillable. Just the same, orders were orders. The division, unable to communicate with General Headquarters, had to move without pause from deep morning darkness until the darkness of night. We, the families, followed in the rear. We could see that we were traveling under much better conditions than any other sleigh train we passed on the road. We had strong horses, sturdy hooded sleighs, all the warm clothing we needed, and an abundance of provisions. We made good time those first two weeks.

Our goal was clear-cut: by February, just before the thaw, we would cross Lake Baikal and reach the Trans-Baikal capital of Chita. Even if we were compelled temporarily to join the forces of Ataman Semenov; even if the only allies who would support us (because they needed us) were the Japanese; even if General Pepelyaev's army had all but disintegrated, whereas the Bolshevik propaganda and the partisan movement were gaining ground—we were still a power; we would still fight on. There was General Kappel, the fabulous White hero, whose army would follow him wherever he led. There were the Izhevsk and Votkinsk Divisions, our First Cavalry, and many other units unswervingly devoted to the White cause. So we still could, and would, fight to the last.

This was what all the younger people felt. This was what I felt, with a sort of rugged optimism, probably inspired by the strict routine of our new life, by the refusal of the mind to think along logical lines.

At four o'clock every morning a sixteen-year-old volunteer, Coco Scheyin (known in Tamborsk as a frail musical prodigy), appointed as liaison between the regiment and the train of families, would ride up to the cottage where we were billeted and awaken us by a few mighty blows on the door. A heap of coal left to smolder during the night in the huge brick oven faintly glowed orange without giving much light; the odor of rising dough, hot bricks, and sheepskin, the odor of living, of shelter against the cruel cold without, were good to wake up to.

A few yawns, a few crackling stretches, a few grunts. A match would flare, a candle would be lighted. Everyone slept on the floor of the kitchen and parlor, the masters of the house either sullenly or fretfully locking themselves in some back room. And soon the samovar would be steaming away, the sound of butter sputtering on skillets. We had to eat all we could to last us until evening, all that the peasants would be willing to sell for our short-lived Kolchak bills. This meal could be sauerkraut reeking to high heaven, dill pickles, or pelmeny. It could be steaming cabbage soup with huge chunks of pork in it.

These peasants tolerated our intrusion as best they could. We were still an army, a power. Thousands had already passed through the same villages, sweeping out their stores of food and forage, crowding them out, playing havoc with their way of life. But how rich they still were, the peasants of these parts—probably richer than any other peasants in the world. At least eight horses, a dozen cows, several hundred sheep were what the average old-time settler family owned in these regions; and land—all they could cultivate. We had never seen, in the villages of European Russia, anything like their so-called five-walled cottages for spaciousness, comfort, or cleanliness. These people worked hard, they ate solemnly and well. Several times we surprised a family having supper. Chewing in ceremonious silence, they would begin with a bowl of thick cabbage soup, followed by a dish of pork with sauerkraut, and then attack the next course of woodcock or duck, before starting their prolonged tea-drinking session. How tired they must have been of this plague of soldiers and refugees pouring day and night through their homes, often leaving the place in shambles, bringing vermin, typhus, chaos! We were hardly conscious of them, however. In our morning haste, we cared only to eat, dress, and leave again. On the whole, anyway, their lot was better than ours.

A chip of mirror was passed from one to another of us young women—myself, Masha, Oksana, Margarita—as we hastily arranged our hair. "Remember powder? Cologne? Going to the coiffeur? Impossible!" It was impossible that anyone at all, anywhere in the world, could still have cologne and powder. We laughed because we enjoyed each other and we had not laughed for so long; because life was so short, and we traveled so unencumbered. Because at last, for a while, the men in our lives were within our reach instead of being under enemy fire.

Countess Cygnen was traveling with us also. The way in which she had taken the despair of being separated from all her family, even the Chief, was amazing. Always composed, ready on time, a down scarf over her sable hat, she would thread her way through the general bustle to take formal leave of the mistress of the house—her contribution to the White cause. "I shall never forget the kindness with which you received us," she would say, or words to that effect, and this regardless of how kind or rude the hostess had been. In fact, the attitude of the peasants toward us was chiefly determined by who had been there before us, by whether any horses had been requisitioned or any chickens "lifted," and by whether we had added any American-supplied brown sugar or rice, of which they were short, to the "Kolchak bills" with which we paid them; and if the woman's answer to the Countess's amenities was a suspicious stare, the Countess's eyes would regain their sharpness and she would add in a mournfully prophetic voice, "And if the Reds come, God help you then."

"There is nothing as hard as undertaking a struggle with one's baser nature," she said to me once, "but nothing as stimulating as carrying on this struggle once you have undertaken it. Indeed, I believe that this is the only way to inject meaning into the confusion of one's day-by-day existence." She certainly lived up to this pronouncement when, instead of complaining of her aches and pains in relation to the floor on which she had to sleep, or instead of giving way to her grief, she chose to rise above all her troubles. "Acceptance is never passive," she explained. "It is a creative act, in which renunciation and sublimation merge." In fact she succeeded in sublimating hardships that were not easy to endure even for us, the young—for instance, the absence of toilets.

"Had anyone told me only two years ago, when I so enjoyed my magnificent bathroom suite—dressing room, bathroom, and"—her enraptured smile and airy little gesture would transport us to her Petrograd mansion on the Moika—"the inlaid marble floors, the great mirrors, the fragrance of my favorite Coty 'Violette Pourpre'! Had I ever been told then that I would have to go out at four o'clock in the morning at a fifty-degree-below frost, to hide myself behind a snowdrift . . ." And now, her pale eyes sharpening with horror, she would draw back, pressing her hands to her cheeks and leaving hollows in them. "Had I been told this, I would have died! Yet when such a fantastic thing really happened" —with an abrupt change of expression, her entranced eyes travel-

ing over the cabin ceiling, her voice lowered to a mysterious solemnity—
"when I come out and see the starlit sky, and stand there gazing at the
myriad unknown worlds overhead, and know myself to be an infinitesi-
mal part of some Gigantic Endeavor of our Creator, the longing to join
Him in this Endeavor exalts me."

I often made Igor laugh by mimicking her, by saying the sort of things
that she might have said on some particular occasion, but even my
most exaggerated inventions stemmed from something in her that was
also in me.

OUT OF the warm soil of our mornings there grew the ice-coated stem of
the day: at least ten hours of driving.

During these endless hours, life was a slice of road, flanked on both
sides by high snowdrifts or by snow-burdened firs; the driver's back in his
elephantine dokha screened the road ahead; our upturned collars prevented us from looking back at what had been left behind. The inner
mind was ice; nothing penetrated it from sunrise to sunset. The absence
of movement, of any responsibility or initiative, numbed it into a state of
rigid endurance. No fears, no regrets, no claims, no thoughts. Just a
dogged urge to get out of the reach of the Reds so as to strike back at them
as soon as we recovered our bearings. My grief over Alik and Father had
also turned into a chunk of ice, its weight heavy on my chest and always
there, but the pain numbed.

We were gradually adjusting to the routine of doing without food and
drink all day, and of being cramped in the sleigh into utter immobility.
On and on, up and down over the ruts, often stopping as the whole line of
traffic would stop. It was during such stops that from somewhere behind
us there would rise a desperate, drawn-out wail:

"*Po-nou-zhaiy!*"

Started by one of the drivers to be taken up by the next one and the
next, this "*Po-nou-zhaiy!*" — "Move on!" —would turn into a continuous
howl filled with the impatience of exhausted, freezing men. It would
hang for versts over the narrow line of road, which swarmed black with
sleighs, horses, and people. *Po-nou-zhaiy!*—a Siberian word that we had
never heard in Russia—was now stamping itself upon the whole White
retreat in Siberia as its nickname.

But then toward four o'clock, when the sun in the west would begin to
dissolve into streams of rose and coral and a luminous bracket of the
moon emerged out of nowhere to rise over the roofs of some distant vil-

lage, life again surged back into us. Straining toward the explosive crackling of birch logs, the odor of freshly baked bread, toward the moment when we would all gather around some kitchen table, keeping the samovar boiling, waiting for the men in our lives to join us, even if briefly.

ON THE very first night of our journey, in the first village where we had stopped, as we were finishing our meal, Colonel Lorinov appeared in the more or less official capacity of General Kostin's representative, to inquire whether we were comfortably settled and in need of anything. Lieutenant Verin, who was with him, doubtless intent on seeing Oksana, had an excuse of his own for coming: an officer of Igor's troop, he had brought me a message that Igor was not yet through with his schedule and would join us as soon as he could.

With their formal bearing, in their tight-fitting sheepskin jackets and clinging felt boots, they looked trim and clean-cut against the generally disheveled state of affairs in our cabin. They had just removed their jackets when my cousin Paul burst in. Masha insisted they all have some tea and sat by the samovar to pour.

The faces around the table burned from the long exposure to the frost. Oksana's cheeks matched the raspberry scarf with which she had tied her chestnut hair at the back of her neck, the same scarf that had been draped around the electric bulb at the regimental party the night before; her earrings dangled with every impetuous toss of her head.

"No, you won't have time to attend to me if the Reds surround us," Oksana was saying to Verin. "Besides, I won't let you shoot me. I would hate for someone else to take aim at me." She gave an exaggerated shudder and then, sending a fiery glance at him, "Not you of all people, with your bloodthirsty look."

"All I meant was to offer my services," Verin said, counterbalancing her blatant flirtatiousness by a markedly formal manner.

"I don't need your services, just give me a revolver. Why don't I shoot you first? I am familiar enough with firearms."

Igor appeared just then. He had walked in quite inaudibly, as we all walked now in our felt boots. "That's right," he said, "don't trust Verin. He will shoot you, and when it comes his turn he will miss himself." This was met with a new burst of laughter. Igor was coming toward me, but I rose to join him at the table.

I avoided looking at Lorinov, realizing that I had made myself enough of an intruder on his aloofness the night before. Still, before I rose to join

Igor at the table, I could not help seeing from my strategic position on the floor that while Lorinov's right hand was raising a cigarette to his lips, his left one found Margarita's under the table and held it reassuringly.

The conversation quickly moved to crucial subjects. Station Taiga stood at the entrance to the most dense part of the forest, Verin told us, and was the largest and oldest of the nearer settlements. And what was the closest city? Achinsk? Never heard of it. And no towns at all for another five hundred versts? And why did we know so little about Siberia, and about how rich the peasants were? Most of what we had heard and learned about it was disheartening: forced labor in the Sakhalin prisons, wilderness, crime; and here we arrive and find nothing of the sort. Then we spoke about Petrovsk, where the Decembrists had been exiled after their rebellion of 1824 against the autocratic regime of Czar Nicholas I, and the conversation swung to how General Kostin had compared us women to the heroic Decembrist wives who had chosen to follow their husbands into exile.

"How ridiculous," I burst out suddenly, forgetting my intention of keeping a distance from the others, or, if I spoke at all, entering the conversation with greater effect than that. "We followed our husbands out of hell, when staying behind would have meant death, whereas they were leaving everything, even their children and a life of luxury, to go to a country that to them was wild and frightening."

"And now here we are instead of them, ninety-five years later!" Masha said with a wondering sigh.

All at once I could see them here, in this room, the Princesses Troubetzkoy and Volkonsky, the beautiful Alexandrine Mouraviev; I could see their tired young faces, their high-waisted Empire gowns crumpled by the trip, their corkscrew curls coming undone. I saw their husbands driven far ahead of them under heavy guard. So recently gliding over the palatial parquets of St. Petersburg, resplendent in their court uniforms, but now shackled prisoners dragging their chains into the depth of Siberia, dejected losers who now doubted the wisdom and rightness of their selfless endeavor, wondering if the suffering they had brought to themselves and others would ever be justified by life and history, whether they had awakened Russia from her doldrums or pushed her backward toward reaction.

And now they were no more. Now, instead of them, here were we in such a different but similar predicament, also ready to die for our cause and also doomed to be obliterated by time, turned into the same phantoms that they were to us now.

As I watched this unusually good-looking group of people around the table, all so young, all so palpably here, I was back to my old device of stepping outside the circle of my life and gazing at this moment from some remote future that none of us would ever see. I intensified my attention on every detail in an effort to salvage this picture before me from the ruthless torrent of time—to hide it in that magic depth of consciousness that seemed to lie closer to the realm of the permanent and indestructible.

Then, suddenly, I saw that Lorinov, who sat in profile to me on my side of the table, half screened from me by Igor and Margarita, had turned and was watching me. Whatever expression he had caught on my face I immediately erased.

"What is especially strange," Masha went on, her speech acquiring a sort of rhapsodical cadence, "is that we, the direct offspring of the Decembrists, are now traveling the same road. My own great-grandfather was a Decembrist, you know; Countess Cygnen is the granddaughter of one of the really prominent ones. Yes, her mother's father was . . ." Masha leaned across the table and her thin lips soundlessly formed the well-known titled name. "Nita's great-grandfather, the poet, was a sympathizer. Why are you shaking your head, Nita? I know he was, just as Pushkin and his whole circle were. And of course we were taught to admire and revere the Decembrists. But," she wrinkled her face into a dubious frown, "now it seems to me that if it hadn't been for their idealistic self-sacrifice, Russia might still be whole and we might not be here today."

Lieutenant Verin, who had been talking to Oksana but evidently had listened to every word, turned quickly to Masha. "Had the Decembrists succeeded in establishing a constitutional monarchy, we also might not be here today," he said.

He was even better looking than he had seemed to me at first. The dramatic line of his eyebrows, frowning over the dark, glittering eyes, was his outstanding feature. Behind the succinct precision of his well-shaped sentences, a richness of erudition loomed as well. Yet as soon as anyone showed a desire to answer him, he would cut himself short, turn to that person with a quick motion of his shoulders, and congeal in the listening attitude of one who was ready to give his full attention to the speaker, no matter what drivel the speaker might have on his mind. His laughter, on the other hand, was quite a departure from the rest of him. It was a boisterous kind of laughter, accompanied by a sharp toss of his head, as if—being in no real need of levity—he were borrowing it from someone else.

"Perhaps they failed," he was saying, "but their lasting achievement was the tradition of liberal thought that they left to the Russian educated classes."

"Which is just too bad," Paul yelled at him, jumping up from the floor. "As far as I'm concerned, the Decembrists were a bunch—a bunch of gullible dreamers, of quixotic Little Lord Fauntleroys who started all the trouble in Russia."

"They were heroes, they rebelled against a state of affairs that was absolutely unbearable!" Oksana snapped back heatedly, bringing the ghosts of her dead parents into the room. "They stood up for the downtrodden, having nothing to gain personally, nothing! And everything to lose. Wait, Paul, let me have my say! Imagine the 1820s: serfdom, medieval autocracy, monstrous class inequality. . . . Any sensitive person is bound to rise against oppression!"

"I wish all these sensitive persons," Igor began, his usual drawl losing its humorous overtones, acquiring a dangerous heaviness (and I could see, with a measure of smug feminine satisfaction, that Oksana irritated him), "I wish these sensitive persons had first made it their business to find out what *real* oppression can be like, as we know it *now*. That" —and now his voice rose to drown Oksana's— "instead of destroying the imperfect that should and could have been improved, and in fact was being improved under our very eyes."

He said this so loudly and forcefully that I seized his hand under the table, then let it go just as quickly. Experience had shown me that this was the kind of maneuver that Igor might immediately parry by asking, just as loudly, "Why are you grabbing my hand under the table?" But luckily Masha called out, her intention of keeping us quiet now completely forgotten. "Yes, indeed, Igor—as we know oppression now. But weren't we ourselves inexperienced and foolish enough before the March Revolution to feel that anything would be better than what it had been then? With the war going wrong, the inefficiency of our government, with Rasputin poking his scurvy beard into matters of state! Oh! didn't we all plan to kill him? Didn't I myself parade with a red flag on the first day of the coup?"

"It would seem then that one should never right a wrong for fear of making things even worse," Verin said sternly. "I would submit that any idealistic enterprise is open to a host of dangers. Who knew that the storming of the Bastille could lead to Robespierre and to Napoleon? And how close the Jeffersonian idea in America came to being swallowed by the monarchist-like Federalists? In fact, mankind has often needed the hard knocks of revolution to be awakened from its apathy. Look at the progress Russia made after the 1905 Revolution."

"Granted," Lorinov said dryly, putting his teacup down on the table, "but, as you well know, revolutions can be useful only when they are quickly stopped."

Verin frowned. "Not if they are quelled by reaction."

"Certainly not. Otherwise why should we be fighting the Bolsheviks? We are fighting them because they *are* reaction. The kind of tyranny Russia has not seen since Ivan the Terrible, only on a larger scale. After all, why did you, Verin, come over to our side with all the risk it involved for you? To fight dictatorship, which is reaction—didn't you?"

These two had sounded like good friends to me, but this time a note of cold challenge came into Lorinov's tone.

Verin's face closed. "That's one way to put it," he shrugged, condoningly. Then everyone began to talk at once, Paul bewailing all that had been destroyed, Masha affirming optimistically that Russian spiritual culture was so alive, so profound, that it would rise from the dead as soon as the present reign of terror was over.

"The rule of savagery can't last," she said, waving her cigarette negatively in front of her face. "Not in the twentieth century! There are spiritual values that don't burn in fire, nor drown in water."

This declaration of hers impressed itself on my memory, because of the objection raised by Lorinov.

"Unfortunately," he said with deliberate nonchalance, "it is the so-called imperishables, such as idealism, abstract thought, the sense of poetry and of art, that are bound to perish first in times of great historical upheavals." And now he turned to look at me, as if he knew that he had voiced my deepest concern.

But it was time for us to part.

"Good night," Masha said, "hope to see you all tomorrow at the same time."

"Tomorrow at the same place?" Igor asked, and we all laughed.

No Russian could conceive of life without evening tea, even if it were merely yellowish hot water, even if the tea were made—as now in Soviet Russia—out of dried birch leaves. It was a ritual, something tangible around which to gather when the day ended.

If the older people had been annoyed by the noise we made that night, they had also been listening to our conversation. The very next evening, when Masha returned from her short visit with her husband at the Command Post (General Kostin considered it impossible to leave it for a moment) with the news that the Chief's Red Cross sleigh train had been sighted behind us, the Countess also joined us for tea.

"I overheard some of your conversation last night," she said, "so I am coming for a cup of hot tea and a few scraps of thought, the rarest commodity on the present-day market."

"THE RULE of savagery can't last, not in the twentieth century," Masha Kostin had said that evening. Our belief in the irrefutable rectitude of the White cause was based on our direct encounter with that rule.

We all were aware that there had been much in our former Russia (and in the whole world) that could be called savage. Yet the longing for justice, for moral and mental growth, for values that exceeded material and personal blessings, had always permeated the air the Russian educated classes had breathed, rightists and leftists alike. It stemmed from our literature and history, our religion, our arts. In the short span of our childhood and youth, until the war, especially since the Revolution of 1905 mentioned by Verin, which granted so many new freedoms to the people, we saw Russia make powerful strides in so many fields. Mental and material freedom, formerly the prerogative of the privileged class, had been broadening fast before our eyes; economic, cultural, and educational advancement, the adoration of poetry, music, the theater, overflowing into all the nooks and crannies of Russian daily life, created an atmosphere of uplifting purposefulness. To stop the process of dehumanization started by the Bolshevists was, we felt, our duty and privilege. I doubt that it had ever occurred to any of us to mind being exposed to dire danger and hardships. Except for the irreparable loss of those we loved, our trials basically constituted the challenge every young person craves. The very magnitude of our purpose, that of tearing Russia out of her agony, made us live fiercely and passionately, in spite of all our tragic failures.

But why had we failed? What had destroyed us? We could have won! We had come so close to winning last spring when our army had practically approached the Volga, and when it was at the very gates of Tamborsk.

We knew that we were fighting against tremendous odds; that our Volunteer Armies, all three of them—the Southern on the Don, the small Northern one, and our Eastern People's Army under Admiral Kolchak—were just thin strings stretched around the immensity of Communist-held Russia. We knew that we were cut off from Russian war industry, indeed from industry in general; we knew that the slogans we were presenting to the masses—such as "Constituent Assembly, Democracy! Free Elections!" —were incomprehensible, empty sounds to them, while those proclaimed by the Red side screamed their meaning with intoxicating clarity: "All Land to the Peasants! All Power to the Workers and Soldiers!" and especially "Death to Your Exploiters! Grab all you want, it's rightfully yours!" All this would seem to have doomed us to failure from the beginning.

But we did not believe so. We had been certain all along that the sheer dedication of our fighting units and the hatred felt for the Bolsheviks in areas that had already experienced their rule were factors powerful enough for us to win in the end. In spite of the latest tragic developments—the surrender of Omsk, the typhus epidemic, the unfortunate attitude of Generals Janin and Syrovoy (these two by now actually in league against Admiral Kolchak)—in spite of growing disunity on our White side, we still believed that we were not fighting in vain. We still could hold Trans-Baikal Siberia, we still hoped for a new start from there.

If indeed our generation had rejected the optimistic ideology of our fathers, with its faith in the progress of the human race, we nevertheless must have inherited some of this optimism, because when, on the first night of our journey, Masha had declared peremptorily that the rule of savagery could not last in the twentieth century, she had simply voiced our common conviction.

8

IT HAPPENS sometimes that a few days or weeks stand out of the general flow of our lives to form a separate world of their own, days whose richness and novelty, despite the misery they may contain, provide nourishment for many lean years to come. Such were the first two weeks of our journey.

Notwithstanding the tragedy in which we were caught, some good things happened that added a luster of their own against the gathering darkness. I could see that for Margarita this stage of our journey was growing into such a precious, separate life because of her infatuation with Lorinov; the same was true for Oksana and Verin; the same was true for me. Even if there was hardly a corner where Igor and I could be by ourselves, there was hope that one of these days we would be assigned a separate cottage, or at least a separate room. Since he was troop commander and constantly needed at the command post, he would usually be the last one to come, and would, in most cases, leave before the other officers. When he left by himself I would come out with him and see him part of the way to his quarters. Perhaps as we hugged goodnight we would exchange only a few words, but in them we compressed all our understanding of tomorrow's uncertainty, all our desperate hunger for each other. Alik had set a poem to music whose simplicity and rhythm held a special heartbreaking charm for me. I would repeat one line to Igor when I had no words of my own:

There is so much I have not told you yet. . . .

And there was indeed something of the utmost importance of which I had not yet spoken to Igor, but had always wanted to since the day we had been married. In our present predicament, the urgency of this "something" had increased. I felt that he must know through what experiences I had come to my unshakable faith in life, and what my credo really was, so that in case I should be the first to die, he could tell our son about it.

THE SAME SNOW, the same huge firs crowding along the road, the same dark balls of birds with frost-ruffled feathers dotting the telegraph lines. Yet we could tell one day from another by impressions that we had at this or that stop, in this or that village—both the good impressions and the bad ones striking and unforgettable.

On top of all that already weighed upon us, some new calamity occurred nearly every day. Someone in the regiment succumbed to typhus—Igor's orderly, of whom he was so fond, had been stricken when we first started out. Then several men of the Third Troop, including the staff sergeant, disappeared when we were passing close to their village.

"I know how you must feel," I said to Igor that night. "But how can you blame those poor boys for deserting."

Igor shrugged. "It's simply the first screw falling out. When you have put all you've had . . . all you've had," he repeated bitterly, "into something as solid and as good as our regiment, to hear it give its first death rattle is . . . hard to take."

Then one day came the report of the death of a highly regarded general. This general had received orders from the army commander that he believed to be unfulfillable. He so informed the commander. Frantic with all the catastrophic trouble on his hands, the latter bellowed that he could not tolerate any insubordination—to which the dissenting general repeated sharply that he refused to carry out his orders.

"If such is the case, you are relieved of further duty," the army commander roared.

"I won't be relieved of duty, sir!"

Suddenly losing control of himself, the army commander snatched out his revolver and shot the general on the spot. This report, although later proven to be true, seemed too shattering at the time for us to believe it.

Then one day disastrous news came from the city of Tomsk. The local garrison, heavily infiltrated and propagandized by the Reds and equally frustrated by our failures, was on the verge of an uprising. Tomsk, an old university city, was the cultural center of Western Siberia, located ninety miles to the north of the Trans-Siberian Railroad and connected with it by a branch line. The population of Tomsk was now pouring down this branch to Station Taiga, where the two lines converged—crowds of panic-stricken refugees riding, driving, walking, dragging their sick on hand sleds, flooding the roads. It was a known fact that between eight and nine hundred thousand people—troops and refugees, almost one-fifth of them by now sick with typhus—had left our White capital of Omsk back in November, and we could imagine what was awaiting us after the throngs descending from Tomsk reached the highway.

Although most of the depressing news was carefully guarded by the officers from us women, it reached us just the same. Yet its import was veiled for us by our instinctive desire to regard news as unconfirmed rumor, and by the hunger for life with which we faced these days, each of which might be the last. In the meantime, one of the good things that happened to me personally was the closeness that had sprung up between Oksana and myself.

One evening—this must have been on the fourth day of our journey—when I came out on the porch to shake out Bibik's blanket, I saw two dark shadows huddled together against the side wall of the cottage: Lieutenant Verin and Oksana in each other's arms. His back was turned to me, but she saw me.

That very night, when almost everyone in the place was asleep, while Margarita was washing her hair in the opposite corner, Oksana came up to me with a blanket over her shoulder. "Look here, Nita," she said, "do you mind if I wedge myself between Margarita and you for the night? You see, I was glad it was you, not anyone else, who caught me. I know that in your family there must be different views on things, quite different; but even if I shock you I would like to have a real talk with you about it all just the same. I feel that you are the sort of person with whom I can speak in my 'total voice.'"

I liked this. I loved the onslaught of eager, all-out confidence in her manner, combined with a sort of devil-may-care flippancy. As she lay stretched on her blanket beside me that night, her head propped on her elbow, her fingers buried in the mass of her hair, she plunged right into the thick of things.

"Remember that regimental party? When you drove away with Igor, Verin said he would walk me to where I was quartered. It was close by, and on our way he spoke to me in that ultra-courteous manner of his about whatever it was. I had no idea what he was saying. I only knew that something fateful, terrific was happening to me. I was quartered in a sort of huge warehouse opening right into the street, jam-packed with refugees, all of them asleep. The only light inside was a candle burning by the entrance. As we stepped in he helped me out of my coat as ceremoniously as if I were royalty, and I just had time to think: how funny, such formality, in this kind of setting. Then he suddenly blew out the candle, whispered into my ear, 'Quiet,' and simply crushed me to himself."

In spite of her trying to keep her voice down to a whisper, the words glittered and throbbed, ready to explode all over the room. "But just then a man's voice called out of the darkness: 'Who's there? What's this?' And Verin replied loudly over my shoulder, 'The candle went out. I'm looking for matches . . . one moment.'" But naturally he was not looking for matches. His lips were on her mouth, then on her throat and neck. "You know, Nita, it was not only . . . I mean, it was the daring, the surprise that was a thrill! Am I shocking you, Nita?"

"No, but you're trying to, so go on!"

"No, I'm not. I'm simply madly, idiotically in love."

As the days went by it became her outlet to tell me all about it. She was not a bit blinded by her infatuation; her critical sense seemed to be as much on the alert as the rest of her. Verin was brilliant, extraordinary, but he actually knew too much. He had read everything, had been acquainted with all the celebrities, traveled everywhere. This was somehow tiresome. The best you could do to impress him was to play the perfect fool, once in a while throwing in some well-aimed insults at him, to deflate his balloon. And yet, what a man! Fearless, decisive . . . the risks he took when he defected from the Reds with all of that important intelligence sewed into his tunic lining!

As she talked I listened, the frustrated writer in me watching the contrasting patterns of our attitudes toward men and love come into sharp focus. "I'm telling you everything," Oksana would say, "partly because I know that you won't repeat it to anyone and also because I have to unburden myself to someone. But chiefly because someday you might be a sort of banister in case I lose my balance. We Belovs are all like that: we rush headlong where others fear to tread."

"A banister of which you would let go whenever it pleased you," I said.

"I suppose so." And we laughed.

As to Margarita, she was in a happy daze that made her utterly inarticulate. Often after Lorinov left she would look at me with a tremulous smile as if to say, "What can I do about it? How can I help it?"

In the meantime I was anxious to straighten out something intangible between Lorinov and myself. Sensing in him a growing awareness of me, I avoided him, and he ostensibly was too absorbed in Margarita to notice my efforts. However, our studied disregard of each other had the half-audible overtones of some subtle, surreptitious game that he and I were playing over Margarita's head. I felt I must channel this whatever-it-was—a subsurface competition in mental alertness, a curiosity about each other—into some direct and open relationship. Or into none at all.

In fact, this whatever-it-was became so tangible to me during the first few days of our trip that I often felt him to be mentally distorting my words into an altogether different meaning, probably just for the fun of it. "No thank you, no more tea," I would say, preparing to leave the tea-drinking group, "I have to attend to Bibik." While the nonchalant blankness with which he would look at me through the smoke of his cigarette changed my words into: No thank you. I'm afraid that my presence might endanger the idyllic romance flourishing before me. I don't wish to participate in its collapse. I want to be a loyal wife and friend, this noble attitude making my person the more intriguing. Meanwhile, the air of unconcern with which I left the table would, in spite of me, reply to these unspoken words that there was a difference between loyalty to a friend and the desire to build oneself up in a young man's eyes.

One night when Countess Cygnen had led us into discussing Pushkin and Lermontov, and what made people prefer one to the other, Lorinov said nonchalantly, his foggy glance sliding around the circle and coming to rest on me, "The fact that I admire Pushkin certainly doesn't rule out my being charmed by Lermontov, does it?"

At this Igor, who was sitting beside Margarita, turned to her with his amused one-sided grin: "Just as the fact that Serge likes singing gypsy love songs doesn't prevent him from dabbling in wireless telegraphy." This remark, taken by Margarita at face value, passed unnoticed by the others, except Lorinov, whose expression went blank for the rest of the evening.

I realized only later that when any wireless messages flew between Lorinov and me, elusive as they were, Igor would usually find a seat beside Margarita and indulge in what he himself called a "heavy barrage" flirtation with her. Flattered, feeling that she was gaining stature in Lorinov's eyes, she would blush delightedly, at the same time shooting furtive glances at me: was she allowed to let my husband court her? Was she, who stood at the threshold of her "seventeenth spring," making me, a doddering woman of twenty-three, jealous? Although I knew Igor too well not to realize what he was doing, and that Margarita rated in his eyes as a charming little bore, her imagining that she could mean anything to him made me bristle. So did my realization of how easy it was for Igor to blow at the iridescent soap bubbles floating between his best friend and me, to show them for what they really were.

Not that what interested me in Lorinov—an aura of uncanny mental awareness—could be entirely reduced to a drop of soapy water.

9

THE DAY WHEN we came close to Station Taiga, General Kostin decided to make a slight detour south from the Trakt in order to escape the jam that had developed at the junction of the Trakt with the Tomsk Highway.

It was one of those windless mornings (actually the middle of the night to us) when the air is frozen to the crispness of glass and every sound engraves itself on the darkness with such precision that you can trace its outline with a pencil.

I had just come on the porch of our cottage. I loved to be the first one to come outside with Bibik to steal a moment of quiet before the noise and movement of departing troops, to gaze at the stars overhead, and listen to my footsteps on the hard-packed snow fall into the silence like notes of music. And yet, how could I? For these were the same stars I had watched with horrified eyes on the night when I fled from home; the same stars at which my father had looked from an open truck just a week later when a firing squad drove him to where he was shot. Never again, I had felt, could I lift my eyes without horror to this unyielding gulf between God and man, hammered in by myriads of frightful metallic nails. So, why should I now come out to catch a moment to be alone with them? How was it possible that again the stars should reassure me of the wonder of life, telling me that nothing great could be really broken or vanquished? At least within us.

Against the black immensity of sky the stars stood out alive and trembling. The row of cottages along the village street squinted half-awake through frosted windowpanes; straight streamers of smoke rose from every chimney. The regiment was forming somewhere close by, and every now and then the shout of a command, the neighing of a horse, would send the frozen stillness flying into splinters like shattered glass.

I was just about to cross the front yard of our cottage when its door squeaked open and Oksana rushed after me. "Nita, listen!" Electric sparks flew from her voice. "I have to tell you something important!" She was holding her carryall but dropped it on the snow and began hurriedly to tie her red scarf over her fur cap. "Do you know what happened last night? When I came back from a stroll with Verin you were already asleep, so I couldn't tell you. . . . Give him to me." She held out her arms to take Bibik.

"You mean when Verin took you out in search of a little fresh air?"

She laughed, dandling Bibik. "I wanted to ask you what you thought of it all. Do you know what Verin told me? He is engaged. Has been for two years, and hasn't seen her for just as long. Yes, because she is in Petrograd under the Reds. This came to me as such a shock!"

"Did he tell you who she is?" We came to the gate and stopped.

"Not her last name, but he showed me her picture—a girl in nurse's uniform—signed 'Nina.' So pretty that it's awful! Compared to her, I . . ." She made a disgusted grimace and hid her face in the fold of Bibik's blanket, although something different from disgust throbbed in her voice.

"In other words she will never see him again. This is terrible."

"Don't think I'm not sorry for her," Oksana said, pressing Bibik to herself by way of expressing the strength of her compassion, and perhaps of her compunction. "But what about me? I make no secret of how I feel about him and am pretty certain that I'm beginning to mean a lot more to him than he expected. Nita, why do you think he told me about her at all?"

The silhouette of a rider, the leader of our train, the same one who awakened us in the morning—Coco Scheyin—had just appeared from around the turn of the street. Our train of sleighs was crawling behind him; their runners squeaked on the stiff morning snow. "Why did he?" Oksana repeated on a lower note, at the same time helping Bibik bounce. "Was he warning me so I wouldn't expect a proposal? Besides, what kind of proposal can there be nowadays? Or, for that matter, a proposition? Where would one go?"

"Hush," I said, with a nod toward Coco Scheyin, who was steering his horse toward the gate. "But if he is engaged and has fallen in love with you, then why shouldn't he tell you about her?"

"And yet why should he? That's what I asked him point blank: 'Why are you speaking to me about her? To tell me about your broken heart, or are you by any chance giving me a warning?'"

The cabin door had just opened, exhaling a cloud of milky vapor through which moved the figures of the Countess, Alenka, Masha, and

— 76 —

others. Oksana's voice dropped to a whisper, "And he said, 'Because I don't wish to conceal anything from you. It all started between us like an exciting game, but I no longer feel it's only a game.' Then I felt . . . well, you know!"

Coco was wheeling his mount to face the train. "Don't delay, ladies! The regiment has formed already. Everyone out!"

I remembered the Coco of some six years ago, a ten-year-old boy in Tamborsk. Dressed in a sailor suit, he was standing on the platform of the Great Hall of the House of Nobles, violin in hand, a frail boy with huge sad eyes and, as people used to say, "with a tremendous future, if he only makes it physically."

Now, having volunteered for the army at fourteen, he had been appointed head of our train. From morning till night we would see him weaving his way on horseback among different sleighs, now shouting orders to the drivers, now dismounting to give a hand to a broken sleigh, now galloping ahead with some urgent report to the regiment, which moved ahead of us. However, I had hardly ever seen his face, only a fur cap coming down on his brows, a scarf bulging over his neck and chin. Thus I had never been able to identify Private Scheyin with the sad-eyed little genius in a sailor suit, nor to fit his violin into the picture.

The bark of a command in General Kostin's throttled voice—or was it a greeting?—had just come from the village thoroughfare where the regiment had lined up, and now came the rhythmic uproar of the soldiers' response. I put Bibik in a sitting position so he could watch the regiment pass. The great moment for us both: he watching the horses, I waiting to catch a glimpse of Igor.

The thud of horses' hooves on the snow, the squeaking of saddles, the occasional snort of a horse came magnified by the darkness. General Kostin rode at the head of the column. His right arm akimbo, his horse prancing under him, he looked like a sculpture of the perennial warrior he really was. His second-in-command, Lorinov, behind him, was making his mare counterpoint Kostin's pace by the unhurried steadiness of her walk, by the nonchalant way she tossed her head. And now Igor at the head of the First Troop, reining his horse toward us! He rode up, produced a small bag out of his pocket and dropped it on my lap. "Crackers from an American can for Bibik," he said. "Keep them under your dokha." His lashes were frost coated, as if made of the same fur as his gray caracul cap. Then he added, a smile climbing up one side of his face, "We're detouring Station Taiga, leaving the general traffic, you know, so we might get a separate cottage tonight. Let's keep our fingers crossed."

"Oh, Igor! Can this really be? What luck!" He nodded happily and rode off.

I was tucking the package under my dokha when a woman's bellow made me start. A peasant woman had burst from one of the cabins and was running toward the moving column screaming, trying to catch at the stirrups of the passing riders, stretching her arms toward them.

"What is it?" Panna asked, startled. I knew what it was. Igor had told me the night before that the regiment had requisitioned a woman's favorite gelding and left a tired horse in exchange. "But one that is no worse than hers, only needs a breathing spell."

I explained this to Panna, but she shifted in the sleigh indignantly: "I wonder what your father or Alik would have said about this."

"Other units simply take what they want," I said. "Any army during any war . . . What else can you do? Leave one of the men behind, to walk?" I spoke aggressively, as Igor would have done. Yet Panna was voicing my own pity for the sobbing woman, and the pity that I knew Igor felt.

Troop after troop, three men abreast, moved by at a gradually accelerating pace. Cousin Paul, with loose, dangling earflaps, was wheeling his horse around, shouting and swearing in his special commander's voice. An artist through and through, he couldn't help feeling that employed in any other capacity he was only acting a part, so he had better put all he had into the acting. "Close it up, you devils," he roared. "Close it up, you laggards, I tell you. What the hell, stringing out like sausages?!"

The last troop changed to a brisk trot, the horses pressing upon the ones ahead. The woman was still running, still screaming; more lights had gone on in the cabins and some dark figures stood in front of them, grimly watching.

Now our train began to move at the same pace as the regiment, and the woman, outrun by the last troop, gave vent to a frantic wail and fell blindly face-down into the snowdrift. She still lay there wailing when our sleigh passed her.

THAT AFTERNOON the sky clouded over, the frost softened, and a gentle snow began to fall. It was gathering, placid and flaky, on Private Doushin's shoulders and on our lap robe. Since we had left the Trakt the traffic had become thinner and our train had been moving at an even pace.

As dusk fell we reached the village where we were to spend the night, a prosperous-looking place with a white church in the center of town, the cottages large, many-windowed, with carved shutters.

There were no other troops or sleigh trains to be seen and evidently plenty of room to quarter our division, for—just as Igor had told me—a large separate cottage was placed at our disposal. It happened to be the last cottage in the street, which had straggled out into the woods. Half hidden by snow-clad spruces, it was reminiscent of something enchanting seen in childhood storybooks. Inside, it smelled of fresh timber and pitch; its front room was an enormous kitchen with a nook where two peasants in sheepskins sat at the table by a samovar, conversing with the mistress of the house, a square block of a woman. As we came in the three fell silent.

Except for this nook, the kitchen and a bedroom next to it were all ours, and Panna was evidently inspired to celebrate the occasion. She made straight toward the tea-drinking group and demanded that the mistress of the house sell her some eggs, milk, pelmeny, whatever she had on hand. The woman, her gruff voice carrying the same impact as Panna's, replied that she had nothing to sell. A cossack regiment had passed through yesterday and eaten everything in sight. To this Panna snapped that she would find all she wanted at some other house. Returning to the bedroom, she handed Bibik's bottle to me. "Will you try to warm it without letting it burst?" The words were packed with reference to all the humiliating defeats I had endured in my struggle with the elements. The milk in the bottle was a chunk of ice.

The safest way to warm a bottle of frozen milk was to put it into an earthenware bowl filled with tepid water and to push the bowl into the center of the oven by means of a special iron fork on a long wooden handle, oukhvat. I rolled up the sleeves of my sweater, pushed up my jingling bracelets, and, oukhvat in both hands, leaned down to the mouth of the oven. The heap of embers glowing in its depth scorched my face and bare arms, the bracelets burned into my skin, the stones in them and in my ring twinkled in the thickening dusk of the room.

The bowl came to rest successfully among the embers, and I was withdrawing the red-hot oukhvat from the oven, when something made me start. Sharply I wheeled around.

One of the peasants—with red-gold hair—stood a few paces behind me, his head thrust forward, bull-like. His protruding eyes, a stupid, greedy blue, were fastened on my bracelets.

"Drop that! Hand me them baubles!"

I stood there clutching the oukhvat with both hands, its red-hot prongs glimmering between me and the man. The realization that the other peasant was no longer by the samovar but must be watching the entrance dawned on me a second later as the door jerked open a crack and he leaned into the room.

"Get moving, Yashka! Beat it! They're here," he hissed.

The redhead leaped for the door, then with a sudden change of mind he turned back on me again. "Drop the oukhvat, *hear*? Want me to pull them baubles off with your arm?"

I was no longer holding the oukhvat: it had simply grown fast to my hands. I could not possibly have had the courage to answer the man, but the other man's words echoed in my ears. "Get moving, Yashka, beat it! They're coming!" I screamed in a frenzied fishwife's voice.

Redhead could have thrown me down with one movement, but just then some shadows obscured the windows, there were muffled outcries, and he made a wild dash for the door. As he pulled it open, Serge Lorinov and two soldiers behind him were already barring the way.

"What's going on here?" Lorinov asked in an extra-calm voice.

My hands and legs suddenly turned into rags. I lowered the oukhvat and stood there propping myself on it. "I'm warming my baby's milk," I said with foolish bravado.

"Is that all?" he asked. "All right, boys," and he nodded to the soldiers, "take this one to the Command Post also."

The man began to struggle and yell, trying to tear himself out of the soldiers' grip, as they twisted and tied his arms behind his back. He had done nothing wrong, he howled, just came here to drink a hot cup of tea, but Lorinov silenced him with a curt upward pull of his revolver. "Be *quiet*! You can tell them at the Command Post how you came here to have tea. They'll want to hear all about it." As the soldiers led the man away, Lorinov called to them from the threshold, "Send over for Doushin. We have to move this party back into the village," and he walked toward the woman in the nook. Her massive back turned to us, she was clearing the table. "Who were those people?" he asked her in an iron tone.

The woman took a rag from the shelf and began furiously to scrub the table.

"Who are they, I asked you?"

"And how do I know who they are?" she burst out. "People come from dawn to night—coming, going, eating, sleeping. You wouldn't know your own father!"

"I'm asking you," —his voice rose— "whether those peasants are from this village."

Although I felt that Lorinov had entirely disassociated himself from my person, I was also aware that but for my presence he would have reduced the woman to a pulp.

"Strangers," she growled, standing in profile to him. "From Sud-janka. Come to buy horses."

"How many have been here, in the village? Will you answer me, or would you rather be taken to the Command Post also?"

The woman's face grew purple. "I didn't see no one but those two." She dropped her rag, took her coat from a peg, and was going to slip into it.

"Not yet." This time his words clicked as if a gun were being loaded. "You are not going anywhere yet." She stopped in her tracks. He threw several bills on the table. "Here. Some tea and what goes with it." He turned to me with a curt aside; "Your milk must have boiled over." I was vaguely aware of the smell of burning milk. Then he ordered the woman to bring some fresh milk, too, and make it quick!

"I have to go outside to the cellar for the milk and butter anyway," she grumbled, "and it's time to milk my cows, but you are not letting me out."

"All right, bring everything and then go and milk your cows. But don't try to leave the premises, understand?" She went.

Bibik had just appeared in the doorway in his turquoise shirt and tiny felt boots, cracker crumbs on his cheeks. I walked toward him and took him in my arms. I was trembling. Was it from the shock of having been threatened by that red-haired fellow, or from having witnessed the scene of his arrest? The important thing, however, was to not be a weakling.

I sat down at the table at my end of the room, Bibik on my lap. Lorinov came up. "I regret having had to put you through all this," he said, unbuttoning his sheepskin, "but it couldn't be helped. May I sit down?" His face was blank, his tone hard and formal. "I'm afraid I'll have to stay here until my men return. Will you tell me exactly what took place before I came?"

"He wanted my bracelets," I said, matching his imperturbable man-ner. "He wanted me to take them off and give them to him. It's my own fault, foolish of me to display them like this, exposing people to temptation."

Lorinov frowned. "What did he do?"

"He simply demanded them. What will you do to him now?"

The only bloody retribution on the part of our "People's Army" that we knew of, inevitable though it had seemed, was the quelling of the Communist insurrection at Koustanay at the very outset of our move-ment. But what if all I had read in foreign papers about White reprisals (of which no concrete cases had ever come to my own attention) didn't apply only to Ataman Semenov's forces at Chita, or the demented Baron Ungern in Mongolia? What if we, of Admiral Kolchak's People's Army, who fought in the name of democracy, the Constituent Assembly, free-dom and humanitarianism, were employing the same terrorist methods? What if Lorinov's soldiers at this very moment were leading these peas-ants into the forest to shoot them?

"You can't possibly take prisoners along with you, so what do you do with them?"

The creases on Lorinov's cheeks tightened. "I see," he said, annoyed, slapping the pockets of his breeches, searching for his cigarette case and finally producing it from a breast pocket. "You are afraid that this character will be shot, so you are shielding him. But you don't have to worry. He'll be forwarded to Division Headquarters and questioned, that's all. Why should you be concerned about the scoundrel?"

Several cups stood on the table and Bibik was fidgeting in my arms, reaching toward them. As I showed him that they were empty, he went into piercing, hungry screams. I went on speaking through his cries. "It would be dreadful, terrible, if we did the same as the Reds do to us. We can't be responsible for what others do, but at least our division . . . Bibik, stop it! Your milk is coming. . . . And if a man is going to be killed because of my foolishness—I know it's war, but . . . ."

Lorinov brought out a cigarette and was tapping it against his leather case, looking at me with impenetrable, clouded eyes. "It's *civil* war, in which the devil himself can't tell what's his and what isn't. May I smoke?"

"Oh, why ask! But, please, Serguey Yury'ch," I injected a note of resistance into the utterance of his name, "will you do everything you can to prevent any violence to this . . . Leave that cup alone, Bibik." I snatched a cup out of the baby's hands. "I am not being sentimental. I wouldn't plead for a commissar or a dedicated Communist, it's they we are fighting!" I had much more pity, I thought, for the woman who had lost her horse that morning—oh, much more!—than for any Commu-nists who advocated terrorism and who might as well get what they preached. "But what does this fellow know about anything? He didn't even know that my bracelets have no value at present."

Lorinov's cheek flicked irritably. He lit his cigarette. "I'm afraid that he knows a lot more than most of us do. However, if anything unfortunate happens to this man it won't be because of what he did to you." (Meaning: You are inflating your own importance.) "Besides, I'm pretty sure that nothing will be done to him at all." He took a long drag on his cigarette, making me feel that the cigarette was helping him to endure the bother of my presence. "The policy at headquarters is to let the peasants be. As to the prisoners we take, we also give them a chance to defect to our side.

Unless, of course," he added, "they are, as you just said yourself, dedicated Communists or partisans."

"I know, but—"

"At Ufa alone we took over twelve thousand prisoners," he interrupted, "and they all came over to us like one man. True, this kind of operation often results in tragedy. There are too many spies and propaganda agents among them, and we are too easily duped." He was shaking the cigarette ashes into his saucer, frowning. I saw that his fingers were long and wiry, the tips of his narrow nails curving down hawklike.

"Generally speaking, these defectors constitute the most dangerous element in our army—Red today, White tomorrow—but we accept them just the same, often blindly. I am speaking only for the army, mind you, and only for the part of the army I know. I'm not trying to whitewash whatever crimes of omission or commission are being perpetrated by the Whites in general."

He was facing the windows. In the exiguous light his eyes looked a darker gray than they had seemed to me before.

"You said Red soldiers defect to our side, but if they don't . . ."

"Then it means that they are hard-core communists—and if so, we have them shot." The word slashed through the air. *"But"* —with a fierce motion he ground his cigarette against the saucer—"we don't pour kerosene over them to burn them alive as the Reds did last spring to two of my best soldiers who weren't even volunteers but mobilized Siberian boys. You probably heard about it from Igor." (I had not.) "We don't sear shoulder straps with a hot iron into the flesh of our prisoners, or shoot their wives and children, as the Reds did at Izhevsk. You may have heard" —and he might as well have said, "You, who seem not to know anything, may have heard" —"what the census showed when Izhevsk was recaptured by our side: eight thousand people machine-gunned! And who could these people be, since all the men, young and old, were in the White ranks?"

I certainly knew all about it. I had been haunted for days by the horror of this massacre. However, at this particular moment my mind was on Lorinov's mounting anger with what to him was my silly feminine sentimentality. I would probably have felt indignant at this, and at the abrasive way in which he was talking to me, and would have enjoyed holding my own if it had not suddenly occurred to me that here before me was the same Lorinov who had led that famous cavalry attack last July in the Urals. The very Lorinov who had, with his own hands, sabered in half the commander of the Bolshevist "Steel Regiment," and probably had sent many others to their death. It was odd that until that moment I had never clearly connected the complex, sensitive, fastidious Lorinov I knew with that ruthless fighter.

"If you think, Serguey Yury'ch," I began, "that I don't understand what it means for a man of your—your exceptional awareness—to carry the responsibility for other people's lives . . ."

He shrugged and said, as if he had not really heard me and was still pursuing his former thread of thought, "You saw this woman. Why did she dare talk so rudely to me? Because she knows by experience and hearsay that we are an indulgent lot, often stupidly so, just as we often are stupidly cruel. In any case, the fellow you are so worried about will be all right. I know the type. He'll be on our side in no time."

It became difficult to keep hungry Bibik quiet as the gloomy *baba* reentered with a bowl of milk, some butter and bread. She set it all at our table, brought over a samovar, and announced sullenly: "I'll go now to milk my cows."

Lorinov turned to her. For a moment he studied her unflinching face with the same cold attention with which one would study a geographical map. "All right. But stay *nearby, hear?* You'll be sorry if you don't."

When she left he stepped toward the window. There he stood for some time with his back to me, his head thrust forward, watching something outside. Then, lighting a fresh cigarette, still standing, he said into the air without turning, "Much nicer without that toad of a female, isn't it?"

I had soaked some bread in Bibik's milk and was feeding it to him. Once in a while he would turn to me between gulps to laugh with happiness. The glow of logs in the oven was building our shadows huge over the opposite wall, and a smoke-flavored warmth swam through the kitchen. In the window one could see the freshly snowed-under branches of firs. A crack had appeared in the clouds massed low over the horizon, opening a cherry-red streak of sunset.

Until this moment Lorinov had positively resented my presence here. Now, however, with his "much nicer without that toad of a female," I sensed that suddenly he was back to where he'd been before, challenging me to the same subtle game he had been playing with me. This was as clear to me as if he had said, *"Enfin seuls."* As he stood there now in profile to me, smoking, I sensed that he was enjoying the silence that had fallen between us, letting it hang like a curtain after an act in a play.

Whether because my own attention had been diverted from his person by what had just happened, or because my intention to arrest the undercurrent flowing between us had gradually grown into decision, I suddenly heard myself say in a most earnest and natural manner, "Thank you, Serguey Yury'ch. Thank you for everything."

He turned. "For what?"

"For the milk. For staying here and watching over us. For arriving at such a critical moment. The timing was miraculous."

"For this you should thank your husband," he said, returning to the table. "Igor learned that you were quartered so far out and asked me to look you up, since he could not come himself. So my appearance here is in no way a miraculous one."

"But it is! At least, when a certain pattern in our experience repeats itself again and again and can't be explained logically, then we call it miraculous. Some tea?"

He bowed briefly and sat down. "What sort of pattern do you mean?"

"In my case, being rescued at the last moment . . . and mostly from a danger of which I was hardly aware."

"Oh! So you admit that you were in danger."

"Well, perhaps," I laughed. "That redhead seemed to be rash and stupid. But anyway, the pattern in my case has been—at least up to this time—that of being rescued at the very last minute." I handed him his tea. "Since we fled from home, Igor has appeared three times and rescued me from the Reds, like the good cowboy in an implausible American film who—"

"—comes galloping wildly to save the life of the heroine and is rewarded by her everlasting admiration. Poor Igor! This one time he had to cede the feat to me."

I let this pass. I felt at ease with him. Now that I had found this friendly tone, I was not going to let him push me off in another direction. I shared my father's inclination to get into direct contact with people who attracted his special attention.

I poured some tea for myself and said, "I am at a loss about what voice to take with you. I have one voice for my husband's best friend, Serge Lorinov; another for the debonair Colonel Lorinov whom I met at General Kostin's party; and again another for the man who . . . well . . ."

"Who almost broke up your marriage," he said, looking at me through the smoke of his cigarette, and waving it away as if to see better how I could stand his gaze.

"Exactly!" Without knowing it, he was helping me to say what I had in mind, and the fact that that was so different from what he might be expecting spurred me on. "That's exactly it! The Serge Lorinov who had been so badly wounded was someone quite different again. He was part and symbol of all human suffering; someone about whom one couldn't think without pain, and without the sense of closeness . . . with which people meet on some different, deeper plane—where everyone is a friend and brother to everyone."

I was well aware that such concepts as "meeting on a different, deeper plane" and "symbolizing human suffering"—ideas so real and alive to me—would have only tickled his sense of the ridiculous, were I not manipulating these words with the same offhand confidence and awareness of their potential power with which he manipulated his weapons.

Frowning and grinning mockingly at the same time, he said, "I wish I had known *then* that I had such a friend. I also hope that you prayed for the salvation of my soul."

"I wasn't sure whether you had one! So all that was left to me was to pray for your recovery."

Why on earth did I say this? Perhaps because Panna entered just then, and I simply fell back on the first words that would end this conversation.

At the sight of Panna, Bibik slid down from my lap and dashed toward her. The door had hardly closed behind her when Doushin appeared. Lorinov rose, and signaled to him to take our luggage. Both stepped into the little room and I could hear them talk in low voices.

"Panna, please—don't unpack anything," I said to her as she leaned low toward Bibik and plunged her hand into the bag with a tantalizing smile, "we shall be moving right away to another cottage in the center of the village."

She straightened up abruptly. "I'm not going anywhere from here."

"How do you mean you aren't?" I dropped my voice to a low, conspiratorial aside. "Do you realize that while you were away one of those mouzhiks here almost killed me?"

"Nonsense," she said. Indeed, what I had said sounded even to myself as silly dramatics, one of those gross overstatements with which I often dealt backhand strokes at her.

IT WAS QUITE dark outside when we left the cabin. A few snowflakes still fluttered in the quiet air. As he helped me into the sleigh, Lorinov said, "I heard you explain to your . . . to Panna Krylocka why I am moving you from here. Frankly, I was not quite sure that you realized who those men were."

"You mean—Red partisans?"

I had spoken to Panna off the top of my head, my only intention being to scare her out of the house, and I was now taken aback. "We have to move out of this village, then?"

"Oh, no, this is just their reconnaissance. Now that they know a whole cavalry division is here and alerted to their presence, they will retreat into the woods. We are too strong a unit for them, nor can they take us by surprise."

"Why not?"

"Because they know that since we caught their men, we'll be on the alert and we'll patrol the village all night. Don't give a thought to them: there are only small detachments of them around here."

I knew this. I also knew that the worst was ahead, that the bands of the partisan leader Schetinkin, who had made a bloody hash of the Whites, were lurking farther southeast around Kransnoyarsk. But Krasnoyarsk was still far away, while the night air was so quiet, the snow coming down with such caressing calm.

"In a way, I can't help feeling indebted, indebted to these partisans tonight." And, cutting himself short, he turned to Doushin who had already climbed onto the box.

"Get on!"

AFTER WE had been moved to the center of the village and again quartered with everybody else, Igor came. He already knew everything from Lorinov and was confident that we were in no danger; the village would be patrolled until morning, the horses would remain saddled; nothing to fear. The night went off quietly. I was the only one of the women who knew that the partisans were somewhere nearby (Panna had not believed me anyway), and I was more preoccupied with the way I had handled my problem with Lorinov, with the step I had made toward an open and valuable friendship, than with the danger of a partisan attack.

I needed Lorinov's friendship because he was the only man who was really close to Igor, and I wanted to be included in their closeness; also, because I was perceiving certain qualities of mind in Lorinov that were congenial to my own, related to the mainsprings of my being. Perhaps I felt the same way toward him as Coco Sheyin would feel toward a valuable violin: I shall only practice on it a little bit, I shall only try out its tone. It isn't mine, I don't wish to take it with me, I have one of my own.

That night it was understood among Igor, Lorinov, and me that there would be no mention of the episode of my bracelets. By morning, however, everyone knew the whole story, and at our next stop, when we rejoined the mainstream of the retreat and gathered around the next-in-turn samovar, the sense of recovered security created an atmosphere of special closeness among us. The conversation was lively and light, and I was prompted to make a funny story of how I had attacked the partisans with an oukhvat, mimicking the gloomy baba, Lorinov's iron voice, and his manner of holding his cigarette, and caricaturing myself. It came out well; everyone laughed, most of all Lorinov, who—both pleased and annoyed—recognized himself. He was quite animated that night, and I felt that I had after all succeeded in untying some sort of psychological knot between us.

The cottage that night was large and bare—no chairs, just benches along the walls, a tiny candle-end that was quickly burning out, and the rest of the room pitch dark. When Paul went to look for candles in the commissary, we also asked him to bring Lorinov's guitar.

That night Lorinov sang even better than at General Kostin's party. He sat on some logs close to the fire, part of his profile and the deck of his guitar catching the faint glimmer of coals, Margarita close to him, the rest of us indecipherable shadows. Igor was beside me, his arm around my shoulders.

Among other songs, Lorinov sang "Autumn Winds." Before starting he turned to Igor and flung him a casual, "This one is for you," and Igor murmured into my ear with good-natured mockery, "Most thoughtful of him, don't you think?" Then, at the very end of that evening, when requested by Alenka Gottel to sing an old-fashioned song that began with the words, "Why should we lie? We know we love each other," and ended with "And so to you I shall be just a brother," Igor again whispered into my ear, "Our family is growing."

"Oh, Igor, stop it! Are you trying to spoil his singing for me?"

"What else?"

Oksana and Verin were in the farthest corner and the darkest.

10

WHEN WE RETURNED to the main highway after having detoured around Station Taiga, the whole manner and tempo of our journey changed. We had traveled several hundred versts and were in the central, windy part of Siberia. The days were sunny, but when a north wind arose, breathing was painful, like swallowing brilliant daggers.

The rumors that the city of Tomsk was on the eve of insurrection, the population fleeing, proved to be true. Crowds of pedestrians and innumerable sleigh trains from Tomsk and from regions north of the highway shouldered into our traffic, playing havoc with it.

The roadbed was being torn up more and more. The heavy sleigh-borne artillery and ammunition trains ahead of us were digging progressively deeper into the snow, turning former holes in the road into a chain of hills and ravines, many of them as deep by now as eight or ten feet. Into these ravines the tormented horses slid, bearing the weight of the sleigh on their backs. At the bottom the sleigh would turn over, breaking down, spilling the passengers into the snow, blocking the traffic.

While the damage was being repaired, the familiar *"Po-nou-zhaiy!"* would arise again and again over the road.

During such prolonged stops, people on foot who walked along the edge of the road, muffled figures wrapped in blankets and shawls or window curtains, would stop by some sleigh to catch their breath and tell of what went on at Tomsk, and what they had witnessed on their way from there. From sleigh to sleigh their stories would be carried along by the drivers:

Stories about the woman who sat in the snowdrift by her dead horse and overturned sleigh, hugging two sleeping babies with alabaster-doll faces and shrieking at those who tried to approach her not to come near, that it was too late. She screamed that she could no longer awaken the babies nor get up herself. She no longer cared.

Stories about young General ("Napoleon") Pepelyaev, who had unsuccessfully attempted to arrest his own commanding officer, General Sakharov. Or about a new antiwar motto: "War to Civil War," apparently proclaimed by the leftist head of the Krasnoyarsk Garrison. Or about a colonel who had committed suicide because his unit had been surrounded by Red partisans and wiped out to the last man.

According to orders, our First Cavalry Division had to move as fast as possible, the objective being to help the combat units get disentangled from the flood of sleigh trains with the sick and the refugees who had wedged themselves in with the troops, breaking the army into disconnected fragments. The impossibility of achieving this goal became clear to the high command soon enough, for no combat unit would submit to sweeping its sick and its families off the road into snowdrifts. Then the First Cavalry received new orders: to repulse bands of Red partisans who were trying to attack us from the roads that crossed the Trakt from north to south.

Just before these orders reached us, things had begun to change: our driving hours had become longer, and provisions scarcer. Paper money, even the so-called Kerensky bills, were no longer accepted by the peasants, and we had to barter the regiment's stores of American brown sugar and rice for whatever the peasants would part with, at the same time lightening the load for the exhausted horses. The peasants looked gloomier every day.

In spite of all this, we, the younger people, were often distracted by many other things. The romance of Oksana and Verin had burst into full bloom. They were keeping more and more apart from the rest of us, taking strolls when we were already getting ready for nighttime. As it was too cold to stay out for long, Oksana still found time to keep me informed on the state of affairs between them: "Verin's fiancée? You know, I'm pretty sure by now that Vladimir doesn't lose any sleep over her. Not any longer. Yes, I'm sorry for her! I know how you feel for all those forsaken women trapped in Soviet Russia. But he loves *me*. And if you want me to be haunted by remorse, that I am not. I'm no Turgenev heroine, to waste my life. To begin with, it's clear that we shall be fighting for years just to hold Eastern Siberia, so they will never see each other again. Besides, do you know what he told me about her the other day? He said, 'She's my past. You're my present.' And I said to him, 'I'd rather you said that I'm your future.'" She didn't tell me what his answer to this was. I suppose he sealed her lips with a kiss.

But there was neither future nor past at this stage of our journey, only great stretches of oppressive blankness against which short flashes of conscious life stood out, intense and unforgettable. "If you tell me that I have no future," Countess Cygnen had once said, "that at my age of seventy-four my life expectancy is nil, I shall have to smile, because life is practically nil if measured in length instead of in depth."

For my part, I had had another conversation with Serge Lorinov, and the thought of it occupied me more than the thought of what was awaiting us all. What was awaiting me had to be left to fate, while the subject of this conversation had to do with the very lifeline I must hold on to, on which I must depend for whatever was in store for me.

Our conversation took place one evening when American-donated canned fruit was distributed in the regiment, and Lorinov, with the officers of the First Cavalry, invited us to their quarters for tea. The huge kitchen was crowded, full of noise and animation. The table was decorated cavalry style: sabers crossed in the middle, two candles stuck on bayonets, surrounded by freshly cut pine branches. Awakened by the sudden warmth, the branches gave out a dizzying fragrance of pine. Crackling sparks shot from the fire in the oven, and for a fleeting instant my heart was lifted by the magic of the scene, just as it used to be in happier days.

Yet I knew the magic couldn't last. Every step taken toward fun and gaiety would serve only to reveal the losses behind us, the hopelessness ahead. Nevertheless, I immediately found myself doing what was expected of us all—scattering light conversation about, exclaiming over the delicious canned peaches.

It was almost nine o'clock, time to go, when Lorinov came up to me. He said that he had been quite intrigued by a few remarks I had dropped when we were stuck in that out-of-the-way village, and now was his chance to probe their meaning.

"I had the queer impression that you were giving me light little shoves toward the straight and narrow path, am I right? I don't mean in the sense of trying to soften my hardened heart with regard to those partisans. . . . In just a few minutes you had managed to touch upon several problems of immeasurable profundity!"

"For instance?"

"You mentioned some 'deeper plane of being.' This intrigued me in particular."

"In fact, I wish I could have talked more of it," I said, "but you didn't give me the chance."

"Right. I didn't give you the chance, but you took it. Now remember, you are always and miraculously taken care of at the very last, most dangerous moment. It's a strange pattern repeating itself in your life. Your karma, is it? Divine intervention? No, please let me have my say! Didn't you tell me that you would have *prayed* for the salvation of my soul—if I had one?"

In the reflections of the fire, there was a blend of hardness and delicacy in the fold of his lips; the slight droop of the left eyelid lent a dreamy boldness to his face.

"You don't suppose," I said, "that I was simply trying to make entertaining conversation with an interesting man?"

"No, you were not. After all, I *have* read some of your poems. The way you spoke of these things of the spirit gave me the sensation that to you they were immensely real and alive. So much so that they took on a certain vitality even for the confirmed realist that I am."

I replied, "I hope you are not under the delusion that you are a greater realist than I? . . . Because to me being a realist means to be aware of the fact that the human condition on this outer plane, even at its best, is a devastating, meaningless tragedy; to know that we are all doomed to annihilation. . . ." I paused, reluctant to go on, but he had followed me to the very word I was withholding from him.

"You mean, we are all doomed . . . unless . . ."

"Oh, is that what I mean?"

"Yes, you mean, 'Unless we face the ultimate ruin of all we are trying to create on this plane and thereupon decide to make a sharp turn and take the straight and narrow path leading heavenward.'"

I laughed. "Not heavenward, no! That road goes inward. And it is a most fearful kind of road. Much worse than the one through the Scheglovskaya Taiga thicket ahead of us."

Although our conversation still had the quality of a game, I felt that beneath it all he was tormented by the same doubts that had once tormented me, that part of him still lived in the gloom into which his past illness had thrown him, and that I should at least try to give him a glimpse of the faith I had come to.

But he went on dryly: "And where exactly is this deeper plane located? Is it where everyone is a friend and brother to everyone else, as you so casually put it? What a deadly bore that would be!"

"Boring or not," I said, "I am surprised that you listened to me as attentively as all that."

He laughed. "Had you not been certain that I was catching your every word, you wouldn't have gone to the trouble of saying all you did. And I admit it was refreshing—this sudden leap from our coarse reality into the realm of the imponderable."

I said very quietly, "A realm you seem to be interested in, or else why this whole conversation?"

Although there was great gaiety at the other end of the table, I could see that Margarita was now casting sidelong glances at us, and I felt I should include her in our conversation. Moreover, Igor was signaling to me that it was time to leave. "Someday," I said to Lorinov, rising, "when you *really* want to know what I believe, I shall tell you."

"DO YOU KNOW that Serge Lorinov won't come to see us tonight?" Oksana asked me the next evening. And she herself answered, frowning, "Because his temperature shot up quite suddenly. I hope it isn't typhus."

I had already heard this from Igor; I was worried. Lorinov certainly pretended to be strong and healthy, but he knew too well that with his past history any illness might prove fatal to him. The thought gripped me now that when he had talked to me the night before he may have been anxious to hear me say simply and squarely: yes, I believe in the efficacy of prayer, because nothing, not a single vibration, is lost in this world; in miracles, for they are a manifestation of different laws of life that, from time to time, break through to us from a deeper level; yes, I believe in a greater life, which lies beyond our trials, beyond death, a life toward which it is up to us to find a path. I should have told him, waving away all my foolish fears of being misunderstood, that my faith stemmed from startling experiences, totally unexpected glimpses of life that must have come from some deeper level of consciousness than any I had previously been aware of. The impact of these moments, their incontrovertibility, had turned all my haunting doubts into cinders.

Lorinov probably would not have shared my beliefs, for when all is said and done people understand only what they themselves have experienced. Still, a burning candle does not have to be your own in order to provide light.

However, in the next couple of days, he reappeared among us and I caught at the chance.

WE WERE APPROACHING the wildest span of the taiga.

The village where we stopped for the night was one of those newer ones we had been warned about, settled recently by poor peasants from the south of Russia and quite unlike the villages of old-timers. The mistress of the house was a young, emaciated woman with quick, flashing eyes, sharp features, angular movements, and a deluge of talk, which she poured forth while both exhaling and inhaling audibly. Her apron, her kitchen, and her whole house were filthy. Her ragged children, broken out in a rash that looked like chicken pox or scarlet fever, kept appearing and disappearing from different dark corners, and whining pitifully somewhere in the background the rest of the time. The woman was obviously poor: her husband, a trapper, had had "chills" all winter; the season had been bad for them. She had nothing to sell us. When we gave her a twenty-pound bag of American brown sugar and another one of rice she repaid us with tales of woe.

"Ou-ou-ou!" A sound akin to the howling of wind in the chimney preceded each of her stories. "Ou-ou-ou! Can't even think how you will be able to get to the village after next. Seventy-eight versts, and the road is narrow. Plenty of ravines and rivers to cross and not a single bridge that isn't falling down."

Next came the story about the "friends of the people," obviously a Red propaganda guard. "They came here a month or so ago. Large parties of them. How do I know who they are? The friends of the simple people, they call themselves. 'We are driving from village to village,' they told us, 'in order to warn you: when the Whites come with their generals and princes they won't leave any of you alive. So your men better be well armed—rifles, axes, whatever you have, and be ready to *give* it to them. And you women with children, hide from them in the forest, lock yourselves in your cellars, because they're after the blood of the simple people, they'll kill you all unless you kill them first.' So when the first regiments came through here we all locked ourselves in our basements and sat it out, because who wants to hide in the forest and feed the wolves? . . . *Sure*, wolves! Two of our mouzhiks went on horseback a couple of months ago and were attacked by wolves, and what d'you think? Nothing was left of either the men or the horses." Then, abruptly thrusting her face forward, "They even ate the saddles. All that was left was the stirrups."

It was a relief to see Verin come in. Unfortunately, he brought the message that Igor had been summoned by General Kostin to the Command Post and would not appear until later. Something in Verin's tone upset me.

When Igor finally came, I wanted to be alone with him, to look at him, talk to him! But he said curtly that he must speak to Verin, and the swift and precise way Verin came toward him made it clear there was something official in the air. For a few minutes they spoke apart, then

Igor turned to us and explained that half of the regiment had just received some special assignment and would separate from us the next morning. "But it's a short assignment," he said and smiled at me.

"Who is going and where? Is my husband going?" Masha cried, worriedly.

"The General is sending a sleigh for you to come to the Command Post," Igor said. "He will tell you everything himself."

Oksana advanced with a mournful look. Margarita stared at Igor with frightened eyes. "You . . . ? You are leaving?"

Igor smiled at her with a flash of comprehension. "Not all of us. General Kostin is leading us, but Serge is taking command of the part of the regiment that will be moving on with you." Verin was staying also to be in charge of the remaining part of Igor's troop. "Yes, I'm leaving," Igor said to me. "But don't worry, we shall be back in two or three days."

I had been aware that we could be separated at any moment, but my spirits darkened.

The Countess, who was finishing her tea, straightened up. "You mean the regiment is to be divided at the moment when we have approached the most dangerous part of the taiga? And if there is only one road in it, how is it possible for you to clear your way anywhere through this traffic?"

"We shall clear it if we have to," Igor replied, a trifle abruptly.

He had to return to the Command Post at the other end of the village—quite a walk—and I came out with him. "Look," he said, taking my hand as we stepped out of the cottage, "I hate to have you go through this section of the road without me, but I'm pretty sure we won't be separated longer than a few days."

"Are you being sent to repulse the partisans?"

"Yes, but there are very few roads around here along which we can be outflanked or attacked, so please don't worry."

The village street was already asleep—not a light in the windows nor in the sky. We had walked some twenty paces, setting several dogs barking frenziedly, some behind locked gates, others running alongside us. "I don't want you to come out too far with me," Igor said, "better run back and get all the sleep you can. As you know, there may be no chance to stop anywhere for the next two nights."

"But I'll be all right. It's you—"

"I hate to be away just at this point, Nita," he said frowning. "But Serge will take good care of you."

"But why is it you have to go, and not he?"

"Well, because he is second in command. I also think he is still running a fever. He does not let the doctor come near him, but the doctor knows."

We stopped under some bare trees. The widespread frozen branches knocked and whistled overhead, and the wind whipped our faces.

"So he hasn't really recovered?"

"Oh, but he will. He says he feels fine. Careful with him, though," Igor said teasingly.

"With whom?"

"You know with whom, Nita. With Serge."

"Oh, Igor," I cried. "It's as if I said to you, 'Careful with Margarita.' Yes, yes, I know, you like to look at her—who doesn't—and to tease her, but it doesn't mean a thing."

"Now, don't counterattack!" He hugged me, and I spoke over his shoulder, scratching my chin on the frosted edge of his shoulder board, dismayed by the thought that he was leaving and that I might have hurt him. "You know how it is between those two, Igor," I continued as we walked on. "I can see that Serge is really in love with Margarita and my role is to help her by providing a background of music for their romance. To fill in the gaps."

"I know," he mocked, "à la Debussy?"

"Why Debussy? What do you know about Debussy?"

"Only what you yourself told me: that in Debussy's songs the main theme usually runs in the accompaniment."

"You know, Igor," I persisted, "I feel that the mental *labor*, rather, the *thinking* Serge must have done week after week, month after month, when he lay in the hospital fighting for his life and probably having no hope of recovery, has resulted in his cynical approach to things on the one hand, and in a dreadful spiritual hunger on the other. You see—"

"For your information," Igor sharply changed to a "now-let-me-bring-you-down-to-earth" tone, "Serge's *chief* hunger is to go me one better in anything the two of us do." With unexpected force Igor let his other stick fly after the retreating dogs. "Oh, yes, he is a loyal friend, but to compete with me in everything is a natural need of his. God knows he doesn't have to try too hard! He is an outstanding officer, has a brilliant mind. What else does he want? And as you know I am not competitive. But now suddenly here is something that I possess that has impressed him, but which he can never have."

"If you mean . . ."

"Yes, I do."

"If you mean *me*, Serge knows only too well that he can't compete with you in my eyes, not on a single score!" I cried indignantly, even though aware that Igor could detect that I was flattered, and ashamed of being flattered, and was trying to cover up both these feelings with my indignation. "Besides, he is too much in love with Margarita—he simply melts away when he looks at her."

Igor had just put his arm through mine, but now, letting go of it, he said sharply, "But why all this? All we had was a few moments together and we had to waste them discussing Lorinov!"

Suddenly appalled, I cried desperately, "But you yourself started to speak about him. I hated to part with you with the feeling that you may resent his attention to me! I wanted to explain that he means nothing to me nor I to him except in a perfectly abstract . . . I mean . . . in an objective way. If you wish, I won't talk to him at all!"

"Now, Nita, that's silly! Talk to him all you want. You know that I don't mind his little game with you; or else, believe me, I would have let you know about it soon enough"—now there was a distant thunder in Igor's words—"but why on earth should you persist in talking to me about him, whom I see day and night, when there is so much else we could have talked about in these last minutes?"

"Oh, Igor," I pleaded miserably, "simply because I'm used to telling you everything, everything! And you know how I like to analyze people and their psychology. It's just an outlet, a substitute for reading, for thinking, perhaps for writing."

"As to the mystery of Serge's psychology, I cracked it long ago." He gave an annoyed chuckle, but as it was against his very nature to dwell on anything unpleasant, especially on what might aggravate our differences, I felt relieved that the thunder cloud was already passing us by. "To hell with Lorinov! I'm sorry. I was simply bored by your harping on him." Again he slipped his arm through mine.

But it was I who was sorry and I clung to him in guilty supplication. We walked a bit farther. Then he said, with a pained frown, "I hate to be unfair to Serge, though. He is the best friend I ever had. Also, he has had it unusually hard, and to lead our kind of life with both lungs shot through takes some doing. So if, as you say, he is enjoying his little interlude with Margarita, the more reason not to spoil things for him by interfering."

"You mean I? *I* am *interfering*?"

"I know you were helping," he grinned, and this time it was his usual teasing smile full of humorous sweetness, and I knew that the air had cleared entirely. "Anyway, though, don't judge men by yourself and be careful with those uplifting spiritual games with them!"

"Oh, Igor," I cried, "even if I don't see it your way, I promise! I promise you that in your absence everything will be exactly as you want it."

The chief thing he asked me to promise him, Igor said, as we hugged again, was not to fear for him. "Something tells me we shall be back in no time. Three or four days at the most," and he cut himself short because we heard strong decisive steps squeak on the snow behind us. We quickly let go of each other. "It's Verin," Igor said. Hastily we embraced and said good-bye.

I was running back. Oh, Lord, had I hurt Igor? Had I been lying to myself, imagining that what I wanted was to help Lorinov by sharing my convictions with him? No, I had not lied. I had acted in perfect sincerity.

But whatever it was, I suddenly was smitten by the realization of what this was all about. That tomorrow Igor could find himself in combat with bands of Red partisans, whose leaders were mostly hardened excriminals and who, in killing a White officer, seared his shoulder boards on his body, cut him to pieces, or burned him alive. And here, in the meantime, like an imbecile, I had been speaking to him about Debussy and Lorinov's spiritual hunger! It also occurred to me that Verin might have caught snatches of what we were saying. How voices carry on a frosty night! How maliciously amused Verin must have been, if he had heard me say that I was providing a sort of background for Margarita's romance with Lorinov!

As I reached our cottage I stopped by the door, pressed my hands in their frozen mittens to my face, and commanded myself furiously, at least—at least—to keep my distance from Lorinov in Igor's absence.

ONE OF THE most powerful Red partisan units, known for its savage cruelty, was the "Schetinkin Band." This band had at first consisted mostly of outlaws who specialized in the wrecking and looting of our railroad trains and in torturing and killing thousands. However, the group had been promptly taken in hand by the Red leaders. Reinforced by their trained men, it was soon organized into an independently operating army, whose ranks were rapidly filling with local peasantry. Schetinkin's new task was apparently to stir a general insurrection against the Kolchak government in the regions south of Achinsk and Krasnoyarsk. This area was populated by old settlers, people who were exceptionally rich, staunchly monarchistic, devoted to their church, and violently anti-

Communist. It was they whom the Reds had to bring to their side first of all. And they did.

One day, still in the summer, Igor had brought me a leaflet with a proclamation signed by Schetinkin. It began with purely standard propaganda clichés: "It is time to finish with Kolchak and Denikin [leader of the Southern Volunteer (White) Army], who continue the dirty business of the traitor Kerensky." Then followed an appeal to the peasants of Siberia "to rise to the defense of our abused Mother Russia." This phrase "Mother Russia" was already odd since the Bolsheviks never referred to Russia otherwise than as "the Soviet Union." But the most surprising part was the next paragraph:

> Grand Duke Nikolay Nikolaevich has just assumed supreme power over the Russian People. He is already in Vladivostok. A general of his staff has transmitted to me his order to take up arms against Kolchak and his myrmidons. Lenin and Trotsky in Moscow have given their allegiance to the Grand Duke and have been appointed his ministers. I am calling upon each and every orthodox Christian to take up arms with me for the Czar and the Soviets.

"Clever so-and-sos," Igor had said, frowning heavily. "These days the more blatant the lie, the better they will swallow it."

WHEN WE had stopped at the "Ou-ou-ou Woman," we were already at the very edge of the wildest part of the taiga. Still, the next village was comparatively close, and in spite of our slow progress we reached it late the same night. The worst, almost roadless Scheglovskaya thicket (inhabited by wolves, sables, bears, minks, ermines, but few human beings, except some trappers and a few witch doctors, or "shamans") began right after that village, and we could hope to reach the next one in some forty-eight or fifty hours at best. The length of this uninhabited thicket was said to stretch for about a hundred versts, the width for two hundred. This last village was another of those new settler places; the cottage in which we were quartered later that night was a shambles.

"A foretaste of things to come," Masha said with a sour grimace.

So Igor had gone, and nothing would be the same until he returned, if he ever did. He had gone, and the brevity of our last good-bye haunted and tormented me. Only now, too, it dawned upon me that others might have noticed Lorinov's interest in me and mine in him and seen it in an altogether different light from what it was I intended. Igor must have realized all this, and if he had avoided pointing it out to me until yesterday it was because to him our total confidence in each other was above discussion. But I must have hurt him just the same.

I was feeding Bibik, crouching with him on the crowded floor, squeezed between Panna and some snoring peasant women with Mongolian faces. Obsessed by belated remorse, cup in one hand and spoon in the other, I was at the same time listening to Panna's running commentary and answering her in a meek, humble voice. To think, I upbraided myself, of all Panna was doing for me—and what was I doing in return? Acting superior, showing no understanding of her unhappiness and loneliness. How would it feel to be she? To love my child as much as I did and have no authority over him? How would it feel to have had the kind of youth she had had, instead of my radiantly happy one? For Panna was the ninth of eleven children, born when the last family money had just given out, a typical Cinderella without a fairy godmother. Like Cinderella, she watched her sisters go to fashionable schools, to balls and parties, be courted and have dressy weddings, while she herself, at the age of twelve, turned into a nursemaid to her younger sister and brother. How did it feel to have hungered in vain for wifehood and motherhood, a home of her own? And I was promising myself to remedy things—at least to make her feel how much I cared for her; that I understood, that I appreciated!

"Well, he likes eggs," my humble voice answered in the meantime.

"I told you that I would make kasha for him—why are you giving him a raw egg?"

"It is not raw. I cooked it. . . . All right, I'll cook it some more."

"Too late. A child can't stay hungry for twenty hours. Let me have him!"

But it was not practical to allow obedience and meekness to go too far, because, my throat suddenly contracting, I saw the raw egg and Bibik's cup through a veil of acrid moisture. "Fine! Here, take him!" But the words cracked dry, devoid of tears and emptied of all my good intentions of a moment ago.

That night Verin was the first to come. As the only officer remaining with his troop, he could not stay, so Oksana hurried into her coat and left with him. Lorinov also came for only a few minutes that night. I was prepared to keep a distance from him; I was going to indicate that what had been all right in Igor's presence would no longer do now; but evidently aware of what was on my mind and intent on keeping a jump ahead of me, he hardly gave me a look, concentrating all his attention on

Margarita. There was actually a tinge of derision in his manner. It seemed to tell me that if I was afraid of his taking advantage of my husband's absence to urge his attention on me, I might as well stop worrying. His life was full and colorful enough without me. But the only thing he actually said to me just before leaving, and this in a brisk, businesslike manner, was that in view of the length of tomorrow's drive we should take with us all the milk we could for our children. "There will be no village for at least twenty-four hours, you know."

"But where and how shall we thaw out the milk?"

"We'll find some way. There'll be bonfires."

"But bottles will burst unless—"

"I know it's a risky business. I suggest you take along some spare bottles."

Bottles were hard to obtain; Masha and I had only one each. I was going to tell him this, but for some reason couldn't. All I said was, "Thank you, we shall," in a foolishly faltering voice.

11

SEVERAL TIMES already during these two weeks of our journey, Oksana had approached Panna with the suggestion that they exchange places for a day's drive, so that Panna could have a rest. It was a strain for Panna to drive in the same sleigh with Bibik and me. She worried about him every moment: now he was not wrapped warmly enough, now too tightly; now he was too silent, was he still alive? But each time Oksana and I recommended that she change sleighs, Panna would turn away in annihilating silence, a gesture particularly infuriating to me.

I was surprised, therefore, when she declared her readiness to exchange places with Oksana, at this of all times, on the eve of our long, dangerous drive. "What luck, Nita," Oksana said. "You can imagine how much chatter I'll be able to spill over you in a space of a forty-hour tête-à-tête!"

The next morning we started out earlier than usual and found ourselves at once in the thickest taiga, our train immediately entangled in a maze of other sleigh trains. It was very dark here because of the narrowness of the road and the density of the fir trees. Neglected by man for so long, the trees now stood locked together against him, grumbling sullenly in a desultory wind. All one could see was the outline of their tops overhead, a tinge blacker than the cloudy night sky, and the shadowy lines of sleighs barely crawling along; all one could hear were the rustlings of the forest and, from time to time, the shout of a driver. Perhaps the only person on the scene who was in the mood for exposing her throat to the intense cold was Oksana.

This was the first chance we had had to be really alone, without the necessity of her hushed, hasty secrecy. Now all she had on her mind about Verin poured through the funnel of her dokha collar. The holes in the road were as bad as ever, and every time we plunged in an especially steep excavation, her voice would break in midsentence, perhaps not as much from the impact with which we rolled down and hit the bottom, as from pity for the horses that had to pull us out. But the moment they did, she would resume her story where she had left off.

Things had changed between her and Verin in the last few days, she told me. "We had really been strangers beneath it all, there was no real rapport between us. When we were by ourselves we simply looked for a convenient kissing spot. And then the other night I happened to ask him, 'Why don't you talk about yourself? I don't even know whether you have any family?' And he said he had two older married sisters, and added that it was only women who talked about themselves. Then I asked him with whom among the officers he was most congenial, and he said that he thought very highly of them all, but . . . ."

As we drove on, first still in the deep morning darkness, then in the thinning predawn shadows, while Bibik slept in my arms, Oksana went on telling me that Verin still felt an outsider among the officers. General Kostin, Lorinov, Igor were all fine, intelligent men, strong characters, he said, but they formed a sort of monolithic whole in their way of thinking, or rather in their purposeful nonthinking, as he put it, keeping their mentality at a medieval level. They were typical knights in armor: *Mon Dieu, Mon Roi, Ma Dame*, and, in other words, to hell with anything else. They all wore blinkers, refusing to see our overall plight, and the tremendous historical crisis the world was approaching: a crisis on a global scale, a reevaluation of values that the Communist coup had triggered, and that from now on would take its inevitable course. But, he said, if he ever attempted to speak to those wonderful fellows analytically and realistically, express his views and doubts with regard to where the White movement was leading us, he knew only too well what would happen: they would think, he comes over to us from the Reds, we welcome him as a hero and accept him as one of our own. But he is still a marginal case, he is still rationalizing things as do most *"groundless intellectuals."*

"So you see, Nita, Vladimir has to keep his thoughts to himself. We were walking back and forth when he told all this to me, and then suddenly he stopped and said, 'This is the first time that I've spoken freely because I feel that of the whole group you, with your family background, and *you alone*, are able to understand me.' And you know, Nita, he said this warmly, impulsively! It was as if a barrier between us had been breached, and all at once I realized how difficult his position has been in the regiment. With his erudition, his academic standing, and all, he is still a wartime officer, an amateur, a subordinate to younger professionals. Well, not much younger, but still . . . ."

I couldn't imagine Verin speaking warmly and impulsively, yet it was clear what this change of tone, this appeal to her had done to Oksana: brilliant, gallant, misunderstood Vladimir, so sure of his superiority and so lonely in it, turning to her for compassion. And pulling the wool right over her eyes.

"What alternative have we except to fight the Reds?" I said this more vehemently than I had intended. "And if there is no alternative, then what is there to discuss?" Couldn't she see that his words smacked of defeatism? Naturally I was also furious with him for imagining himself to be Igor's intellectual superior. And Lorinov's. "What does he have in mind, anyway? Compromise? As if you didn't know," I said, "how many real idealists have tried to collaborate with the Bolsheviks out of purely unselfish motives. And what were the results? Prison and death."

It appeared, however, that Oksana had already said all this to Verin herself. "Nita, at any other time I would have simply jumped on him. You know how I despise any kind of wavering back and forth when it comes to the White movement. But this was no wavering, it was just a moment when he began to open up his innermost thoughts to me! Still, I must have spoken too vehemently, because he said very sternly, 'Now look here. If I hadn't believed in fighting the Reds, why should I have defected from them to our side? Which, however, doesn't mean that those who have a mind to understand the historical and political aspects of our situation should silently swallow the way the White movement is being conducted by some blockheads. Thinking people should at least discuss things among themselves in order to be better prepared to meet all sorts of eventualities, particularly when it might be a matter of saving hundreds of lives entrusted to them. After all,' he said, 'if we, the three officers who defected from the Reds, had not trusted each other implicitly and had not discussed things among ourselves, we would never have gotten away from the Reds.'"

"That was a different situation," I said sharply. But instead of taking this in, Oksana exclaimed on a higher note, turning down her collar, her face in the red scarf now clearly distinguishable in the thinning darkness, "Please don't repeat any of this to Igor. If you do, Verin will kill me."

It was not my business to repeat anything to Igor, because obviously it was not the predicament of the Whites that was under discussion, but Oksana's own predicament in regard to Verin. Indeed, the next thing I heard was that since that conversation his whole attitude toward her had changed. "He began to need me as a human being, to rely on me. I felt I was no longer simply a toy for him to play with for the duration of the trip.

"The trouble is—at least, *you* would call it trouble—that when it comes to the physical side, I don't mind a bit becoming a toy in his hands. I know that you will despise me for this, but the sense of his superiority just exhilarates me. That time when it was dark in the cabin, remember, and he and I sat away from the others, he put his arm around my waist and then reached under my blouse, and I—I actually didn't care a hoot whether anyone could see it. At that moment nothing existed in the world except him. I was simply fainting in his arms. You resent this kind of conversation, Nita, don't you? You are so conventional and uncompromising in your . . . sort of otherworldly aspirations. I must sound too earthy and coarse to you. But to me anything that has to do with Vladimir becomes poetry, sheer magic! Especially now, since I know he really cares! Because he does. This is why I feel free now to go as far with him as I wish. I do, too! Why would I care now? Whom can I hurt? Myself only, but it will be worth my while."

I didn't exactly resent this kind of conversation, but such outspokenness in personal matters was to me incomprehensible and, by the same token, intriguing. As to her problem with Verin, she already knew my views on that matter, and it was as simple as ABC: to be really appreciated by a man of Verin's type, a man spoiled by women, a young girl ought to make herself hard to get.

"Listen, Oksana," I said to her now, "haven't you noticed that what you call my otherworldly aspirations never interfere with my practical sense? I mean, when it comes to the psychology of human relationships? Be careful that your unconventional ideas don't place you in an inferior position with respect to Verin. You'd hate that. After all, it isn't a woman's freedom to act as she wishes that makes her free. What does? Primarily a creative alertness in regard to the psychology of the man—her foresight, control of the situation, and—"

"And her sense of dignity," she finished for me mockingly. "A sure way to turn your life into a dust rag!" But then, a warm laughter in her voice, she said, "I know, Nita, you're trying to do what I asked you to: to be my banister in case I begin to lose my balance. But do you know what? It's too late now. Besides, who needs a banister in this wilderness?"

The trees here rose to a height of over sixty or seventy feet, the sky between their tops had grown lighter, the silhouettes of sleighs and of motionless bundled-up figures in them were coming into focus. As the morning wore on, the cold began to penetrate under our collars, and we had to bury deeper into them where the fur had not yet turned into icy needles. Our throats were sore from talking. Soon we fell into a torpid silence.

DURING THIS longest day, the character of our drive had been gradually changing. Earlier, two lines of sleigh trains had been crawling in dreary submissiveness; now, different teams began aggressively to bunch together, attempting to pass one another. Some of the horses, crowded off the packed-down track, sank into the snowdrifts and desperately struggled in them. All over the road blackened by traffic, over the agonizing melee, over the quarrelsome outcries of the drivers, there rose and fell, and rose again the familiar "Po-nou-zhaiy!"

Every now and then, Bibik awoke, and I would lull him back to sleep. Thus crept the hours, through the rapidly deepening gray of the afternoon and into the dark of night. No villages, no food, no more talk. Nor had the wind ever been so penetrating and the mind so oppressively void.

But then—how did it happen? When? Oksana and I couldn't tell, but at some point around midnight, everything became different. Neither of us had slept a wink, but it was as if we had suddenly awakened from a depressing dream to realize that somewhere along the way an amazing change had taken place. The wind had abated, the road became smooth. No more noise, no ruts. The snow under our runners felt so fluffy and deep that the sound of horses' hooves and the squeaking of sleighs ahead and behind were lost in it.

The same two great walls of forest stood on either side of the road, opening only a narrow strip of ink-blue sky, but that sky had cleared and the stars—clusters of stemless glittering flowers—were closer and bigger than ever. After all the confusion of the day, the purity and depth of silence around us was like a message from a familiar former world.

We no longer felt hungry, our throats were better, we began to revive, again fell to talking. Strange, wasn't it, to be hungry and not to feel it? And then we spoke of how important it was to be put through all the physical hardships we had been experiencing; how much more sensitive we would be to other people's deprivations if we survived all of this. And yet to be starving among the starving was merely physical torture, while to starve among the surfeited was a soul-corroding degradation. So we hadn't experienced the worst of it yet, not the *real* thing. "Ours is the Gumilev wartime kind of hunger," Oksana said, "the proud kind." And she began to quote Gumilev's poem: "Well he knew the pangs of thirst and hunger . . . ," and we tried to remember the poem line by line, then other poems of his, and those of Anna Akhmatova, once his wife, both our favorites. Those two and Voloshin were the greatest poets of our time, we agreed.

The horses continued to move very slowly. The proud and valiant beat of Gumilev's verse against the amazing stillness of the night was returning us to our vanishing selves. "'I, the grim and arbitrary mason / Of a temple rising in the night,'" Oksana began and then, "Listen! Don't you think that if a man is deprived of the sense of beauty he stops being *really* human? Don't you think that where there is no poetry there is bound to be frustration? This is what I miss in Vladimir. This is what he lacks," she said. "He knows poetry, quotes it. I mean, he's always doing something with it instead of *it* doing something with *him*."

We understood each other, we agreed. Then we spoke of how easy it had been to lose our material possessions compared to losing the sense of beauty, the awareness of some higher imperishable level of life that at times burst through this crude and perishable one to let us know it existed. Yet indestructible though it was, our connection with it could be lost if we didn't watch out. Lost, crushed by the cruel prose surrounding us. What was it that Lorinov had said once about the so-called imperishable perishing first at times of great historical upheavals? And we spoke of how we were losing our artistic sensitivity, our capacity to think. Art, we said, was our link with that higher level of being, and what, we wondered, must be the life of those who had no such link? Utter devastation. How sorry we were for such unfortunates. And then we became sorry for Doushin. Judging by his hunched-up back, he was dozing. It was easy for us women to sit chatting in the sleigh, propped up and protected from the wind; but he had to do the driving, he had nothing to lean against, nothing good to talk about. He would have been a lot happier riding with the regiment, we decided.

Then all of a sudden the horses stopped. Doushin's slouching form jerked forward and straightened up with a start. Turning a gaping, bewildered face to us, as if to see whether we were still there, he jumped down from the box and began to twist his head right and left. I leaned forward to look around also, when I suddenly heard him gasp, "Holy Fathers! Where are they? Where's our train? Looks like nobody's there."

"What's the matter, Doushin? Isn't there anyone behind us? Has everyone passed us?"

He didn't answer. Facing the road ahead of us he cupped his hands to his mouth, "*Po-nou-zha-a-a-i-i-y!*"

For a few moments we sat there, bewildered, not yet clear as to what this was all about. Then, as the truth began to dawn upon us, we straightened up, straining our ears in the hope of hearing some response. Not a sound. Nothing. Just a scarcely audible whispering of the trees.

"I better go see why the horses have stopped," Doushin muttered. He walked up the road, his footsteps crunching in the darkness. "Looks as if we're lost," Oksana said; then, leaning over the edge of the sleigh, she called after Doushin: "What's happened? Are we on the wrong road?"

He came back, shaking his head. "Ya, well . . . we must've . . . they must be someplace back of us, I reckon."

"Why not ahead?"

"No road there. A steep drop."

"Is that why the horses stopped?"

He nodded, and again cupping his hands to his mouth gave the driver's call, this time facing the direction from which we had come. And again his voice sank forlornly into the void.

Oksana said, "We must have made the wrong turn. You probably fell asleep, Doushin."

He replied evasively, "They say there's just one road, so how could the horses get off? And where?" He scrambled back to his seat. "We can't take chances staying here. Have to go back." Then he wagged his head fretfully. "Too many wolves in these parts."

"You have a gun, in case . . . ," Oksana answered resolutely.

"Ya. But who'll do the driving?" He was reining the horses ahead to an open spot at the top of the grade.

"Do you think you can make a turn through the snowdrifts?" I asked.

"Nothing else to do. Not so deep around here."

"Just in case, give me that gun," Oksana ordered. "I can't drive, but I certainly can shoot. How many cartridges do you have? Five? Is it loaded? Fine. I'm a good shot, you know."

"Well . . ."

We both knew that Doushin was alarmed, but obviously not enough to give his gun to Oksana. He only bent down a moment, probably to make sure the gun was there. But I was not afraid, nor was Oksana. Courage, was it? No. It was just that by now our minds were able to comprehend only that which was actually there. If we were not afraid of the Reds who were at our heels, of the Schetinkin bands who might attack us at any moment, why should we be afraid of wolves?

We had made a turn at the top of the hill and were returning to the spot we had left, Doushin now whipping the horses into a brisk trot. The change of motion must have awakened Bibik, for he began to stir uncomfortably in my arms—and this time I was frightened. Should he fully wake up, it would be terrible! He had had no food for almost twenty hours. His milk and a slice of bread tucked inside my coat were frozen solid. I began to rock him as much as my heavy sleeves would allow.

At that moment something happened. Something must have startled the horses. They began to snort, jerk, and all of a sudden bolted violently forward, dashing headlong down the sloping road, the sleigh jolting so that I could hardly hold Bibik.

"What is this, Oksana? What happened?" And now in my voice I heard the same horror that was in the snorting of the horses, and knew what had happened. "They even ate up the saddles." The dreadful words of that "Ou-ou Woman" exploded in my mind shattering it. "Nothing was left of either the men or the horses. . . . All that was left was the stirrups."

I pressed Bibik to myself with all my strength, as if my arms could protect him from what was coming. Hazily I knew that Doushin had thrust his gun to Oksana, and given a hard push to our hood. It collapsed. Oksana was already kneeling on the seat, the gun at her cheek. She fired. Bibik gave a piercing scream. All I could see was Doushin's stiff back and the hooves of our side horse beating a savage rhythm, hurling clots of snow into my face and onto the lap robe. Oksana fired again. We can't be far from the main road, I thought. . . . Oksana is shooting that gun just to scare off the wolves in case . . . no, she wouldn't waste cartridges unless . . . and the horses know . . . and then I didn't think anything, only prayed the furious prayer of the savage, of the terror-stricken primeval man.

FOR ENDLESS minutes we galloped at this maddening speed. Once I turned to see what was behind: only the sloping road running away from us. Then Doushin shouted wildly to Oksana, "Hold on! Don't fire no more!"

I was still concerned about exactly what had happened, as we went flying ahead, but then the horses slowed down, apparently on their own. For a while we were silent, then Oksana asked hoarsely,

"Doushin, do you think they're gone?"

"Ya, aah . . . for the time being, anyway."

For the time being . . . something caved in inside of me. Then a faint, drawn-out sound wafted toward us from the distance "—zha-aa-i-iy!" Doushin slapped his side in frantic joy and emitted some sort of wild, soblike guffaw. "No farther away than quarter of a verst from here!" Reins in one hand, his free hand curled around his mouth, he exploded into a roaring "Ponouzhaiy!" of mixed triumph and entreaty.

FOR SOME TIME we had been standing at the crossing where our side road entered the Trakt. The night seemed especially dark here, so narrow was our roadbed, so tall the trees. But darker than all else was the black snake of sleigh trains crawling at a right angle to where we stood and from where Doushin had been trying for some time and in vain to enter the general stream.

"Let us in, boys!" he was wailing. "Have a heart! Hold it a second! Open up and let us in! We barely beat the wolves. . . ." And derisive voices shouted back through the darkness: "Where d'you think you're going? Hold it yourself, you ———. Wait for your goddamn turn!"

"Damnit, let us in! We got lost!"

"Who the hell asked you to get lost?" A torrent of trenchant profanity followed. Oksana turned to me: "Doesn't the swearing sound like the song of a nightingale to you? To be near everybody!"

"You are wonderful, Oksana! Wonderful."

"I'm not. I missed them. I only scared them away."

"What do you mean, you missed them? Did you *really* see wolves?" She looked at me, and in the darkness I could see her eyes flash.

"Nita, what do you think I was shooting at? The trees? Of course I saw them. Not the wolves but their eyes—several pairs of eyes, at least six or seven. Quite close. Didn't you?"

"Hold on, fellows—*let us through*," Doushin was imploring. "We've been standing here freezing for an hour—a *baby* is freezing!" But no one would stop to let us in. I stuck my face out of my collar and called at the top of my lungs, my voice harsh and shaking: "Any trace of the First Cavalry Division?"

"Sorry, sister. No private telephone lines here."

Bibik, amazingly quiet until now while we were moving, suddenly burst into convulsive shrieks. Perhaps that was what did it, for finally the silhouette of some team stopped: "Well, damnit, go ahead."

We entered the general stream, and were creeping along the Trakt with the line of traffic, when there came whiffs of smoke from the distance, the crackling and spitting of burning wood, some remote humming of life. After a while we saw that the sleighs ahead of us were making a turn off the main road and soon the wall of forest opened on one side. A tremendous bonfire some fifty feet wide was burning in the middle of a great circular clearing. Tall flames, higher than the forest walls around, capped with whirling black smoke, roared upward. There was a dark ring around the fire's edges, the shapes of sleeping soldiers. The rest of the clearing was black with people churning about, a shifting mass encompassed on all sides by the great wall of the taiga.

"What's this, Doushin? A village?" Oksana asked as we stopped again at the entrance to the circle, and I could hear a tremble in her voice.

"Don't see any village. Just a bonfire, a zaimka at best." He scrambled down from the box. "Have to feed the horses somehow. They can't go on."

And I had to feed Bibik. He lay motionless, silent, in my arms. Oksana helped me out of the sleigh. "I'll go scouting," she said. "Someone might have seen our regiment pass."

HOW STRANGE, I thought, getting out of the sleigh, my legs unwilling to support me, my heavy dokha swaying about my feet as I walked toward the bonfire—how strange to have come to the very depth of the most frightful forest in the world, about which we had heard so many fantastic tales in our childhood. But it was even stranger suddenly to hear a languid feminine voice exclaim in drawing-room tones: "Oh, look! Here's Nita with her baby! Where have you been all this time, Nita? We were worried!" It was Alenka Gottel. I stopped holding my breath. So the regiment was here! Our only home, our only family left, the only fatherland remaining to us—the regiment!

Alenka was sitting beside the bonfire. Several soldiers lay asleep by her in the snow, one dangerously close to the coals and to the metal pot that stood at the very edge of the fire and from which she was eating porridge with a huge wooden spoon. She was swathed in a heavy shawl, red and black shadows darting over her Madonna-like face. "Here, Nita, have some porridge. Give some to your baby and sit down before they take these logs from under us to feed the fire." She moved aside to make room for me.

"Is the regiment here? And everybody?" I asked.

"You were the only ones missing," she said. "Serge Lorinov has been worrying his head off about you. Isn't he touching!"

"*Pardon,*" I said mechanically in French as I stepped over the legs of one sleeping soldier, then the head of another, at the same time constantly searching the faces around, looking for Masha, Margarita, Lorinov. But they were not there.

Bibik was now sitting up in my arms, watching the flames, fascinated. "Did you ever see such a bonfire?" Alenka said, handing me her spoon as I sat down beside her. "That poor little farmer! How long he must have worked to chop all that wood that we stole from him! Can you imagine what your father would have said to this? He always worried so about the peasants." Then, interrupting her drawing-room chatter: "Do you know about your Panna? Do you realize that if it hadn't been for Lorinov you would have lost her?"

The rice porridge was boiling so hard that the kernels were popping out into the fire. I had just dipped the spoon into it, and dropped it there. "What? *Panna?*"

"Oh, she'll be all right! Lorinov has managed to squeeze her into the house. Her sleigh broke down some seven versts from here. The driver rode off on the horse and left her on the road, so she had to walk all the way here. Nobody would pick her up."

"What? She walked in her leather shoes? How . . . but her legs and feet must have been frostbitten, frozen off!"

"Oh, no, no. Don't jump up. Feed your baby first. She'll be fine. Lorinov took her inside and gave her a whole cupful of vodka—actually poured it into her. And had someone give her a rub. So she's coming to."

I sat down. Alenka took the spoon out of the boiling porridge and carried it straight to Bibik's lips.

"You'll burn him," I cried, frightened. "It's boiling!"

"Oh dear, no." She quickly touched my cheek with the spoon. I could hardly believe it: the rice was already stone cold.

"I'll feed him and then try to see Panna," I told her, dipping the spoon into the bubbling mass and nudging Bibik to open his mouth. He did, but spat out the rice and feebly, pitifully began to cry for milk. . . . I must warm his milk. . . . I must see Panna. . . . I simply had to get into that house.

I was about to rise when Oksana burst out of the darkness into the ring of light. "They're all here," she exclaimed. "Vladimir isn't—he was just sent ahead reconnoitering. But I found Serge. He's pulling whomever he can into that farmhouse. He got Margarita, Masha, and the Countess in."

Oksana must have been running, she was out of breath. "He's coming to take you inside. Here's your milk . . . you left it in the sleigh." She handed me the bottle. "Oh, Panna is better, but Serge says it's impossible to get through to where she is. Too crowded. Now, come with me."

I followed her. Around the farmhouse the crowd of soldiers was packed solid. They were trying to make way for an officer who was coming toward us but who could hardly squeeze himself through. All I could see was the top of his head, but I knew it was Lorinov. "Here she is," Oksana called to him. "For God's sake get her inside—her baby's getting quite sick." And to me: "You can't squeeze through in this dokha. Let me take it back to your sleigh."

Someone was always helping me, doing things for me. And now Lorinov took the bottle that I was holding against Bibik: "I'll carry it. Hold on to my sleeve." He began to force his way back toward the door.

"But I can't hold on to you. I need both hands to carry Bibik."

"Then I'll hold you by the sleeve."

We could hardly inch our way ahead. "Step back just a bit, Ivanov, can't you?" I heard him say to someone. "Trying to, sir. Sorry, sir." How polite they still were!

When we reached the door Lorinov leaned hard against it with his shoulder, but it wouldn't give. "I have to let go of you," he said, turning his face toward me. "You hold on to me for a moment." Some reflections of the fire wandered over his lean cheeks. "Hold on. I don't want to lose you again."

Even in the semidarkness, even suffocating in the crush, straining my muscles to protect Bibik, I felt the force of his gaze. He gave another powerful push to the door. At last it opened and a wave of heat, reeking of thawing felt and smoke, tore out to us, turning into whirling steam. The crack widened. We pushed inside.

We couldn't see much through the crowd of soldiers pressed shoulder to shoulder against each other. The low hum of voices in the enormous barnlike room was torn by the screams of someone else's infant. A kerosene lamp hanging from the ceiling gave some scant light. Anyway, I could see only that which was at the level of my own eyes: faces, faces, drawn youthful faces; unshaven cheeks of frost-burned red or perhaps of fever red, many with eyes closed, asleep on their feet. But how; on what were they standing? This was incomprehensible, because the floor was strewn with the prostrate bodies of soldiers, dead asleep. Over these bodies I walked, moving behind Lorinov; now feeling an arm, now a hip under my felt boots, afraid to step on someone's face, for I couldn't see where the floor was. But they felt nothing. They didn't budge.

"Nita, *you*!" someone said right into my ear. One of the young faces with black stubble on it had almost brushed against mine.

"Oh, my Lord! Misha!" One of Alik's closest friends, a young poet—a volunteer. "You here also! What unit are you with? Kappel's . . . Oh, Misha!"

"Is that your baby? A boy? Doesn't cry. Amazing."

"He's weak from hunger. . . . Tell me about yourself, Misha."

"I? Fever," he said. "Probably typhus."

"How can you stand on your feet?"

"I'm not standing, they're holding me." He nodded at the crowd. "Saw Margarita, she's in the next room. Where are all yours?"

"Igor is covering the retreat. I don't know where. Oh, you mean my family, the Ogarins? They stayed on—Red territory—I know nothing about them." The way was entirely blocked now. We could talk.

"So did mine. You know my father has been executed."

"Mine also."

"I have also heard about Alik."

"*What?* What did you hear?"

"Why, wasn't he . . . I was told that he was mortally wounded last spring on the Tanyp."

"Yes, he had been counted for dead, but later there was a rumor that he was alive, taken prisoner by the Reds, recovering. . . ."

"Is it possible? Such a genius! Such as he should live on and on." He produced some sound that was supposed to be mocking. "Only . . . where?"

I was about to say, "How unbelievable, how implausible for us to meet in such circumstances, when less than two years ago . . ." But he wouldn't have heard me. I had to step forward and someone was pushing me from behind. I could hear him call after me, "Happy to . . . I remember your poems . . ."

I turned. "I remember yours."

This was a large farmhouse, the front room enormous, kitchen and parlor in one, the stove at the opposite wall across from the entrance, the crowd around it an unyielding human wall, the heat suffocating. I was afraid Bibik would be crushed. He was not crying, his head lying limp on my shoulder. He was still drawling out one of the several words he knew—"*m-i-i-l-l-k.*" Inch by inch Lorinov was making his way toward the stove.

Something was boiling on it, steam rising, whirling upward. Hands holding tin mugs stretched over heads and shoulders; a child's wail pierced through the general noise. From among the backs and heads of the prostrate there suddenly flashed a woman's fur-capped face, contorted with tears. I didn't recognize Masha at once. I had never imagined that Masha could cry. If something had happened to her husband—then to Igor, also. She saw me through the confusion and her despairing voice called, "Nita! My bottle just burst! Aliosha is going into convulsions from hunger!"

Not Igor, then! Not yet. And from behind this momentary seizure of horror and the instant relief, a new fear: what if *my* bottle bursts too? Everything had collapsed, everything was ruined, lost—what was the use of pretending to oneself? Gone was Russia, doomed was our cause, perhaps doomed was the whole world. But just for this bottle of milk not to be lost! Even if I had to share it with Masha, who had always shared everything with me . . . even if there wouldn't be enough left for either of our babies . . . even if sharing it would be the same as tearing a leg or arm off oneself. All I craved for now was that this bottle would not burst.

Then—happiness! Exhilarating happiness! The warm gurgling of milk in their throats, life coming back into their faces as both boys swallowed spasmodically. And there was enough for both. "Oh, Lord, look at them!" Tears in Masha's great turquoise eyes made them shine.

LATER EVERYTHING became hazy. New parties of soldiers were pushing into the house, others out of it. Then, at some point Oksana appeared, took Bibik from me, picked up my coat, and said that now I could get through to Panna. She was out of danger, sort of half awake after the cup of vodka, and nowhere frostbitten. At the very moment Oksana took Bibik, Serge Lorinov walked in the front door and stopped, searching the room with his eyes.

There was something in his face that had never been there before. I pushed toward him without knowing why and what had happened. Something had—to whom? To Igor? He came up to me. "Now, if Oksana will hold your baby, I'll take you to—"

"To see Panna?" I asked quickly, shielding myself from the blow.

"No. A Red Cross sleigh train is just moving out—a train with typhus patients—"

"*Oh!*" I regained my breath. "You gave me such a start, I thought. . . You mean *our* Army Red Cross train? Yuri Molsov's? Is he here? Does the Countess know it?"

"No, it's another train. But someone just told me that your older brother is among the sick. They have been standing there in front of the bonfire for some time. It seems about to leave now."

I plunged headlong past Lorinov toward the exit. I knocked against someone, tore the door open.

"You're crazy! Your coat!" Oksana screamed after me. "Stop her, Serge—she's lost her mind!" But I was already outside.

The bonfire was still burning, its flames no longer as high. This was all I saw except for a long train of sleighs creeping around it. Leaving already! Just as he and I and everybody are about to die, they want me to put on my coat, something inside me was crying. I ran savagely in my sweater and cotton skirt after the front sleigh of the train. Who's crazy—I or they?

I had run about twenty paces from the house when someone caught me by the elbow and held me in a dead grip. I tried to tear my arm away. Lorinov, of course. But I didn't want any of him or anyone else. Yet, holding me viselike, he threw my coat over my shoulders, and not to seem hysterical to him, I halted long enough to slip my arms into the sleeves.

I hadn't yet caught up with the front sleigh when I saw Dimitri in the second one. He was alone in it, half lying in a narrow, hooded *koshovka*, covered up to the chin with a sheepskin blanket, his drawn face emaciated, his head resting on a pile of straw, eyes closed. In the crimson glow of the bonfire, I could see how his cheeks had caved in, his features sharpened.

"Dimitri!" I cried. But no, it wasn't a cry. I called his name in a low voice, afraid to startle him, for he obviously was semiconscious. But this "Dimitri" sounded like an invocation, as a summons to all that once had been his and mine—immense, undying, and lost.

The sleigh was hardly moving, and I walked beside it, leaning forward toward him. "Dimitri, it's I, Nita." He heard me. He had heard it all. He opened his eyes. They were enormous and transparent, and I could see that he was trying to smile. True to himself, even now, avoiding a direct show of emotion, he said—straining hard to get out the words— "The greatest gaffe . . . I've ever committed . . . was to fall ill at such a time." And he relapsed into unconsciousness. His sleigh was creeping away farther and farther, but I ran after it until some horseman came between us, blocking my way. I stopped, watching the sleigh out of sight.

"Let's go. Don't stand there. You'll freeze without your dokha," Lorinov's voice urged behind me.

I was going to say something, but could not.

12

I HAD NEVER HEARD Igor criticize his superiors except in strict confidence, and at that he would either give vent to a strong epithet or invent some preposterous nickname for the person who had annoyed him and deliver it with special angry gusto. For the commander of our division, General Svitovsky, he had recently brought forth some variations: at first he was Svitovsky Spitovsky, which lately grew into the Russian equivalent of Svitovsky Spitovsky Don't-Give-a-Damnsky.

The general was driving with his staff at the head of our train. I had never seen him but had heard that he was a most amiable gentleman with a silky curling mustache, but no quick thinker, and like a mule about his decisions once they were made. In other words, one of those officers of the old school who were totally unfit for a civil war. Suffering from an attack of sciatica and apparently unable to endure this kind of traveling, he decided to escape the chaotic mainstream of the retreat and at a certain point to make a sharp thirty-mile detour along a narrow road that ran parallel to the Trakt. This he did on the very day we emerged from the Scheglovskaya thicket. This smaller road turned out to be amazingly smooth and free from traffic.

Exhausted as we were, we did not ask ourselves at first why the large village where we arrived that night seemed so uncrowded that our party of fifteen were this time accommodated in two separate cottages. Ours had large windows, cross-stitched curtains, highly polished floors. On the table a sparkling samovar, a fire in the arched oven, a *lampada* burning in the icon corner.

I stopped before the icons. For a few moments I stood still, watching the tiny spot of light, the dark earnest faces of saints, waiting for the fog in my mind to settle.

And time also stood still with me and watched them.

Verin came first that night. He came late and couldn't stay. He had stopped by just to make sure that we were comfortable. He had command of the troop in Igor's absence and would not even sit down.

We said we were comfortable—just think of having two separate cottages! He also had a nice separate cottage, he said. "The general has really outdone himself for us all," and he tightened his lips in an inscrutable way. "There are even some books in my cottage."

"Just show me a book." Oksana was already pulling on her coat. "I'll come with you, just to see what a book looks like."

He made a show of protest: "It's a long walk and I won't be able to walk back with you. Lorinov's hands are too full tonight."

This evidently meant that Lorinov would not appear at all.

But a little later he appeared for a moment. Masha suddenly remembered that she had some Cognac and insisted that he have some. At once ecstatic, Margarita rushed to pour tea for him and I came to the table, trying to look cheerfully passive.

"Now let's have it out, Serge," Masha said. "Why did we have to leave the Trakt, losing contact with the combat echelon and losing time?"

"Oh, we won't lose time on this," Lorinov said, taking the cup of tea from Margarita and giving her a special smile, but putting his cup aside to sip the Cognac.

"Our wonderful White leadership, the Lord help us," Masha sighed.

"Well, anyway," Lorinov raised his Cognac, "here is to a successful passage and . . . ," he mimicked General Kostin's bombastic speech back at Novonikolaevsk, "and to the remarkable fortitude and steadfastness" — now his eyes were on me—"displayed by you ladies."

If he had wanted to embarrass me, he had succeeded this time. From the moment he came in I had the feeling of something false and unnecessary emanating from me. Because there I sat, intent on keeping a distance from him, while the awareness of all he had done for me during this last drive had accumulated in my chest and tied itself in a knot of unexpressed gratitude and admiration. If it had not been for him, Bibik might have gone without food for two days; I could have lost Panna; I could have pneumonia if he had not rushed after me with my coat when I ran out to see Dimitri. And it was to him that I owed this glimpse of Dimitri. So how could I sit here looking as if I had taken it all for granted, the unapproachable and irreproachable straw-widow who had foolishly assumed that she meant more to him than she really did? And this, of all things, when I could plainly see how utterly fascinated he was with Margarita, her youth, her beauty.

When Lorinov rose to leave I also rose and impulsively put my hand out to him. "If Igor had seen all you did for me during this drive . . . he would have . . . ."

I didn't know what Igor would have done, but my voice said it all and, judging by the response in Lorinov's eyes, more than I had intended.

I didn't hear Oksana return that night; I was fast asleep. When I opened my eyes in the morning, I saw that she had installed herself at quite a distance from me, which, I decided, was for the best. I even turned my back toward her, occupying myself with Bibik—an act of mixed embarrassment and consideration, as I knew her too well by now not to realize what must have happened in that separate cottage. But a little later when we met at the washstand, she grabbed my wrist and said into my ear, "Don't imagine that I want to play hide-and-seek with you." She had just washed her face, her skin was wet and glistening, she smelled of our American soap. "Remember, you are my conscience and I'll tell you everything, no matter what you think of me!" And she pressed her towel to her face to hide it.

But what could I think of her? That she was madly in love, and nothing except the intervention of providence could stop her from doing as she wished; that such a thing as social opprobrium no longer existed; that the rules and standards on which I was dependent because their aesthetic value and practical soundness sustained and enforced my inner independence and freedom meant exactly the opposite to her. So she might as well have what she wanted, as long as she was ready to take the consequences. The chief thing was that the convictions of her dead parents sanctioned and encouraged any fearless break with convention.

"Nita, there is just one thing I want you to know," she said to me that morning. "I have no regrets; on the contrary! I am thankful I snatched at least one hour out of this terrible mess. When I think of all that lies ahead of us . . ." And then, "He hopes to have a separate house all to himself again tonight."

This last annoyed me.

In the evening Oksana disappeared right after our meal. Again our party was billeted in two different houses. Panna, Oksana, Bibik, and I had a separate room. Even if its squeaking door never quite closed and there was only one narrow bench for furniture, this was luxury. However, with Oksana away, Panna ill enough to keep a stony silence, Margarita certain that Lorinov would be too busy to appear, and Masha and I worrying about our husbands, the general mood was so low that even the usual tea-drinking did not materialize.

I was settling for the night and Panna was still working in the kitchen, when Oksana suddenly reappeared. "So soon?" I asked happily.

Without answering, she began to spread her bedding next to me, her movements jerky, her face taut. Then she went to the door, which was open a crack, crossly pushed it shut, muttered "Damnit," slammed it again and again as it kept reopening with pitiful squeaks, and finally returned to her blanket, angrily mumbling something under her breath.

So she was waiting for me to start her talking. "What is wrong?" Oksana made a furious downward sweep with her arm. "I'm losing my mind, that's what," she said, "losing my mind! Only it isn't what you think."

"Then what?"

She sat down on her blanket, pulled off her thawing felt boots, and pushed them irritably toward the wall. "I have no right to tell you anything. I have promised not to!" This was an angry groan. "But I can't keep it all with me, either. Oh, Nita! I don't know what to do!"

"To do about what?" I asked impatiently. What could she do except what she had already done? "Better tell me frankly what it's all about," and I blew out the candle, which had begun to smoke. Now the only light in the room came from the crack in the door. "Go ahead!" I said. "Has anything new happened?"

"New! I should say it is new!" This was a bitter sneer. "Only I swore not to say a word of it to anyone. . . . I swore it to Vladimir. But . . . Nita, Nita!" She let go of her knees and turned to face me, her voice suddenly flooded with desperate pleading. "But—but if I tell it to you, you alone, I won't consider it a betrayal. Because I trust you more than I trust myself. Only it's got to die with you, understand?"

I was baffled. "All right. What did he say?"

She lay down and dropped her head on the floor with a thud. I folded her sweater and stuck it under her head. "What he said was something we all feel in our bones, but never let ourselves think," she began in a heated undertone. "We are so unprepared for what is ahead of us."

"Unprepared for what? Death?" I said, shielding myself with irony from whatever was coming.

She rolled on her side to face me. Her eyes plunged into mine, intense, burning. "He is doing something that none of the rest of us are willing to do: he *thinks*! He is looking for some way out of the hole we are in. It's sheer idiocy." And now anger, Verin's anger, was seething through her half-whisper, "Sheer idiocy on our part, he says, to go like a herd of cattle straight to the slaughterhouse without even—"

"We are going to take a stand at Lake Baikal," I interrupted her sharply, enjoying a certain show of courage, "and try to hold the Trans-Baikal territory. Slaughterhouse or not."

— 120 —

"Oh, Nita, are you blind as everyone else? So you think you are very brave! But before we get to Lake Baikal there is Krasnoyarsk, which is already as good as in the hands of the Reds."

"Listen, Oksana. Why should Verin speak about it to you at all? Just to scare you? What can any of us do about it?"

"If you knew what I know," she said, her eyes glittering at me in the dusk, "you wouldn't speak to me in this supercilious tone! Although I suppose," now she was sarcastic, "that as long as you are Igor's wife and he chooses to wear blinkers, you want to wear them too."

"In fact, the opposite is true," I suddenly bristled up, "because it's you who tries to see everything the way Verin sees it, losing all critical sense."

This must have been a master stroke of unconscious provocation; I must have pinched the right nerve. Angrily she hit the floor with her fist. "So that's what you think! If you are that slow to understand, then you might as well know the worst! Do you realize where we are going?" She raised herself on both elbows, her eyes slanting at me like those of a frightened horse. "We are moving right into Schetinkin's hands! Yes, we are. He is right on the road where this silly ass of General Svitovsky is pushing us. We are moving to Krasnoyarsk through Nazarovskoye, and Schetinkin's main forces—a huge army, mind you—are also approaching Nazarovskoye from the south, from Minusinsk." She jerked herself up into a sitting position, her glossy hair tumbling to her shoulders, and illustrated her point by stretching her right arm horizontally in front of her and bringing the fingertips of her left one perpendicular to it. "There! Do you understand what this means?"

"Now look here, Oksana," her anxiety was turning in me into cold anger toward Verin and especially toward her—she was disturbing my peace of mind. I had to make an effort to keep my voice low. "At this moment Lorinov is in command," I said, "and he is no less clever than Verin and no less informed."

"Oh, naturally! In cleverness he comes right next to Igor."

I ignored this, but my voice hardened. "And if what you say is true— which I am sure it is not . . . !"

"You don't understand, Nita, you don't!" she burst out furiously. "Lorinov is so *military* he will never go against his superiors! If you think Vladimir is trying to frighten me . . . Well, he is trying to do exactly the opposite—to *save* us all from Schetinkin! Wait a minute, let me finish! He says that there is still one thing we can do." She began nervously to slap the blanket with her hand at every other word. "We can return to the Trakt and be reunited with the regiment. If we don't make this turn north sometime tomorrow, then, well . . . we are as good as finished! Finished!" She repeated the word this time with a high-pitched squeak. "Then Vladimir will . . . but this—" She suddenly buried her head in her hands and shook it. "Oh, no, no!" she cried. "This I swore to him never to tell anyone."

"You might as well tell me all! Or I'll think it's worse than it is."

"How do you mean 'worse'? What Vladimir is about to do is real self-sacrifice, real heroism! He will attempt to save us from Schetinkin at the risk of his life!"

"And how will he do it?"

"I can't tell you how, but he will act on his own."

I sat up aghast. "How can he? What can he do?"

She also sat up abruptly and tossed her head. "He'll go by himself, try to reach the headquarters and explain our situation to Kostin. He knows too well that he may be court-martialed for insubordination, but he will do it just the same. Insubordination, my Lord! When everything has already gone to pieces. And if he can manage, he will take me along."

"What do you mean?"

"I mean that I begged him to take me along, and he wants to! He can, because he has to take a sleigh with some supplies with him anyway. And I know he wants me to come! He can no more part with me at this point than I with him. But Nita. Nita!" She suddenly hissed desperately, squeezing her head between her hands and looking at me with horror, as if awakening to the realization that she had spilled it all to me. "Do you understand that if you repeat a single word of this to anyone at all, it will be the end of Vladimir? Lorinov himself may kill him! He is so obsessed with loyalty, discipline, and all that, that he may simply kill him! Oh, yes, he is perfectly capable of it! Nita, swear to me . . ."

Not for a moment had the reality of all she was saying penetrated to me. "Now listen, Oksana. First you say that we shall meet with Schetinkin. Then that Verin will be court-martialed. Then that Lorinov will kill him. Piling horror upon horror. It's just as if you were someone else. You know perfectly well that Lorinov would not lead us toward Schetinkin. You know perfectly well that neither you nor Verin are going anywhere tomorrow, except where we are all going. You especially."

"But he needs me! He does! In case something happens to him on the way, if he is arrested or—" she faltered for a second. "I'll be the only one who can explain to the regiment why and where he was going. Besides, I didn't say tomorrow. I said if we don't turn back to the Trakt tomorrow, only *then* will he go. And I with him."

"So much the better," I said, in my most forceful and authoritative manner. "If it isn't tomorrow, let's wait and hope that in the next twenty-four hours Verin and Lorinov together will be able to persuade the division commander to do what is right. We still have a whole day ahead of us."

"You know, Nita," she suddenly turned on me angrily, "there are times when your idiotic serenity simply infuriates me!"

NOT THAT our predicament was unclear to me. My mind knew it all, and even as I spoke to Oksana, I was dimly asking myself how it could be that the horror of death that had haunted me in the abstract all through the years of the war could have lost its reality *now*? Now, when a violent and ugly kind of death was menacing me and my child from all sides? Who, what was protecting me, I was asking myself.

It could be emotional exhaustion, the unwillingness of an overtired mind to take in reality. It could be my youth. It could be my faith. No, I was no longer living my faith as I once did. My mind was becoming opaque; I was losing a dimension. My conviction that man should be prepared for death—that he was entitled to step consciously into a higher state of being, lest all his love and suffering and effort toward spiritual growth be wasted—had been steadily losing its outlines. Just the same, there was this treasure of higher knowledge within me—diminishing, but still there—and the fact that I was living on its dividends seemed irrefutable to me.

IN THE MIDDLE of the next morning, our sleigh train stopped on a narrow road. The frost was less intense than usual. It had snowed during the night, and occasional snowflakes still floated in the air, looking amazingly white against the gun-metal blue of the clouds hanging low over the forest. A reluctant wind rustled in the firs, lifting whiffs of crystal dust from their branches. As the minutes went by, the drivers strolled up and down the sides of the road, stomping their feet, some playfully boxing with each other, exchanging jibes.

Doushin was among them, his ruddy, pancake face grinning, revealing broad white teeth. I was telling myself that if it were true that Schetinkin was coming close, the drivers would have certainly heard about it from the peasants and wouldn't have looked so carefree and cheerful. I was not going to agonize about things over which I had no control.

Now that Doushin was not screening my view, I could see the line of sleighs stretching ahead and disappearing behind a bend in the road, the dark silhouette of people and horses etching itself into sharp relief against the fresh snow. In the sleigh right in front of me were the absolutely immovable humps of Alenka Gottel and Countess Cygnen's figures, the contours of their shoulders and heads looking like those of two peasant-crafted wooden dolls.

Now suddenly two horsemen appeared from around the bend in the road—Lorinov on his brown mare, and his orderly. They were coming toward us, working their way through the double line of sleighs. My heart began to pound against my chest. Until now I had felt no responsibility for Oksana's confidence, but my ambiguous situation of divided loyalties suddenly dawned on me: loyalty to the regimental commander and loyalty to my friend.

But here he was. And if I must tell him at least that rumors of Schetinkin had reached us, this was the moment to do it. Yet how could I, what would I say? I watched him halt his horse on the other side of the road and slide down from his saddle. Yes, something was wrong, terribly wrong, I thought; and as I watched his stern, almost stony face, last night's conversation with Oksana suddenly leaped into focus, acquiring a menacing shape. Something was wrong, or else why should he be here instead of with the regiment?

With a brief salute he stopped by my sleigh. "I avail myself of this delay to have a few words with you," he said in a hard undertone. "A tree is blocking the road, so I could take the time to come."

He glanced at Panna; she had pulled her scarf over her eyes against the falling snow, her head lying on her shoulder. Worriedly I freed my face and ears out of my collar.

"What I have to ask you is more than private." He turned and glanced at Doushin to make sure he was not within earshot. The look on his face made my heart sink. "Olga Alexan'na," he said sternly, "I have to speak to your friend Oksana, but I would rather spare her by speaking to you first. You understand that this is entirely confidential?"

I nodded.

"You know that after your husband's departure, *Lieutenant* Verin was the only officer left in the first troop? Well, just now the first troop's sergeant reported that Verin had left early this morning, allegedly summoned to the Army Headquarters. He took along his orderly. Did Oksana by any chance know of his intention to leave?"

"What? This morning? Already?"

"How do you mean, *already*?" He stiffened even more.

"I mean—where to? I mean, who summoned him?"

Lorinov's jaw set. "Who could have summoned him over my head? All orders come through me. He couldn't have made a step without my knowledge."

I began hurriedly to scramble out of the sleigh. "I shall ask Oksana. I'm certain that she has no idea that Verin left." But Lorinov indicated for me to stay where I was. "I shall speak to her myself. All I had to know was whether she knew anything about Verin's plans, because if she did, you would also know." He turned away from me with an almost insulting sharpness and started toward Oksana's sleigh.

My head was whirling. I couldn't believe that Verin would have lied to Oksana, using Schetinkin as a cover for his intention to defect to the Reds, or simply to proceed to the east on his own while it was not too late. Then something Oksana had mentioned and to which I had paid little attention at the time came into focus: "If anything terrible happens to Vladimir, if he fails to reach the Army Headquarters, then I will at least be able to explain what he had planned to do!" she had said. In other words, he had intended that Oksana should whitewash him in the eyes of the regiment and the White command in case he failed with whatever his real plans had been.

Lorinov was already standing by Oksana's sleigh, helping her out of it. They stopped out of my range of vision, screened by a tree and by the figure of one of the drivers, who was lustily beating his hands, swinging his arms out wide. In just a few moments, however, Lorinov was back. He strode past without a glance at me, but I couldn't stand being left without knowing what had happened.

"Serge, please," I called, making it sound demanding rather than pleading. "Please!" He stopped. I could see that he was still unwilling to talk to me, but he came up, his face set, his lips pressed together.

"You knew it!" he said in a furious undertone. "You knew that Verin had boasted of being in possession of information about some imaginary danger and that he intended to use it as an excuse for deserting! Don't you realize," he said, his eyes boring into mine as if I were not I at all, but only the source of his fury, "that you should have told me about his intentions the very *second* you heard about them? I believed in your judgment. I thought you were not like other women!"

"He was not going to desert!" I cried, trying to keep my voice as low as his and yet to strike at him as hard as he had struck at me. "And what's more, I knew nothing about it until late last night. Besides, I had every reason to think you knew no less than Verin, and it was none of my business to inform anyone of things that I heard secondhand."

"Inform!" he repeated with scathing scorn. "Don't you see what will happen if people learn why he ran, and if the men in our regiment get the same idea? Don't you realize that had I known of this plan last night I could have stopped him?"

Indeed he could have. Such was the set of his lips and jaw as he spoke these words, that I realized he would have stopped Verin even if he had had to kill him. Oksana had been right, I thought. But I was going to beat back his anger with my own anger at finding myself mixed up in all of this and at the way he dared to speak with me, pouring at me all his accumulated frustration.

"I told you that he was not going to desert! Didn't Oksana explain everything to you? Verin's intention is to save our part of the division." And now I craved to believe every word Oksana had told me. "He's risking his life to save us because he is sure that we are on the wrong road, that we are . . ." —now I might as well tell it all— "that we are heading toward Schetinkin."

"In other words," Lorinov snapped back, "because Verin took into his head the improbable notion that we might have an encounter with Schetinkin and would have to fight our way through, he decided to save us by deserting the troop entrusted to him." Giving me no time to answer, he briskly raised his hand to his cap. "Sorry. We have to move on now," and rapidly strode toward his horse.

"Improbable notion." Even as Lorinov had pronounced these words, I knew he was only sparing us. What else could he have said to a woman who was like all other women; and as I watched him ride off I felt my last link with the regiment, with Igor, with security begin to snap. More than that, so far I had felt no fear. Fear had been galloping somewhere ahead of me, so I could see only its back in the distance. But it had abruptly turned about-face and was now staring at me out of its hideous eyes.

Now I was alone with Bibik in my arms, moving toward a terrifying end.

13

AS WE FOUND OUT later, it was on that evening, December 12, that the combat echelon of our division, having beaten back some partisan bands from roads that crossed the Trakt, entered the town of Maryinsk, where the headquarters of our Second Army were located at the time. The first thing General Kostin learned at the headquarters was that our part of the division under the command of General Svitovsky had left the Trakt and taken a southern road, toward which, according to the latest information, the main forces of Schetinkin were moving from Minoussinsk. This meant we were bound to collide head-on with Schetinkin.

Infuriated, the commander of the Second Army issued urgent orders for General Svitovsky to return to the Trakt, but how to deliver these orders to Svitovsky was a different matter.

General Kostin sent for Igor posthaste, met him on the porch of his cabin orders in hand, and barked out the situation. "In other words they're bumbling straight for Schetinkin; otherwise, their exact whereabouts are unknown. Aside from me, you are the one who has good personal reasons for finding them. I can't leave, naturally, so take a detail of twenty men, be sure the horses are the best, and cut straight south. I don't know where they are, but you find them and bring them back to the Trakt. You found them several times before, you can find them again."

Igor and his men started out at two o'clock in the morning and rode all the next day through the intermittent patches of forest and stretches of steppe. The sun was just going down when they came out on a long, bare plateau along which one could see at least some fifteen versts. The day had been clear; the sunset was fiery red, stretched over the whole horizon. Against its glow they could see a dark line of tiny moving figures.

"They're ours, Captain, ours!" the soldiers yelled. "See our pennants?" Igor could hardly make out the line of figures, and even then he was not sure at first that they were moving and that it was not a line of trees. The distance to this line was about ten versts as the crow flies. To find roads that would lead to them in the quickly condensing darkness was another matter.

JUST AS we arrived in the next village and I was about to get out of my sleigh, a message from Lorinov in a sealed envelope was delivered to me by a dragoon. Hastily written in pencil, it said that he would try to see us later that night; for the time being, in case anyone should ask about Verin: Verin had been dispatched by the division commander on some special duty. "Please pass this on to Madame Kostin and Oksana." There was a brief P.S.: "No cause to worry. Everything under control."

As I came to the last words all my muscles went limp with relief. Then I reread the note again, foolishly looking between the lines for something more, perhaps an expression of regret for his abruptness that morning; yet I knew that the very fact that he had addressed the note to me was enough of an apology.

With this note folded in my still shaky hand, I went toward Oksana just as we came inside the house where we were quartered. Her head high, her face rigid, she made a show of walking past me. "Think whatever you wish," her expression said, "but I know that he is a hero." Silently I showed her the note. She read it and turned to go. Intent on carrying out my diplomatic mission, I crossed to the other end of the kitchen to a bedroom where the older women were sitting. Addressing them all, I said, "Don't be astonished if Oksana doesn't eat with us and if she looks miserable. She is upset because Lieutenant Verin has been dispatched somewhere by the Division Commander . . . where to? I have no idea. On some special duty."

None of the ladies seemed interested in this piece of information.

Then I went over to where Panna was settling down with Bibik and said to her in an artificial voice, "Lieutenant Verin was sent away this morning to establish contact with the combat echelon. Poor Oksana is so unhappy she won't even eat with us."

A short but pregnant silence ensued, after which Panna said, "What do you mean he was sent? Nobody sent him. He was clever enough to go by himself."

"Why, Panna!"

"Do you think I am altogether deaf?"

"Panna, dear Panna, if you heard my conversation with Lorinov this morning, then for God's sake don't—"

"I never say anything anyway. It's you who lead endless conversations with everyone," and then she told me that for a change I could *do* something instead of talking. There was a large sack of flour standing by the oven and she wanted me to pour some of it into a smaller, handier bag of her own. She must have been really exhausted to have entrusted me with such a responsible task. Then, handing the bag to me, she said, "Why should Verin have stayed when your husband and Paul and other officers have gone long ago?"

"But Panna! They're fighting! They are with the combat echelon clearing the Trakt for the rest of the army to pass!" I cried in exasperation, giving an angry shake to the bag in my hand. "And you know it!"

Of course she knew it; this was only her peculiar way of giving vent to all the anxiety and gloom that had accumulated in her and to which she could never give any direct expression.

And now I stood in front of the flour sack, looking for some implements with which to scoop out the flour, but finding none. Finally deciding that the simplest way to scoop the flour would be with my cupped hands, I went to the washstand at the other end of the kitchen to give them a good washing, and returned to my flour sack just as Lorinov came in. I called to him, my hands buried deep in the flour, "Serguey Yury'ch, just for one moment! May I ask you a question?"

He turned to Margarita and I heard him say to her that he must speak to me—that I probably was worried about my husband.

He came up. His face was drawn but, quite unlike that morning, extremely calm. "You know what my question is," I said. "I would rather hear the worst, I want the truth. By now I know too much not to know the rest of it."

"Olga Alexan'na," he replied, "all I can tell you is that there is no more reason for you to worry about anything. None." He spoke very slowly and calmly. "This morning I was stunned by simultaneous blows from different sides. I was crudely impertinent and I apologize. Now, however, I am absolutely at peace. I have made my decision, and I give you my word—you don't have to worry any longer."

In fact, the calm with which he spoke had a depth, a power almost hypnotic. Both my hands still immersed in the flour, I stared at him, forgetful of what I was supposed to be doing. "Can you tell me what this decision is?"

"I wish I could," he said, "but what really matters for you is to be sure that everything is under control." He paused and the hint of a smile tinged his earnestness. "In fact, there are many other things I wish I could tell you, and never will. But this too is unimportant, for it has nothing to do with the matter at hand." And he immediately interrupted himself, as he often did, sweeping his own words out of the way, by an abrupt change of tone. "What's this you are doing? And wait—where's your ring?"

I had just withdrawn my hands from the flour sack and glanced at my left hand. My emerald ring was missing.

"To begin with," he said, now speaking with tranquil irony, "this is no way to handle flour. Look! Everything is on the floor and on me." He brushed some white dust from his breeches. "Second, I love this ring of yours. The emerald has an unusual combination of rare depth and play. So let me try to fish it out before you have it buried entirely in this sack." He looked around, took a ladle that hung on the wall, rolled up his sleeve, and began to scoop out the flour with it, slowly pouring it over into my bag. In a minute my ring, the green of the emerald feebly glittering through the coating of white, was in his hand as he was rubbing it against his sleeve. Then he raised his eyes to me.

I was dusting flour off my hands, realizing that I should be laughing and saying, "Oh, how silly of me, oh, thank you," or something of that kind. But his silence, the immobility and force of his gaze paralyzed me. "Let me have your hand," he finally said, holding the ring in readiness to slip on my finger.

Counteracting his intention, I held out my cupped palm to him, but he slipped the ring on my finger anyway. He did it with a deliberate, unhurried motion as if about to say something yet deciding to leave it unsaid. Just the same, this something that emanated from him was like a heaving wave about to break against my chest. And it was really amazing that at this very moment the lamplight flickered from a sudden onrush of cold air, the heavily padded front door creaked on its frozen hinges as it opened and slammed shut. Masha's voice behind us screamed, "Oh, Lord, you are back! Where is my husband? Where are the others?"

When I turned, Igor was already standing in the middle of the room. His papakha in hand, he was brushing the snow from it. Snow was melting on his shoulders and at his feet. I made a wild dash toward him, but Lorinov was already beside him. Igor gave me a brief, almost indifferent hug, his whole attention on some envelope that he was producing from his breast pocket. He handed it to Lorinov. "This is the copy of the order from headquarters that I just delivered to General Svitovsky. Kostin was anxious that you should have it."

I was helping Igor out of his sheepskin, nervously calling to Masha, "He is frozen! Masha, where is your Cognac? Bring your Cognac!"

Saying words that I didn't hear but hearing those that cried within me: had Igor seen it? Lorinov had been facing the door through which Igor entered. Did Igor notice his expression? Could he have imagined . . . at such a moment when . . . ! "Have you come alone, Igor? Where is the regiment?" Someone was asking. I didn't even know who was asking this. Perhaps I, perhaps all of us at once. "Where do you come from? Any losses?"

Before Igor spoke he swallowed in a single gulp the Cognac that Masha had poured for him, as if it were vodka. "Several men have been wounded," he said. "Paul was the only officer among them, but his is just a slight wound in the leg. He's getting along all right. But several men in the Simbirsk Lancers regiment were killed"— he stretched his empty glass to Masha again— "one more will do it." And he again drained the glass in one gulp and wagged his head with a sort of desperate satisfaction. "Oh, Lord! What an unbelievable piece of luck to have found you again." Then his face changed abruptly and became serious as he made some sign to Lorinov. "We two must first discuss business, excuse us," he said. Together they went aside to the far end of the kitchen and I ran to the stove to heat up some soup and buckwheat kasha for Igor. My hands were trembling.

Again he had arrived at the most crucial moment, coming to our rescue without sleep or food, to snatch us out of Schetinkin's claws, while we were preparing for a good night's sleep and losing rings in flour! He must have seen Lorinov as he slipped the ring on my hand. Of course he had, or else he would have said something quick and tender to me when I threw my arms around him! But he had not. Instead he had turned to Masha, addressing everyone, not me. He would have hugged me harder! He would have paid more attention to Bibik. To think that I should find myself in the position of some frivolous, vulgar army wife engaged in a little intrigue with her husband's best friend while her husband was under enemy fire! And how could one explain, what could one say? Even all that I had said until now was wrong, because in my nervousness I was putting on an act, and Igor certainly sensed it.

Then they both came in, Lorinov just to salute us from the threshold, wishing us goodnight in a blankly polite voice. Falling back on the official manner of Igor's superior, Lorinov said to him, "Be sure to take a rest here before you join me in my quarters."

A few minutes later Igor settled down at the table to eat the steaming soup, and everyone surrounded him, firing questions at him from all sides. He ate with relish (no, he hadn't noticed anything!), once in a while drawing a huge sigh of relief, looking around the circle with happy wonder, as if still unable to believe he was here.

"Listen, Igor," Masha was saying to him, "don't try to spare us, just tell us if the rumor that Schetinkin is somewhere close is true. No? Are you sure? But he is somewhere in this neighborhood, moving toward our road, is that it?"

Igor waved this aside. "All that no longer matters now. I brought to General Svitovsky the army commander's order for this part of our division to turn north the first thing tomorrow morning; we shall take the Trakt at least twenty-four hours before Schetinkin can reach the road on which you are now. Nothing to worry about at all."

"Igor," I said, removing his empty soup bowl, my hands still unsteady, "how is it that you always manage to find us in the midst of nowhere?" But I didn't really care how he did it. All I knew was that he never gave any thought to himself. And even if he had seen Lorinov slip that ring on my hand he would have understood everything as it really was.

When he finished his meal, I spread my blanket in a far corner of the kitchen for him. He stretched out with a happy groan. I sat down beside him and he took my hand and kissed it several times. "What a relief to have found you! Did you really suspect that Schetinkin was coming your way?"

"I thought that I was the only one who knew," I said. "To me it came through Oksana, Verin told her—you already know, of course, about Verin. But mind you, Igor, that whatever the truth of it is, Oksana is certain that he was risking his life in order to save us. And perhaps he was—"

"He was what?" Igor suddenly exploded. "A traitor. A defector, that's all. As far as I am concerned, he is dead and buried."

"Well, let's not talk about him," I hastened to say, sorry to have started on the subject. But lifting himself on both elbows, Igor hissed, "To leave his men who were entrusted to him and to run like this!"

"Oh, Igor, please! If Oksana hears you! Please spare her! Let's just keep our minds on how we have been saved from Schetinkin, from such unimaginable horror! Saved by you!"

"It is unimaginable horror, all right," Igor said, sitting up all of a sudden, still ruffled all over, but his mind evidently darting back to the vision of what had been awaiting us. "Only as it turned out, I didn't save you from anything," and he began to tighten his belt, which he had undone, preparing to rise. "But I saved Serge, this I won't deny. Or rather, I was instrumental in saving him."

"How do you mean? You saved him, him alone? Not all of us? Just him?"

"Now, Nita," he frowned and spoke in a stern undertone, "remember that what I am going to tell you can never be repeated to anyone. Never! But you might as well know," and he began to button up his shirt collar, "that Serge had strong suspicions that you were heading straight into Schetinkin and that after another day of driving there would be no road north by which to escape from him. But that fool of Svitovsky could not be persuaded to change his orders. So today Serge made the decision to arrest Svitovsky and his chief of staff and to turn back to the Trakt tomorrow; then to present himself to the Army Headquarters to face a court-martial. Which, you understand, under the circumstances, with some of our high command losing their minds, could have meant good-bye, Serge. This is why . . ." He rose to his feet. "This is why I'd better go and join him. And you have your sleep. Tough as Serge is, he's had it pretty hard these few days, sandwiched between Verin and Svitovsky—"

"But you had it even harder, Igor!"

He didn't seem to have heard me. " —so that I don't really mind that farewell gesture of his. He was really saying good-bye to you and to *everything*."

"What?"

"Well you know what. Let's forget it."

Something had flared in these last words that made me feel light-headed. But I knew that the conversation was finished. And if the topic were ever to be reopened, things might not end well at all.

14

THE SO-CALLED Outer Taiga between the towns of Maryinsk and
Achinsk was less dense, more populated, and on the dazzling morning of
December 17 we suddenly came out of the wilderness into a wide expanse
of open steppe. The steppe was a flat silver glitter as far as the eye could
reach, except for one spot in the northeast where it rose steeply to a
narrow plateau. I straightened up in the sleigh, jerked down my fur
collar. In the distance on the plateau there loomed something that looked
to me like the kingdom of Czar Saltan, from Pushkin's fairy tale. Against
the frozen azure of the sky, the jagged contours of snow-capped buildings
and the golden domes of churches sparkled in the sun. This must be
Achinsk—the city where we had been promised a twenty-four-hour
rest—a landmark! Western Siberia was behind us now!

"*Is* this Achinsk, Doushin?"

He half turned in his seat, smiling incredulously, "Yea-ah, seems to
be," he drawled.

A city! To be able to stretch oneself full length on the floor, to give
oneself a hot sponge bath! We might even be billeted in a good house,
perhaps with a separate room for Igor and me! And if we had a whole day
of rest tomorrow, I would try to go to church. Church . . . a world in
which nothing had changed, against which you could always watch and
measure your changing self.

"Look, Panna, this is Achinsk! We shall stay here until tomorrow. We
are in *Eastern* Siberia now."

Soon we could see the entire line of our train in front of us, coiling up
the winding road. The head of the regiment, with its flying pennants,
was already at the top of the slope and disappearing behind the buildings.
But what was this again? Another abrupt stop. A group of men who had
appeared at the crest of the road were gesticulating, speaking to someone
in a sleigh. In a few minutes, however, we were on the move again, soon
entering the fringes of Achinsk.

Had we perhaps approached this fairy city from a different side, not the one we saw at a distance? For we were now driving between rows of dismal-looking shacks, which had nothing in common with Czar Saltan's kingdom; along streets blocked by trains of sleighs like ours, by artillery, by refugees and soldiers, gathered into agitated clusters. Soon the story of what had happened here in Achinsk just a few hours before began to crawl through our sleigh train like a poisonous snake.

"The ammunition train at the railroad station . . . blown up by the local Reds."

"No, no! By Schetinkin!"

"Thousands killed, burned to death, mutilated . . ."

"Scores of trains were massed at this station, waiting for fuel, when it happened!"

"All *our* trains, Russian trains! The trains with the foreign missions have all passed through."

"You should have seen what went on at the station: screams, moans. The platform, the station square, crammed with victims with torn-off arms and legs. Carcasses of burned cars still smoking; the road downtown blocked. Orders to detour the town and stop on the eastern outskirts."

Panna said to me, "I told you so." She added anxiously, "Where is Dimitri? They didn't put him on a train, did they?" It was difficult for my lips to form a reply.

What sort of town was Achinsk? This I was never to know. After having circled through some dismal suburban streets we finally landed in the basement of a dilapidated house. Outside there was a greenish puddle of frozen slops, inside a mob of refugees—utter confusion: the smells of rancid food, garlic, and sickness.

I sat on the floor, Bibik on my lap, hoping Igor would come soon. My body was numb with passive endurance, my own existence obliterated. Most members of our group sat nearby, squeezed on all sides by strangers. Glafira had managed to clear a place for the Countess to lie down between two snoring soldiers. Oksana, saying that she would rather freeze than stifle in this stench, had rushed out of the house, obviously in hope of hearing something about Verin.

Finally Igor came in and threaded his way toward us. He was not smiling. His smile, whether happy or mocking, or just lurking secretly in his cheeks, was so much a part of him that without it his face took on a forbidding sternness.

"I'm sorry we were unable to find anything better for you," he said, addressing us all; but this was brushed aside by anxious questions—was anyone we knew killed or injured in the explosion? Igor replied that the reports were still confused, then turning to me he said firmly, "Dimitri is here, and he is pulling through. Still unconscious, but the doctor says his heart can stand it. I took him to my cottage."

I jumped up, hurriedly handing Bibik to Panna, and began to slip on my coat—missing the armholes and tearing the lining—but Igor said that I couldn't see him now, not yet. And again he spoke to the others:

"I only know that there are few survivors left in General Sputnin's private car, in which my family had been supposed to go. The Georgievsky family got the worst of it. His wife and daughters, Madame Georgievsky and Nina . . . well, they were burned to death, and the younger girl lost an eye." I hid my face in my hands. So I had been spared, spared again! But not they.

Igor raised his voice over the horrified exclamations of the older women. "This is all I know so far. Nita, will you come out with me a minute? I must speak to you."

We came out on the porch and I stopped. Hungrily I gulped the crystal air, but its way toward my lungs was blocked. "Igor, but you swear to me about Dimitri, you promise me? Why can't I see him now?"

"You may later. Right now the officers are cleaning up and dressing. You can see him after we leave."

We had just come down the porch steps and as I blindly slipped on the frozen slop puddle, Igor caught me by the elbow. "How do you mean, 'after we leave'? You told us that we were to stay here until tomorrow morning, that the horses couldn't go on."

"Nita, listen. Let's go up there, where we can talk."

We turned into a side street that climbed a steep slope. Some vacant snow-clad lots on its top glittered in the afternoon light. It seemed to me that it was from the glare that the bones of my forehead ached. "You see, my dear, the regiment has new orders."

We came to a broken switch fence by one of the lots. A torn poster with the half-obliterated words, *"Freedom! Constituent Assembly! Free Elections!"* hung from a broken pole. Igor stopped. It was as if the weight of what he had to tell me made him stop.

"We are leaving within the hour. We can't take the families and the sick with us anymore. Your train will leave to detour Krasnoyarsk, taking a longer but safer road."

I said, "I know, and you will have to fight your way through Krasnoyarsk because it has been occupied by Red rebels."

Now he took both my hands in his and spoke slowly and firmly. "However it may be, you understand the situation. There is a good chance we still may temporarily lose track of each other. It may be only for three days, or it may be for three years. At best, you'll be put into railroad trains and taken to Vladivostok while we reorganize the other side of Lake Baikal. At the worst we may be cut off by the Reds." And then he said that which so many lovers have said to each other at wartime partings, "But we shall wait for each other, wait and hope, even if it is as long as three years."

Three years! Why three years? And then there flashed through my mind the vision of the September night when we had first fled from Tamborsk, and I was sitting on a heap of straw in a gloomy peasant hut, holding on my outstretched palm the red bag with my jewelry that he had just handed me, and asking him, "Two years, Igor? Why in Siberia? Why two years?" Because he had just said, "On these diamonds you can live as long as two years in Siberia." At that moment, just fifty versts from Tamborsk, Siberia to me had seemed as remote as the Sahara Desert. Now here we stood on the snowy slopes with a new deadline, a new probation period: three years. But I knew that his voice had really said, "Perhaps three years. Perhaps never."

There was not a soul around. Taking off our right-hand gloves, we made the Sign of the Cross over each other, embraced, and said good-bye. Then, looking down the hill over my shoulder Igor frowned. "There comes Lorinov—what the devil does he want?" He let go of my hands.

I turned. Lorinov was coming up the hill with fast, furious steps, his jaw set, his face haggard. His formal salute and the cool shadow of a smile with which he apologized for interrupting us were evidently supposed to indicate that he was too polite to let me realize that at the moment neither my person nor the tender farewells of a couple in love were of any importance to him. The important thing was his fury.

"Igor," he said, "they are detailing me to stay with the train of families. What does this *mean*? Who *did* it? I'm on my way to General Kostin to protest these orders."

"You know very well not *who*, but *what* did it," Igor answered. "You have bronchial pneumonia. The doctor said you would have to be driven, or you will soon fall out of the saddle."

"I have nothing of the sort. Not any fever today, none, and I won't be driven."

"Too late, anyway."

"We shall see."

I said, "Good-bye, then. If you succeed in having your orders changed, it may be good-bye for good." I stretched out my hand.

"That's right," he replied, nothing but asperity in his voice. Then, in the same voice, he explained his sudden intrusion upon us. "Igor, I have to have a few words with you. I shall be at the Command Post." He raised his hand to his cap and walked down the slope with furious strides.

"The hell he has to have a few words with me," Igor said. "He knows perfectly well that the orders can't be changed, and there is nothing more to talk about."

"You mean . . . ?"

"He simply came to show that he feels bad, staying with you when I have to go."

"If he stays with us," I said in a desperate voice, suddenly admitting to him that which I had never yet admitted to myself, "then I swear to you, Igor—even though none of this matters any longer—and never did . . ." My heart was breaking in two, because this time I knew it *was* good-bye. "Just the same I swear that everything will be just as you would want it. I swear it to you, Igor." I crossed myself.

AN HOUR LATER the regiment was gone. We did not see them leave, but Oksana burst in with a ravaged face and told us so. Lorinov was to stay with our train, raving mad, she said. She also brought the names of more acquaintances who had been in the explosion—killed, blinded, maimed. Many had been put into cattle cars, piled up there like firewood, because they screamed that they would rather freeze to death in cattle cars than be left to the Reds. What she did not tell me was that she had been reconnoitering the area hoping for some news of Verin.

We hardly had time to give Bibik the semblance of a bath when a great wave of cold air rushed in and Coco Sheyin burst into the room.

"Anyone from the train of the Tamborsk Dragoons," he shrieked in a desperate childish voice, "immediately into their sleighs!"

Wild confusion ensued—shouting, pushing. I thrust bewildered Panna into her coat, Bibik into his, and in a minute we were carried toward the door by the crowd. "The suitcase! Your suitcase," Panna cried; but Coco had already grabbed it half open and was pushing balking Panna across the threshold.

The profile of the moon, still a narrow but brilliant bracket, was climbing over the roofs against a blue-black sky. The sleighs of our train already crammed the street. When Coco shoved Panna into ours, and I jumped in with Bibik, he threw my suitcase into the driver's lap. The suitcase opened, and something fell out into on the snow. The horses bolted forward, other sleighs knocking against ours, machine-gun fire somewhere behind us, screaming and shouting all around. Through my conviction that it was not we but the regiment that was in danger, I was unable to make sense of what was happening. My chief worry was about what had fallen from my suitcase. Had it been Alik's diary and the pack of his letters?

The sleigh bumped madly over the ruts of the road. There were no more trees, no more people, except for one soldier who was running up the hill right in front of us, his elongated blue shadow beside him. Suddenly he threw up his arms, fell on his shadow, and rolled down the slope. So the bullets were flying after us.

All at once there was a forest on our left and we were driving along its fringe. On our right undulating hills shimmered in the moonlight. Doushin, who had been standing erect in the sleigh savagely brandishing his whip, sat down with a smothered grunt of relief, and held in the horses. The sound of firing, the screaming and shouting were behind us. So was Achinsk.

"What was this firing, Doushin? From where? A partisan attack?"

"No, a revolt. Seeing that the Reds are coming this way, this gang is now going to try to whitewash itself by turning against the Whites!"

The highway here must have been in the hands of the insurgents, for we soon veered into some side road, narrow and obviously rarely traveled, plunging deeper and deeper into some endless nowhere. One hour passed, two hours, three. . . .

Bibik slept. Panna's profile in her scarf had dropped to her chest. Although I could never sleep in a sitting position, I felt neither tired nor worried. Nothing. "You are empty," the ever-present observer informed me. "You are like a house in which everything has been packed into trunks, all the furniture under slipcovers. I am the only one still alive wandering around in this desolation, and reporting to you."

IT WAS PROBABLY after three in the morning when, with a sudden downhill descent of the road, our train found itself in front of a dark, narrow building. It had leapt at us from nowhere, a two-story protuberance standing by the road, ghostly and bleak in its loneliness. No shed, no outbuildings, no trees around it. We came to an abrupt stop.

Coco Sheyin and some other men had already run up the steps and were hammering at the door, first with their fists then with butts of guns. Against the shackled quiet, the blows at the rickety door were thunderous. "Eh, you in there, open up!" But there was not a stir in the house.

"All right, men," Lorinov commanded, "go ahead. Break it down!"

However, even before the door caved in, some blood-curdling bellowing, like the howling of an animal being led to slaughter, burst from the house. Lorinov himself stood on the porch watching us file in, now directing his flashlight onto the steps, now onto the hall through the broken door.

"What is this screaming?" I asked with terror as I climbed up the steps.

For a moment the light pinned in its beam the face of a kerchiefed woman with popping eyes and the dark hole of an open mouth from which the wails were erupting.

"Nothing. It's just a woman who got scared. Seems to be entirely alone here," and he went toward her. "Eh, you there, Grandma, stop it! Quit it, I say! We won't touch you. Where is the master of the house?" But the screams, interspersed with a loud clattering of teeth, only redoubled.

From the crazy screams of the half-demented woman we could make out that some armed detachment had broken into this house in the middle of the night, just as we had. Only it seemed that they had been shooting into the windows, had killed someone, had taken someone along with them, had pillaged the house (while she had buried herself in a snowdrift), demolished the shed for fuel, and led away her horse and cows.

"Who do you think did it all?" I asked Lorinov as he came in, bringing some candles. Never had shadows cast from a candle looked so sinister, so oppressive.

"A gang of bandits, probably," he replied. "Just the same, the Reds will claim that the Whites did it and we shall say that the Reds did it. Well, we'll have to make you somewhat more comfortable in your Hôtel du Nord." He shouted to one of the soldiers, "Some firewood! If there isn't any, start on the fence, and fix that front door again. Quick now!"

DURING THE YEARS of war, when the spectacle of so much misery sent me groping for some irrefutable meaning of human life, I had been afforded a few glimpses of that tremendous, elating possibility within which we all lived, although I was unable to put it into words or call upon it at will. I also had experienced the stirrings of some capacities entirely new to me. One of these was the ability to identify with other people: suddenly, if only for a moment, to become some other person and to have a glimpse of life through a mind altogether unlike my own. It would seem that with the onslaught of personal tragedy and hardship one's sensitivity toward other human beings should grow and deepen. And in a way it had. Yet now that life was whipping and kicking us hither and thither, it was the surface layers of the mind that were dominating conscious thought, recalling mine from that new, indefinable realm toward which it had tried to work its way in former years.

However, when late that next morning we all sat around the lopsided samovar (the only object left, by some miracle, in the frightened baba's house), there were moments when I was more she, this baba, than I was myself. It was as though I too were hiding somewhere behind the door, peering with popping eyes through the crack. Out of the darkness of a horror-shattered mind, I was watching this queer breed of people who broke into my house in the middle of the night, smashing their way inside with gun butts; who now sat there eating, talking, seemingly enjoying themselves, and for some incomprehensible reason hadn't killed me as yet.

For a fleeting second I would be this baba and measure the depth of her horror and of her mental blindness. Then I would return to myself, endlessly grateful for my life, for being part of the little crowd whose presence in this room had miraculously transformed it.

Everything seemed less hopeless to me today; we still might catch up with the regiment; we still had a chance to get through to our destination; and the fact that the unknown object that had dropped out of my suitcase on leaving Achinsk had turned out to be my manuscript didn't seem as disheartening as it had when I had discovered its loss the night before. Alik's diary and letters were safe, and this was what mattered.

Lorinov didn't have us awakened until late morning, and we had slept luxuriously wrapped in our dokhas, unconscious of the stench, the filth, the humid cold. Now, huddled together on our bundles, boiling rice in the wall stove, we gloried in our extra hour of rest. In the steely glare of the morning the drippy wall, the cobwebbed windows, stood out in all their hideousness, but the mood of the place was entirely changed. Spooning a tepid rice porridge out of my mug, I was listening to the conversation around me and wondering at the lightness of everyone's mood. This, after all that had happened yesterday, in the face of all that might be awaiting us tomorrow, if not today. Was it simply because our time was so short, our moments of rest so rare, that they became doubly precious? Or was it that, our material needs having dwindled to the minimum—a cupful of tea, a piece of bread, a place to sit on the floor— we, without having the slightest intention of devoting ourselves to the ideas of freedom from earthly wants pursued by saintly men, had been allowed to taste the magic fruit of this freedom?

Bibik, pink-cheeked and blue-eyed, was unsteadily wandering among us, stumbling and falling, taking little unconcerned rests on people's laps while being hugged and squeezed. Masha's Aliosha, quick and sharp-eyed, was looking for narrow canyons between people, decisively mincing his way through them, and wiggling out of hugs and kisses that blocked his progress.

For a while already we had been comparing notes on our reactions to the varied hardships we had had to endure since our flight from home. What had been the hardest for each of us to stand—hunger, cold, filth? Lack of light and foul smells had always weighed the heaviest on me, and the Countess said that next to sleeping on bare boards—her chief nuisance—had been the ugliness of surroundings. We all had to agree, however, that it was not the deprivations or discomforts, but the people with whom you were thrown, that meant the most. Human relationships could reduce your physical hardships, at least in retrospect, to next to nothing; they could also provide light and warmth and food, and the sense of security, or rob you of it all.

"People, people! And not only those who are, but those who have been," the Countess cried, the palms of her hands joined before her. She was sitting on her suitcase, feet swaddled in a plaid blanket, her Glafira in attendance. "How the very memory of them, their thoughts, their words, support us in moments of stress! There are certain sayings that I always carry with me, which I call my magic staffs. I lean on them whenever I am about to slip or fall, and they hold me. For instance, this from Marcus Aurelius: 'It is sinful to anticipate misfortunes that the Gods may not have meant to include in our destiny.' Or this from our contemporary Vassily Rosanov: 'Only toward the very end of our existence do we realize that life was a lesson during which we were unwilling and inattentive pupils.'"

"My magic staffs mostly come from the Upanishads," Masha said, and I quoted a line from the Amiel Journal, dear to me. I wanted Margarita to say something also, but her mind was not on it, because the sounds of steps and of men's voices were now heard on the stairs.

An open map in his hand, Lorinov stopped on the threshold, asking permission to enter.

"We are so grateful to you for letting us have some sleep," Madame Tongovsky twittered, as if she were greeting a caller in her drawing room. "Will you have some tea?" He declined the tea, and his terse answers and the expectant posture automatically silenced the room. "We may have a few difficult days ahead of us before we join the regiment," he finally said. "We had to make a detour to the north and will move farther north for a while, but shall return to the railway line to catch up with the regiment after we pass Krasnoyarsk."

"But they say that Krasnoyarsk has already been occupied by the insurgents, whoever they are!" Alenka cried.

"We'll get around it. Don't be alarmed if today and possibly for a couple more days we shall have a difficult drive. Here" —he raised the hand with the map— "we are to take a rarely traveled road and might run into some steep hills, but at least for a while we shall be away from the immediate confusion. We are to start out," he glanced at his wristwatch, "quite soon."

"Do you really hope we shall catch up with the regiment?" I asked.

"We have to. This would certainly be the wrong time for you to lose your special brand of mystical optimism," he replied in the casual, friendly tone we were trying to sustain with each other these days.

WE MIGHT run into some steep hills, Serge Lorinov had told us. And so we did the same afternoon.

Such things occur sometimes as bad dreams: before us an almost perpendicular scarp, about a hundred feet high; an unscalable cliff that one must nevertheless scale since all other routes were already cut off. The people in the sleighs all got out—everyone except women with small children, like Masha Kostin and myself. They began to climb, like a file of black ants, along a spur of the cliff, flailing over the snowdrifts, grasping at bushes, falling and rising again, plastered with snow. The drivers wallowed along beside their sleighs, trying to help the struggling horses, which again and again kept gaining almost the top of the scarp only to slide backward, raising showers of snow dust. At the middle of the slope stood Lorinov, tight-lipped, mercilessly using his whip on horses that came by him. At the top were his men, hauling on ropes those of the rigs which could not make it by themselves. Alenka Gottel was walking, someone pulling at her to help her; Panna walked, falling, rising, never letting go of her little suitcase.

My sleigh still stood at the foot of the slope. Now it was our turn. Doushin turned his round red face toward me. "Well, with God's help, we'll make it, eh?"

In a dream such things are always frightening. In a dream there is

— 143 —

some terrible unknown truth that invests the insurmountable cliff, the floundering attempts to scale it, the refusal of one's muscles to obey. Here it was different, everything so clear and real. The sleigh jerked forward. I found myself leaning back almost head down, clutching Bibik, who had rolled under my chin. Lorinov's face flashed by, and I became aware that he was pushing the sleigh from behind. I felt the straining of Lorinov's arms, of the horses' muscles, the desperate clawing of their hooves on the snow. At each moment we could roll down again. But we did not.

When we reached the summit and stopped on a clearing I sat without moving. I did not want to watch the others struggling upward and sliding down; the poor horses being whipped to go on; Lorinov helping other teams to push themselves up. How could he, with his lungs shot through? Oh, Lord!

Great, snowed-under fir trees crowded about. The soldiers who had typhus and who also had had to climb the cliff on foot, now lay prostrate here and there on the snow. A doctor, his face swathed in a wool scarf, went in and out among them, leaning down and making them drink something out of a flask. The older ladies who had been helped up with ropes lay side by side on blankets, motionless, Countess Cygnen piercing the pale-gray sky with a pale-gray accusing stare.

When, by some miracle, all the sleighs had at last reached the summit and the troops had deployed along the slope on the other side, a ten-minute halt was declared to let the horses rest. They were steaming, their flanks working in and out like bellows. Then I saw Lorinov come toward my sleigh, a cigarette in his mouth.

"Well," he said, stopping beside me, "I wouldn't be surprised if we owed our miraculous ascent to your spiritual optimism." He drew in his smoke with relish. His hard task having been successfully accomplished, he seemed to be in the mood now for some light badinage. But not I.

"Oh, Serge," I exclaimed, suddenly using his first name and hearing my anxiety for him erupt in its utterance, "you know too well to whom we owe it! Are you all right? When I saw you pushing on my sleigh I simply couldn't stand it. How much easier it would have been for you to have stayed with the regiment instead of with us!"

He produced some sort of soundless chuckle. "That's right, a lot easier," he said. "It's Igor who should have been assigned to be with you. Then all would have been well. Well for him, for you, and . . ." He paused and with a sharp, impatient movement flung the cigarette far into the snow, ". . . and for me. And you know it."

"But you also know," I said, catching at the thought of Margarita, whose image I felt I must immediately force between us, "that your being here with us is a matter of life and death for someone to whom you and you alone mean everything in life."

"I and I *alone*," he repeated, making me feel I had implied something that I had not meant to. Yet what of it? This was the end of things anyway.

Margarita came up and stopped before us, holding her canvas bag open. "Lump sugar," she said. "I'm passing it around because we may be unable to eat for a long time." Under the white rabbit-fur cap her eyes were so touchingly, so ethereally blue, that for a moment we both stared at her in admiring silence.

Panna had been standing a few paces away from us, brushing the snow from her coat, still breathing heavily through her nose. Now she was ready to climb back into the sleigh, and Lorinov turned toward her to help. He answered her decorous "Thank you kindly, Colonel," with a formal brief salute, of which each of us was apparently invited to accept an equal share.

15

FOUR DAYS HAD PASSED since we left Achinsk, and the last time we had slept and eaten was at the house of the poor half-crazy baba. There had been only a few brief stops since then, to feed the horses at some hamlet or farm, a place already jammed with other transports, teeming with freezing, hungry people, all trying to get their children, their sick, indoors.

No one knew anything. Where was the regiment? Disconnected rumors (later proved to be true) had it that Admiral Kolchak was on his way to Irkutsk, but that the commander of the Czech forces, General Syrovoy, had given orders to switch his train to the congested line, where it would be stalled; that, on top of this, they had refused to supply Admiral Kolchak's train with coal. The garrison at Krasnoyarsk had revolted and the city was occupied by some sort of insurgents, which meant that Kolchak with his staff was cut off from his own army.

The Czechs being in full control of the railway, there was no chance for anyone to come to Kolchak's rescue. General Kappel, that shining hero of the White movement, now Commander in Chief of the Army, was reported to have demanded, by wire, from General Syrovoy, immediate passage for Admiral Kolchak, and that apologies be made to him and to the Russians for the insult suffered. This demand having remained unanswered, General Kappel, helpless and indignant, challenged Syrovoy to a duel. It was said that the two Allied generals, Syrovoy and Janin, after a brief discussion between them, had laughed it all off and sped on eastward. Another version was that Syrovoy had accepted the challenge, postponing the duel—a mockery—until the time when the Czech evacuation was complete. We also heard that uprisings were spreading through all the cities down the rail line, and to many villages. We had to detour around those, meandering over almost impassable roads, the Reds at our heels.

Out of the wash of those windy, gray-skied days and pitch-black sleepless nights, certain moments would jut out forever, like hard rock formations on a beach:

Masha and I are standing in a crowd of women with children, all of us pushed and jolted by those others who are trying to fight their way into the house, pressing on frantically toward the stove, the water faucet, the table on which several mothers are changing their whining babies. Underneath the table lies the regimental doctor, asleep in coat and hat, pince-nez on his nose, and some sort of apparatus on his chest. His felt-booted feet stick out from under the table for everyone to step on; but he feels nothing; and I envy him his luck. "You have never known envy," I say to myself. "Now see what envy is: how bitter, how poisonous."

My arms can no longer hold Bibik. One more jolt from behind and I will fall. No, I won't, for there is no place to fall. People around me are standing shoulder to shoulder. And I cannot fall, for Bibik would fall also. He is silent, he looks ill. Someone passes a mug of water to Masha and me—there is, of course, no vestige of food or milk left in the house, and we are grateful, grateful for the water. In the meantime an aggressive howling is growing behind the doors: "You've been in there long enough! You're holding up the wounded, the sick, the frostbitten!"

Or something else: the sky is overcast, it's early evening, and several people on horseback are painfully weaving their way through the dark and narrow snake of sleigh traffic. They bypass our sleigh; the last rider, who is lagging behind the rest of them, an uncouth, swaddled figure, is wailing in a desperate woman's voice, "I can't, I can't!" And all of a sudden this shapeless, wailing bundle rolls down from the saddle into a snowdrift, and as it begins to struggle and flounder in the snow, another small bundle wrapped in a dirty blue blanket—the American Red Cross—donated type—flies out. Her voice breaking, the woman screams, "Somebody take my baby! At least take my baby!"

"Doushin, stop! Stop at once!" I cry. I strike him on the back with all my strength, although aware that he is insulated from my hardest knocks by his dokha. I am also aware that I can't, I don't wish to take this baby, that I hope someone else will do it—and yet I know only too well that to her, to this woman who is trying to scramble out of the snow, her child is the same as Bibik to me, and that I shall have no peace from now on unless I do by her what I should.

"Stop, Doushin, I'm telling you!" I cry hoarsely, and our sleigh stops indeed, but only because at that moment the teams ahead of us have stopped also. Turning on the box seat, Doushin waves his mittened hand down at me placatingly, "They'll take him, that sleigh behind, from the

— 147 —

other train. Y-a-a-a, someone is taking the baby already, so don't get upset, Olga Alexan'na."

"And what about the mother?" We have already passed her, and I am trying to turn around and stretch up so as to see what is going on behind us. With relief I see that someone is helping the woman back to her feet. I have a short glimpse of her flaming face, her strangely unfocused eyes—typhus. And Doushin says, "Why, she has her own horse . . . somebody'll ride her horse and give her a place in the sleigh instead."

"Who will, Doushin, who?" But I want to believe him so as not to feel miserable and ashamed of myself. So I believe him.

Then there is some sort of small hamlet, a short street of some twenty houses facing each other, bare and lonely in the middle of an empty field, a tall fence, a dead horse before it, with white frosted flanks; a few bare trees alive with cackling blackbirds. A dark, churning crowd mills around the houses. We halt while our horses are fed some straw, which our drivers have pulled from the roofs of sheds.

Suddenly a cannon booms. There is a pause in the din around. Heads turn. Another detonation. The stirring in the crowd becomes feverish. The bombardment, however, is still far away, and we are not under fire as yet; but the sudden, dry crack of a pistol shot and the ripping screams of several women's voices are right here in our midst. I prepare to get back into my sleigh. There is a surge forward in the crowd toward the shot, and also a straining away from it. Oksana's sleigh is somewhat ahead of mine, and I see her come toward me.

"It's someone we don't know," she says, "a colonel from that other unit. Yes, he shot himself. He heard about the humiliation of Admiral Kolchak and said he couldn't take it. Yes, he's dead." Angrily she presses her working lips together. "At least he could have waited until the last moment. This isn't the very last moment as yet."

Inwardly I say, I can't take it in, and no sense grieving about this colonel. Soon all of us too . . . But then the explosions of shell after shell, through the windy grayness of steppe and sky, give me a slight nausea. This isn't going to be the end of someone whom you have never seen, the unrelenting Taskmaster within me says contemptuously. This is going to be those very "all of us" that means you yourself, and this you can take in perfectly.

I DIDN'T KNOW how or when we got on the railroad embankment, but the next morning we were suddenly caught in a furious flood tide of traffic, rushing along right over the ties.

A range of hills loomed through the fog ahead of us, screening the horizon. The rails were zigzagging across a narrow ridge that dropped precipitously on either side. Now and again we were clattering over iron bridges in whose bars the horses' legs caught and sometimes broke. At dawn that morning both front legs of one of our horses went through and Doushin was trying to lift it, screaming in a despairing falsetto to other drivers who flashed past us, "Stop, you devils! He-e-elp! Don't you see, you scoundrels!" And someone finally tried to help—not drivers, but some pedestrians who were dizzily weaving their way between sleighs, with blankets thrown over their shoulders, and with oddly crimson faces and swimming eyes. They were a group of typhus patients whose sleighs must have broken on the way. They tried to help, to hold our other horse so its legs would not slide between the bars also. But this horse could no longer keep its balance, nor could the helpers.

Then Lorinov appeared from nowhere, as he often did at critical moments, and began to hack at the leather traces to separate the injured horse from the team and help it rise. But, both legs broken, it neighed and struggled in agony, while scores of teams crowded us from behind in a din of screams and swearing. Then—a shot, and I saw Lorinov return his revolver into his holster. A thin thread of smoke curled from it.

I couldn't see it all in this melee. I only heard a heavy thud somewhere under the bridge. Doushin, the muscles of his cheeks and lips working, waved his hand down dejectedly and jumped back on the box. As we drove on with just one horse, I could see him once in a while wiping his eyes on his sleeve.

Trains were still running in this region. A couple of times already the approach of an eastbound train had caused a panicky crush, a crowding of sleighs to one side, and now, just as we started moving again, after we had crossed the bridge, the heads of all the drivers and our own briskly turned back at the menacing whistle of a locomotive somewhere behind. Then, almost simultaneously, another oncoming train swept from behind a range of hills that blocked the horizon. It was bearing down on us. What could this mean? Where was it going—west to the Reds? We could already see two wings of steam fluttering on either side of the engine's black belly, and hear the threatening rhythm of its breathing, and here we were rushing along the spine of the ridge, away from the train behind, and head-on toward this one. Pedestrians, sleighs, horses that crowded the double track, mingled into one struggling, screaming lump. I had time to glimpse the sleigh ahead of us veer sharply, heading toward the incline, which was as high as a six-story building. Doushin turned a panic-distorted face to me. "Hold on, Olga Alexan'na!"

Our runners squeaked over the rails. Doushin was leaning backward, almost standing erect in the sleigh, his head in the rabbit cap touching my chin. I was wildly pressing my feet against the driver's box so as not to fall forward, squeezing Bibik to myself. Deafened by the thundering of the train over our heads, we plunged dizzily into blinding whiteness. Then there was a hard jolt and the sleigh was rolling down, the hood over me scooping at the snow like a ladle. Another jolt and I lay on my face, snow in my mouth, in my eyes and ears, struggling to get from under whatever had pinned down one of my legs. The deafening rumble of two trains passing, screams nearby, and the neighing of the horses stunned my mind; still I knew that this was not all, that something else dreadful had happened to me. For there was nothing in my arms. Bibik!

Where was Bibik? Where was that anchor that held me, the meaning of it all, the reason for living, for fleeing, for fighting? I finally managed to push off the felt boot of my captive leg, with one stockinged foot freed myself from under the sleigh, and began to thrash about in the snow. Where was he? Why no sound from him? Were he alive, I would have heard him! The snow was so deep that I was in it up to my waist, sinking deeper. "Bibik! *Bibik!*" My voice was lost in the din around.

Then suddenly there was something firm under my foot, like a tree root or bush, and just as I stepped on it, it gave way under my weight, sinking further, and I cried out in horror because it was the top of Bibik's head in the khaki hood. Deaf to the chaos around, the floundering of horses, the flashing of whips, the cries of people falling or climbing all over the incline, I grabbed him, together with a heap of snow. He lay face downward and motionless. With a jerk I turned him toward me.

Two bright blue eyes over two explosively pink cheeks on which snow was melting, were staring at me with intense curiosity. His cap, stuffed with snow, sat askew on his little head, and a sudden spasm of wild laughter caught me at the throat, shook me, choked me. "Panna, Panna!" For there she was, crawling through the snow also, rowing with both arms like a swimmer. "Look at him, Panna, look! He is—he is wondering—he is thinking! He's trying to puzzle it all out!"

How we had climbed back up the incline to find ourselves clattering alongside the rails again, I didn't know. But we were once more racing in the chaos.

ANOTHER WHOLE DAY without rest or food. One o'clock in the morning . . . two . . . three . . . Blackness all around; up one hill, down another. No place to spend the night? Why not, we can take it. Hungry, freezing? Never mind, we're used to it. Just as long as we are moving away from the Reds. This was what I felt. This was what we all felt, because by now our train, the horses, the drivers, the driven, were one semirational being, blindly dragging itself through the snow.

Then the word "village" pierced the column like an electric shock. Indeed there it was and, judging by its blinking lights, a huge one. But to enter it was impossible. Horses, artillery, sleighs blocked the street. Several enormous bonfires burned in the middle of the main thoroughfares, and around their edges the snow was dark with the bodies of sleeping men, huddled together. Our train stopped by the village gates.

Bibik was silent. To the touch his face was like red-hot iron. It was frightening. He must have contracted the illness, whatever it was, at the house with sick children where we had stopped a week ago.

Lorinov came up to speak to me for a moment. "I gave orders to Coco Scheyin to take care of you and Bibik before anyone else. First, because he is ill, and second—" Lorinov had lost weight, his face had become like one on those ancient icons of Roubilov, but he still had to be true to type.

"How do you feel, Serge?" I asked him.

"What a pertinent question."

"It would be pertinent, perhaps, to speak to a friend as to a real friend, at least now before it all ends," I said.

A cruel north wind arose, tearing at the bonfire. Our horses stood motionless, half dead.

Coco Scheyin rushed from one cottage to another. "At least let the women and infants in!" we heard him cry.

"But you can't get in. See for yourself! See that unit—General Kappel's men—all out in the street, freezing! Hey, stand aside! Here they are bringing more of the frostbitten ones in."

When Coco finally came back to us, he said there was perhaps a chance of getting one of us at a time into different cottages. "You, Madame Volotskoy, come with me now."

COCO HAD JUST pushed the door of some cottage open for me, and a wave of stifling warmth, the stench of illness, filth and disinfectants burst into my face. Holding me by the sleeve so I wouldn't stumble over the sick who covered the floor, Coco pushed me across the threshold. The reflection of the bonfire outside was the only light here; the air, like rancid soup, was filled with snoring, groanings, delirious mutterings. Coco said, "I shall push this fellow here a bit to one side, and make room for you."

"Don't touch him, Coco, don't touch him! Careful!"

"Never mind, this one is unconscious, and he won't feel a thing. Put the baby down; you'll rest for a few hours and then we shall drive on. Oh, don't worry about the others. It's almost morning, and Kappel's division will be moving on soon. There'll be room for everybody."

I put Bibik on the floor. Freeing his dry, burning hands from his coat, I leaned over him, peering into his face. It was dark with fever. He breathed fast, eyes closed. My feet no longer held me, and I crumpled on the floor beside him. Oh, my God, save him!

But happiness, what is it indeed? From where does it sometimes burst into our lives? Why is it that often, when everything has been made ready for it, it simply won't show itself? And suddenly when there is neither door nor window, not even a chink for it to creep through, it explodes upon you to flood everything with its glow?

Could it be that such a glow broke through to me now, simply because I could lie down and stretch out after four days in the sleigh—and at that, lie down in this stench and filth in the midst of dying men from whose bodies swarms of typhus-bearing lice immediately descended upon me and my sick child? Could some inner door within me have opened because of this momentary lightening of the physical burden, to let out a flood of such happiness that in spite of my utter exhaustion, this flood lifted me up like a feather and brought me to my knees, standing me strong and erect, arms flung out wide, as if to free myself from the dimensions of my body, as if to make room for more gratitude than I could hold. If this was only the physical relief of lying down, then why did I rise? What was I thankful for? What was it that had happened, who was it that had touched me, I was asking the darkness. But no, I wasn't asking anything. I knew. Someone else in me, reasoning, logical, and curious, someone *secondary* in me was asking these questions; someone who did not know and would never know, and was not worthy of being answered.

WE HAD JUST stopped by the railroad tracks, our horses standing stockstill with sinking heads. The profile of one of the old-regime passenger trains—a string of *wagons-lits* cars, each with a small French flag on the roof—loomed nearby in the predawn darkness. I could see the silhouettes of Coco Scheyin and of Lorinov's orderly standing by a dimly lighted car that had the broad, smartly curtained windows of a diner. The latest information relayed to us down the line by the drivers was that Lorinov had a high fever and could no longer lead us, but that he had sworn to prevail upon the French officials, whoever they were (not General Janin—he was far ahead of us by that time) to make room for us in their train.

And then I saw Lorinov come down the steps of the dining car. An officer in French uniform with raised collar followed him out and gestured toward the rear of the train. Then they exchanged salutes. Lorinov turned, made a few steps, stopped, wavered, and fell flat on his back.

By the time I had scrambled out of my sleigh, his men were already carrying him toward the tail end of the train. A few minutes later we were all ordered aboard, into one of the rear baggage cars indicated by the French officer.

16

THIS WAS OUR third day on the French train. Now hardly crawling, coming to frequent stops, then starting with a jerk to roll on at a breakneck speed and stop again, we had covered about 150 versts and were approaching the city of Krasnoyarsk.

By now we knew for certain that Krasnoyarsk was in the hands of the insurgents; that insurrections which had allegedly been started by Socialist Menshevik groups (but in all probability by Communists who had infiltrated themselves among them) had grown during this last week into a bloody civil war within a civil war; that the Krasnoyarsk railway station was in the hands of the rebels. Anyone connected with the Kolchak forces was said to be dumped out of trains, arrested and "put against the wall"; but in our car all future problems were obscured by immediate ones. At least for me, anxiety over Igor and over Bibik, who was burning with fever in my arms, outweighed all else. For Margarita, it was Serge Lorinov's illness. Although we had been told that he was over the worst of it and improving, she didn't believe it, and there was no access to his "typhus car."

Like our windowless baggage car, which was already overcrowded when we were admitted, and into which daylight penetrated only through the cracks in the boarded walls, so were our minds dark and overcrowded. Just as our limbs had grown numb, squeezed into utter immobility by other people's hips and shoulders, and were refusing to obey us, so was our imagination unable to make the least move either forward, backward, or sideways. At least, such was the state of my mind and body, for the only way to take a rest from the position—that of a Buddhist monk, in which I had been sitting through these three days on the upper shelf of the car—was by scrambling down to the floor and standing there for a while stamping one's feet. This descent, however, was a major and risky undertaking. Forty of us, refugees with our bags and bundles, were crowded here—this in addition to the trunks and suitcases that belonged to the members of the French mission. The space between the shelves designed for baggage was so small that people on the lower tier could hardly sit straight. On the topmost one, the heads of taller persons like myself almost touched the ceiling. So the easiest way for me to rest my legs was by pinning my skirt with a huge American safety pin to the top of my felt boots, then raising my feet and propping them on the car's ceiling. At such times Bibik, whom I held in my arms, would lie on my chest, or I would hand him to Oksana, who sat next to me. Panna's place was down below at the very wall where the draught was the worst, so she couldn't be of any help.

Porridge and water were being continually boiled on the iron stove in the center of the car, its flimsy walls glowing red, its mouth breathing fire. Because of lack of space around the stove, most of us had burned holes in our clothing; a huge round one gaped in my skirt, showing the tops of my felt boots. The heat around the stove was scorching, but just a couple of paces away from it people had to keep themselves covered, as a cruel wind could blow through the car's boarded walls.

Just the same, were it not for Bibik's illness, things wouldn't have been so bad. When we were still in Novonikolaevsk, Igor had said to me, "Even if the worst comes to the worst and you are traveling in a freight car, you won't be alone." And I was not.

Masha with her little boy and maid was on the upper shelf opposite mine; close to her was Margarita; Oksana right next to me. On my left was the beautiful brunette, with her four-month-old baby, who had magnanimously made room for me. "Squeeze in if you can. I don't care what illness your baby has, you have to sit somewhere." She was called Veronika and her name became her. She had a proud profile, rose-petal nostrils, a queenly manner of speaking. Heavy braids of glossy dark hair were wound in a crown around her head. She told us that the last time she had combed them out was on the night before we, the families of the Tamborsk Dragoons, had descended upon the place. You couldn't touch her braids now, not enough room around. "I simply have too much hair. It comes to my knees and could be in the way of the people below." She was proud of her hair and wished she could show us the snapshot her husband, the cossack colonel, had taken of her, her hair covering her all over, like a tent, and she peeping through it at the camera with just one eye. She was also excessively proud of her husband and his extraordinary exploits. A great hero. Seventeen years her senior, but she worshipped him. She had no idea where he was now, but there was a chance he had already joined Ataman Semenov. He was one of those eight desperadoes who, two years ago, led by Semenov, had overthrown the Bolsheviks and liberated Eastern Siberia from them in one fell swoop. Just like that.

She had written a poem about it. Yes, she was a poetess. Without poetry and heroism, life was a dirty mess, not worth living. She would tell this to her son as soon as he was able to understand, she said. She recited this *poème héroique* to us, head high, and then many other poems of hers. Some were dedicated to her husband and his heroic deeds, others to some luckless admirers and pretenders to her hand. Those, however, being lesser heroes or not heroes at all, the ringing beat of her verses trod them to dust.

At times, particularly at night, when she rocked her baby to sleep, she would fall into reminiscences of the pretty gowns she used to wear "before all this began" and intended to wear when all this would be over. That is, unless we were all massacred sometime soon, possibly in a couple of days at Krasnoyarsk; naturally, no pretty gowns then. She also liked to speak of the Volga. She had been brought up in the district of Saratov, where her father had been superintendent of some large estate right by the river. She would tell us of how the Volga looked on moonlit nights, how it would change colors at sunset. First it would shimmer dazzlingly, both sky and water in the west gradually turning into a bonfire, the air cooling, the fragrance of linden trees in bloom breathing from the shore. "I would row away in my boat all by myself and every now and then lift the oars. I would watch and listen and dip them in again. Splash! and again . . . silence. Then I would begin to sing." Could she sing? Yes, she had an operatic voice.

We listened to her, fascinated, Oksana and I, stimulated in spite of ourselves to quote our favorite poets, to hum some of our favorite songs by Rachmaninoff, Rimski-Korsakov, Borodin, to the words of Russian poets. "What a ridiculously inspiring idiot," Oksana whispered into my ear once.

Life on the upper shelf was bearable.

It was bearable despite the fact that all this went against a continuous buzzing of other conversations, of children's crying, of grunts and groans of discomfort, or sporadic spasms of wrangling between some of the women. True that the wrangling also provided a certain amount of entertainment, most of it coming from a birdlike, coquettish, and totally uninhibited brunette—the wife of a long-limbed young engineer with a bandaged head, and mother of a four-year-old boy; both husband and boy were named Nicholas and both of whom she called Nikusha. Among ourselves we referred to them as Nikusha-père, Nikusha-fils, and to her as She-Nikusha, or simply "She." Often at night, when the exhausted passengers were already asleep, they would be suddenly awakened by the sound of violent kisses coming from the Nikushas' corner on the upper shelf across from ours, at which everyone uneasily pricked up their ears; kisses to which she responded by tearfully irritable moanings, "Nikusha, dear, why do you torture me? Why don't you leave me alone, my love?" Then as the gloomy four-year-old voice replied, "I'm not torturing you, I'm kissing you goodnight," a ripple of relieved laughter would flutter through the car.

A companionship of sorts had established itself in the car, a constant exchange of fears and hope, a rechewing of political rumors. These rumors usually burst into our car together with an icy wind and glare of day whenever the train stopped and the doorway was rolled aside. The bearers of these rumors were chiefly porters sent by the French Mission for some pieces of their baggage. Although we had not seen any French people and did not know who they were, we appreciated what we thought was their desire to make more room for us. In fact, before we had reached Krasnoyarsk, most of their trunks and suitcases had been gradually removed.

Even though we all professed to be secure enough in this Allied train, nevertheless, when it began reluctantly to edge its way into station Krasnoyarsk, the atmosphere in the car stiffened. Faces darkened, voices became strained, private conversations stopped. Nikusha-père took a stand by the doorway, opening it just wide enough to put through his head in a tall astrakhan hat stuck over the bandage. "Something seems to be going on," he would report; and then, "All I can see are standing freight trains. . . . We seem to be moving to a siding—no, we are approaching the station building. Yes, indeed, it is Krasnoyarsk, all right."

"But what's all this noise? Are they shouting or singing?"

"For God's sake, let's lock ourselves in and keep quiet," Alenka lamented. "As long as ours is a baggage car . . ."

"As if they won't know how to open it, if they want to! Bang! And that'll be that," Oksana mocked.

"Nika-Nikush, hold on to me, hold on to Mama," his mother cried, as the train stopped with a jerk.

"Who's holding on to whom?" I whispered into Oksana's ear.

A little while later, when "She-Nikusha" saw that her husband and several others, among them Oksana and a bearded gentleman with glasses who had introduced himself as Professor Hertz, were making ready to jump off the train "to do some scouting," she screamed, "Have you lost your minds? What if the train starts without you? Do you want to be killed? Where are you going?" But no one paid attention to her. They would keep close to our car, they said, and be back right away. A few minutes after the doorway shut, the train gave a sudden jolt, started to crawl for about a hundred paces, and again came to a standstill. The screams of Nikusha's mother mingled with the noise of gunfire and the shouts of people who were running past our train. Presently a prolonged and piercing woman's wail made us all catch our breath. Then again all this turmoil ebbed away from us.

You're not afraid, the familiar voice within me was informing me. Is it because you don't believe that you are in any danger or because your mind will no longer function? Or is it that all that matters to you is Bibik's illness? You also don't care anything about the others, even about Oksana. You are certain that they will all be back in a moment. And, indeed, just as the train gave a few more jerks, there came a wild knocking.

"We don't know much. . . . We had no time to find out exactly. . . . We saw our train move and we ran after it," Nikusha-père was saying to his wife. Each of them seemed to be in a hurry to return to their places—he, to be near his family, Oksana to be with me.

Professor Hertz didn't speak at all. He only shook his head as if to get rid of what he had just seen. But, instead of climbing up on our shelf, Oksana stopped in front of me, looking first at me and then at Veronika with a stare she was trying to make blank. In an undertone she said, "Shall I give it to you straight, girls? Well, then: they're leading people out of trains, taking them straight to the wall; and they shoot whoever it is."

"Who's 'they'? Not the Socialists! They wouldn't . . ."

"The insurgents, whoever they are. Probably Bolsheviks, sheep-skinned as Socialists. Nita!" Oksana's tone changed, a plaintively crooked smile so unnatural to her twisted lips, "this is not to upset you, but we have to face it. . . . I mean . . ." She choked on what she was about to say, but then got the words out with such a fierce effort that they sounded almost rude. "I mean, if our turn comes, and if they take you first, Nita, will you let me . . . will you give me Bibik?"

"No!"

The impact with which I hurled this "No!" at her was not only rude but cruel. I knew that I had hurt her but felt nothing. You are becoming hard, feelingless, I thought, as my arms drew Bibik closer to myself. I felt no remorse for having sounded the way I did in answer to her outburst of whatever it was—love for my child, pity for us both, horror at what could swoop upon us at any moment now. I must say something, ask her to forgive me. I could see that her eyes still held the vision of what she must have witnessed a few minutes ago, the sight of which I had been spared. But I also knew that if they took me first, her turn and Panna's would come soon enough.

And it wasn't at *her* that I had hurled this "No," but at the vision that had emerged before me with her words, a vision constantly there, in the background of all else: Bibik alone, as so many other children were today, lost in this mess of blood and ugliness and crime: Bibik pushed and kicked by bloodstained boots.

It was at this vision that I had aimed my answer so as to smash it, break it into bits.

Then, all of a sudden, the train started. Everyone in the car fell silent, tensely listening, exchanging questioning glances, afraid that we would soon stop again. However, the train was gradually picking up speed. It even whistled in a rather independent manner and soon acquired an even rhythm, as if nothing were the matter.

"Is this real?" Nikusha-père finally asked, with an incredulous grin.

"Too soon to be hopeful. They still might . . ."

"Well, God willing . . ."

Later that night the mood in the car became wonderful. The train had made several long stops along its way, but Krasnoyarsk was left far behind. On the opposite upper shelf Nikusha's mother laid her head on her husband's shoulder, listening to him. "*Gospoda*, think only," he was saying, "think only of normal human living! We have forgotten what it is, but how much, how much of it went unappreciated in the past? Should we live to see it again, could anything seem monotonous to us? Never. All we would have to do is remember this bloody muddle we're stuck in now, and everything would become Heaven! *Paradise!*"

Veronika said, "Think only how we shall appreciate our morning coffee! An armchair of our own, a book! How precious it will be to sit on the kind of chair from which you don't expect to be dragged to prison, or put to the wall. If I live, I shall write about it! I shall cry at the top of my voice for the whole world to hear: 'When you sit down on a comfortable chair, appreciate it! Remember what it could have been instead!' I shall call this article 'The Magic of the Armchair.'"

Oksana nudged me with her elbow. Margarita was quiet in her corner. Whenever our eyes met she forced a pitiful smile.

LATE THE NEXT morning we reached Station Klukvennaya, about a hundred versts from Krasnoyarsk. This was a triumph: just another hundred versts and we would reach the out-of-danger zone.

This was another dazzling-blue-and-silver morning. Our doorway was open. A hoarfrosted tree by the depot glittered joyfully against the turquoise sky. Some of the passengers were promenading along the platform, keeping close to their cars in case the train suddenly started.

I saw two soldiers go past, toward the rear of the train, carrying empty stretchers. Margarita's back was turned to them and over her head I watched them stop in front of our car, putting the stretchers down on the snow. One of them, a big, burly, redheaded fellow in a shaggy hat, stuck his face into the car. "Families of the Tamborsk Dragoons here? A message for the Tabakov lady from Colonel Lorinov in the typhus car."

Margarita caught at the edge of my shelf to steady herself. A fragment of brown paper handed to someone by the soldier was rapidly traveling from one person to another until she seized it. The soldiers took up the stretchers again.

"What are those for?" someone shouted in their wake. "Did someone die?"

The redhead turned with a contemptuous shrug of his shoulders. "Of course somebody died. Who doesn't, nowadays?"

"Is it from Serge, Margarita?" As I heard myself ask, I could hardly recognize my own voice, for it had occurred to me just then that the note could have been delivered posthumously.

A moment later, red spots on her cheeks, eyes like two blue lamps, still wet with tears, Margarita showed me the note. Written in Lorinov's hand, but on brown paper, it was half-legible. It said that he was quite well, that his illness had not been typhus. What still kept him in the typhus car was the fact that all his clothing had been taken away to be fumigated. He would come and join us in our car as soon as he got his things back, probably tonight.

This note had kept our spirits up all through that day, for the train didn't start until late that evening.

When it did, we were on the move for about two hours. Relieved, the older inmates of our car began to settle down for the night, when the train stopped again, this time with a violent jerk. Bibik almost rolled down from my lap. Down below, someone's tea splashed on Countess Cygnen's knees, and there ensued the usual nervously apologetic expressions of mutual concern and annoyance, mingled with surmises about the origin of the jolt.

"They must be changing the engine," somebody said. "We must have come to another junction."

Oksana said to Margarita, "If we stop here long enough, Serge Lorinov will be able to move into our car. His clothing should have been returned to him by now."

It had.

17

IT WAS CLOSE to midnight when the sliding section of our car gave a frozen squeak and rolled open with a hoarse, grating sound. Revealed for a moment was a square patch of moonlit sky and snow; almost immediately, the dark shape of a man in a tall fur hat leaped into the square. For a split second, his dark silhouette with outstretched arms between the sides of the opening formed a dark cross against the moonlit background. It was Lorinov.

So here he was, as he had promised, only there was something in his stance that said he had not come to join us and stay in the car. It was clear from the anxious tone of exclamations and greetings that flew at him from different sides that I was not the only one to feel this.

"Good evening," he said. He stepped inside, gave a sharp pull to the door behind him, rolling it shut. His eyes swept the place, found Margarita's, and held them for a moment. "Good evening, everybody," he repeated; there was a depth in the sound of his voice that had never been there before; it made my heart sink.

"I am sorry to have come for just a few seconds," he said, making a slight movement with his left hand, which held a khaki grip, "and this only to tell you that which I hate to tell, and you will hate to hear. So be very calm and courageous."

In the breathless silence that fell in the car, there was heard only the lurching forward of bodies, the creaking of luggage on which people sat on the floor, their heads straining forward or leaning down from the shelving. I tried to scramble to the edge of my shelf to have a better view of him. The reflection of fire that seeped through the flimsy, red-hot walling trembled a dark orange and black on his emaciated face. The shoulder boards on his sheepskin jacket were gone.

"I have asked you to remain calm, because I am, as you probably already know, the bearer of bad news."

"We've been cut off, haven't we?" Nikusha's mother shrieked. "The Reds have overtaken us! It *is* the end!" Several voices hushed her.

"Stop it and listen!" her husband snapped.

"They have not overtaken us yet," Lorinov said, "but they're closing in on us from three sides and will be here by morning."

"So there is still time! We still can—" someone began.

"The trouble is," Lorinov said, "and this is what I hate to tell you, that you can no longer move on. This is why I beg you all to be courageous. Our engine has gone. No, no, it isn't frozen to the tracks, but gone. The French Mission has left a short time ago, and they took the engine along with them. All that remains of this train is your car and three more freight cars with the sick."

Subdued gasps rose from all sides. Lorinov raised his voice. "Don't blame the French Mission. This is not their mess. Not yet."

Someone groaned, "Oh, merciful God!" Someone said heavily, "So, it's happened." Several hands rose, making the sign of the cross. Nikusha's mother emitted a couple of tentative tearful shrieks, but at once gave up the endeavor, attacked by other angry voices, mine included.

Lorinov raised his hand. "Please let me finish! I can't stay with you any longer." The arresting quality of his tone brought another silence. His eyes traveled over the many, many familiar faces, almost indistinguishable in the shadows, as he continued. "My duty now is to try to catch up with the regiment, to be with them when they resume their fight farther east. My presence would only incriminate and endanger you. Without me you are only refugees fleeing from embattled territory, so please stick to this version. But—to leave you here, stranded, is"— his eyes were again on Margarita—"is dreadful for me."

Her place was at the other end of my shelf, farthest from the doorway. She was prevented from moving toward him by the crowded state of the floor below. "But where, where can you go?" she cried.

He smiled at her. "Eastward. There are several roads and villages in these parts."

Nikusha-père said, "But if we are surrounded, and Irkutsk is already cut off by Red rebels?"

"I shall try to get through."

"You're still sick! How can you go anywhere?" Margarita cried, and I could see her hand pulling at her rabbit coat behind her, and I knew what she was about to do. So did he, but at the moment, speaking to the people on his right, he said, "Excuse me," and squeezing his way between them, he made a few steps toward Oksana and me.

"Olga Alexan'na," he said, in such a low undertone that I alone could hear him through the hum of voices that again rose from all sides. "If you

— 162 —

ever happen to hear from a peasant of the Irkutsk Province, an electrician named Ivan Popov. . . ." With a half-perceptible gesture he indicated some paper that protruded from his breast pocket. "Ivan Popov," he repeated, as if to stamp the name on my memory. ". . . Do remember, do remember what a heartbreak it has been for him to part with you. . . ." And now louder, shifting his gaze to Oksana, ostensibly continuing the same sentence, ". . . to have to part with you all at such a crucial moment." Then, without letting us answer, he turned to face the others, saw Margarita slide down from her shelf, and with an abrupt change of manner, again his usual self, precise and debonair, he raised his hand to his cap. "Good-bye, good luck."

He jumped off.

The murmur of stricken good-byes was dying down, and someone inside was about to push the door shut, when Margarita's voice shrilled, "Wait, don't close it, let me out!" She had just slid down off Professor Hertz's lap. Evidently taking it for granted that she was rushing out for the privacy of a last good-bye with Lorinov, the professor was fussily trying to help her recover her balance and to make room for her to pass toward the door, but on seeing the traveling bag squeezed under her arm, he began to mutter something in a disconcerted, anxious voice. "But you can't do that! You'll only delay him, you shouldn't . . ."

Masha cried, "This is insane! You can't go with him, Margarita!" But Margarita rushed frantically toward the door.

"Why don't they leave her alone," Oksana said to me with a painful grimace. "Serge will turn her back at once anyway." I stretched forward and called after her, "Margarita!" but didn't know what else to say, and she didn't hear me for Panna's voice covered all the others: "Slide that opening shut! There's a sick child in here!"

SERGE LORINOV was not only a friend; he had also been our guardian. Through him we had still kept connection with the regiment, or felt we had; in him were our hopes of some future, mine for joining Igor. Now all this had collapsed, gone with him into the darkness that was closing upon us.

While he had still been there, people forgot all the questions they had to ask. These questions lay unconscious in them, knocked out by the blow, however expected. But now they began to struggle upward, dazed and futile, turning into a general nervous buzz. How could the French Mission have . . . What were we to do now? Where were we? How far from the main highway? From some village?

There were also other questions, mute ones, whose weight was too overwhelming for them to be flung about. One of them was creeping from the lower shelf where one of the passengers, a taciturn ex-government official sat silent; on his lap lay his valise in which, as She-Nikusha had by now discovered, there lay together with a toothbrush and a snapshot of his family, his prized possession, a loaded Browning.

For a while, Nikusha-père stayed by the door with the intention of letting Margarita in as soon as she would knock. As no knocks came, he finally opened the door a crack. We all thought that Lorinov had gone, and could imagine her standing there in the snow, crying.

"Is she there?"

"No, she's gone with him. I can see them."

"Impossible!"

I did not know what people around me thought; I didn't listen to what was being said. All I knew was that the air of the car, quickly filling with the putrid smell of defeat, was becoming unbreathable; that I couldn't bear to sit here passively through the long night, doomed to either death or enslavement, and wait for the verdict. And I said so. Loudly, belligerently I heard my voice say so, oddly finding relief in this belligerence.

"And what do we propose to do now, wait here for them to come and take us? I won't. If Lorinov thinks he can get through, why can't we? We too might catch up with the regiment. At least I will try." If tomorrow were to be the end—darkness and ruin—there was still one point of light beyond it, toward which my whole being strained: Igor, the regiment. And I began, as much as space around me and my free hand allowed, to go through the motions of getting Bibik's coat, which lay crumpled in the corner.

They said I was insane. "How can you! With Bibik in this state!"

"I'm staying right here," Panna's basso welled forth from down below. "If you wish to kill your child and to carry him and your suitcase all by yourself, go ahead."

"But the frost outside might be better for him than the drafts in here. I'll go too!" Veronika said.

There was a general movement in the car now; people talked louder, protesting, of course, the foolhardiness of youth, and yet stirred by something alive, a choice, an attempt to be made, a last risk to be taken. Masha conferred with her maid; she was coming with me, too.

"But all the roads are blocked!"

"You'll be stuck in the snowdrifts before you get to any village."

"You'll freeze to death, darling!" cried Madame Tongovsky.

"But she wants to join her husband and so do I!" Veronika declared with finality. "And if she can carry her child, I can carry mine! If the roads were impassable, Lorinov would have sent Margarita back by now."

Oksana said she was also coming, and would carry my things for me. "Panna," I called, in that authoritative voice she detested, "please let Oksana take my suitcase." But I knew Panna was coming with me.

WE HAD JUST come out of the car: Masha, her maid and baby, Oksana and Veronika, Panna and I with Bibik. The night was motionless and clear, cruelly cold. The full moon, a luminous slab of frozen ice, rode high upon the immense sweep of sky, and the steppe blazed such a bright silver that it seemed not to be really night, but day at the bottom of a blue glacial sea. For a few moments we stood there, heads lifted, held by the purity of silence, perhaps by a vague sense of kinship with the frost-shackled steppe, its barrenness, its desolate acceptance of doom. Our heavily clad figures loaded with bundles cast grotesque, bluish shadows on the glittering snow.

We looked around. No one. By now Serge and Margarita must have gone quite a distance. We saw their footprints, which sank deep into the snow, and at first followed them single file, but the footprints soon disappeared. They must have crossed to the other side of the railway tracks. A broad expanse of open field lay before us. On our left it was broken by a strip of forest that propelled its dark fringe about half a verst eastward. In the distance ahead, on the railroad tracks, a square patch of black looked like the back of a train or of a few forsaken cars. Quite a bit nearer to us, to our right there loomed a clump of trees. With a little wishful thinking one could imagine a farmhouse standing behind them. I was carrying Bibik and leading the way, and, perhaps, had it not been for this house that I had imagined to be there, I too would have crossed the tracks in the hope of catching up with Margarita and Lorinov. But no. No, this I wouldn't have done.

My arms in the heavy sleeves could barely reach around Bibik, who was wrapped in a blanket over his quilted coat. The snowdrifts were high and crumbly. With every step we sank into them, so that the top of our knee-high felt boots scooped the snow. After a week of having squatted motionless with my legs bent under me, I could hardly pull them out, and we hadn't made fifty paces before my heart was hammering mad-deningly against my chest, pulsating in my throat, in my ears, choking me. Behind me I could hear the heavy breathing with which Panna followed, her bag in one hand, a bundle with provisions in the other. Suddenly I remembered she was walking in her leather shoes. How could I have let her—no!—made her, yes, made her go with me? And this with her heart condition.

I stopped. "Panna, sit down, put your bag down, let it sink into the snow, and sit on it, try! Or else, if you want to, we shall . . ." But I could not say it. I could not return; I had to make it to someplace—some village, some train! At least to those trees that really looked as if they were sheltering a house.

"Don't be disheartened, my friends," Oksana quoted in a voice strained and panting, but which she obviously meant to sound swash-buckling. "In that next world, everything will be exactly the other way around."

She passed me, and we started again, trying to step into her footprints. And now new voices reached us from behind, cutting sharply through the silence: "W-a-i-t, w-a-i-t!" I turned. Our forlorn cars loomed dark in the moonlit distance, merging with the slanting square of their shadow on the shimmering snow, and dark silhouettes of people were jumping off, waving their arms at us. We waited. When we resumed our walk, filing behind us were Madame Tongovsky, the Nikushas, and several others.

Had it not been for the clump of trees, we might have dropped with exhaustion, but we were becoming more and more sure that a house was indeed lurking behind these trees. We saw no lights in it, but through the bare lacing of branches we could by now distinguish a chimney. A thick veil of smoke seemed to trickle from it. Even if the smoke were only our imagination, even if this were some forsaken building, we still could spend the night in it, make a fire, feed the children. Then, quite unexpectedly, we came out on a hard-packed sleigh road and sat down on the snow for a few minutes, hardly able to breathe or move. But move on we did, for by that time we could plainly see the house before us.

THERE WERE TEN or twelve of us, dark figures in the moonlight, standing in a semicircle by the front porch of the deathly silent house, our foreshortened shadows lying at our feet like dark bits of rugs. Behind us were the picket fence, the locked gate across which we had climbed.

The house looked like some primitive school building. A snow-capped shed stood by, but there was no vestige of life around, no horse, nor cow, nor any sleighs in sight. No light came through the shutters, but the smoke trickling out of the chimney was clearly visible now.

Oksana ran up the steps first. She knocked. The rest of us stood there tense, listening. No sound came from inside, no stirrings. In the silence the frozen *swish-swish* of a lazy breeze in the trees came to the foreground. Oksana took off her mitten, knocked again, harder this time. "Is anyone in there? Open up! Please, please!"

Silence still.

The feeling was that someone was playing dead. Nikusha-père came up the few steps and shook the door handle. "Look here," he called, "if you want us to think the place is empty, nothing will prevent us from breaking in. So you had better open."

"They can't hear you this way," Oksana said. She leaned toward the window and hammered at the shutter, shouting, "You there!" Her voice carried far through the frost-bound silence. "You there, want us to break in?"

Again we waited. But when a man's voice suddenly burst through an invisible crack in the door, we all started.

"What's all this, comrades? This is the middle of the night. What d'you want?" The voice was hoarse and rough, but it was also a scared voice.

"We are not comrades, we are women with children," Oksana called through the crack in the door. "Let us in!"

Nikusha's mother cried in a sob-laden voice, "We're refugees, we're left on the tracks—we are about to drop dead! Have a heart."

The crack widened, and the shadowy face of the tall lanky man behind it was a ghostly gray spot. "Have a heart yourselves! You're obviously Whites, and you want me to let you in just as the Reds are coming! There are two villages near here, just a few versts away. Why don't you . . . ?"

"But we can no longer move, we can't!"

We argued with the man, we insisted, we pleaded, when suddenly Panna came to the door. Her intention to push her way inside past the man was so obvious that he stepped outside and stood shielding the door with his back. His bare, scrawny neck showed from under the shawl collar of his fur coat. In the moonlight his face with a stubble beard looked gaunt and greenish.

"Don't you realize what you are doing to me, citizens?" he wailed. "What will happen if I let you, Whites, stay here just when the Reds are supposed to appear any moment? I am the schoolteacher here. I have a sick wife in the house, who has typhus. If the Reds find you here, it'll be the end of me!"

"See here," I said, finally finding the strength to rise from the steps where I was sitting. "All we want is to feed the children and to find out how to get to the nearest village. The Reds won't come until morning. Where can we hire some horses?"

"All the horses you can get are dead ones, as many as you want along the road. What are you talking about? And once I let you in," and his voice gave a high, desperate squeak, "how shall I get you out before morning?"

"We promise," I said firmly. "Just let us get a rest and get warm, and we shall leave before daybreak."

"And how can I tell who you are? Perhaps you're a general," he pointed to Professor Hertz. "If you have any papers on you, anything incriminating, like White documents or letters or passports . . ." But he was weakening, and we were by now already pressing toward the doorway.

"The man is a professor, a teacher like you!" I said.

"We will destroy all our papers, we swear to you," Madame Tongovsky cried. "We'll have to, anyway."

"If you swear to me to leave before daybreak, and before that to burn all compromising stuff—and I mean every bit of paper you happen to have on you or with you or—"

Several of us, speaking at once, said we promised, swore to it, and he was now letting us enter, still prophesying calamity in a breaking, sinister voice. But we were already inside.

An iron *proletarka* stove stood in the middle of the room; through its square opening a few coals twinkled crimson in the darkness. The man struck a match, and as he lit a candle on the rough board table, I saw his hand shake. The table was littered with bread crumbs, crowded with cheap, dirty dishes. The copper of a samovar caught the candlelight, and seeing everyone's movement toward it, the man cried, "No, no, first get rid of all your documents." With a nervously dangling hand he indicated the stove. "Tea will come later, please! The samovar is cold anyway. All right, all right, I'll heat it for you, but first of all . . ."

ONE AFTER the other, people knelt before the stove, feeding it with their papers. Soon it would be my turn. Meanwhile I sat on the floor, legs outstretched before me, holding Bibik. His face burning, his eyes closed, he lay motionless in my arms asleep. Still I rocked him, rocked him for my own comfort; by way of conveying to him my pity, my tenderness, my gratitude. Sick, unwashed for days, in the same dirty blanket, and never a sound from him, never a cry. Panna had put a cup of warm water with sugar beside me, and once in a while I would try to force a little of it through his lips. Panna, Veronika, and Oksana were fussing around the stove preparing to cook something, trying to placate our nervous host by offering him whatever food we had.

I was not thinking of the morning, of where we would go, of what awaited us. I was thinking of the papers I had to burn—Alik's diary, his letters. I had to fulfill my promise to this man; I could not possibly keep the diary, written on the front by a White volunteer, without endangering not only myself, but everyone else around.

It was about five o'clock in the morning when I finally took all the papers I had with me out of my bag and came up to the stove. By that time, too tired to sit up, people lay on the floor around the walls, or sat crumpled at the school desks, their heads in their hands. The odor of wet, thawing felt and furs, of smoke, and of American canned food hung in the room. No one slept. Panna sat in a corner with eyes closed, holding Bibik. I crouched before the stove at such an angle that she could not see exactly what I was doing.

The stove by now was red hot. I slipped off my sweater, took out my passport, opened it for a last look. "Olga Volotskoy," it said, "wife of Lieutenant of His Majesty Alexander the Third's . . . hereditary noblewoman." I tore it in two, stuck it in the narrow mouth of the stove. The fire flared up, hot on my face. Then, without looking, trying not to see the lines in Alik's still schoolboy hand, I began to tear page after page out of the gray copybook and feed them to the stove, tearing, crumpling, and burning all that remained of Alik's genius. And I also was tearing and burning the hope to which I had frantically clung through these months, the hope that he could still be alive. For I no longer wanted him to be alive. Not in this world where I was. As I rose from my knees, brushing some light ashes from my skirt, a glacial deadened voice within me was repeating, Never. Never.

But this "never" was related to myself, not to Alik. For I realized that together with his diary and letters, I had also destroyed something infinitely smaller, utterly insignificant now, yet something around which my whole being had been wrapped: my yearning ever to achieve anything in art or creative thought. For whatever gift I possessed, it had no more right to be, this gift so immeasurably inferior to Alik's. Not now when nothing was to be left of his genius—not now that I had burned the last of him. And as I stood there pulling on my sweater again, my life before me—if any—was a charred empty field, one in which nothing but a few stray weeds could ever grow again.

"Don't hurry us so! We've promised you to be out by daybreak, and so we shall," I heard Nikusha-père say to the host. "It's only half past five."

Oksana came up to me. "Well, it seems the only thing left to us will be to try those cars we saw on the tracks. Can you imagine the temperature in them? The closest village is eight versts away. No horses left anywhere, he says."

I stared at her blankly. Horses? Villages? Hadn't we known all along that there were no horses? That there weren't any villages nearby?

Making an effort to move my lips, I replied. "I burned Alik's diary."

THE FIRST THING we discovered as we climbed up the railroad embankment toward the stranded railway cars was that the Trans-Siberian Highway lay close behind it. We knew it by the line of sleighs that emerged from the edge of the forest on our left, and moved at a maddening speed. We stopped, transfixed. Then someone said:

"The Reds."

The highway ran parallel to the railway tracks at a distance of some hundred feet and the sleighs were swiftly coming close enough so that we could decipher the figures in the crowded sleighs, the drivers frantically brandishing their whips.

"No, not the Reds! Our people, refugees! There are women in this sleigh, see? See that blue shawl? A woman."

"The fools, why are they galloping like that, if we are surrounded?"

"Perhaps hoping for the same thing we were," Oksana said crisply.

"But to drive at this rate is the surest way to attract their attention."

I said, "Don't worry." We were speaking just to ease the tension. "They'll be attentive enough even if they find us standing still."

"Let's get into one of the cars," Masha said. "At least we can play dead for a while." And suddenly Oksana cried, "Oh, my Lord, oh, good heavens! Look!"

A group of horsemen were coming out of the forest and galloping after the sleighs. Five or six of them first, then more, a reconnaissance detachment probably. We could hear the furious thud of horses' hooves, the shout of a command, and, as their pace increased, we could see the spots of red on their caps and sleeves. Except for Panna, who, with her head to one side like a balky horse, proceeded straight toward the cars, we all stood there petrified, our eyes measuring the diminishing distance between the sleighs and the horsemen. And then another command that sounded like "Ah-oh, oh-oh," and almost simultaneously the silver ribbons of several sabers flashed in the sun over the horsemen's heads. They were close to the last sleigh when it lurched, rolled sideways at a turn in the road. "Oh, Nita, Nita!" Oksana cried, covering her eyes with her mitten.

"Why are we standing here looking at it," Alenka groaned desperately, rushing after Panna toward the car, "when we ourselves . . ."

But I saw it all. I saw it because my eyes refused to close, my legs to move—saw the sleigh, the driver, the passengers, the horses become one mass, frantically floundering in the snow. I saw the horsemen's sabers crash down upon the mass, and then screams, piercing women's screams rent the air and drowned all other sounds. I saw the rest of the detachment gallop after the sleighs ahead.

We entered the first car that was not locked. The cold inside seemed worse, smelled of rusty metal and frozen linoleum. It was a first-class car with a large section, a drawing room in the middle, and several compartments, yet it was only a dead skeleton now. Everything, including the upholstery of the bunks, had been torn off, wrenched out. Walls and a roof was all it had. Whose car? Who had done it?

Still silent, our eyes still full of what we had just seen, we tramped through it. Unable to stand with Bibik in my arms any longer, I sank down on the frost-stiffened canvas of a bunk.

PART
THREE

Krasnoyarsk

18

A GRAY, FREEZING January morning. Oksana, Veronika, and I were preparing to leave the building of the Krasnoyarsk railway station. We had been brought here the evening before and had spent the night with a crowd of other refugees on benches and on the floor of the waiting room. Now we were told to vacate the building before dark. To go where?

It was three weeks since Krasnoyarsk had been occupied by the Reds. Three weeks, which we had spent in our "purgatory" car, as we called it, forgotten by the new rulers, who had more important souls to take care of. But it had been clear to us for some time that the only road out of this purgatory was a one-way track to hell.

It so happened that all our co-passengers on the French train had eventually found and joined us in this car—all except for the taciturn man with the revolver, toothbrush, and family snapshot. On the morning after we had been cut off by the Reds he had come out on the ties, considerately walked some distance away into the snowdrifts, and shot himself.

Joined to the torture of hunger, cold, and sleeping on the frozen floor, the awareness that we were hell-bound had been crushing all our thoughts and desire to talk. Even Oksana had hardly spoken to me. The only conversation among us had been about whose turn it was to walk to the Klukvennaya station, less than a verst from where we stood, to barter our last cups, forks, and towels for food that was still being sold by the peasants; or about who was to go to the forest to pilfer some wood for the iron stove in the midsection of the car.

I had been spared all these activities because Bibik, although recovering, was still so weak that I never released him from my arms.

It was also at the station that all sorts of announcements, orders, and news issued by the Reds were posted. Nikusha-père would be the first to read them and then, returning to our car, give us the dreadful truth plucked from a maze of propaganda clichés, invective, and lies. Thus we learned that the train of Admiral Kolchak, on its way to the next "White

Capital" of Irkutsk, had been caught between the few remaining Czech trains, and that simultaneously, after a leftist insurrection and a short struggle, Irkutsk had fallen into Bolshevik hands.

The bulk of the retreating White army was still some three hundred miles west of Irkutsk, and this gave a free hand to the railway officials (always Red sympathizers) to block the passage of these last Czech trains. As the Czechs' only goal was to go home, their leader, General Syrovoy, decided to betray Admiral Kolchak to the Red rulers of Irkutsk in return for safe passage for the Czech trains through the Red-occupied Irkutsk territory. General Janin, chief of the Allied Command, gave his consent to this betrayal. Thus on January 14 the car of Admiral Kolchak and his staff was surrounded by Red guards and immediately entered. His fate was the Red tribunal.

We could not believe it. We had heard too many lies from the Reds to believe anything. Also, there seemed to be no room in any of us for more than what oppressed us already. But it appeared there *was* room for more.

Just a few days after this news, we awakened to an iron clatter and a rough jolting, our car evidently being hooked to a train. By evening we were at Krasnoyarsk, to be disgorged there at the station into a crowd of other hollow-faced refugees. From them we learned that since the day three weeks ago when Krasnoyarsk had been cut off by the Reds, it had been filled to bursting by thousands of Red officials and army men on one side and captured Whites on the other. The separation of the sheep from the goats had not yet really begun, they told us. There had been many arrests, of course, but the main units of the Cheka—the state security force founded by Felix Dzerzhinski, which was later to evolve into the KGB—had not arrived yet. It wouldn't be long, though. All businesses had been nationalized immediately, and government food stores had been opened, with long queues freezing at their doors. So far private homes were still untouched, but every house was jam-packed; to find a place to stay was impossible.

However, on the next morning, a burly, leather-jacketed commissar appeared and began to storm at us, threatening everyone with arrest unless we cleared out of the station building before dark.

So now Oksana, Veronika, and I were on our way. Masha was no longer with us; she had contracted typhus and had been taken to some hospital; they did not tell us where. So had Countess Cygnen, with an attack of angina. But Bibik was a trifle better, his fever subsiding. It was a relief to leave him with Panna, go somewhere, do something purposeful, no matter how unachievable, instead of just sitting there.

As we worked our way through the crowd and out the front entrance, we ran into an odd queue of people, refugees like ourselves. Dead silent, they were inching their way along the station wall, searching it with intense, hungry eyes. The wall was practically covered with scraps of paper tacked to it, fluttering in the wind.

"See that? See the notes?" Oksana cried. "Oh, Lord! Let's look! There may be something for us too!"

I pushed my way close to the wall, my eyes seizing one note after another.

Sasha, my dearest, we passed through here on December 15. Mama died of typhus before she knew about poor Kolya. You are all I have now! If you make it to Irkutsk leave a note for me at the church nearest the railway station. Your Katya.

Good people, I beseech you! In the name of the Lord have pity. If you run into my five-year-old boy, Misha Somov, blue-eyed, blond, lost on Christmas Eve at Station Taiga, notify Vera Somov, Chita Military Hospital.

You our great Leader and hero General Kappel and your Kappelites . . . You whose courage and martyrdom give us the strength to bear our crosses, Russia will never forget you!

Anyone from Tamborsk, look up Kyra G. at Military Hospital, critically hurt in Achinsk explosion. Her mother and sister burned to death, her father sick. Writer of this can't visit her—Wanted.

This last "wanted" was written in French in one word instead of three, " *Onmecherche*," as if it were a signature.

And I had been slated to be on that very train, in that very car!

That day we went from house to house, first the three of us together, later singly, and made our little speeches: we had nowhere to spend the night. We had babies; they might freeze to death. And with me walked the blurred specters of people who had often appeared at the back door of our servants' hall. Aunt Katya or someone would come out to them, talk to them, have them fed, clothed, helped. But I never did. I was too busy at the piano or in a rush to go somewhere. And so now it was my turn. Ringing and knocking at door after door, I was not oblivious to the poetic justice. Deep down I was even grateful for the chance of repaying a debt.

How they imprinted themselves on the memory, those doorways! Framed in them forever would stand those different housewives, so different, but so alike in the belligerence with which each protected her own little kingdom from suspicious-looking intruders. Especially from such as we, who looked like beggars and were beggars, but did not talk and act like the usual ones.

"Sorry, comrades." This from that first young one, who looked like the red geraniums and the snow-white curtains, full of unyielding starch, in her windows. "Sorry, you ought to know better, the whole town is overcrowded. We have hardly any place to sleep ourselves. Even our parlor is occupied by two comrades commissars, so don't waste your time." Or the long-nosed angry one, who scolded us through a narrow crack in the door: "They come and come . . . they ring, they knock. Don't you understand, citizens, that it's dangerous for us to take in the likes of you? If my son came and saw you, ex-Whites, in his house—Oh, not that we like the Reds; still . . ."

Well, of course. As simple as that.

There also was that polite, nervous-looking woman who let us enter and warm up a bit, but there was typhus in the house. And then again door after door opened and closed before us, leaving us outside. By twilight we could hardly walk; while only brisk movement could keep us from freezing.

Still, only part of my exhausted self was trudging from house to house that day, asking strangers for shelter. Some other part, still free and unruffled, went on thinking, comparing, repeating to myself that millions of men and women had been doing this from the beginning of time, and so why not I? For "Ye have the poor with you always." Even in a land of Utopia there would be famines, floods, fires, and wars—yes, wars—on this outer plane, until the very nature of man changed. Was it Countess Cygnen who had said this? Never had I felt so strongly that my real home was on that other level, of which I had once attempted to speak to Lorinov, and that at least some part of my being was looking at this outer Olga Volotskoy from that shelter. As we went on with our tramping, my awareness of this steadied my faltering feet and my starvation-dizzy head, blocking out any fear of tonight and tomorrow.

There was a moment that afternoon that thrust itself with particular force out of the impressions of that day. We had just reached an intersection of a deserted street when Oksana suddenly stopped short. "Look, Nita, *look*!" Her hand in the frosted mitten gripped mine. "See there?"

A man had just appeared from behind the next corner and was now crossing the street. For a moment I saw his profile, then only his back; yet something in the set of the man's shoulders and his stride struck me with its resemblance to Verin. But Oksana was already shaking her head in violent deprecation. "No, no! How silly of me! Nothing in common with him." But her voice was trembling. "I always thought that mirages could be seen only in extreme heat, not in extreme cold." She waved her hand in a dejected downward gesture.

We were still standing there paralyzed, when the man suddenly turned and glanced at us. He did not have Verin's close-trimmed mustache and his cap fell low over his eyebrows, so that his face looked square. "No resemblance at all," I said energetically. "None whatsoever," Oksana echoed. Even though her cheeks were aglow from the frost, I saw her face draw in sharply, her features tighten. Perhaps she knew as well as I did that it *had* been Verin.

WE WALKED ON. It was dark and we were becoming more exhausted, hungrier, weaker as we kept circling the town, but the certainty that something would eventually come to our rescue had not failed me for a moment. The magnetic power of this certainty proved itself again when we all found shelter in a hospital near the railroad station that night.

How this happened none of us knew; but just as we returned to the railroad station in the darkness of the evening, a man's voice suddenly shouted from somewhere behind that this was where women with babies and the sick should go: "Just two blocks away, follow me!" Was it because of my optimistic faith, or because the man leading us had noticed how ill Bibik was that I, with him in my arms, was the first to be admitted into the hospital building and given the only free bed, vacated just a few minutes before by a typhus patient?

I threw off the filthy woolen blanket, spread my coat over the sheets, put Bibik on it and lay down next to him. Where was I? Where was Panna? Where was everybody, and everything, anyway? Had I lost Panna, and all my friends forever?

But no answers came. Even though immediately attacked by hordes of lice left behind by my defunct predecessor, who had bequeathed his bed and its contents—and perhaps his fate—to me, I was already sliding down through layers and layers of sticky dirty cotton into a blissful nowhere. The gray, trampled-down snow of front porches, opening and closing doors, were still vaguely flashing before me. Then suddenly Igor broke through this vagueness, his face so clear, so real, his eyes bright and intent, and said, "The horses are ready, we must go!" Then Lorinov appeared from behind him, held his hand to his cap with aggressive blankness: "Good night." And the central section of the baggage car rolled shut behind him. "Good night," I replied.

Good night, I said to them all. To Igor! To those I loved and had lost back in Russia; to those I loved and was about to lose and who would lose me. And to all men born to this earth I said good night and good-bye, with abysmal tenderness and pity.

I WAS STILL in bed the next morning when Oksana appeared, from where I did not know, and said that we had to go to some place nearby to see a certain Red official who might arrange for us to stay in a neighborhood school. Then dear Panna also appeared, unperturbedly took Bibik from me, and we all soon found ourselves in an office. There, a heavyset man with a pince-nez and a cultivated manner of speaking sat at a desk. With a broad flourish he invited us to be seated also. He addressed us as "comrades," but was trying to show that even though we looked like paupers he was well aware that we were ladies, giving himself credit for his magnanimity and perspicacity, and for the fact that he, although compelled to work for the Reds, was a gentleman. It was Oksana who did the talking this time. Veronika sat there in proud, demanding silence, I defiant and numb. A Red official. Our first personal encounter with the enemy. However, by the end of a few minutes, he granted us permission to stay a while in the Krasnoyarsk Land Survey School a few blocks away. "The building is empty," he said, "I mean overcrowded with people in the same predicament as yourselves, but empty of furniture. I suppose under the circumstances . . . ?"

We thanked him and rose to go. He bowed with a deferential "I did my best." Later that morning, when we all walked to that Land Survey School single file, carrying our babies and our few possessions, one further eventful thing happened. We were passing a wooden fence upon which bulletins from the *Krasnoyarsk Pravda* were posted. This time several identical ones with enormous headlines had been freshly pasted on in a row. Oksana and Veronika, who were somewhat ahead of me and Panna, stopped short, their eyes first on the bulletin, then furtively on me. I came up.

"The First Cavalry Division of the retreating White bandits," the bulletin said, "was surrounded by our valorous Red Army and annihilated after two days of fierce battle at Station Zima. Their officers, to the last man, have been killed or taken prisoner."

"What nonsense," Oksana whispered furiously. "Our division couldn't have as much as reached Station Zima yet!"

Veronika said, "This is their usual cruel method: whenever they're beaten they tell the opposite to hypnotize the people. They couldn't possibly be near there." But she glanced at me worriedly.

"Let's figure it out," Oksana said. "Today is January twenty-fourth. We parted with the regiment in Achinsk on December seventeenth, right? How could they have made that distance of about nine hundred versts to Zima? Fighting, at that. *Impossible!*"

It was hard for me to speak, so I nodded.

19

YURI MOLSOV, chief of the Red Cross train on which I had left Omsk in November, suddenly appeared in the doorway at the other end of Auditorium Number Two of the Land Survey School, where we had spent the last two weeks. The February dusk was condensing behind the windows, but there was enough light for me to see the anxious frown with which he was searching the overcrowded place. He had lost weight drastically and his sheepskin minus the shoulder boards fitted him loosely. I waved to him, and with a quick flash in his eyes and an answering wave of his windmill arm, he started toward me, threading his way among the ragged figures sprawling on the floor. I would have rushed to meet him but was afraid to wake Bibik.

Molsov squatted down beside me, clutching my hand, his broad shoulder a welcome barrier between me and my neighbor, a sickly Buryat peasant woman. Seeing Bibik's ravaged little face, he made a sort of *tsk-tsk* pitying sound with his tongue. Back in the Red Cross train he and I hardly ever talked, but suddenly that train was our precious mutual home in a world of struggle and freedom and of shared purpose.

"Igor?" he asked, frowning, and his eyes told me he was ready for the worst.

"I know nothing," I said, "and what the papers say can't be true."

He nodded forcefully. "The usual garbage. But mind you, a lot of people here know that the First Cavalry fought the Reds off at the outskirts of Krasnoyarsk and really messed them up, and that your regiment bypassed the city on their way east. They ought to be approaching Lake Baikal by now."

I was about to sigh with relief, but he added, "I hope they get to Baikal before the thaw; it's their only access to the other shore. No, I've heard nothing either about my children. But," and again his face gathered into a bitter knot, "the Countess is with me, really very ill." The hasty way he spoke made me feel that he came with something else to tell me.

"I have been looking for you all over town," he finally said. "Someone from Tamborsk told your brother Dimitri that you were here. Yes, he is here too." My heart stopped. Dying? In prison? My arms contracted about Bibik.

Molsov said quickly, "Dimitri, thank God, is recovering. Still can't walk, though. Aftereffect of typhus, you know—excruciating pain in the legs. Another problem: savage hunger. And, of course, their food ration is just a few potatoes."

Dimitri was living in a huge attic across town, Molsov said, with a group of stranded Whites, patients and staff of a hospital train that had been cut off by the Reds on Christmas Eve. "I'll tell you how to find him." Then, to cheer me up, he said that there was a bright side to Dimitri's situation: he had found himself in good company. "There are several former has-beens and several friends of his in that attic, anyway, his own kind."

I thought, So it will be easier for the Cheka to arrest them all at one blow; and I felt my face change. He saw it. "No, no! The Cheka won't come around for them for some time yet. It's just beginning to do searches for concealed weapons, and hunt for army officers.

"Moreover, they need us, educated people. They can't possibly manage the administrative part without us; they've bitten off too big a morsel. Of course we have to work for them. Yes, it's terrible, but what's the alternative? Starvation or execution. Too late for anything else. I myself already have a job. I'm in charge of dog kennels on a farm, and I'll try to get Dimitri over to this farm. With his height and looks he will be too noticeable in Krasnoyarsk. Another good thing: when the Reds cut off this typhus train, Dimitri was unconscious, and the staff passed him off as a private mobilized by the Whites, and so that's how it stands now in his identity papers: hospital orderly. By the way . . . ," he wrinkled his face into that pained knot again. "Is it true that Igor's friend Colonel Lorinov was not with the regiment when it was cut off? Too bad! It seems that some soldier, a Tamborsk Dragoon who has just been released was interrogated by the Cheka about him. They're looking for him. You probably know that it was he who sabered down their famous commander of the Steel Regiment. So you can imagine what's awaiting him."

"I know," I said and looked down at Bibik.

Bibik opened his eyes and for a moment they gazed at me, earnest and sad.

I couldn't go to see Dimitri until Panna returned. Not only because there was no one with whom to leave Bibik, but also because I had nothing to take to Dimitri unless Panna brought our bread rations. But if she came empty-handed, as often happened, I would find something to take him. I would break myself in two, but get him something I would! The *upravdom*, custodian of our building, who lived in the basement, would barter some provisions with me. His duties were to take care of the building; but this being next to impossible, with plumbing lines broken, corridors flooded with puddles of putrid water, and electricity having gone out of order with the advent of the Reds, he found himself speculating with the last possessions of the refugees. Mostly jewelry, and jewelry was all I had left. This bold-faced, thick-set man seemed to like me and at times was magnanimous. "For this interesting trinket [a Fabergé brooch], you may come every day for half a bottle of milk for the next two weeks."

With both rations of bread—because Panna had given me hers also—wrapped in a scrap of towel, which Dimitri might need, I set out across town to where he was staying.

NO ONE IN surrendered, overcrowded Krasnoyarsk ventured out after dark. It was not yet seven o'clock and the curfew did not start until eight, but the streets were already dead. From time to time the heavy silence was sliced by the roar of a madly speeding car. That was all. Communist officials alone had automobiles. One of these zoomed past me, then all I could hear was the crunch of my hurried footsteps on the hard-packed snow. At times I would almost be running, slowing down only to regain my breath. And finally there I was, opening the garden gate of the corner house, skirting the building, as told, running flight after flight up the dark rear staircase. At the very top was the door to the attic. I leaned against the wall to rest, closed my eyes. Green and red circles pulsed inside them. Except for Bibik, Dimitri was all that was left to me of my family, my Russia, of my happiness with Igor! Of my own self. And this that was left was about to collapse as from a burning roof and be turned into cinders.

In the dusky light of one lone electric bulb in the ceiling, the huge attic was a scene out of Gorky's *Lower Depths*. Swaddled silhouettes of men in sheepskins and greatcoats were sitting and lying on the floor, some standing by the iron stove in the center of the room. It smelled of smoke and frozen mildew; a low murmur hung in the air. And then I saw Dimitri coming toward me. The ceiling was low and the top of his head almost touched it. As he came near, his face closed into perfect impassivity, which I knew so well and which betrayed to me the force of what he felt and also of how painful it was for him to move around.

We shook hands, unable to speak. In his emaciated face the sea-blue eyes looked enormous; his dark brown hair and the Vandyke that he had lately grown, and the deepened Ogarin planes in his cheeks emphasized his pallor. I didn't wish to feel anything, I didn't wish to ask him any questions or hear what he was asking me about Igor, all I wanted was to give him the bread I had brought, give it to him in such a way that he would eat it by himself, at least most of it! So I signaled for him to come out with me on the landing.

"Eat it," I said, fiercely shoving the package into his hands as soon as we stepped out of the attic. "Eat it at once, or I'll throw it away. Oh, yes, we have plenty, plenty of flour and so on. It hurts you to stand, sit down on this windowsill and eat it at once!"

He took the slender package from me. His long fingers now looked like wax candles and, for a fraction of a second, his former hands moving over the piano keys flashed before me. Then with ecstatic eyes I watched him eat, promising that I would bring more tomorrow, talking without stopping so he would go on eating. I told him about our friends who had been stranded here with us, about those who had been imprisoned or killed, and I also told him about Igor's regiment—there were rumors they had fought their way through the Red encirclement and were approaching Lake Baikal. If this was true everything now depended upon their reaching it before the thaw. "Colonel Lorinov, you know, was in charge of getting us out of the Red trap, but fell sick and had to jump off the train. Somehow the Reds knew it and are hunting for him. So I suppose by now he either has been killed or has committed suicide."

"Igor's friend?" Dimitri asked frowning.

"Yes, mine also." But Dimitri's mind was not on Lorinov. "And nothing new from over there?" He had been anxious to ask this question since he saw me. No more Red and White border, the postal and telegraph communications had been reestablished for some time, but no one we knew had heard from European Russia yet. "Everyone feels that we—I mean the Whites—might endanger our families by writing. And how can they, back in Russia, write to us? They have no idea where we are." But we both knew that we were also afraid of hearing the worst from home. Starvation, epidemics, executions had been sweeping all over Russia. So I did not dare express to Dimitri any conjectures about Sonya, his wife, and their children. We did not mention Alik either. Had Alik been alive and on the Red side, some rumor would have reached us by now.

It was cold on the landing. We reentered the attic and Dimitri led me to his corner. There was not much else we wished to put into words.

We settled down on his army blanket. Whatever last rag he had would always be carefully shaken out, brushed, folded. I smiled and pointed: "Nero and his fiddle." And the happiness of being together again began to filter through our shattered state, coming out in little gasps of laughter. No one around seemed to heed my presence or hear us; and Dimitri, indicating to me with his eyes now this, now that grotesque, beggarlike figure, would tell me who they really were.

"That big bearded one by the stove, who looks like Grandmamma's coachman, is—you know who? Yardin, that ferocious general-in-chief of the Volga Military District. He too was sick and in a typhus train. The prognosis is not too good. And that other one, in the opposite corner, the criminal type, straight from Sakhalin, wouldn't you think?" And Dimitri grinned, rubbing his hands together as he always did when he was amused and delighted. "Prince K———, a Colonel of the Guard, a graduate from the School of Pages. He knew Mother and Father intimately. You should meet him. If he shaved off his bushy beard, you would see what I mean."

"Do they all look like this because they can't help it, or on purpose?"

"Both. They can't hide their identity for long, but at least for a while. Here in Siberia the local Bolsheviks have no notion of the difference between the names Naryshkin and Otryshkin."

And we laughed, because it was fun to marvel at the tricks life could play on people. In the past we had always marveled at things together, gazing at life as though from some faraway horizonless homeland to which we had once belonged and of which we still remembered enough to measure things against it. And now, both caught in the dark crevice that had closed in on us and where we would probably smother, we recognized this remote inaccessible homeland in each other's beaming eyes, and for a few blissful moments it was ours.

THE MONTH of February was the weight and color of lead. Typhus throve on the filth, overcrowding, and starvation, toppling people right and left. In its wake crept its predatory twin, recurring typhus. The Cheka by then was fully deployed, hunting for dangerous Whites and suspicious-looking residents. Police roamed the city, roared in the middle of the night through the streets in their "Black Ravens," making people sit up stiff and hollow-faced, waiting for gun butts to pound on their doors. Dwellings were searched, people taken away. Queues of freezing women, carrying their last scraps of food to their men, wove a dark line outside the city prison gates. Every single day, people we knew died from one cause or another.

Soon after I saw him, Yuri Molsov was arrested. In prison he contracted typhus, and that was the end. The night they led him away, Countess Cygnen had her last attack of angina. When I had seen her a few days before, she had said to me, "It is a tragedy to be old and ill and yet to be even more interested in life and people than when one was young." It was also a tragedy for me to hear her say this. I had hoped that old people were tired of life, attached to it as lightly as drying leaves to their tree.

At least she had been spared the blow of Yuri's death, I tried to console myself. But as I went through the joyless chores of those days, trudging every morning across Krasnoyarsk to an orphanage where I taught music, Molsov's eyes kept following me, telling me that he would never see his wife and youngsters who would be waiting for him, perhaps waiting and hoping for years. For who would let them know? How? Where?

Admiral Kolchak had been executed. General Kappel, who had led his army out of Red encirclement by detouring Krasnoyarsk and fighting his way through Red-occupied territory, died late in January of frostbite, gangrene, and pneumonia. We heard that the Czechs had offered him a berth in one of their trains, but Kappel had refused to accept any help from the men who had betrayed Admiral Kolchak and our whole army. In spite of his agony, Kappel chose to continue in his sleigh, and died on the journey. So went the greatest man of the White movement.

It was all like a Shakespearean tragedy: by the last act there is no one left to tell the story. Some of our Tamborsk families that had been spared in 1918 were now annihilated in one sweep. Every man in the family of Dimitri's wife, Sonya, had been wiped out: her younger brother committed suicide when his unit had been cut off by the Reds; the older brother died of typhus; the brothers' teenage sons, White volunteers—the pride and hope of the clan—had been found shot, lying face-down in a snowdrift in the forest near Krasnoyarsk. Sonya and her sisters-in-law, who had remained in Tamborsk, would have to hear all of this from us when the postal service was reinstated.

There were no more coffins available. Hastily knocked-together wooden boxes were all one could get. This was the way Oksana and I buried Colonel Georgievsky, the one whose wife and daughter had been burned during the Achinsk explosion. Their beautiful younger girl, who had lost an eye and lay prostrate in some overcrowded basement ("Glass is still filtering from my wounds," she had told me once), asked Oksana to come with a sled for her father's body. Someone else would provide the box. Her father, a brilliant, energetic man, had died of a heart attack.

Late that afternoon we pulled the sled with the box on it somewhere far out of town following a lame priest, whose long hair swept to and fro in the glacial wind, our voices constantly breaking as we sang after him whatever was supposed to be sung. Then we shoveled down clods of frozen clay. They rattled on the box like grapeshot.

Death roamed all around us, peering at us from all sides, watching us. Oddly, although I had been constantly haunted by the awareness of my mortality when death was so far from me personally, I had no fear of it now. All that I had left of will and mind was now focused on just one purpose: not to stoop, not to falter under life's blows. ("Never give way to dejection, always believe in the creative spirit of life and let it work its miracles." —Father's last letter.)

There was much for which I had to be thankful: Dimitri and Bibik recovering, Panna at my side, no typhus, no prison. Also there is the bitterness of being alone in misfortune. This the inhabitants of Auditorium Number Two were spared. There were all kinds among us, but all were ex-Whites, sharing the same fate, the same feelings. When stretching out on their bedding at night, people would move closer together and their private unburdenings would rustle on and on. About the chances of escaping. To Mongolia. To China. To Persia through some subterranean rivers. The risk was great, but what we had to live with was worse. Or about the families left behind in European Russia. They had been waiting for two years, praying, hoping, despairing. They had no idea where we were, whether we were alive. Would it endanger them if we wrote? And if we did, what would we hear in reply? The idea of hearing from them was frightening. But people in our Auditorium shared their fears, their last bread, also their daydreams. Against the darkness in which we lived, these daydreams were like red-hot rockets that would blind us by their glow, then burn out and singe the heart.

Veronika dreamed that our troops that had fought their way out of the Krasnoyarsk encirclement would unite with those of Ataman Semenov. Supported by the Japanese, they would swoop down on us. Veronika's husband was with Semenov, the cossack hero! She believed that only the fearless cossacks, fierce and cruel as they might be at times, had what it took to "clear out the Red rot."

Oksana, of course, dreamed of a possible meeting with Verin. She was now certain it had been he whom we saw on that first day in

Krasnoyarsk. "I am sure of one thing: whatever he did, he did it because he believed it to be right." The fact that Verin had intended to take her along and then had left her without a word of explanation had also changed color in the light of her craving to see him. "It was *I* who insisted that he take me! He had never promised it, never!"

She was working as a typist in an office called Up-San-Arm and did everything possible to find out if anyone had heard about him. She often lingered in the street after work, talking to acquaintances. The town was full of people we knew from Tamborsk and from Omsk; the air was full of rumors, which spread with uncanny speed. Somehow, though, no one had heard anything about Verin.

IN THE LAST DAYS of February it snowed continuously, and a fierce north wind blew. This was particularly disheartening because we had been told that we would have to clear out of the Land Survey School by the end of the week. Where to go? What to do? At work Oksana had heard about a cottage in some out-of-the-way street, whose inhabitants had recently all died of typhus. It stood there empty, with the front door torn off its hinges. Whoever got there first could have it.

It took her some time to find the miserable shack in question and when she found it, it turned out to be already occupied by some refugees. Tired, frustrated, cursing under her breath, she took a shortcut home through a deserted uphill alley. It was there and then that she ran into Verin.

He was coming down the hill with another man, talking to him in an earnest, businesslike manner. With dusk gathering and the snow falling in thick diagonal streaks, he did not see her until they had almost passed each other. He wore his old military sheepskin, but there was no kind of Red insignia on him. If he passed by, pretending not to know her, then everything everyone thought about him would be true: a traitor to the cause, a traitor to her.

But Verin did not pretend not to know her. Obviously controlling his surprise, he raised his hand to his cap in a gallant gesture, smiled a little as if he had seen her yesterday, and immediately resumed talking to his companion. But a moment later she heard him take leave of the man and hurriedly come after her. Then he called her name. She didn't dare turn even then, but he was already at her side. "Oksana," he said. "How I have watched for you! I knew you were here!"

But I heard this from her later. When she returned to our school she didn't say a word to me about the encounter. This was suppertime, and together with a group of our newly acquired friends we were crowding around the wall stove taking turns to cook our flour-and-soda butterless pancakes, discussing the probability of soon finding ourselves in the streets again. When Oksana entered I noticed how her face glowed, but this was only a snapshot my eyes took at random, to which I paid only the slightest attention.

We had hardly finished eating when I saw her slip into her coat. "Where are you going?" I cried, astonished. Without looking at me, she said she had to go to the city library to look up something about Karl Marx for her boss. Whatever was really afoot, I would soon know in detail; and I did.

She poured it all out to me later the same night, in exuberant whispers. When they first ran into each other, Verin had an urgent appointment and suggested that they meet in an hour at the public library. She was supposed to look for a book on Karl Marx and pretend to read it in the rear reference room. As he came in he sat down opposite her and opened a newspaper.

"But there was not a soul around, and later we could talk and he told me everything! Oh, Nita, I was right! He is an extraordinary man! When I tell you all, you'll see."

It appeared that the night he had left he had at first briefly fallen asleep, but soon woke up with a start, struck by the realization that to leave the next morning might be too late. He must go immediately. Better to have everyone believe that he had deserted than to have us all tortured and hacked to pieces by Schetinkin's men.

He was right not to wait until the next day; it took him over thirty hours to reach the Trakt. The melee on the Trakt was such that he had to go with the tide, his only goal to reach General Headquarters, which rumors claimed had already moved to Achinsk. He rode on through the night, hoping to make Achinsk the next morning, but was confronted by one personal misfortune after another. First that scoundrel, his orderly— a boy he had trusted—disappeared in the general confusion together with his sleigh and provisions; then his horse fell with exhaustion; he had to shoot it ("It was like committing suicide") and make the last twenty miles on foot with a long file of others who had lost their units, constantly forced off the road to flounder in the snowdrifts.

Achinsk was so overcrowded that all approaching units were being diverted to bypass it. The only way for him to catch up with our division was to overtake it farther east by getting on a train. He rushed to the railroad station, jumped on a Polish train already in motion, and hung on to the handrail until he was finally taken on. The train was slow. It came to Krasnoyarsk right in the middle of the Socialist uprising; and there he was stuck.

"He wants to tell everything to you himself. You'll see that he outdid himself to catch up with the regiment. You'll see how true he is to his innermost convictions! I even have the feeling that he has some plan—some hidden plan." This last came in a frightened whisper.

"Do you mean he is plotting something?" I asked, incredulous.

"If he were, he wouldn't tell me, but I can swear to you that he is. Honestly. I feel it in my bones. Anyway, when he accepted the position offered him on the newspaper—"

"What newspaper?" I interrupted, although I knew there was only one newspaper here now, the *Krasnoyarsk Pravda*.

"Oh, he isn't really. This is a purely technical job printing or editing or something, and anyway he had to accept it."

I was taken aback by hearing that Verin was working for *Pravda*, but of course I also knew that refusing to take the job would have meant the end of him. "But why on earth does he want to talk to me?"

"Because you are Igor's wife and to him Igor is the regiment. If you see Igor before he does, you can explain everything to him. But it's also *I* who need your help! Please, Nita, please come with me!"

BY THAT TIME Krasnoyarsk was crowded beyond capacity, but the someone on whom I always depended helped me again. That very morning Panna, standing in a bread queue, met with the ex-secretary of the Tamborsk nobility, Stephan Ivany'ch Stankov, a sad-eyed little man with a drooping mustache. In the past I often used to see him sitting stooped over in our reception hall at Tamborsk with a portfolio of papers ready for my father's signature. Now, as Panna saw his stooping back, she rushed straight toward him and told him about us. "What?" Stankov cried, "Alexander Lvovich's daughter? With a baby?" What wouldn't he do for us in my father's memory! They were six in their room, but it was large and devoid of any furniture, enough space in it for four more. There was the use of the kitchen.

"Your father is helping you again," Panna said, her eyes filling.

The next day we moved to the Stankovs. Their flat was across town, almost on its outskirts, close to the Yenisei River. Panna carried our suitcases; I carried Bibik, who was still too weak to walk. As we reached the front porch of the two-story house we both had to drop down on the steps and sit there, Panna breathing hard, the muscles of my legs and arms trembling. This was where Stankov's soft-spoken wife found us. What a forgotten experience it was to be greeted by a sweet singing voice, to be welcomed and hugged.

The room we were to share was indeed empty, except for six piles of folded blankets, but it had large windows and the electricity was in order! Light! Now I knew what it meant to have light.

Oksana had decided to spend another day at our old place. She also had to see Verin that evening, because of some "terrific developments." When she moved in with us the next day she explained that Verin and part of his office were being transferred to Irkutsk and were looking for a typist to take with them. He had recommended her. If she accepted, she would have to leave by the end of the week, Verin and the chief editor later, when the office was already set up. She would have to decide immediately. What should she do? What did I suggest?

"You know that I hate for you to work for *Pravda*."

"But my job would be something else; he made this clear. I'll do general typing. And I can't lose him now, Nita!"

The following evening Oksana came home in a frantic state. "Could you come with me to the railroad station right after we eat? Vladimir wants to see you! He'll meet us at the corner behind the cathedral. Nita, please."

"You don't mean that you're already leaving?" My heart sank.

"No, not yet! But in case I decide to take this job, he must obtain some order blanks for me to fill out beforehand, or something."

"But why on earth should he want to see me?"

"Well, he does, and so do I. Because I want you to feel him out! If he really intends to marry me and spells it out to you, it will make me less afraid to go to Irkutsk. Please talk to him, Nita! I shall find some pretext to leave you two alone."

"Has he ever mentioned his fiancée? Or does he expect to hear from her?"

"He might hear. But now he knows that he loves *me*! He is also certain that she has given him up long ago."

THE EVENING was dark, moonless and starless. A frosty haze enveloped the streets. Between five and six o'clock, when people were still returning from work, was the safest time for meeting a friend in the street and having a talk without being watched. The desire to be fair and open-minded toward Verin did not prevent me from feeling that I was advancing toward a battlefield in full combat readiness, performing an unselfish and fearless act, looking foward to a show of strength. But as he suddenly emerged before us out of the fog—the same Lieutenant Verin of a month or two ago, walking with the same assured stride, head up, so tangibly carrying with him the atmosphere of our recent past, as if nothing had happened between then and now—I had to ask myself with a sudden sense of awe whether I should have come at all. And what would Igor have thought of this meeting?

"Good evening," I said dryly, as he raised his hand to his cap and fell in step with us. He replied in a tone that I had never heard from him before. "How good to see you, Olga Alexan'na." The tone was gentle and earnest, the kind in which he must have often spoken to Oksana, but which he had never used with me or with anyone else in my presence. "I was so anxious to know what happened to all of you. I had no news at all. And now there are so few of us remaining . . ." His brilliant eyes were looking at me with concern from under the characteristic frown.

Verin asked some questions about the regiment, about Igor and Lorinov, and I said curtly that we had heard nothing, although rumors had reached us that our division had crossed Lake Baikal, many of the men with frozen limbs and gangrene, many dead.

I presumed that he knew a great deal more than we, but I did not ask. Instead I said in a blank voice, "I understand that you are leaving for Irkutsk and will be working for the newspaper."

"I have already told Nita of all that happened to you," Oksana interrupted nervously, and she quickly glanced around to make sure that no one was coming up behind us.

"Well," he said with a shrug, "things seemed to conspire against me. If you are interested . . ."

"We have certainly been wondering about your fate," I said.

"Fate," he repeated on a deepened note. "Actually, the strangest thing that happened to me was that at the unfortunate moment when I found myself here in Krasnoyarsk, with that Polish train going no farther, I learned that a cousin of mine was here at Krasnoyarsk. He had always been a radical, this cousin, and I understood that now his name was ranked high among the Socialists. He is the ascetic, impractical type, you know, but a saint in his own right, the kind of whom our present masters make such good use for their own purposes. It was only after I saw him that I remembered how you once spoke of fate."

"Did I ever say anything worth your remembering?" I asked coldly.

"Yes, indeed," he smiled a little. "You spoke of how certain entanglements of events often seem to have been plotted by a superior living mind. You find a road you were about to take suddenly blocked, while another road opens for you just as suddenly. Such was this day for me. Because my cousin was not going to help me to proceed east, as I had hoped he would; on the contrary, he made me see that by trying to escape from the Reds I would merely be saving my skin."

Cousin or no cousin, I thought, Verin went to ask a Social Revolutionary for help. But not one of those SR's who were now the Communists' worst enemies, but one of those starry-eyed romantics who had instigated revolutionary terrorism in Russia before the war and had betrayed the White army by blocking its retreat.

"My cousin insisted that I stay here where I could still serve my country," Verin went on. "Men of goodwill were needed desperately to counteract the other kind—sadists and criminals who had pushed into the ranks of the Bolsheviks."

Verin probably knew the town well. As he spoke, he led us to the railroad station in a roundabout way, along some deserted streets, past a row of empty lots with broken fences and some sort of windowless barns where no one could overhear us.

"At first I flatly refused to stay. I might be called to serve in the Red army, which would mean fighting against my friends. However, my cousin promised to see to it that I had a full discharge from military service. I knew he could do it; he was close with some of the most powerful men in Moscow, Bukharin for one. I began to weigh all the pros and cons. My personal survival hardly came into question, for whether I tried to escape from the Reds or stayed with them, in either case I would be a hairsbreadth removed from death, as I am now. It was clear to me what lay ahead of the White movement: its final ruin. The utter impossibility of counteracting the tremendous power of a ruthless tyranny by our disunited front was obvious, especially after Admiral Kolchak had relinquished his powers to Ataman Semenov. What would be left for the survivors except leading a miserable, utterly fruitless, selfish existence in Japan or China?"

"But what can an ex-White officer do except be arrested?"

"I'll take this risk." This came out with conviction and force. In fact, his whole speech inspired confidence, so that I felt my hostility diminish and regretted having shown it. Almost without pausing he added, "I am sorry to have led you through such a gloomy district, but at least we could talk. We shall come out on the railroad plaza presently."

IN CONTRAST to the rest of the town, the railroad plaza and the station building were flooded with lights. There was some traffic outside, but inside the building was half empty, the infrequent sound of voices and footfalls echoing forlornly in the void. We had hardly entered the waiting room when Oksana mumbled some garbled excuse—she must locate somebody or something—and disappeared. I had not expected her to leave us so soon.

We sat down, leaving a suitably formal distance between us, I feeling that, ready or not, I must attack Oksana's problem at once. But he anticipated me.

"I am so thankful for having a moment alone with you, Olga Alexan'na. There is so much I would like to tell you. I am well aware of the bond that exists between you and Oksana and how badly she needs your advice. She actually has no one except you."

"And if she leaves for Irkutsk she will have only you," I said quickly. "Are you certain nothing will detain you here?"

"That's exactly it. Whether she decides to go or to stay, I want to make it clear that I am not trying to influence her one way or the other."

"But, barring acts of God, or rather of the devil, are you certain that nothing will detain you here?"

"I wouldn't have offered this job to Oksana if I hadn't been certain."

A gray-whiskered, gloomy-looking man in deep galoshes was passing by us, the galoshes squeaking a worried rhythm, and for a moment Verin relaxed against the back of the bench. When the man passed he picked up what he had been saying, but in a still lower voice and going over to French.

"I am reasonably sure that neither being recalled from the job nor being arrested threatens me in the *near* future. But I repeat: much as I long to have Oksana there, near me, and certain as I am that her new job will give her much better rations and living conditions, I am not using the slightest pressure. On the contrary."

Suddenly provoked, letting go of whatever diplomacy I ought to have used, I said, "Vladimir Vladimirovich! Aren't you talking to me like an old-fashioned bridegroom to an old-fashioned parent? 'I can give her this, I can't give her that.' I am not her father or mother, and, besides, this is usually done after a proposal of marriage has been made." This last simply shot out of me. I knew it had sounded arrogant and attempted to veil it with a little laughter. "Has one in fact been made?"

"I am glad that you came straight out with it, Olga Alexan'na," he replied with outward courtesy, although I detected a shade of condescension toward the intrusive female who was indeed taking herself for an old-fashioned parent. "Oksana must have told you that I want to marry her. Yes, I do. But my position is still too indefinite. In a few months I shall be clearer about my standing and whether by marrying I might not endanger her."

"Please!" I said impatiently. "Please don't take me for a match-maker. Personally I don't want Oksana to work on a newspaper that feeds monstrous lies to the whole world, and am extremely sorry for you if you have to do it!" This had sounded too aggressive and, since I had not come here to spoil things and to quarrel, I added on a softer note, "Even if it is only a temporary expedient on your part. Which I *know* it must be."

"Naturally. It is my bad luck to have been trapped into newspaper work," he said casually. "But haven't we all been trapped into doing whatever we know how to do?"

"What do you mean!" I said, anger rising in me again. "Vladimir Vladimirovich, are you the kind to be so easily trapped into anything? And if I am giving music lessons to orphaned children or if Oksana has to type some fool medical documents, it is not the same as to be working in *Pravda*, which is an official organ of Communist propaganda." Oh, Lord, what was I saying, perhaps ruining myself, perhaps insulting a decent man.

Instead of getting excited or insulted, he turned to me with that sharp movement of his well-shaped shoulders. "May I remind you, Olga Al-exan'na," he said sternly, "that in the position in which you and most ex-Whites are—I mean, giving lessons or working at hospitals—you cannot be of any real help to your cause, can you?" He paused and his eyes forcefully plunged into mine. It was the way he said it, the tenacious look in his eyes that took me aback and made me feel that our conversation had suddenly veered at a right angle, and I was confronted with something quite unexpected.

"I don't quite understand you."

"This is all I dare tell you. If you were not you, whom I know so little but for whose integrity and reserve I can vouch, I would *not* have tried to see you at all. Do you realize this? I am perfectly aware of what you must think and what Igor must have thought of me since I left the regiment. This last is what plagues me most. Perhaps it is because Igor's opinion is so important to me that I felt an urgent need to see you and explain. I repeat that I trust you completely, I trust your understanding of me, of my integrity and my credo. I also know that you realize that what I just told you cannot possibly go any further."

"But what have you told me?"

"Indeed, what have I told you?" He paused while his lips curved into a smile, but his earnest eyes, riveted on mine, went on telling their different story. There was a sort of disturbing, mournful sincerity, an appeal to my understanding in the way he sounded; and I was at once baffled and excited and ashamed by my suspiciousness. I rose from the bench and he did too.

"If you are saying what I think you are saying," I began hesitantly, "then you are—"

"As good as dead? This is exactly it. When you asked me if I had proposed to Oksana . . . Anyway, you see now what my real position is." And this time the undertone in which this came from him was so convincing that I believed him. "As my wife, Oksana would have to share anything that I suffered."

"And your cousin also?"

Verin suddenly stiffened. "I hope that I didn't give you a false impression," he said almost severely. "He and I don't follow the same road." So now he was protecting his cousin.

Oksana must have been watching us from behind one of the doorways, because just as we both rose, her red scarf appeared at the other end of the waiting room. And now I wouldn't know what to say, how to behave if left with both of them together; but his eyes were on me dark and grave, and all I was able to utter was "If I understood you correctly, then—then may the Lord help you." And in the way with which I put out my hand and spoke these words there suddenly escaped a touch of admiration that I had not known I could feel toward him.

20

A GREAT DEAL happened after Oksana left, and it was only after her departure that I understood how much of her vitality I had been absorbing through that winter and how it had been sustaining me.

Once the train started moving on that murky February afternoon when I was seeing her off, her face in the red scarf framed in the car's window looked childish and frightened. She was making desperate signs to me, now pressing her hands to her bosom to indicate how horrible it was for her to part with me, now holding her head and shaking it as if to tell me how unsure she was of what awaited her.

Soon after that I began to receive letters from her, desperate ones. She was losing her mind. There was no news from Verin. Despite meeting several Tamborsk friends of ours in Irkutsk, she was wild with despair at having left me. So to the beginning of March, when everything changed: Verin had arrived. She had never known before what real happiness was like! They were living on a volcano (she wrote "on Vesuvius," obviously hopeful the Red censors would think Vesuvius was the name of a street in Irkutsk); he was just a couple of blocks away from her and came every day. When he was busy in the evening and didn't appear, she felt like jumping out of the window; but as soon as he came, nothing else mattered.

There had been days when writing a letter to a friend was a moment of poetry, of creative rest, but that was long ago. In answer to Oksana's effusions I wrote back colorless communications about what was happening in our life.

"Dimitri has recurring typhus. The first attack was terrible, I don't know how his heart stood it. The next attack is expected in about two weeks." Behind these words pressed the vision of how someone had brought me a note saying that Dimitri's temperature was over 42 Celsius and I must immediately find a doctor, and how I had rushed about the town, from door to door. An unexpected thaw had set in that day, after a long period of frosts. My felt boots slopped on the wet, dirty snow. Stuck in my pocket was a five-hundred-ruble Romanov bill that Igor had given me for the greatest emergency: the only kind of money that represented some value.

Most of the doctors apparently lived in the very center of town. The main street, Voskresenskaya, crowded an hour before by people returning from work, was rapidly emptying; dusk was gathering. My left hand closed with a dead grip on the bill in my pocket (I had bartered away my purse long ago). With a stone in my throat, I rushed up and down from one address to the other. Again, as on our first day in Krasnoyarsk, doors were opening and quickly closing before me. "No, no use waiting for the doctor, he's out with patients night and day, hardly has time to eat or sleep!" And at the next address, through a narrow chink in the door, a sobbing voice together with a strong whiff of disinfectant, "The doctor has typhus himself. Unconscious for three days!" Finally that house where the door stood open: "Don't stand in the way, please. They're carrying the doctor out; he died from typhus." It was then that my heart, which had been wildly racing before, began oddly and nauseatingly to slow down. What shall I do if the moment comes, perhaps tonight, when they say about Dimitri, "Stand aside, they're carrying him out"?

I had never yet admitted to myself that Dimitri could die or be killed. My whole future, if any, was pivoted on the hope that at least the last man of my family would be spared; that together someday, somewhere, we would carry on all the beauty that had been bequeathed to us by our father. And all at once the world was an abyss under my feet, and I and Bibik homeless wanderers slipping into it. This was the moment when my will not to stagger and fall under life's blows suddenly deserted me. I was going to give in to grief, and to admit my despair to myself. But this was also the moment when, no longer looking for a doctor, staggering along the street, I found myself in front of a door on which a large copper plaque said, "Dr. S. M. Shapiro." A tall young man with a doctor's bag was hurriedly coming toward the same door from the other side of the street. He walked with a light stoop, evidently dead tired. I ran up to him.

Yes, he was Dr. Shapiro. Was there anything he could do?

"It's my brother, doctor! He has just recovered from a bad case of typhus and, now, recurring typhus. Could you possibly . . ." I spoke fast without caring how wretched I sounded, my breath failing me. "His heart might not stand it. If you would just come with me *now*!"

If he refused me, I was going to renew the attack. I would tell him who Dimitri was—a genius, a composer, an inventor—that if all the best, most gifted men in Russia were dying, who would be left? That he—

Dr. Shapiro said nothing. He simply nodded and turned to follow me, his profile inclined against the gusty wind. Then softly, sadly, he began to question me about Dimitri's symptoms.

I was incoherent in answering him, too grateful that he was coming; I had been running too fast. When he asked about Dimitri's temperature I said twenty-five, thinking that he wanted to know Dimitri's age. Then: "No! his temperature is forty-two, and he is so terribly weakened by his previous illness, by hunger." I also heard myself say, "the last man of my family," and knew that I had said this so he would not suddenly be called away by someone who would also run toward him in the street, just as I had. These words, which I had meant to utter in an undertone, erupted from me like an explosion.

But I did not really have to say much. Those who had been coming to this doctor day and night through these last months, imploring, conjuring him to see their dying ones, were all like me. And yet how closely he was listening! He asked where I was from, his dark eyes watching me, as if trying to picture me somewhere else outside of this moment. He even asked me what happened to the rest of my family. It helped me to talk to him. I told him that my father and uncle and cousins were executed over a year ago, my younger brother killed last summer; this brother's wife and small children were in Tamborsk, that I knew nothing about my husband and might never hear. There was a sober intensity in his eyes as he listened, and something more, which made me add guiltily, "It is the same with everyone."

WE WERE STANDING over Dimitri. This time he lay on some raised boards. There were a couple of men beside him, shapeless in their bedraggled sweaters, one of them wringing out a dripping towel. Dimitri's eyes were closed. In the dusty light his face, so gaunt, so handsome, glistened with perspiration.

Taking the thermometer out of his mouth, Dr. Shapiro slowly wagged his head and looked at me. "Thirty-four point eight," he said. "A steep drop. Alarmingly steep."

Just the same, he gave Dimitri some sort of injection, held his pulse. There was hardly any. "There is nothing more I can do," he said, frowning. He could not even stay here and wait for the effect of the injection. "He might pull through, though. His heart must be amazingly strong to have stood it this far."

I followed him through the attic, crowded with sitting and lying figures to the landing. "I don't want to give you any false hopes," he said, "but if he makes it this time, be prepared for the next attack. By that time he'll need a special injection." He spoke as if he were sharing my grief, and I felt that although he must hurry to some other sickbed, he also hated to leave Dimitri. Leaning against the wall, he wrote down the name of the medicine on a bit of paper, which he admitted was almost unobtainable at this time, unless, by chance, a certain Dr. Meyer might have it.

I thanked him in an awkward, overwhelmed voice, and stretched out my hand to slip the five-hundred-ruble bill into his, afraid and ashamed to do it.

He jerked his hand away almost as if I had burned it.

"How can you? How can anyone take money for—for such suffering?"

I could not speak. I watched him go hurriedly down the stairs—so young, so slender, but already stooping under the load of misery in this world; and his oddly shaped sentence, together with the look of horror in his eyes, stamped itself on my memory as if it had been written in fire.

DIMITRI RECOVERED that time; but there was little hope that he would survive the next attack unless I could get hold of Dr. Meyer. I finally found him at home, exactly on the day when Dimitri's fever started up again. A maid in starched cap opened the door to an elegant apartment, the kind I didn't know still existed, and Dr. Meyer—handsome, fortyish, carefully groomed, an expensive relic of twentieth-century civilization—came out to speak to me in the hallway. An injection would cost a thousand rubles, payable immediately. He had only a couple of ampoules left. He would be there at seven o'clock sharp. It was five o'clock, and I had no money. None. In the time since Dimitri's last illness, the five-hundred-ruble Romanov bill had gone.

I rushed home for some of my remaining jewelry, wrapped it in a handkerchief, stuffed it in my coat pocket; then on to the basement of the Land Survey School, to see the custodian there from whom I used to get Bibik's milk.

He lived alone. It was already dark when I came, and there I stood before him holding out the glittering things in the palms of both my hands. That this coarse-grained speculator did not simply take the things from me and throw me out, when he could have done it with full impunity, was amazing.

He inspected each thing through a magnifying glass, chose an almandite-and-diamond necklace of Fabergè, and a diamond pin as security, and gave me a thousand rubles. "If you return the money in a week, you can have them all back."

"What will I owe you then?"

"Oh, to hell with it." He waved his blunt fingertips a little self-consciously, his moonlike face spreading out benevolently. He even said, "Good luck to your brother."

Later the same night, Dr. Meyer appeared in the attic of the gabled house. I was waiting for him by Dimitri's side. Dimitri was still conscious, his fever mounting, his bones aching unbearably, his lips hardly opening from the pain.

In his beautifully creased trousers, Dr. Meyer picked his way through the gloomy attic, trying to avoid contact with the people who crowded the floor. He asked no questions. He simply gave Dimitri the injection, carefully cleaned his needle with alcohol, dabbed some on his fingers, folded the thousand-ruble bill into his wallet, and departed, never to be seen by me again, and forever to be wondered about. And perhaps pitied. Yes, pitied.

Dear Oksana,

I can finally tell you that Dimitri is not only out of danger now, but he can walk and work normally. On March 1 he was appointed head of the central disinfection chamber at the City Hospital because he was the only one who at once made out how to operate the heating devices there. He now calls this place and himself "Centro-Louse." I go to see him whenever I can. As usual, the people who work under him are ready to eat out of his hands, but I don't know how long this will last, because when I was there the other day . . .

But I could not tell Oksana about that. Not about the state of red-hot fury in which I had found Dimitri that last time. He was walking up and down his room, rubbing his hands, as if soaping them, with convulsive movements, cursing the Communists so loudly I was terrified someone would overhear him.

What had happened that day was this: some high-up commissar had dispatched a messenger to the head of the disinfection chamber with an order to have all the clothes of one of the dying typhus patients delivered immediately, to have him dressed and out of bed. For some reason, the high-up commissar wanted to execute him personally. Dimitri replied that at the moment the door to the heating chamber couldn't be opened, and the commissar would have to wait.

"Comrade Disinfecter," the messenger roared, "if you don't deliver the man's clothing right away, the commissar will come here himself and make you do it! He is here, in the hospital this minute. He won't allow this White bandit to die his own death."

Dimitri said with that rude carelessness, the only manner that ever worked with the present rulers, making them suspect that their interlocutor had connections higher than theirs, "So tell the commissar to come and take the clothing himself. If I go in there now, there'll be nobody to operate the place." And he immediately turned up the heat to the highest degree.

The commissar appeared soon enough, flew at Dimitri shaking a revolver in his face, and ordered him to open the chamber.

"Go in yourself and see what I'm talking about," Dimitri said with the same insolence, and he opened the door full blast on the man. The wave of terrifying heat that rolled out of the chamber made the man jump back with a wild growl, purple-faced. "What do you figure, that I can't get him out naked?" he bellowed.

And he had his victim led out in his nightshirt. Two soldiers half-carried, half-dragged him outside and threw him down by the hospital wall, where the commissar took some time to curse him before he shot him between the eyes.

Since then Dimitri's state of mind, as well as his position at the hospital, had changed abruptly. He was seething with hatred for the Communists and could hardly conceal it. He also became aware that he was being watched closely; that it was time for some move, however risky.

21

ANYONE FROM the outside world with any heart at all would have buried his face in his hands in order not to see the way we lived. However, no foreign spectators were admitted to watch us, and even had any such persons appeared, they would have been unable to apprehend all the deadly, dehumanizing currents that were poisoning us. One of our ordeals that would have remained imperceptible to an outsider was the constant struggle to preserve our human dignity under the onslaught of crude physical force; the struggle not to cringe before those in power (every Red official, no matter how low in status, was a power with regard to a conquered White). To counterattack might easily cost your life and the lives of those closest to you, while not to do so was self-betrayal. There were times when I would parry the arrogance directed at me by being even more arrogant in return, then would shiver that night awaiting the consequences. On the other hand, anytime I tried to compromise with the Reds, I felt I had been untrue to myself, a coward, and would react doubly next time, putting myself and others—Dimitri especially—into jeopardy.

Another bitter trial was the necessity of fostering a constant mistrust of people. So many men and women had been released from prison on condition that they would inform on those around them; and any subsequent foot-dragging was punished by persecution, most often execution. Naturally, even well-meaning people were often unable to withstand the pressure and gave in. There were also the kind who went into such activity as eavesdropping, with a will and with gusto. You had to watch your every step.

"What? He has informed on her? How could he?"

"Well, the poor man sat for twenty-four hours in the ice chamber and discovered he could."

One day we were told that an ex-officer named Paul Melikov, who had recently been released from prison, had apparently spent some time in the same cell with someone we knew, but it was someone whose name he would not disclose. The Melikovs were a Petersburg family well known both socially and historically; our parents had known some Melikovs. We were excited: probably someone we could trust, with whom we could speak the same language. Who could his cellmate have been?

The day he was to come we baked some bread of our own and boiled a few potatoes to offer to him with the tea that we had made out of dried potato peelings.

He appeared in the early afternoon. There he stood in the doorway, rather short, nondescript, a dilapidated coat disproportionately widening his shoulders, dark smudges under his eyes, sunken cheeks. He looked and spoke neither like an ex-officer nor like a Petersburgian. I tried not to show my disappointment. I seated him on my suitcase in our corner of the room, served him a mug of our imitation tea, and offered him some bread, which he refused.

"I understood that you were in prison with someone I know," I said.

"Yes; well, not exactly."

"Not exactly?"

"I was in prison too, but it was an uncle of mine who was in the same cell with your . . . friend, not me. But my uncle, he's very sick now, too sick to see anyone."

"But didn't *he* have to bring me a message from this friend?"

"Yes. This is why I came here."

"But a message from whom?"

"Oh, I should have told you this in the first place! The name is Ivan Kapitonovich Petrov."

"Kapitonovich?"

There were plenty of Petrovs in Russia, but I didn't know a single one, let alone an Ivan Kapitonovich. "I don't know him."

Melikov spread his hands, nearly covered by the coat's long sleeves; his fingers were grayish and they trembled.

"He seemed to know you. At least he had asked my uncle to find you and to tell you he was still alive, here at the Krasnoyarsk prison."

"There must be some mistake," I said, crestfallen. "Did this Petrov give any other message for me?"

"Yes. For you not to try to get in touch with him because this might endanger him. I mean: not to bring any food to him, nothing."

This sounded especially suspicious to me, as if Melikov was afraid that by taking some food to Petrov in prison I might find out that no such person existed, and if so I would know for sure that he, Melikov, came just to snoop around. And yet his pale, exhausted face, his reticence about helping himself to our bread, and the way his fingers trembled, made me ashamed of myself.

"But when—how long ago did your uncle see this Petrov last? Two weeks? Do you think he is still in prison?"

"Had he been released he would have gotten in touch with my uncle; but not so many come out alive, you know."

And this was the only sentence that came out of Melikov with mournful sincerity. Yet the reason for this sudden easing of tone may have occurred because he was already rising to take his leave, glad to be free of me and of what had obviously been a painful and frustrating experience.

I was seeing him off, still unable to escape from my suspicious mood, still held in its grip. Suddenly he heaved a huge, bitter sigh. "Sorry . . . I wish I could have told you more about this Ivan Popov but as long as you don't know him—"

"What? What did you say?" I cried, my heart suddenly sending all the blood to my face.

Melikov turned to me astonished, unable to understand what I was asking, why this abrupt change in me.

"Until now," I said, "you called this man Ivan Kapitonovich Petrov, but now you call him Popov!"

Melikov suddenly came alive. "I don't know what came over me. Well, yes, Popov is the name. So you know a Popov!"

The last time we had seen Lorinov in the French baggage car, he had said to me: "If you ever happen to hear from a peasant of the Irkutsk province, an electrician named Ivan Popov . . . ," and he had touched his breast-pocket, indicating what apparently was a false passport.

I wanted to keep Melikov from going, to start the conversation anew, but instead I heard myself say casually: "Yes, we knew him. He was some sort of electrician. A good man, who knew his job. I hope they let him out soon."

"You can never tell about *them*," he said despondently.

That night I could hardly sleep. I was tormented by remorse and pity for the miserable, probably innocent man whom I had rejected and humiliated; I was harassed by the thought that Lorinov was here, in prison, still alive, although perhaps not for long.

Dimitri was the only person to whom I could speak about it. I would try to see him in the morning. But Dimitri's situation had lately become even more of a worry to me than all the rest. He was still quite weak, conscious that his every step was being watched, and in a state of boiling hatred for all that went on around him. Heading for a nervous breakdown, I felt. Indeed I did go to see him, but not because of what had upset me the day before.

The morning after Melikov's visit, just as I had stepped out on the porch on my way to Dimitri, a telegram was handed to me by an old, emaciated postman. "A telegram for you. Came through the post, though."

From Oksana? Who else? Who else had my address and would telegraph? But I must have known better, for in my hurry to open it, I couldn't control my hands, and the telegram tore in half. Holding the torn pieces together, I read:

"We, Aunt Katya, Aunt Vera, Sonya, and the children are alive. Please write Aunt Vera's address."

That was all. I clutched the torn telegram to myself, unable to believe it, to understand how they, in Tamborsk, knew my address, unable even to put my finger on what the telegram did *not* say, but aware that a black chasm had just opened in the very center of my joy. Panna saw me from the window and came out on the porch. She read the telegram and knew at once. Her face blanched.

"So Alik is not there with them. So they have not heard from him. How many times have you told me that Alik might be there in European Russia!"

"Oh, Panna, but I hoped, I hoped!"

"But you always knew it was not so. Why did you lie to me? So he is dead."

The other name that was missing was the name of Aunt Vera's husband, Piotr. I wired back: "Brother, Bibik, Panna, I all fine. Love you. Writing."

Soon after this, letters began to come, first one from Aunt Katya; I read it sitting on the edge of my suitcase:

"You realize, don't you, Nita, what we all felt when we heard about you. Some people who had just returned to Tamborsk from your parts brought us your address and said that you and D. were alive, that they had seen you, talked to you! Then came your telegram."

My eyes hungrily consumed the closely spaced lines written in Aunt Katya's even hand on cheap brownish paper, the firm simplicity of her diction screening the ruins into which her life had crumbled, and yet crowding me with visions of all I had tried hard not to see through these last years. They had known about Alik for some time, she said. My telegram had only confirmed what had reached them as a rumor. Aunt Vera's husband, Piotr, had died too. (How? When?) The last man in the family. Aunt Vera was bearing her grief and all the rest heroically, her energy directed to the upbringing of her three children and her work at a child-care home of which she was superintendent. "I don't know how she can do it. She hardly eats or sleeps." And I could see Aunt Vera's head tossed upward, her gray eyes shining out of her thin narrow face. Aunt Katya wished she could live with her, but she was temporarily staying with Sonya and her four babies, who needed her even more. Sonya had been allotted two rooms in the basement of what had been her and Dimitri's home; this was where the seven of them, including old Niania, lived now. Sonya worked all day; Aunt Katya also earned a little giving lessons in French and English in exchange for potatoes and flour. Our former house was occupied by a school.

All the intervals between these bits of information in the letter were filled with words of such tenderness and concern for me that as I read them my hands began to tremble. Then that sudden surprise at the end, "Did you know that Polya is also here in Tamborsk? Very ill after all she has been through, but of great moral support."

A FEW DAYS later a letter came from Sonya to Dimitri, in care of me. Again I raced with it wildly across Krasnoyarsk and had almost reached the city hospital when I ran into Dimitri in the street.

"For you! From Sonya!"

Briskly he took the envelope, unfolded the letter, but just as his eyes took in the first few lines, his hand jerked to cover the text and uttered a sentence that was to stay with me for good:

"To see her handwriting is . . . is unbearable."

More letters began to arrive from her and Aunt Katya, telling us, mostly allegorically, of what had passed during the last two years—Aunt Katya's tone resigned and calm, Sonya's passionately impatient; Aunt Katya asking questions, but never suggesting to me what I should do next, Sonya urging Dimitri to return. She gave us to understand that there was some powerful man in the Moscow central Cheka, the son of one of our former stablemen in Sinniy Bor, who had always been devoted to Dimitri, with whom Dimitri always had held himself on equal terms. In case of trouble, Sonya could appeal to him. She also had a friend, a doctor, in a Red Cross train that was bound for Krasnoyarsk. This doctor had agreed to take Dimitri into his staff in some administrative capacity for the duration of the trip back to Moscow and for as long as Dimitri wished to keep that position.

But was the doctor himself so sure of his own position?

Late in March, on the very night that this train arrived in Krasnoyarsk, a confidence-inspiring, old-regime Moscow doctor came to see Dimitri at his Centro-Louse. Everything had already been arranged for Dimitri to fill the position in question and to board the train that same week. Here at Krasnoyarsk Dimitri's predicament had become extremely dangerous; and he longed for his family. Nevertheless, when he came to say good-bye to me, he could hardly talk. With a sad smile, he said, "I know that by going to Moscow I'm asking for the noose, but then it is the same here also."

Earlier I had told Dimitri that if he left, I would also return to Tamborsk. I, too, would have to wait for some chance, for some free transportation at least as far as Perm north of Tamborsk, and then board a Kama-Volga steamer.

Until now, the thought that I could not go any farther away from Igor had kept me here; that, and the hope that I would somehow escape eastward with some group fleeing through the Gobi Desert to China. In fact, certain groups had already fled that way, naturally never to be heard of by any of us. But how could I ever escape with Bibik and Panna? And now with Dimitri's departure, when the last link that held me here was breaking, I saw with perfect lucidity that there was only one place where I should be: in Tamborsk with Aunt Katya, and all those that remained of the family, who in the last two years had taken all the worst blows upon themselves head-on. I loved them, they loved me. To be with them was my duty, a precious duty. Perhaps I had known this all along.

However, for the time being, here I was in Krasnoyarsk. There was no Dimitri, no Oksana; Panna was in one of her heaviest moods, hardly talking to me, furiously working in the kitchen. "Never give way to depression," Father had said in his last letter. "Always . . . rejoice in the ever creative spirit of life and let it work its miracles." I held hard to this after Dimitri's departure. And, indeed, a small miracle happened: one day Masha and her little boy appeared from nowhere, looking for a place to live somewhere close to us.

THE PROXIMITY of people whom in normal circumstances we would have avoided at all costs was another major hardship. One day an old couple who lived in a room next to ours told us that they were returning to their home in European Russia, come what may. I pounced on the chance of getting a permit for Masha to move into their room, but it turned out the room had already been requisitioned by the Cheka for one of its members and his wife.

Even though Masha was temporarily admitted into the house next door to us, this was a blow. Having to deal with Cheka people would be horror, while to shun them could turn out worse.

However, as soon as they moved in, it became clear that the man, Boudkin, and his wife lived by the clock; so it was easy to avoid any collisions with them. Boudkin, a solidly built, fair-haired cheerful-looking fellow, would usually appear in the kitchen at seven in the morning when Marya Ivan'na Stankov was just starting the oven; he would pour himself a glass of vodka, which he kept by the sink, bolt it down, his head thrown back as far as it would go, and at once noisily stamp away to the Cheka. His wife, a jaundiced blonde who managed to resemble both a moth and a weasel ("My wife, a former prostitute," was the way he had presented her to the Stankovs), and who spoke an incomprehensible combination of Latvian, Polish, and Russian, would run after him with mincing steps; and we wouldn't see them until late at night.

At night they usually came home drunk and half asleep, except for the times when they returned in the company of a few fellow Chekists, bringing armloads of bottles and groceries. On such occasions they were very much in evidence. Their supper would run far into the night, the loud guffaws, the curses, the toasts keeping the whole house awake. Once the guests had left, Boudkin, dead drunk, would become engaged in chasing his weasel around the room with the clear intention of killing her, all the while informing her in frightful gasps of what he thought of her, and cursing the devil who had bamboozled him into marrying an ugly old tramp. To these frightful gasps, she replied with piercing squeals, but so far had been spared the coup de grâce.

Finally there came the night when I was awakened by a dreadful fracas in their room. Something had just crashed to the floor, and Boudkin was bellowing at the top of his lungs, "This time I'll finish you, you dirty bitch! This is where you have pushed me!" Then came her frightful shriek for help.

At this point I jumped up, wide awake, slipped into my coat, and, candle in hand, strode with a menacing step toward the door, intent on saving the prostitute's life. By then the Stankovs were sitting up, holding their ears, their teenage boys covering their heads with their blankets.

"Where are you going?" Panna hissed, horrified, and I replied with mournful decisiveness, "If no one interferes, he will murder her."

"You can't interfere; he's too drunk. He'll attack *you*!"

But I had already stepped into the corridor. In my wake, Panna shouted furiously, "At least button up your coat!"

This sobered me. I halted in the corridor and considered withdrawal. But at the same moment the woman's last scream came on a shattering pitch, which suddenly turned into an odd, nauseating gurgle. I realized that Boudkin was strangling her, and that it was too late for me to retreat. I banged on the door with all my might.

There was another sickening sound of choking, then convulsive, pitiful gasps. Apparently the man had just let go of her throat. "Open up at once!" I shouted.

"Who's there? What d'you want?" he screeched back. It seemed to me that he was scrambling up from his knees. In the hardest voice I could muster, I said, emphasizing every separate word, "We would appreciate getting some sleep."

There was a short pause. Then the door jerked open, the man stepped out, banged it shut behind him, and stood there ferocious and drunk, exuding vodka, sweat, and frustration. A muffled moaning could be heard from within. In order not to lose momentum, I held my candle above me like a torch.

Boudkin, his shirt unbuttoned, his forehead and neck glistening with sweat, suddenly stepped back, spread his arms in a broad gesture, an imbecile drunken smile coming over his face. His tongue tangling over a misquotation of Pushkin, he chanted,

> A moment, moment I remember
> When thou appearest before me . . .

"Good night," I said sharply, "let's have some quiet! For your own sake and for ours."

"Quiet, quiet, blissful quiet!" he chanted, rocking in rhythm to the words. Then, quite suddenly enraged, pointing back into his room, he yelled, "Yeah, but why should that dirty svoloch have any quiet?"

"DO YOU KNOW what?" Boudkin said to me one morning soon after, when, thinking he had already gone, I came into the kitchen. "I'm mightily indebted to you, and I don't mind telling you so. I don't remember all that happened, but I could have mangled my wife for life,

— 211 —

that I remember." Again he was standing by the sink, pouring a glass of vodka for himself. He gulped it down and added with jolly astonishment: "That's what life can do to a man: you just keep rolling and rolling along and finally you get there!"

I said, turning to go, "What is important is not what life does to a man, but what man does to life."

"Now listen," he said, "if you could have your way with life you wouldn't be stuck here today, would you? You were with the Whites, right?"

I stopped and turned, looked hard into his eyes. "Of course. Where else?" This had sounded belligerent, but by now I was certain that no harm was coming from this man.

"Well, that's where I was also."

"What?"

"Yeah. A White, that's what I was at first. So I fought on and on until I began to see that there was no real order on the White side. Kolchak and his people had their own ideas and Ataman Semenov different ones, and all the Allies thinking only of how to get out of our mess, and so forth. Everybody pulling in a different direction and no real leader! So I said to myself: the Whites are doomed, what's the use?"

"We had strong, wonderful men," I said. "General Kappel, to begin with."

"Kappel, Kappel," he sneered. "And when was he appointed to lead the army? When it was too late. What sort of power did he have until then except to fight? A leader must have power! The people must have faith in his having power. And who did the Reds have? Lenin! See? Lenin himself, who has the whole of Russia and holds it in his fist and won't let go of it. Why on earth should we fight when it's clear there's no way we can win? I asked myself. If we had a czar it would've been different. So I simply waited for a suitable moment and went over to them."

"And they accepted you just like that?"

"Oh, no, they aren't that simple! Not like the Kolchak intelligentsia. But you see, I wouldn't have defected all by myself. There was another volunteer in our battalion, but one planted there by the Reds, so he kept explaining things to us all along, convincing us. A clever devil, I admired him! I said to myself: Now this is business. This is organization, this is the way to put on an affair on foot, using all available means."

"Did it never occur to you that if nobody listened to these spies and propagandists the Whites could have won?"

"Not a chance. I'm telling you we had no real leader to unite us. This man said to us: 'You're fighting with windmills like Don Juan, that's what you're doing.'"

"Certainly," I said, "Don Juan is the man."

"Well, anyway, whoever he was, our comrade said, 'It's only medieval knights who had nothing better to do than to shed their blood just for fun.' Sure, the Reds could have shot me, but I was pretty certain they wouldn't because I am an auto mechanic, you see, and they were short of them, so . . ."

"So you became a Chekist."

"Now listen! If they had made me arrest people and shoot them, that would have been different. But they'll shoot people anyway without my help. My business is only to repair their cars. Their cars are mostly junk. Even I myself have to walk to work, they're so short of them. I am doing no harm to anybody; on the contrary."

"What do you mean, on the contrary?"

"You never know. They like me there. I might even have a chance to help somebody out someday. Why not?" and he suddenly glanced at the clock. "Well, time for me to go."

He was already on the threshold when he turned. "Well, thanks again." His face broke into a jolly, friendly smile. "Hope I might be of use to you someday, too."

TOWARD THE END of April the weather grew warm, and as soon as we removed the double winter panes a special kind of people began to appear at the windows. They would stand there and wait, silent, for someone to speak to them. They were all young, dressed in rags, with faces the color of dirty melting snow, and great immobile eyes. It seemed that they stopped because they did not have enough strength to move on, but, we knew what they needed and who they were. We did not have enough bread, of course, but we would rush to offer what little there was. These were the men left over from our volunteer army: soldiers just out of prison, deprived of the right to have even the rations that we had, wandering over the city with nowhere to stay, many of them lame with frostbitten feet.

We gave them what we could spare, even what we couldn't. It made us, Masha and me, feel better. For Masha with her little Aliosha and her maid had moved into our house at last and we became inseparable. So did our boys.

Those soldiers framed in the window, how much worse off they were than we! We would ask them to come in, but they never did. "Oh, no, no. You would get the typhus. The typhus in prisons, you know, is the bad kind. It gets everybody." And holding our pitiful piece of bread in their waxen fingers, they would shuffle on, barely moving their feet, through the hungry barren city.

I had been particularly struck by one of them, by his intelligent, suffering face. "Are you a White volunteer?" I asked. Even with his gray transparent skin he did not look more than nineteen, and I suddenly groaned, "Oh, my Lord, what you have been through!"

He replied in a ghostly voice, "Well, it's not as bad with me . . . now, I'll tell you." He was obviously too weak to talk and paused to gather his strength to go on. "You see, they threw me out of the hospital when I still couldn't stand on my feet. Our doctor, Magdalina Alexan'na, a sort of . . . looked like a little girl . . . afraid of nothing. She was the kind who performed miracles with us. Anyway, took such care . . . an ex-White too. 'I won't let you leave,' she said, 'I'll fight for you with the commissar.' And then, later, I heard the commissar bawl at her in the corridor so that we could hear it in the ward." The soldier halted, took a deep breath, and broke off a piece of the bread with his shaky, transparent hand; as he chewed it, I could see every bone on his face working with the effort. "So this commissar bellows: Out of fifteen people in this ward, thirteen are White bandits, Kappel's men! What did we fight them for if you're going to coddle them night and day?' And so forth. In other words, they pushed me out on the street that same day. At first I fell . . . then on all fours . . ."

Again I gasped, "Oh you poor—" but he shook his head impatiently,

"But I'm telling you I'm not the poor one! For two nights I was put up by someone I knew, but he had room only in the hayloft for me. It was still late in March, as cold in the loft as outside. Well, on all fours or not, I went to the hospital to see my wardmates, the only place to get warm for an hour or two—besides, I felt lonely for them. But envious of them too: why should they be taken care of and I thrown out half-dead? And then, what do you think?" He halted again and shook his head, eyes closed as if driving away the vision of what he wanted to tell me about.

"See, I get there, and meet that woman doctor right there by the entrance, and she hisses at me: 'Get away from here, get away while you're whole!' I sort of stood there—aghast—and she goes on hissing—'or else the same will happen to you.' At first I didn't know what she was talking about. You see there was a yard behind that hospital and this is what they did the next day after they kicked me out: got all the ex-White patients in our ward into that backyard, carried out those who couldn't walk yet, shot them all; then into a truck and out to the taiga, to the dump heap."

I began muttering something incoherent, calling him inside. "Please, please, I have some hot soup. . . ." But he wouldn't come in.

"My friend will think I'm dead. I left a long time ago. I have your bread now to share with him—thanks a lot for that."

I stood there immobile, watching him; how he wobbled on his feet, how he held on to the walls of houses; how in his young exhausted body he carried all the pain bequeathed to this world from the beginning of time.

22

I HAD LAUNDERED my Valencienne negligee—all rags now—and was on my way to hang it out to dry in the garden. All through the three months I had spent in this house, the garden had played no part in my life. A few dark tree trunks and an entanglement of bare branches sweeping a metal sky were all I could see from the kitchen window. However, now, in the middle of May, this garden had miraculously burst into wild bloom and stood around the house densely green and shady. It was fenced off from the backyard driveway, and in its deepest part there stood a wooden bench and a round table, whose recrudescence as the snow melted had been a gift from heaven.

It was well past nine o'clock and already dark when I came out. The air, cooling after a hot day, smelled innocently of fresh earth and lilacs and of a possible warm rain. I crossed the back porch, wringing out my negligee on my way, cold drops falling on my stockingless feet, and was looking forward to the moment when I could sit down on the bench and rest. Aside from teaching music at the orphanage in the afternoon, I had spent all morning at the black market, at the former bazaar square, the only place in the dead city that had not died and was by now bursting with color. A bright bandanna on my head, I had kept my spirits up by acting a boisterous young baba and finally managed to barter off my old caracul coat for a chunk of butter and a basket of eggs. Rare luck. Even Panna had not minded this. She didn't even ask me, "What will you wear in winter?"

Through all these last weeks I had been tormented anew by the latest rumors about the First Cavalry. They had crossed Lake Baikal, inching sixty versts of their way over ice during a ferociously windy February frost, leading their horses in leash, the horses slipping, breaking their legs, or falling from exhaustion to freeze on the ice. The march had lasted all day and night and all of the next day. Thousands had reached the shore with frostbitten limbs, had developed gangrene and had their legs amputated later in Chita; thousands died of exposure. But I was not going to think of these rumors now. I didn't dare. All I wanted was to breathe in the fragrance of resuscitating nature. If there were no chance of any renewal in my own life, still, spring was there for the taking.

The air was motionless, the nearby backyards deserted, the street already asleep. There was some sort of clothesline in the back garden, but I was too tired to look for it, so I spread the negligee on a lilac bush, hoping it would catch the smell of lilac. However, just as I sank on the bench, I heard someone walk into the yard and up the driveway.

It was not the footsteps of Boudkin; and while it was still too early for searches, it was also too late for visitors. Judging from the hesitant quality of these steps, whoever had walked in was unsure that he had come to the right place. Then I saw the shadow of a man approach the garden gate and stop by a clump of bushes.

Although he wore a soldier's cap, something in the outline of his shoulders, in the bearing, made it clear that he was not one of those starving soldiers who constantly appeared by our windows. A ragged jacket hung loosely from his erect frame. I rose from the bench. The man saw me and stopped abruptly, holding on to the garden gate. I went toward him. "Are you looking for someone?" I asked with hasty sympathy. Then my voice broke.

He did not answer but pushed the gate open and entered the garden. A weak ray of light from the kitchen fell onto the garden path; as he walked into its beam I gasped, afraid to call him by name. "You!" I finally muttered in a stifled whisper. "From where, Serge, from where?"

He grasped my hands, his eyes holding mine, with an intensity that paralyzed me. Then he answered, "From prison. They released me this morning. It's wrong of me to endanger you by coming, but I won't stay long." Even in the semidarkness I could see that his face was tallow-white, the skin drawn tightly around his jaw. He must have asked me about Igor, I him about Margarita, and we both must have replied that we knew nothing, that we hadn't heard for months. "But you must stay with us," I said desperately. I could not stand the thought of losing him now, come what may. "If they just let you out of prison today, you'll be safe for at least a little while!" Without releasing my eyes or my hands he shook his head, "I can't have you run this risk. You see, they released Ivan Popov, but they're still looking for *me*, and I have to be on my way."

Just the same I couldn't let him go. There had been no raids on our house since Boudkin moved in; and he and his wife were never home until about three in the morning. But if they were to come earlier tonight, well . . . Boudkin had hinted he might even be helpful in case of danger.

"You will be safe here, Serge, I am certain, safer than anywhere else! How long can you stay? Two hours? Oh! At least that! You must tell us about yourself, you must eat something—" I hardly knew what I was saying.

Then came the sudden roar of a car up the street. I stiffened. Perhaps they were coming here; they might have already tracked him down. The car passed. Instinctively, we both stepped back farther into the shade. And now, letting his head drop low over my hands, he began to kiss them.

Perhaps it was the constant crowdedness, the impossibility of ever having a moment alone, that had given our relationship a touch of mysteriousness and unattainability, that had intrigued him and teased him along, and that had been my protection against any complications between us. But too much had changed since we parted: I, without Igor and almost without any hope of ever seeing him again, even were he still alive; he, on the brink of death and without Margarita. What had not changed between us, however, was our crowded state, for just then Panna appeared in the lighted doorway, forcing me to tear my hands from his.

"Please, come in, and have some tea with us!" I could hardly articulate the words. He was not only himself, he was also all that was left of our demolished lives, of our broken hopes, of Igor's regiment, of all we had fought for.

Panna came out on the porch. "Nita, where are you?" she called, unable to see us in the dark. "Masha is here looking for you." And immediately Masha came out after her on the porch and took a few steps into the garden. Seeing a man at my side, she froze in a ready-for-anything attitude. I ran toward her and said into her ear. "Careful, it's Serge! Don't forget he is *Ivan Popov!*"

"Oh, my Lord," she gasped. "How on earth . . . ?" Then, rushing toward Lorinov, she did what I had longed to, but had not dared to do— impulsively threw her arms around his neck.

WE SAT BY the narrow kitchen table, Lorinov, Masha, and I; Panna as usual radiated hospitality, slicing bread and pouring tea for us. That day Masha had gotten hold of two packs of cigarettes; she gave one to Lorinov and he was smoking with a sort of angry relish. The doors were closed, the curtain drawn. The sensitive Stankovs, immediately aware of what was afoot, had gone out on the back porch to keep watch just in case.

Masha and I had already told Lorinov in a disjointed way, interrupting each other, about all we had heard of the regiment, about ourselves. I had started to speak of Oksana and Verin, but the sudden cold unfocusing of his eyes made me change to my intention of soon returning to my family in Tamborsk. He told us that he had spent three months in prison, right here in Krasnoyarsk (yes, indeed, he had given a message for us to one of his fellow prisoners); that he and Margarita had parted early in January in some out-of-the-way village.

For a few moments I hardly knew what he was saying. I was in turmoil, and I watched him more than I listened. A candle burned on the table between us (using electricity after nine was prohibited), and under its light his eyes in the emaciated face had a new luminosity, a depth that had not been there before. My concern about what I would say to him before we parted, what words to find, words that would help him on his way, often made me lose the sequence of his story. What words? As if the realization that he no longer needed words from me, except those that I would not tell him, had not struck me the very moment we had met in the garden.

How had he allowed Margarita to follow him? Well, he at first assumed, as had the rest of us, that Margarita had jumped off the train to say good-bye and would then return to us. But she declared that she intended to follow him, no matter where. This angered him. There was no time for argument, so he swung her around by the shoulders to face the train and then, without a backward glance at her, walked rapidly along the ties. "Now, you probably remember that the moonlight was dazzling," he said to us with a bitter grin. "The air crystal-clear, not a sound . . . sheer delight."

We knew, we remembered.

There was a sleigh track running below to the left of the ties. He could reach it by descending the steep bank through huge snowdrifts. He started down, pretending not to know that she was moving behind him, but suddenly realized that if she came down the incline, she would be unable to climb it again. He then turned to her and shouted, furiously: "Margarita, go back! You can't go with me! I can swear to you that they won't touch you, or any one of those women there, in the car. But if you are found with me it will be much worse for you!" She burst into tears, crying out that if he left her behind she would stay where she was and freeze to death. "Why should I die alone and not with you? Shoot me before you shoot yourself," she sobbed.

"I won't shoot myself," he roared at her. "I have to try to reach my regiment. They need me. Don't you understand that you will slow me down on my way?" But she was already sliding down through the deep snow, beating at it frantically with her arms and muttering through her sobs that he would be safer with a woman than by himself.

He could not leave her there alone to freeze to death. He gave up.

I could not have repeated his story the way he told it but I could picture every bit of it. They walked fast along the deserted, moon-flooded road (theirs was a good hard road, which took them in the opposite direction to ours, running north), Margarita trying desperately not to lag behind him. At some point they stood on a hillock; before them was a village. It could be occupied by the Reds but he did not think so. On the way he drilled Margarita in his false passport information: Ivan Popov, electrician, peasant by birth, twenty-seven years old, born in Omsk; their train had frozen to the tracks; they had decided to walk and had lost their way. To the Whites he would be a White, to the Reds, a Red.

The first thing Lorinov realized as they entered the village gate was that it was not Red-occupied, no sign of any troops anywhere; oddly, long black flags were hanging from most of the housetops. In the center of the main street stood a church, its square-shaped whitewashed wall bluish in the moonlight, and next to it a cottage with feebly lighted windows. They went to this cottage; they knocked.

The door opened almost at once, just a crack, and the gaunt face of a long-haired, grisly priest peered out. "Just a minute," he said and his voice was calm and resigned, as if he had sat there waiting for someone. "I'm ready. Who is it this time?" A sheepskin was thrown over his cassock, he must have indeed been waiting for a caller, but then saw who it was, and for a moment stood there gaping at the two striking figures, so unlike the ones he must have expected to see.

Lorinov gave his rehearsed speech: Ivan Popov, lost his way, and so on. The priest nodded hastily, closing his eyes as if he already understood all the rest and led them inside the dingy little cottage. It smelled of warmth ("some stuffy kind of holiness," Lorinov said), hemp oil, and cabbage soup. A *lampada* flickered in the icon corner. I had no idea how Lorinov managed, with muted gesture or the slightest change of intona-tion, to project such a clear portrait of this priest, but I could see how this Father Nikon, suddenly excited, began to fuss about the kitchen, heating the samovar, the soup, looking in vain for clean dishes, muttering something to himself; how in his hurry some of his motions ended in nothing, and then he would wave his hand, as if annihilating what he had just begun to do, hastily starting something else and talking with Lorinov at the same time.

"The black flags? They are for smallpox. How long ago were you vaccinated? Well, fine, then you can stay here for a while," he said. "Nobody will touch you here. Whether Red or White, as soon as they see the black flags they go right around us. Even if you are an electrician, a laborer sort of" (but obviously he knew better) "—you were with the Whites, just the same, so it is safer for you to be here."

Lorinov realized in what a backwater they had found themselves, if people in this village had never been vaccinated. Night and day the priest was giving communion to the dying and burying the dead. His wife had died of typhus that fall, and he seemed happy to have somebody in his house.

Lorinov did not dwell on what a wonderful man Father Nikon must have been. He only said with a humorous twist of his lips that he reminded him of Dostoyevsky's Idiot. "A sort of poor edition, but the same idea."

Next morning Margarita seemed revived. "Unfortunately, it was I who was drooping," Lorinov said. He fell violently ill. This next part of his story was not clear at all and he seemed not to wish it to be clear. At first he thought he had typhus. He vaguely recalled blacking out, coming to, seeing Margarita beside him, suffocating in a repulsive mishmash of nightmares that lasted endlessly. He would charge, kill, lose his horse, lose the battle; his revolver was just a toy and wouldn't go off. One night in the middle of some such nightmare he saw the face of Father Nikon leaning over him, a large crucifix in his hands; saw the lampada light burning. He must have made efforts to speak to him, probably talking unintelligible nonsense. Then all this collapsed into blackness.

One day he suddenly woke up dripping with sweat and with the feeling that everything that had happened to him had been unreal, a dream. He was able to lift his head and look out the window. It was one of those brilliant February mornings when deep blue shadows have been poured into every footprint in the snow and when the branches of trees weave a sharp pattern of glittering black against the sky. Father Nikon walked in, bringing a cup of hot tea, and said, "Serge Lorinov, God is merciful to you. You must have passed the crisis. You coughed up blood. I'm pretty sure you had a bad case of pneumonia."

At first Lorinov took all this in his stride; the tea tasted to him better than champagne. But then it dawned on him that Father Nikon had used his real name, "and soon enough it became clear that this Holy Father knew everything about me: who I was, who Margarita was, and all that story about the Red Steel Regiment. Everything!"

Masha and I both thought that it was Margarita who had given it all away, but Lorinov shook his head. Obviously he had done it himself when he was delirious, he said, and Margarita had been obliged to fill the gaps.

This was all he told us. But we understood, at least I understood, that the priest had chosen a moment when Lorinov had been more or less conscious to give him communion. Prior to that he had had to hear his confession, in the course of which Lorinov must, at least to some degree, have unburdened himself of things that had been weighing on his mind—a feat that he probably would never have accomplished except in a state of half-delirium. Although he didn't put all this into words, I had the feeling that not only had it been so, but that he also wanted me to know about it.

As Lorinov began to get better, Margarita was suddenly stricken with typhus. Now it was she who was burning with fever and tossing in her bed, moaning, mumbling in her delirium. One day, when she was at her lowest ebb, Father Nikon said to Lorinov, who was preparing an ice pack for her in the kitchen, "This won't help her much. There is only one kind of cure left for this girl," and he paused to let this sink in. Lorinov waited, vaguely aware of what was coming. "Only one kind of cure: to be married to you. I know all about her feelings. You are a bachelor, aren't you? You have not made promises to any other woman? Fine. Just as soon as she comes to—if she does—I'll call in two trustworthy witnesses and marry you. I shall marry you as Ivan, but to myself I shall whisper Serge. The good Lord will hear and forgive this. Fate has brought you and this girl together; don't fight against it. This is your chance to save a life; she might recover from sheer joy. Moreover, you'll never find a better wife anyway."

He said: "But how can I marry when my duty is to get back to my regiment and fight the Reds? You will marry us while she is prostrate, and the next day I will be gone. Rejoining the regiment is my only concern, and the only reason I am still alive. This is why I got myself a false passport, and on this I won't yield."

Father Nikon replied decisively; "Well, if you go, you go, but for the moment she needs to know that she is your wife, and if she dies, let her die knowing this." Then he added with complete candor, "You don't have much chance to live long yourself, and she knows it too. She will be a wonderful nurse for you in case . . .

"Now listen to me, Serguey Yury'ch," he went on, "how are any of us going to get out of this bloody mess? So it's best for you to do a kind deed, and make your accounting to the Lord easier. There is no reason for you to be afraid of marrying her. Look at me! Am I afraid of keeping you in my house?"

That decided it. As soon as Margarita had a moment of lucidity,

Father Nikon told her that he was going to marry them, but that if Lorinov would have to leave she should not try to detain or follow him. She agreed to everything.

The marriage rites took place, she in bed, Lorinov standing by; and Father Nikon gave him a certificate that corresponded with his passport: Ivan Popov, age twenty-seven, married to Margarita Tabakov, age seventeen. Anyway, Father Nikon was right, it must have helped. She was still quite ill, but conscious most of the time.

A few days later a peasant rushed in to warn them that a Red scouting party had appeared in the next village. He also said that they might come at any moment, that Lorinov should go immediately. As for Margarita, what could you do about her, sick as she was? Just a girl dying at that. The Reds would not give a damn.

Lorinov decided to leave at once. "As a memento I left with her the amulet I had worn throughout the war." Then he went to get his revolver, which Father Nikon had buried in the backyard while Serge was ill. But the timing was bad. Just as he was going to retrieve it there emerged on the back porch a peasant whom the priest suspected of being in sympathy with the Reds. Lorinov pretended that he had come out to shovel snow from the porch. The peasant entered the yard and stood there talking until Lorinov cleared all of the snow off the porch. By then there was nothing else Lorinov could do but go back into the house. But just as he entered from the back door, three young fellows, Red army men, came through the front entrance.

"I never could have imagined in my wildest dreams," Lorinov said to us, "that I would fall weaponless, and married at that, into the hands of the Reds."

The next day he was put on a train with other White prisoners. They did not know where they were heading, but were prepared to be shot. And shot Lorinov undoubtedly would have been if he hadn't played the part of a man of power whom they had mistakenly arrested. He told them that if the commissars found out that these soldiers had arrested him, Ivan Popov, specialist in electrical communications—in such short supply— they would be taken care of, fools. As a result, Lorinov soon found himself in the Krasnoyarsk city prison, where he passed the next three months. It was there that he heard in disbelief what had been done to Admiral Kolchak. He also heard in prison that our forces had crossed Lake Baikal, that it had been a terrible crossing, where hundreds had frozen on the way or had lost their legs. And yet how he envied them!

The prison was, as expected, a nightmare of starvation, filth, and mismanagement. Lorinov was interrogated only twice and succeeded in stuffing them full of lies, which they swallowed whole. He, for whom they were looking, in their eyes one of the worst White criminals, had been spared, even released, while countless White teenage volunteers or mobilized peasants had been shot almost without being interrogated.

The day of Lorinov's release, he saw another tattered man like himself slowly walking ahead of him along the deserted street, an oddly familiar figure. As the man turned to see who was behind him, Lorinov saw with a shock that it was a sergeant of Igor's squadron from the Tamborsk regiment. If in the prison they had succeeded in converting or terrorizing this man, it would be Lorinov's end. So Lorinov walked past him with a haughty swagger, looking straight ahead. For some time the sergeant— the sturdy, heavyset type of Siberian peasant, his bones now sticking out of his emaciated frame—followed him, obviously trying not to lag too far behind; and Lorinov thought this was indeed the end. Then, choosing a moment when there was no one at all on the street, the man caught up with Lorinov and whispered, "Colonel, sir, were you there too?" There was wild amazement in the whisper.

In prison the sergeant had been questioned over and over about the Tamborsk regiment: who were its officers, who was at the head now, but especially where was Lorinov, that lackey of the czarist regime, the one who . . . and so on. So "they" knew that Lorinov had been separated from the regiment and could be found somewhere around Krasnoyarsk.

The poor sergeant had had it much worse than Lorinov himself: he had been brutally beaten, questioned night after night, prevented from sleeping, "put on ice." So now his only urge was to escape. He was going to see some local people, his late father's friends, and lie to them that he would be looking for work in Krasnoyarsk. In reality he wouldn't even stay here overnight. Since he was the son of a trapper, he knew the shores of the Yenisei River like the palm of his hand. So he and Lorinov decided to escape together and to start this very night.

THIS WAS Lorinov's tale. He told it in dry, matter-of-fact tones, with occasional bitter sarcasm. He had been smoking as he spoke, and perhaps it was this habitual casual handling of his cigarette, narrowing his eyes from the smoke and negligently shaking off the ashes, that had made his sentences fall into a certain rhythm and had helped him tell it all. When he finished he said, "So this is all there is to my idiotic adventures."

Masha breathed, "Incredible! I still can't take it in! To think of all you've gone through and that now you are married, and yet . . . don't even know . . ."

"I am not married. It is electrician Ivan Popov, from whose pocket my orderly got this passport, who is married posthumously. On the whole, a total mess."

"You shouldn't talk like this, Serge," I said forcefully. "You care for her, you made her happy, perhaps you saved her life; and she'll be waiting for you and have something to live for."

He looked at me. It was a heavy, wondering gaze. Was I thinking that what I had just said was a noble effort at self-effacement? Was it a cruel and selfish demonstration of womanly virtue? Whatever it was, he didn't think much of it.

Panna said with meek reproach, "But as long as during the ceremony Father Nikon whispered your real name to himself, then in God's eyes your wedding was not a sham. It was real."

Lorinov glanced at her with a surprised little smile; then his face darkened again. "The only thing that is real in this whole affair," he said, putting out his cigarette and screwing it with fierce concentration into his saucer, "is that if Margarita is still alive, I shall never see her again. I may be married to her in God's eyes, but not in my own. Another thing that is real," he glanced at the kitchen clock and suddenly rose, "is that it's high time for me to vanish." Then, probably to destroy the tension, he added casually, "It's most annoying to have no watch. Mine, of course, was confiscated in prison."

One of the greatest treasures still remaining in my jewelry bag was a small gold watch of my mother's. I would give it to him. "Wait a second, Serge," I said. "I shall be back at once." I wanted him to have this watch; and I also had to have a moment alone. I had to stop the turmoil within me, hold it and decide what to do with it. For something must happen now, before he left, and what it was would depend upon me. From the first moment when we had met in the garden, and all the time he was telling his story, he had made me feel his need of being alone with me, and I could not fail him. However tenuous, he had been my link with the life of thought, with poetry. And perhaps I would have known what I had come to mean to him had I allowed myself to know it, instead of shielding myself from this knowledge with Margarita's image. But never until now had it occurred to me that the threads that had stretched between us could become tangible enough to draw me into any sort of "situation."

Of course, I realized that there was hardly any chance I would ever see Igor again. Even if he were still alive, the iron wall between Red and White would stay on and on. It was too late to demolish it. But this was not the point. Yes, indeed, deathless poetry was an approach to eternal truth, but more so was total fidelity to the bond of love with the person whom you once chose to be your own.

When I returned to the kitchen, the watch tucked in my skirt pocket, Masha was saying good-bye to Lorinov, her arms about him. Her eyes were full of tears. She left. Panna was doing something by the kitchen sink, and now as Lorinov stood before her to take his leave, she handed him a neat little package. "Just a couple of hard-boiled eggs and some buttered bread for your journey." He shook his head, "Please keep it for Bibik." But I took it from Panna. "I shall see Serguey Yury'ch off and will make him take it," I said.

THE SHORE of the Yenisei where Lorinov had to meet his companion was a five-minute walk from where we lived. There was not a soul in the street, no lights in the windows as we came out.

Just as we stepped off our porch, I began to talk very rapidly, keeping my voice as low as I could, forcing Panna's sandwich on him, hastily building a screen of questions and answers between us. What had been the chances of Margarita's recovery at the time he had left her? "Very slight." Would he want me to write to her, or to Father Nikon, and indicate in some roundabout way that he, Serge, was alive, that I had seen him? "Under no circumstances." And I knew that I was straining his patience.

When we turned a corner and came out on an unpaved street with sparsely scattered cottages, at the very edge of town, he simply stopped answering my questions, and we made a few steps in silence. The ground underfoot was soft and smelled of humid earth and young grass. Still silent, Lorinov put out his hand to me. I gave him mine.

"This is not the way I had hoped to meet you," he finally said. "I hoped to the very last minute before I was arrested that I would be able to catch up with the regiment; that there would still be a chance for us to take Krasnoyarsk back from the Reds, that I would see you again at least once and tell you all I wanted you to know."

He spoke unhurriedly, with the same precision and economy of intonation with which he sang his songs. "Shall I begin with the recurrent dream I had in prison? It was a total fraud, this dream, but such a convincing fraud! It had a startling clarity and precision of detail, a logical sequence. Anyway, we had beaten the Reds into a pulp and were entering Krasnoyarsk, just as we entered so many other towns that we had taken a year ago. Crowds cheering, church bells ringing, people shouting 'Christ is risen,' and all that . . ."

"Oh, Serge, I also had the same dream!" I said desperately. "And to wake up to what we were living in was . . . horror!"

"But your dream was probably not quite like mine," he said. "Let me tell you. I was riding with Kostin at the head of the regiment and knew that this was where I would find you. Igor rode behind me in front of his troop, and all I had on my mind was to be the first to reach you. Before he did. But I also knew it was impossible."

He had been looking ahead at the road, but now turned to face me. "I knew it was impossible," he repeated. "There was in this dream a promise of elation mixed with the sense of impending disaster."

"And how well I know it!" I said.

"You probably do. Yet you have to be actually locked up with little hope of coming out alive, in order to learn to what a white heat desire can mount. This was the point I had reached in my craving to see you at least once more before we parted for good, and to tell you what I wanted to."

He paused; and the rustlings of our cautious steps on the road became audible. "I had to tell you that during the darkest moments in prison I found myself going over some of your words that I had listened to without really taking in. Waiting from minute to minute to be led out and put to the wall, I had something to hold on to: your faith. I had, really, only a blurred idea of what your credo was all about, but it was yours and the kind that held a promise of victory over the meaningless mess life is. To me this faith of yours was like a sealed envelope with orders from Headquarters. Sealed and stamped Secret, to be opened at the last critical moment. Anyway, having this envelope was what pulled me through in prison and what may pull me through now."

I didn't know what to say. I felt suddenly crushed, humbled, as if I'd been given an undeserved gift.

The street ended where it ran into a narrow dirt road leading to the riverbank. Tall, scraggy pines and wild undergrowth stood dense on either side of the road. We had neared the spot where the other man was supposed to meet Lorinov to lead him through the thicket to the river.

"Don't go yet," he said and his voice stiffened as if he, no longer trusting it, had to hold it hard. "Don't you have anything to tell me that I can take with me to . . . wherever I'm heading? I know too well that you are following your own road, that I could never have turned you from it to where I wanted you to go. Nor am I asking too much. I only want to hear you say what I've dreamed of hearing, even if it is a last good-bye."

"Oh, Serge, you know that what you feel for me is different from what you feel for Margarita," I was finally able to say. "And that for you she now must come first, as Igor comes first for me. And it shouldn't be our last good-bye. I don't want it to be that. You will rejoin the regiment; you must! And I shall also try to escape somehow. Even if I go to Tamborsk first, later I shall try to escape and we must be reunited, all of us!"

"I know that Igor comes first and that you will try to join him. Someday you may succeed," he said bitterly, "whereas I hold no hope of ever seeing Margarita again. The whole story is too unreal and crazy anyway. But if you don't find Igor and if I, by some miracle, am still around . . ."

At any other time I would have cut him short, I couldn't have my greatest fear voiced by anyone, by him especially. But at the moment he was not simply Serge Lorinov to me; he was one of all those heroic young men of Russia who had risen against a savage enemy and now were haunted, trapped, perishing, but going on with the fight. He was also Igor's best friend, who had watched over me and my child in Igor's absence, cared for me, helped me.

For some time already I had been hearing branches crackle farther down on the footpath, heard cautious steps approaching. It hardly mattered. This was the last I was seeing of Serge. Aware that he was saying farewell not only to me but to hope, to Russia, to life, to everything, I threw my arms around him impulsively. Then, tearing myself away from him, I slipped the watch into his pocket and said good-bye. The shadow of a man had just detached itself from the wall of the forest.

"Wait!" Lorinov cried desperately. "Wait! There's one more thing I must tell you!" But I did not wait. Pushing myself away from him, I broke into a wild run.

INSTEAD OF going straight to my room that night, I went into the farthest corner of our garden and sat there on the wet grass, stifling my sobs with my hands. None of them would come back. Lorinov wouldn't. Igor wouldn't either. Igor! There was nowhere for them to come back to.

And what had come over me that I hadn't waited to hear Lorinov's final words? Whatever it was that he had wanted to tell me, I would now never know. How I must have wounded him at the very last moment.

When I awakened the next morning, I could hardly open my eyes, so swollen were they from crying. It was late. The sun was streaming into the room through our curtainless window. Panna was giving Bibik his milk, and I caught her inquiring and sympathetic gaze on me. I turned away. But she said to me in her sweetest and most reassuring tone, "You'll see! Someday Igor will come also!"

This was what I wanted to hear.

PART FOUR

USSR

23

WE REACHED the Tamborsk pier at midnight. As our Kama-Volga River boat docked, all the passengers were ordered immediately to clear their cabins. This did not mean that we were free to leave, however. We were told we had to spend the night on the boat because the gates of Tamborsk were closed until dawn.

It was a stormy, glacial September night. Barely a light in the sky, either aboard or ashore. A furious north wind was raging over the Volga, lashing the deck where we, huddled on our luggage, were trying to hide from the gale between huge cargo sacks, rough sacks against which we pressed our backs and scratched our faces. My only concern was to save Bibik from catching pneumonia. But whistling and wailing, the hurricane swirled between and around the sacks, tearing off the blanket I endeavored to hold over Bibik's face, choking me, turning my fingers into icy sticks. Panna twisted this way and that to shield Bibik, all to no avail.

This cruel game of hide-and-seek with the storm had already lasted for several hours. Why had they thrown the passengers—most of them local peasants and laborers, for whom the revolution had been presumably made—out of cabins that would be standing empty all night? Oh, but the reason was always the same: to make it difficult, to exhaust, to intimidate, crushing all strength and initiative out of people, to make them incapable of resistance. It was all part of the scheme, and we no longer questioned this treatment. Being exposed to the elements was becoming the natural way of life.

The only feeble light in the general blackness came from a yellow square of window in a barracklike building by the dock, in some sort of office. I jumped up. I was ready for anything. Trying to hold Bibik's blanket down with my chin because the wind was beating it back into my face, I said, "All right, Panna, take him. I must do something."

As I ran down the gangway toward that lighted window, one hand clutching my beret, the other sliding down the rough wooden railing, my inner voice was saying, So this is Tamborsk! Tamborsk, which two years ago had crashed into nonexistence because of its inaccessibility, because the mind refused to accept the horror of its fate.

The yellow square of light revealed the profile of a man in a military cap. The silhouettes of several other men in peasants' greatcoats in front of the window were scooped out of the darkness. I went toward them.

"Do you know who is in there?" I asked in the foolhardy, decisive manner in which I had learned to speak nowadays, the only tone that hit the mark. "Is this the steamship office?"

"The commissar on night duty is there. Only too busy, you see," one of the men replied, and his familiar Volga accent broke my heart. There was a vexed and yet humorous acceptance in his sneer. "Just look at him! Busy as a beaver. Won't talk to no one until morning."

"I must see him *now*," I said, and moved close to the window. The commissar, a boy of about twenty-two, was sulkily frowning over some papers and occasionally taking sips of muddy tea out of a glass. A naked electric bulb hung over his head. Like the tea in the glass, his long face was an unhealthy yellow; his lips were puffed out and his lower jaw was slightly loosened as if weighed down with the burden of responsibility and power. I had already seen so many of these self-important pouting lips. How quickly they would shape up into youthful alertness at the approach of a superior; how instantly they could stiffen into cruelty and impudence at the sight of a potential prey. Where had they all come from, this new breed of people?

But it was funny that as I came up to the window I forgot all I knew about them. Funny that as I gave a sharp knock to the rain-and-dust-streaked glass I was not the helpless prey, but the former Nita Ogarin with all the attributes of optimism, confidence, in men and in myself. The Nita Ogarin to whom no harm could come from this boy obviously standing far below me on the cultural ladder.

Holding his hand visorlike over his eyes, he leaned against the window. "What d'you want?" It was a hoarse bark.

Forcing my voice through the glass I said, "See here, let me inside for a couple of hours. I have a small child, and the cold is terrible."

He half opened the window, stuck out his face. Then, the wind whipping between us, I said aggressively, accusingly, "My child will get pneumonia this way; there is no place to hide him from the gale."

"How old's the child, comrade?" Frowning austerely he stuck out his face farther, searching mine.

"Just two. He won't disturb you, he'll be asleep."

The man nodded briskly. "All right. Go get him."

"At least this," I rejoiced as I raced back up the gangway, "at least not to tremble for my child." A few minutes later, with Bibik in my arms, I stepped into the building, and as a gust of sheltered, musty warmth burst upon me, the man who opened the door suddenly bellowed at Panna, "And you, you old witch, where are you trying to push?" He was about to slam the door on her but I cried, outraged, "Let her in, this is—this is my aunt!"

"You crazy?" He turned on me, coarse, violent. "What the hell do I need you here for with an aunt?"

I wheeled around, pushing dazed Panna out through the door.

So this was the way my city met me. . . .

The words rang through my head as I came down the steps, struggling with Bibik's blanket, conscious that this phrase belonged to a poem, that I would always remember it, and that more lines would follow someday.

"This is the way my city met me *once*," I repeated, holding tightly to this last word, craving for it to propel me into some remote, better future from which I could look back more calmly at this sordid *now*. At the same time, the ever-present detached overseer within me laughed at my own naïveté and that of Panna, who could not possibly have made head or tail of the brief scene that had flashed out of the stormy darkness and vanished back into it.

I was not going to stay here another moment. A peasant cart was all I could afford to hire, and a peasant cart was probably all that was available anyway for reaching Tamborsk. I knew that it would move at a caterpillar pace, the driver probably walking alongside to ease the load for his starving nag, and that it would take ages for us to reach the city limit. I said so to Panna.

She had taken Bibik and blindly walked behind me, as I groped my way down a slope toward the muffled sounds of men and horses, sounds carried to us on blasts of wind.

"You fellows there," I called into the darkness, "are you drivers?"

A shadow of a man seemed to approach us, a sleepy voice replied, "Ya, that's what we are."

"When are you allowed to start out for Tamborsk?"

"Well, you may start any time. It takes about an hour to the city gates. You aren't supposed to reach there before six, though."

"Could we perhaps start out now and go very slowly?"

"Doesn't matter to us," the shadow came closer. "Only should we get there before six, they'll arrest you and turn us back."

"Then perhaps we can wait somewhere on the way, before we get to the gates."

"Can be done, why not; only it'll cost you more." He named a prodigious figure. I had just that much left.

"Fine, let's start at once."

It was somewhat less windy here, on the road. The darkness was a solid black, but evidently the horses' legs knew the way. The cart jolted on the ruts. So did my thoughts. I was coming back to Aunt Katya, back to a home that was no home. No husband, no father, no poetry, no music, no more capacity to think—bankrupt, intellectually and artistically; as empty as this road. And very likely no brothers, either—Dimitri had not been heard from since he left Krasnoyarsk. I realized that we must now be nearing the grove where they killed my father, but this I still couldn't understand.

Yes, I was returning to Tamborsk three days short of exactly two years after I had fled from it. Just as then, when shock had swept me clear of any thought, when my only link with reality was the words, "Father has stayed behind"; so now the words "I'm coming home" were my feeble link with reality. My thought-resistant mind clutched at these words as at a life belt. I was not tired, not sleepy. The wind blew my hair about my face. No lights anywhere. It was better so. Better not to see anything, either outside or within oneself.

Panna was silent. She seemed to have fallen asleep, as did the driver, whose breathing had become suspiciously slow and tranquil. I had no watch, no idea of the time. Then suddenly—

"Halt!"

The cart stopped with a jerk. I veered around. Right ahead of us was a cluster of buildings; a feeble light gleamed in the nearest windows. We had stopped in front of a gate; the silhouette of a sentry in a peaked Red army cap was already standing beside our horse.

"Your pass!"

I jumped off the cart. "My documents are here. If we are too early we shall wait outside the gate."

The driver, who was supposed to have stopped on the road in order to approach the roadblock by six was now hastily, helplessly justifying himself. "Ought to be about six now. How can you tell with light-saving time?"

"They know it's against the law to approach the city before six, but no, they will do it! They *want* to get in trouble, as if there wasn't enough of it already." The sentry was trying to sound cross and yet his was just an annoyed grumbling. "Now I have to arrest you and upset the commissar.

You think he likes to be awakened at this hour? Come on now, you're under arrest."

Panna, obviously dazed, wanted to take Bibik but I was afraid to leave him: too many children had been lost like this. I told her I would be back shortly, and took him with me. He was still asleep.

A desk and a few chairs stood in the center of the otherwise bare office of the commissar. A portrait of Lenin hung on the wall, a low-shaded lamp on a rough wooden table cast a circle of light on a torn, ink-stained blotter. I sat down on a bench by the door and waited. Bibik awakened, looked around the room astonished, and a blissful smile began to stretch his lips. "*Domik*," he said, "a little house." He had not been in a house for quite some time. "A nice little house." So it was.

Through the door I heard heavy footsteps and a coarse, sleepy voice talking to the sentry. When a heavyset man came in, buckling a revolver on his leather belt, all I felt was a pitying tenderness for Bibik's un-awareness.

Without a glance at me, the man moodily dropped his bulk on the desk and took a pen.

"Your name." He spoke in the usual rough, barking manner with which they all spoke; no better and no worse.

"Olga Volotskoy."

Arriving from?"

"Siberia, Krasnoyarsk."

"Place of birth?"

"Tamborsk."

"What were you doing in Krasnoyarsk?" His voice rose menacingly.

"Working as a music teacher," I replied, his challenge echoing in my answer.

"Husband?"

"Divorced." I still remained sitting on the bench.

"Ex-White, eh? I can't hear you from there. Come closer." There was thunder in his voice now.

I rose and moved closer to the chair this side of the desk. Bibik had suddenly grown too heavy for my arms. But it was not only because of this that I knew I must sit down. To remain standing would be to admit my subservience. Admit your weakness, waver, and be crushed.

But before I had time to sit down, the commissar, his eyes on the paper before him, his pen poised, asked this worst of all questions:

"Maiden name?"

"Ogarin."

The pen froze to the paper. He shot a quick sideways glance at me, furtive and incredulous. This was the first time he looked at my face and saw me. And I saw him. Saw the thick protruding lips, the heavy nose, the narrow slits of eyes; and from the weight of the last years, the sound of a name leaped forth: "Shurka."

He said, "Your patronymic," in a voice that struggled to remain even. Before me rose a picture of the reception hall of our Tamborsk home, the tall carved chairs on which petitioners who came to see my father sat waiting to be admitted. Among them, the sulky-looking schoolboy—fat, uncouth, homely—who used to reappear month after month, year after year, an orphan out of the slums, cared for by my father, fed, clothed, talked to, put through school. Shurka.

There was a short silence, through which we both sat, looking down. Then he scribbled something and, still without looking at me, rose abruptly, took a few ponderous steps to the door, and called to the sentry.

"Let this citizen straight through."

The clock on the wall showed a quarter past five.

THIS COULDN'T be true, it couldn't! The unpaved road had ended; the wheels were now rattling over the cobblestones of the suburb of Volnaya Sloboda. The outlines of low-roofed houses on both sides were a trifle darker than the sky; another half hour and we would be there.

The fantastic dream of reunion that had haunted me through these years, changing with the change of events, gradually darkening, shrinking, had stabilized into one dim vision of my dropping to my knees before Aunt Katya, before all her suffering and the strength with which she bore it. But this vision had always been permeated by the sense of its impossibility. Now that we were getting closer to the familiar parts of Tamborsk, and night was giving way to a dense gray dimness so that one could distinguish the houses, recognize the streets, the implausibility of what was actually happening turned within me to something between laughter and a nervous chill.

There were no lights in the houses, none in the streets, of course. Even if people were getting up, which they must be, there would be no lights used; or, if used, it would be stolen light blacked out by heavy blinds, the electric power being only for the powerful. No sound either, save for the rumbling of our wheels and the clumping of our horse. The usual fear-shackled silence.

As we approached the main elevated part of town and were close to what had formerly been the smart shopping district, our miserable nag seemed hardly able to trudge uphill. I jumped off the cart, as did the driver, and walked behind it. Here it was no longer windy; and to be in motion was easier. When we reached the top of the hill where the great bulk of Trinity Church was foggily outlined at the corner, phantoms of the past began to rush at me, crowded and indistinguishable. My inner gaze darted from the old images to the new, attempting to grasp reality, tossing between the reality in whose brutal grip I was being held, to the ghostliness of a vanished world, but one that still endured in me, for of it I was made. Those two unbridgeable lives, past and present, were linked only by a thin, tightly drawn thread: incomprehensible words, "I'm coming home."

The tramping of my worn-out shoes on the asphalt, on its sharp-edged, caked-up, frozen dirt, and the lazy rambling of the cart's wheels echoed through the cadaverous stillness. There was enough light now for me to see the empty windows of shops. Broken windows, boarded doors. The former Café Europe—could that be it, its windows filled with hay? The former flower shop Eastern Flora, now piled with cartons. The music shop where we used to buy every latest piece of Rachmaninoff, Scriabin, Glazunov, gaping into the street with black, glassless holes. I caught up with the driver, who was now walking alongside the horse.

"Turn to the right! Don't let's go down Trinity Hill—not along Smolensky Street. The other way, over there." I couldn't bear going past the Nobility Assembly, or by the skeleton of the burned-out Opera House, or anywhere near our house on Pushkin Square.

As we crawled on and on, I was hardly looking about me. Bibik had awakened and was sitting up, staring, interested.

"Here, stop here, this three-story house on your right."

Sonya's house was dark, the street dead. Panna with the suitcases, I with Bibik in my arms, tiptoed through a side gate to the backyard, our shadows almost indistinguishable in the narrow well that led to the back entrance between the houses. I whispered into Bibik's ear that we had come to Aunt Katya's and Aunt Sonya's house, that they must be still asleep so we should not make any noise. Perhaps he understood more than I said. I knocked. We waited. How many times during this year had we crawled in the dark to various doors, knocking, whispering, waiting, those behind them afraid to open.

In the silent predawn grayness, the hammering of my heart filled my head, the empty yard, the world. Then cautious huffling steps approached the door. In the window next to the porch a curtain moved. There probably was enough light now for whoever it was to see my silhouette with a child in my arms and to realize that this was not a next-in-turn search. The door opened a crack.

"Who is it? Quiet, quiet." Then a horrified gasp, "Good God, Olga Alexan'na, get inside quick!" It was Sonya's nurse; hastily she nudged me in. Holding me by the sleeve, she led me through the pitch-dark corridor into the kitchen, muttering under her breath. "My goodness, we certainly didn't expect you. Katerina Lvovna will certainly be startled. Did you receive her telegram not to come?"

"Not to come? Why?"

"Because of something that came out in the paper the other day. *They* knew you were coming . . . a sort of warning . . . but her telegram must have missed you. Anyway, I'll go wake her."

She struck a match, lit a candle on the kitchen table. Panna put our luggage down. Neither of us spoke. Somehow it didn't matter what that newspaper had said. Warning or no warning, none of us were safe now, here or anywhere else. I looked around. This was Sonya's former kitchen; now also dining room, living room, and the nurse's bedroom. Some of the children's expensive toys, remnants of former days—little Nicky's large wooden horse Lava, a tricycle—stood in the corner. Bibik began to tug toward them in my arms, trembling. He had never had a single toy. I could hardly hold him.

"A horse," he cried, but the nurse hastily hushed him. "Sh-sh-sh! Our neighbors are Bolsheviks," she whispered into Panna's ear, "spying after us, planted here to report on us. Careful." She went toward the bedroom door. But Aunt Katya had already opened it and was standing on the threshold.

She was hurriedly tying the sash of her ancient flannel dressing gown. Her graying chestnut hair was drawn back tightly, night fashion, which made her forehead look too high, her face too thin and narrow. In the dim light I could see that the two sharp furrows that bracketed her mouth were congealed into a ready-for-whatever-was-coming firm-ness—a search, an arrest. When she saw me standing there with Bibik, she dropped the sash, threw up her arms, and gasped in a dismayed half-whisper, "Nita! My telegram! Didn't you get it? Nita . . . Nita! Why have you come?"

Unable or unwilling to absorb her meaning, I stood there peering over this dear face, the hair flattened over her head. I could neither move nor speak. I could not withdraw my eyes from hers—my eyes, which independent of my will, were peering deeper and deeper into the frightful chasm of these two years of our separation.

"Aunt Katya," I finally heard myself say. "I came to be with you."

She put her arms around me and Bibik, then took him from me and, pressing him to herself, began to apologize for having frightened me with this horrible greeting. She had hoped that I would be coming through Moscow and had sent the telegram to my brother because of a notice in last week's *Tamborsk Pravda*: "As to former capitalists and aristocrats," it read, "such as the Ogarins and their like, who for ages drank the blood of the poor, they had better stay where they are, lest they suffer the same fate as has befallen some other members of their family."

"You have not frightened me, Aunt Katya," I said. "Why should they care about such an insignificant person as I?"

"They care about everything," Aunt Katya replied. "Everything. Hence their strength."

Awakened by our whisperings, Sonya suddenly appeared on the threshold of her room. She wore the red velvet robe of her trousseau, so becoming to her, so familiar to me. Her dark hair was curling gypsylike around her beautiful face. She stretched her arms toward me, her eyes brilliant in the dusk. "How wonderful that you came! And how dreadful!" Then she rushed toward Bibik and took him in her arms. Politely he waited to be released so he could get back on the horse. "I heard you," she said breathlessly, "but couldn't believe it! I knew you wouldn't go through Moscow, and yet . . . Have you slept? Eaten? Tea? Some potatoes?" Yes, Dimitri was in Moscow; she was waiting for permission to join him there. So far they were letting him be; they badly needed able administrators. But I felt that she was worried. Had I heard anything about Igor? She asked me.

"No," I answered automatically. "No news. No rumors. Nothing." It was always like this now when, after a long separation, you met someone you love. Their pains, their despair added to your own, the pity for them and for all humans broke your heart; yet the mind remained blurred, unable to understand how one could take it all in without screaming and beating one's head against the wall.

There was no room in me on that first day of my arrival for any fear of being arrested. The details of what my family and friends had had to go through in my absence were themselves more than I could absorb. Only later was I able to realize how strongly Aunt Katya and Sonya—who had been constantly harassed by persecution, searches, and arrest—had felt that fear for me.

However, they did not come to arrest me either that day or the next. After a while, we learned that the shake-up in the local Cheka, which had almost coincided with my arrival in Tamborsk, had resulted in the appointment of a fairly young man as its new chief. We had known this man in our childhood under the name of Goga, as the teenage son of one of our gardeners at Sinniy Bor. A rebellious, aggressive youth, Goga had been a constant trouble to his family, and indirectly to mine. Aunt Vera had been running a boarding school for needy gifted teenagers, financed by her mother and my father. She had recognized Goga's potential, accepted him in the school, and had especially tried to set him on the path of "idealistic service to humanity," as she would have put it. He had always received the special attention of my entire family, was encouraged in his friendship with Dimitri, talked to, cared for.

And now this bitter irony: his taking over the Tamborsk Cheka had not changed the pattern of arrests and executions, which, with his arrival, continued all over the city and the whole district. But it had magically stopped at the threshold of our family. For how long we did not know.

24

ALMOST TWO YEARS had passed since my return to Tamborsk. Life had been hard, but I had never regretted coming back. My place was clearly here with Aunt Katya, with those I loved and who needed me. Yet in many ways, to be a refugee in Siberia was easier than to be at home, nailed down against the once familiar, the sacred and now defiled. No Father . . . No Alik . . . Dimitri away in Moscow, where Sonya and the children had joined him. Dimitri was still working, needed by the government as inventor, engineer, administrator—yet constantly under threat of arrest.

No news about Igor in all this time. From the newspapers we learned that our White forces were still fighting, gradually retreating, yet constantly counterattacking and retreating again, by now somewhere east of Khabarovsk; but not a word about the First Cavalry.

In Krasnoyarsk we had been strangers to the land, protected by a certain anonymity. No attachments held us there, and our wild dreams of escaping, hiding in the taiga, taking dire risks, had made our trials seem temporary. Also, at the time we were there, the process of dehumanization had not gone as far in Siberia as it had in Russia proper. In Krasnoyarsk, I had never witnessed scenes of such beastly cruelty as I had here in my native city, formerly so peaceful and dignified.

Once, in the market square, where I was bartering our things—an old tablecloth, a feather boa, an old clock—for black-market food, I saw a man who had apparently stolen something being beaten and killed by the crowd. Locked in the crush, I couldn't escape seeing his bloody head disappear and bob up from under flying fists.

Another time, early in the morning, I saw a bedraggled young working woman in dilapidated shoes shuffle past our house, bending low under a sack of potatoes. At the window I was watching her doubled-up profile, and thought of how much more fortunate I was than she, this poor wreck for whose benefit the revolution was supposed to have been made. She was obviously bringing those potatoes from some village and must have planned to reach the city unobserved while it was still dark. But she had taken the wrong route: the militia station was right at the next corner. And indeed, a few seconds later, a man's bellow tore into the early morning silence: "What's that you have there, potatoes? Are they communal?" The next moment I shuddered from the crack of a shot. Not a single window opened in the street, not a single face showed. For the edification of the local population or perhaps out of sheer negligence, they left the woman there, lying on her back and congealing in a mire of blood, for another hour. By that time passersby on their way to work would stealthily kick the scattered potatoes with their feet until they felt it was safe enough to pick them up and stuff them into their own pockets.

Yet these people were only strangers, part of last winter's pattern of life. Later, in spring, I was on my way home when a slender boy who looked oddly familiar swung from around the corner and ran past me, his knees flying high, his face distorted with fear. Almost immediately around the same corner there burst a crowd of hoodlums hooting, shouting. All I heard clearly were the words, "White bastard."

For a moment I froze, then tore wildly and stupidly after the crowd, screaming "Stop it, stop it!" in a piercing voice that no one could hear, except some ashen-faced passersby who shrank against the walls. But the crowd, now lustily joined by some militia men, was already upon the boy. He was a bloody heap within a moment. Who? Who was it? Oh, but I *knew*. It was Coco, the little musical prodigy, the leader of our train: Coco Scheyin.

I turned back, caught at the first lamppost, and stood there awhile.

Night raids, searches, and arrests were constant. True, since Goga had become chairman of the Cheka none of us had been touched. Nevertheless, it often happened that our whole block would be cordoned off in the middle of the night. Waiting for the sound of gun butts at our door, we would hurriedly destroy every bit of paper that lay around, for an unfinished letter or a poem would be avidly pounced upon by the searchers, some secret meaning ascribed to it. Writing had become impossible. I didn't even try to memorize the lines of poetry that sporadically would rise in my mind, those desperate words accepting the impossibility of ever being reunited with Igor.

I had hardly seen a single person in Tamborsk whose life had not been ruined. Our former servants; the cobbler down the street, whose son had been executed and who told me about it, wiping his eyes with a dirty rag; my father's former secretary, Luba Mercutov, whose husband had died in prison; the former prima donna of La Scala, Baronelli, from whom I now took singing lessons, paying her a bowl of soup an hour; all were half-starved, sick, orphaned, afraid. Even peasants from Sinniy Bor would drive over to see us to complain bitterly of the losses and offenses they had suffered at the hands of the village commissars and even the young generation of Communist-propagandized hoodlums—their own children. Although these visits to us, their former landowners, endangered them, these older peasants came just the same, surreptitiously bringing tokens of their loyalty: a few eggs, some flour, and butter, as scarce by now in the country as in the city.

At times to go on living as we did seemed impossible; yet even here I continued to be more fortunate than millions of others because of the love that surrounded me, because of the unshakable courage with which both my aunts bore their lot: running to everyone's help, sharing anything they had with those even worse off than they. There again we were blessed, by still owning things to sell and especially by having milk. Aunt Vera had managed to keep a cow. It was called Krasotka, or "Beauty." Since several attempts had been made to abduct Beauty, she had been given a place of asylum in the storage room, next to the cubbyhole where Panna, Bibik, and I slept. Through each night we would hear torrential rumblings and plops, and the whole house was often awakened by forlorn mooings. But it was worth it. All the more so because the morning cleaning up was done by two of our former servants who had stayed with Aunt Vera, asking only for food and shelter in return for their work.

I became especially aware of the extent to which I depended upon my aunts' indomitable spirits when one of our closest family friends died. Aunt Vera and I and several other women had to take turns carrying the coffin to the cemetery. There were no men left in the city to whom we could turn for help. No horses, no sleigh that we could afford to hire.

The afternoon was a leaden gray; tiny needle-sharp snowflakes stung the face. It was a long way to the cemetery, and we often changed sides in order to change hands. At times we stopped to rest, our breath coming out in thick white vapor; we stood there, Aunt Vera and I avoiding each other's eyes. Once we stopped in front of our former house—before the walnut front door, the rows of tall windows through which I used to look at such a different world! And all of a sudden, past and present clashed in my mind with such violence that I felt as if something must be breaking loose in my brain. In desperation I looked at Aunt Vera. There she stood, her head tossed, staring at the windows, an almost exalted brilliance in her eyes. Holy martyrs went like this to the stake. They did not go insane or have nervous breakdowns; they glorified God and thanked Him. So, I knew, was she now thanking Him and this old house for having inspired and nourished all that she would carry with her to the end.

It had not seemed possible for the conditions of our life to sink any lower. Yet the previous spring, 1921, a disastrous drought had killed the crops all over the Volga region. By summer, the famine had reached its peak. Thousands of cadaverous peasants came staggering from remote villages to fall in the streets of Tamborsk and die there unattended. Rumors of cases of cannibalism began to reach us; cholera broke out in the city; and the government hardly raised a finger to help, except to ask America for assistance. Or was it, perhaps, the Americans who offered it themselves?

They came, indeed, like the good cowboy in American films. Herbert Hoover's American Relief Administration began immediately to establish food stations all over the Volga region. They rescued millions. They also rescued me, because they hired me as a translator.

As the Reds gradually fought their way eastward, many Tamborsk people who had been refugees farther east in Siberia than I had been returning to their hometowns. But all I learned from those I saw was that two years before, when we had been cut off by the Reds, the First Cavalry had bypassed Krasnoyarsk, the fighting no longer led by General Svitovsky, who had decided to give up, nor by General Kostin, who had been severely wounded at that time, but by a brilliant young Colonel Semchevsky, who took over command at the request of the officers.

The returnees also said that in spite of the help of the partisans, the movement of Red troops had been slow because of the stubborn resistance of the remaining White forces. Once the Whites had crossed Lake Baikal to Chita—the stronghold of the cossack Ataman Semenov— they at least nominally had to recognize Semenov as their commander in chief. No more help came from our allies, who had all gone home long ago. The only people still interested in the anti-Communist struggle in Siberia were the Japanese, and they had put their support behind Ataman Semenov.

So, if he were alive, Igor was still free to fight, and he would, to the bitter end. That was a lot to be thankful for.

AT FIRST I kept in touch with Siberia through Oksana. It was clear that many of her letters did not reach me; then they stopped coming altogether. The next-to-last one, which I received in Tamborsk, must have been written in a moment of frenzied despair. From our previous correspondence I had already been aware that things between her and Verin were not going smoothly. He was not coming to see her as often as before; he no longer mentioned marriage. They had indulged in a few heated arguments. But this time they had had a quarrel, a really vicious one. The cause of it was Grisha. Or at least Oksana thought so.

Grisha was a boy her own age who lived in some dark closet in the same house as she. A dear lad, with earnest, watchful eyes and a tender, childish smile, he was great for evenings of heart-to-heart talks, for reciting poetry, for laughing with one about things about which one really should have cried:

> You understand, Nita, that he was desperately in need of sympathy and help because of his critical illness. He suffered from a virulent case of *anaemia pericolosa*, meaning that he has too many white corpuscles in the blood, too few red ones. [Of course I immediately knew what she was trying to tell me.] And, as you know, there is no cure for it. This illness is not contagious, but V. is afraid to catch it by coming into close contact with Grisha, so that I had to ask Grisha not to visit me anymore. Which was horrible, because Grisha lost all his family, all his friends, just as I have. I was furious with V., but decided not to antagonize him, and to act as if nothing were the matter. But you know me, Nita!
>
> The very next day at the office he introduced me to one of his colleagues, a man who gave me the creeps, a sort of white spider, and I said to myself, Well, I may as well treat V.'s colleagues as he treats my friends. So I was very short with that man, to put it mildly. Then V. left town on business. I decided that this was the end, he had left to punish me, and you can imagine how I felt. If it had not been for Grisha I would simply have jumped into the Yenisei. I mean it. But I could not do that to Grisha. By now he was like an adored brother to me. Mind you, he knows everything about my love for V., but in spite of it he insists on marrying me. His only chance of improving his health is fresh air and exercise, changing climate and living in a pine forest. This alone can save him. [Fleeing, she meant—hiding from the Reds in the taiga.]
>
> If things don't get any better between V. and me, I am thinking indeed of leaving with Grisha. Please tell me what you think. I'm in the mood to listen and obey. I will at least be myself again and be needed by someone. . . .
>
> P.S. Remember our friend, Serge? He had the same illness as G., and we just heard that he died of it. Hope the rumor is false.

25

AFTER SEVERAL DAYS of early March thaw, a severe frost struck, turning the pavements into unyielding, kinked glass. Even in felt boots, one had to walk slowly and cautiously to avoid slipping.

I had gone one night to visit an old friend whose husband had been arrested the day before. Houses where arrests had just taken place were particularly dangerous to visit, and Aunt Katya would be worried to death about me; besides, I had promised Bibik to come home early to tell him his bedtime story, and he was old enough by now to know that a promise was a promise.

So I walked too fast down dark and deserted Smolensky Street and, only a few blocks away from home, suddenly missed my footing and crashed full length on the ice, hitting my back and head. I knew I had not broken any bones but I lay dazed, reluctant to move.

My fur beret had slid over my face. I pushed it back and was surprised to see a clear, starry sky over me. So the stars still exist, I said to myself, my eyes traveling over the limitlessness that had opened before me. After all, there still was such a thing as spaciousness, limitlessness . . . and how easy to forget about it when each of your days is a cell, a rattrap.

I tried to sit up but the pain in my shoulder made me stop. And yet it was a good thing, this fall, I thought. A reminder of something else. To see nothing of the tragedy of earth, but the sky alone; to be reminded of those magnificent nights in the taiga nearly three years ago! Magnificent because Igor was there with me. If he was still alive, he must be in the Trans-Baikal region now, but where? "The miserable remnants of the demoralized White bands," said the *Tamborsk Pravda* recently, "tried again to recapture Khabarovsk [Oh, had it been taken by the Whites before?] but were repulsed with heavy losses by our valiant Red cavalry." So by now Igor should be somewhere close to Vladivostok.

One of my gloves had flown off, and as I groped for it my bare fingers slid over ice.

When we were saying good-bye in Achinsk, Igor had warned that we might not see each other for as long as three years. Three years would soon come to an end, and so would "never." Oddly, all that was not Igor had receded into fog. Each day was now like a prison cell that walled us all off—from past and from future. Restrictions, night searches, arrests. Death.

I finally retrieved my ice-encrusted glove and, propping myself on my elbow, felt my neck with my cold, still-ungloved hand. Although it hurt, it obviously was nothing serious. Still, to stay put for a few more moments seemed best. After all, someone lying on the pavement was not such an unusual sight. A passerby, probably half-starved and worn out as we all were in those days, feeling unable to help, would simply cross to the other side, pretending to himself, especially at night, that he was seeing a drunk. How many cadaverous-looking people prostrate in the street had I myself stepped over last summer during the horrid Volga famine?

I started to rub the back of my head, shook it this way and that. Apparently nothing had happened to it, or to my brain either, which in any event had been functioning at a dismally low level. And why not? Did I need a brain to do what I had to do nowadays? To be a file clerk at the American Relief Administration? Did I need a brain to hold government-issue matches, one in twenty of which would light, to light damp government-issue kindling in the morning? Did I need a brain to stand in a queue for bread or to sell our things in the black-market bazaar? Thank God I still had enough brains for bringing up Bibik and giving music lessons to children. To keep my mind from utter deterioration I had tried to write the other day, even though I knew too well that any writing that was found in a search could become the cause of arrest and execution.

Suddenly I realized that I was no longer alone in the street. Someone's heavy steps were stamping over the ice from around the corner. Before I had time to sit up, a woman's fat face in a thick kerchief bent over me.

"What's wrong, citizen? You dying or something?"

The voice was the energetic factory-activist kind of voice. It was rough, but concerned.

I sat up. "I am not dying, no. I just fell down and couldn't get up right away."

"Broken something, maybe?"

"No, I was just counting the stars. You see them better lying down." I thought this might amuse her.

But she was all action and enterprise. "Here I was walking along," she said with businesslike gusto, "and saw someone lying there and I thought: another victim of the pavement. Want me to help you up?"

She was a broad-shouldered, big-boned woman who could probably have moved a piano singlehandedly. Before I knew what had happened, she grabbed me by the elbows, lifted me to my feet, and began to brush the snow from my back. "Icetime is no joke," she said with a gloomy pout. "The other day some citizen slipped on the ice and . . . bam! Her skull broke right in half. I read this in the paper." Then changing from chitchat to a tone befitting the printed word, she added, "And that's what the caption said: 'Victim of the Pavement.' All right, are you? Can you walk?"

I was all right. I knew that she must be one of those peasant women, one of those few human beings who, without being a potential criminal or one of those power seekers, had profited by communism; who had found new lives in no longer being enslaved by their husbands. I thanked her. "Are you a commissar, or some chairman, or some sort of an activist?" I asked.

"Sure! I'm the secretary of the Tamborsk People's Health Department. And you, citizen?"

"I—I am . . ." What was I? "I am a stargazer of sorts . . . formerly a specialist in woolgathering," I said. She nodded vigorous approval.

I HAVE ALWAYS wondered whether I would have remembered that night, that fall, this woman, had it not been for what happened later.

The front of Aunt Vera's house was occupied by strangers, so I had to skirt the yard and come in by the rear entrance. It was half dark but warm in the kitchen; the elbow-shaped pipe from the samovar was still plugged into the flue in the wall, the steam purring up around it, the coals at its base still glowing red. They had kept it going for me. I slammed the heavily upholstered kitchen door hard behind me to announce my arrival, and immediately Aunt Vera's voice called out from the depth of the former study, now the whole family's bedroom. "Here she is!" There was tension in the exclamation, an excitement that sounded more than simply relief from worry. And at once there came a shuffling of chairs, Aunt Katya's hurried, almost running steps through the narrow dining room, Aunt Vera's children racing ahead of her and her strained, nervous voice calling into the darkness, "Is that you, Nita?"

"What did you think? Did you think that I was arrested?" I asked brightly. And then suddenly we were all crowded in the dining room, people and things: both my aunts, Panna, the three youngsters, their old grizzled and ever-grumbling French governess, the couch on which she slept, the grand piano, the dining room set and heavy bookcases of former days. There was in the room a tingling, anxious anticipation puzzling to me. Aunt Katya's hand was extended toward me, holding an open envelope.

"Please forgive me, Nita," there was a tremor in her voice, "but this letter was addressed to me at our old house. It reached us just as you left so I couldn't help reading it."

"From whom?" I asked, almost in awe.

"Well, guess!" Aunt Vera cried, head thrown back, an ecstatic light in her eyes.

And one of her boys, Kolya, hopped up, wedging himself in front of me. "From your husband!" he yelled.

The envelope was postmarked Moscow; the handwriting was not Igor's—could not be.

I pulled at the thin sheet of paper inside; it stuck. I muttered apologetically, "My fingers are still numb, it's so cold outside," and quickly dodged away from Kolya, who was about to help me take the letter out. But yes, it was, it was Igor's handwriting! "Dear Nita, If this note reaches you . . ." It was dated January 3. So he was alive then, two months ago!

Impatient, they watched me read. The tension was growing; I sensed that they wanted to rejoice with me, to celebrate with me, regardless of what this letter might mean to them. But, in order to be able to read it through to the end, I felt I must try to make myself stonelike.

"Someone I know," wrote Igor, "who is on his way to Moscow promised to mail this to you. I live by the hope of our being together again someday. I am well but traveling constantly [yes, I knew, fighting!], so I have no permanent address. Write care of Aunt Liza in Harbin." I couldn't think of who on earth Aunt Liza was, but it didn't matter; Aunt Katya seemed to know, and the address was there. Then came a few more precious words, over which my eyes slid hurriedly, words I would read later, alone, when I was free to understand what it all meant and to break down if I had to. Because anything might have happened to him in these last two months; because even if Igor was still alive the Soviet government would never let me out of here to Harbin, a territory still in the hands of the officials of the old Russian regime; because this was the time of death and despair.

But they were waiting for me to do something, to say something. And suddenly, still unable to take it in, I threw my arms around Aunt Katya wildly, elatedly, and everyone began to hug and kiss me. And only then did it come to me that he was alive and waiting for me.

AFTER I HAD received Igor's first letter I wrote him several times, addressing him as if he were a girl, calling him "Iga" and trying to dwell on the bright sides of my life. I told him that Bibik was extraordinary, sweet, intelligent; that the spiritual strength of Aunt Katya and Aunt Vera were an inspiration (upon rereading this, I felt that it was best to strike out the dangerous word "spiritual" and recopy the letter). I also wrote that it had been a great help this winter to work in the American Relief Administration. The food rations—butter, sugar, flour—that the Americans gave their Russian employees were literally saving us. But here again I had to change the sentence, dropping the Americans out with the butter and sugar, so the final copy read: "The special food rations we receive are a great help." I also wrote that I was making every effort to move to Moscow early that spring. My brother and his family, crowded though they all were, seven people in two rooms, wanted us to stay with them. Once there I would start to make arrangements to join Aunt Liza. The very thought of it made life worth living. I also knew that foreign passports were issued only in Moscow.

Another letter came from Igor in the course of the next month. The envelope was addressed to me by Aunt Liza (who was no aunt to me at all, just a distant connection) in her aggressive, pointed handwriting. As I opened the envelope I could feel my heart violently hammer in my throat and chest and my fingers go cold—until a crumpled bit of paper written in Igor's handwriting fell out of it. There were just a few words of endearment and hope that must have been written in a hurry, perhaps on the eve of a battle. At least the date coincided with some newspaper reports about the "fleeing White bands still attacking on the way to Vladivostok." Just the same, the last words were, "Do everything in your power to come to Aunt Liza as soon as you can."

Enclosed was also a note from Aunt Liza. If I ever came to Harbin, it said, my child and I would always find a bed in her house. This was especially generous of her because although she had loved my father, she hardly knew me, and having been a famous beauty of St. Petersburg some fifteen years before, she cared nothing for women in general and for young ones like myself in particular.

CERTAIN MEMORIES slowly fade with time and die; while others remain indelible. There are also those that grow with the years like plants, like trees, whose potential gradually reveals itself in all its fullness when it is too late to do anything about it. Of this kind was the memory of one evening at the end of that winter.

Both my aunts were sitting in Aunt Vera's room by her work table that night. I came in and sat down with them.

The circle of light cast by a low-shaded lamp in the middle of the table fell on a heap of themes written by Aunt Vera's pupils; her pale, nervous hands gathered them into piles. Aunt Katya, across from me, bent over a gray stocking she was darning, her face set into tense concern that obviously had nothing to do with the stocking.

"And so what do you intend to do?" She raised her thin narrow face from her work. "Frankly, I don't see how, run-down as you are, without money, and with a small child, you can start out for God knows where." And she looked at me, her huge questioning eyes stern, prepared for the blow.

Did I or did I not realize at that moment that I held a dagger over her? That my answer, "Yes, yes, I want to leave, to go to Manchuria," would be a heavy blow to her? But my decision had been made long ago, at the very moment when Igor's first letter had come. Still, the answer shot out of me resolute and relentless.

"I want to go look for him wherever he is."

"But if you do, of course you will take Aunt Katya," Aunt Vera cried. You can't possibly think of leaving her behind, she meant.

"Naturally," I exclaimed, "if Aunt Katya agrees to come."

And this was terrible. It sounded as if I had said that with her or without, I was going just the same.

"But these are only dreams, Aunt Katya. Too soon even to think of it!"

Even to receive a permit to leave for Moscow, where one had to go in order to get an exit visa, would take months. Years to get a foreign passport. "You see, Aunt Katya, it's only in principle I have decided to go. I want to be with Igor and to take Bibik to him. However, it's next to impossible."

Aunt Vera said emphatically, even belligerently, "I think it is insane of you. If you knew exactly where your husband was, it would be different."

No, she was not thinking of herself, of what it would mean to her to be left alone without her chief support, her older sister, whom she worshipped; she was standing up for her, fighting off the pain I was inflicting upon her.

Indeed, I had returned to Tamborsk in order to help Aunt Katya live. And I had succeeded, but now I was dropping her! At a time, of all things, when she was too weak to undertake a trip, for she had been suffering all winter from frequent attacks of some unidentified pains accompanied by high fever. Suffering for days at a time.

"My health may make it impossible for me to go with you," she said firmly. "Where will you be if I fall sick on the way? It's better for you to go with Panna. She will be a real help."

"We shall take Panna too, or else you will follow me later, Aunt Katya! Please, please! As soon as I am established somewhere . . ."

But, against my will, my pleading voice also said that nothing could stop me now from trying to join Igor, and she knew it.

AFTER LONG, strenuous efforts to procure some identification and permits to go to Moscow, Aunt Katya, Bibik, and I (Panna would come later) were ready to leave Tamborsk. It was June.

We left on one of those tender June evenings when nothing stirs and the air is fresh with yesterday's rain. Loaded with our suitcases and bundles, we emerged from the tramway onto Railroad Square. The sidewalk around the square was full of people also burdened by bundles and hurrying as we were, but the bare asphalt of the square itself was empty. Exactly in its center, by a mute fountain, lay, spread-eagled, a little blond boy of about seven in a clean light-blue shirt.

Why no police, no doctor, no people around him? There wasn't anything to do, of course; it was perfectly plain he was dead. Too late. And, anyway, everybody died. I quickly shifted my position so as to screen the boy from Bibik.

I never wanted to see Tamborsk again.

26

ONE MID-AUGUST DAY in Moscow, I was suddenly gripped by a fear of arrest, a fear so violent that I could hardly contain or conceal it.

Almost three months had passed since Aunt Katya, Bibik, and I had come to Moscow, overcrowding the three rooms of Dimitri and Sonya's flat. There were seven of them already there: Dimitri and Sonya, their four children, and their nurse, who managed to keep the place in regal cleanliness and order, an extraordinary accomplishment in now unrecognizable, shabby, dirty Moscow. Three months since I had applied at the Department of Foreign Passports of the Moscow Cheka, now renamed GPU, for a permit to leave the USSR. Three months of days spent in a waiting room crowded with applicants, all of whom were called in ahead of me and ahead of one other applicant, a slender, tight-lipped older woman in a worn tailored suit. She and I usually sat in opposite corners, pretending not to see each other, as if avoiding a glance in a mirror. It was only at the last moment before closing the office that a clerk would stick his head through the door and call: "Citizen Roukov and Citizen Volotskoy, be here tomorrow at nine." What sort of game were they playing with us?

Thus passed week after week of stagnation and anxiety. Panna had, meanwhile, arrived in Moscow, prepared to leave with me.

The hours I did not spend at the GPU I spent dashing back and forth across Moscow in search of some "reliable speculators" who could turn my remaining jewelry into inflated Soviet money. By now two third-class tickets to Manchuria cost over eighty million rubles.

It had become clear enough lately that my long sessions at the GPU were not leading to anything good. And indeed, that day in August, things vaguely sensed until then suddenly sprang into sharp focus. I was trying as I had tried a few times before, to stir things up, speaking to one of the officials, asking what was delaying my case. But the clerk whom I approached this time, a big man with sagging eyes in a fleshy face, brought me abruptly to my senses. "If you don't want to wait your turn,

Citizen Volotskoy, you can bloody well pack up your documents and get the hell out of here while it isn't too late. Though it may be too late— understand?"

My attempt to stare him down in answer proved to be a mistake, because as I turned to go he yelled after me, "Better go and wrap it all up as I just told you, hear?"

So they had discovered something to my discredit. They knew I had a husband in Manchuria and had tried to conceal it. A husband who was an enemy. A White officer.

They intended to arrest me.

Aunt Katya was very ill. When I came home that evening, she lay on the sofa behind the screen of the former living room, a room crowded with antiques that Sonya and Dimitri had managed to save from Sinniy Bor. Portraits covered the walls. I sat down on the edge of Aunt Katya's sofa. Through the dusk I could see how her features had sharpened lately; the lines that framed her mouth had deepened. A wet towel lay on her head. I didn't want to worry her, but could hardly speak.

"Tired?" she asked. I nodded. She knew by looking at me that things had gone wrong. Although the thought of my departure terrified her, she wanted me to go just the same.

"Has anything new happened?"

I was going to say, "They will arrest me tomorrow, if not tonight." Instead I said, hardly able to push the words through my lips, "The same old story. Nothing moving."

She took my hand—it was icy—and held it with her burning fingers. "Nita," she said, "tomorrow is the eve of a great holiday; why don't you go to church? When did you last go to Confession and to Communion? You know how one sometimes gets new strength from the effort of praying."

How she must have prayed nights for my father, for Alik to be spared, to live! Yet she still believed in prayer?

Not that I was able myself to pray at this time. Still, the denial of the power of prayer was to me tantamount to the denial of the power of human thought and will. Yes, I also believed in prayer.

MY NARROW, old-regime summer slippers echoed emptily over the ceramic tiles as I crossed the enormous church and stood behind the old woman in front of one of the side altars, waiting for the pre-mass Confession. The sun slanted down in wide sheaths from the high window. It poked at my left shoulder and left cheek and warmed me. If I turned my head to the right, I saw my clear-cut shadow stretch over the blinding bright tiles and knew that my hair had turned gold. Which no longer mattered to me or to anybody. What do you do with your hair in a prison? No water, no soap. Squalor.

So now, although still worrying about being arrested, I was also thinking of my hair and of my white summer kid shoes, instead of concentrating on my sins and what to say about them to the priest. "So many, Father," I would say, "but such ordinary, dull, and inextricable— yes, inextricable—sins, just like everybody's." And then of course I should try to tell him of what really weighed heavily on my conscience, my greatest guilt. The very root from which all other guilts grew. Only . . . how could I put it into words?

A few moments before, a bald little priest had entered the side door of the altar with hurried, mincing steps, and I knew without looking back that the church was beginning to fill with people. The tall windows were all open, and the tolling of the church bell rose serene and pensive on the crystal air. On this same kind of morning three years ago, Igor and I had gone to Communion at the cossack cathedral in Omsk. The times were bad enough even then, but how incomprehensibly everything had lit up and blossomed for us that day! However, those years had still been years of hope: Igor and I had still been together. I was seized anew with despair of ever seeing Igor again, and remembered about Confession only when the priest's voice, feebly intoning some undecipherable words of prayer, reached me from the altar. When he came out, carrying a golden cross and a Bible, he stopped in a niche behind a screen, waiting.

His soft-featured face was kind and attentive. ". . . But, Father," I said, "what weighs the heaviest on my conscience is that during these last years I have lost, squandered, all the spiritual inheritance bequeathed to me by my family, and that I do nothing to recapture it, although I realize—"

"Do you believe in God?" he interrupted.

"Oh, yes. Absolutely."

"Do you say your daily prayers?"

"Very briefly. Not always."

"Do you go to church regularly?" The questions were out of a religious primer, but his voice was meek and concerned. "Oh, you don't? Do you observe the Lents?"

This sounded exactly like Levin's confession in *Anna Karenina*.

"No, not really. Except—except that there is not much to eat, anyway," I hastened to add in self-justification. The clash between my penitent manner and the conversational tone of this offhand statement struck me as ridiculous, and I felt that little nervous bubbles of laughter, filled with longing to be what I was not, could explode at any moment into sobs.

"But if you believe in Our Lord, then you should observe . . ." Speaking with mild rebuke, the priest said what he was supposed to say and asked if I were married. Then with a heavy, ready-for-the-worst sigh, "How do you live with your husband?"

"I haven't seen my husband for three years, Father. No, I'm not divorced. He is on the other side, with the Whites."

"I see." He sighed again, grievously this time. "Have you succeeded in being faithful to him?"

"Oh, yes," I waived the question, the answer to which was too self-evident, and said, crestfallen, "I'm trying to leave and join him, only—" I had to cut myself short. Quite unexpectedly, I was on the verge of sobbing, and I could hardly finish. ". . . Only they won't let me go. It seems impossible."

A funny, amazed little squeak in the priest's throat, as if he had swallowed wrong; a slight pause; then, "So you have kept your marriage vows?"

"Oh, that was only natural, Father."

"Natural?" He raised an astonished, almost stricken face to me. "This is the first time in years. . . . But how is that possible nowadays? Now, when everything all around is soiled, everything defiled! Praised be the Lord for helping you to keep the purity of your marriage!" His hand was making fidgety Signs of the Cross over me. "I'll pray now that He help you join your husband. Thank you, my child, thank you for comforting an old man!" He spoke in a confused, breathless stammer.

"But, Father!" I cried shamefacedly, shrinking from this undeserved praise, feeling that I had somehow misled him. "To remain true to my husband required no effort, but I have done worse than be untrue to him. Oh, no, not worse, but just as bad." I did not know how this came to my lips, how the something of guilt that had obscurely loomed in me until then broke to the surface to tighten my throat and cut into my voice box, but I had to go on now. "I have been encouraging another man who really cared for me. I mean . . . I was playing games with him." The realization of how this must have sounded to the priest made me shrink with embarrassment and I muttered through my constricted throat, "And when this man was on the brink of death, my chief concern was not to smear the purity of my marriage, of *my* life, and of *my* peace of mind."

"Did you love this man?" the priest asked forlornly.

"No . . . no! This was not love, this was—I had brought things to this point for my own diversion, to forget all my other sorrows, and then fled from him when he needed me most. I didn't even wait for him to tell me what he wanted to say, although I knew that it was our last good-bye." I was fighting for breath, shocked into sudden despair by the truth of what I had just heard myself say. "And now he is dead and I can't forgive myself."

The priest fumbled with the parchment stole with which he was supposed to cover my head at the end of the Confession and said softly, "Perhaps it was good for him to love an honest woman, perhaps he felt. . . Now get on your knees!" And now I was on my knees, sobbing desperately into my palms, while his voice, suddenly firm and solemn, rose over my head in a drawn-out chant, which absolved me of all my sins.

A FEW MORE DAYS passed since my spasm of fear about being arrested. The fear ebbed, but the realization that I would never be allowed to leave was beginning to garrote me. Aunt Katya was still quite ill. A friend of Dimitri's who lived in the same flat had been arrested because of a forbidden French novel found in his room; Dimitri knew he would be next, but walked around with an especially unruffled air; some fat baba with stony nostrils had been installed in the room of the arrested friend, obviously to spy on us.

It was a murky, late afternoon. The sky, an asphalt gray, sowed thin, off-and-on drizzles; a sporadic wind smelling of humid earth tore yellow leaves from the linden trees of the Moscow boulevards. I had spent all day, vainly as usual, at the passport office and was taking a shortcut home along an old crooked alley, walking fast, hands in the pockets of my seedy prewar raincoat, when a tall man in commissar-style leather jacket appeared from around the corner. He walked with a purposeful gait, head high, but even in the growing dusk I could see that his eyebrows were heavily, almost mournfully knit. There was hardly anyone else around. But even so he would not have noticed me had I not stopped in my tracks watching him.

Verin.

It was a shock. What was he doing now? Why was he here? Where was Oksana? The questions went off like gunshots in my mind. If he did not stop, if he pretended not to see me, his position would be clear. Or would it? For if he were really doing subversive work he would certainly try to avoid me, an ex-White. But the opposite might be true, too: he might wish to involve me in some underground scheme. Was I ready for that?

He had noticed that someone on the opposite corner had stopped to stare at him, and as our eyes met I caught his momentary hesitation in recognizing me. The very next moment, however, he was crossing the street toward me.

"At first I couldn't believe it was you, Olga Alexan'na. I never expected . . ."

I held out my hand. Neither of us smiled. "I thought you were in Petrograd," I said, instantly introducing Oksana between us by these words and conscious of the challenge in them.

He looked the same as before except for his hair, no longer sleekly parted on the side, but negligently combed back and glistening from the rain. He must have cut himself when shaving. A tiny dab of rust-colored cotton, of which he was obviously unaware, was stuck on his left cheek, and I wished the rain would wash it off.

"I was in Petrograd, yes, on a temporary assignment, but that was two years ago." Gone and forgotten, his manner said. Lowering his voice, he asked, "How are things with you? Any news of Igor?" And as I shrugged my shoulders, wondering what to say and what not to say to him, he asked me, "Have you at least a general idea how and where he is?" But he was really asking whether Igor was alive.

"Igor was all right four months ago, in April, but I don't know where he was," I said.

Verin nodded. "So far, so good," he said. Then, with his characteristic heavy frown, "I suppose our old outfit is still fighting. Probably with its back to the Pacific Ocean by now." His tone said: What a tragic waste.

But he still called it *ours*.

"If you still work for *Pravda* you must know where our outfit is and what is happening to it," I said coolly.

"No, I'm no longer with the newspaper. It was only a temporary device, and I did my utmost to be transferred to book publishing, which I am doing now. It is most important work." He turned to look at me, his brows knit, and for a moment the dab of cotton on his cheek came into view again. "I'm presently in a position to give an extra push to some talented young writers who are not—" Some people were coming behind us, so he waited until they had passed. Then he finished: "To help some young writers who are not entirely subservient to the rules of . . . the new game."

He seemed to have stepped on firmer ground as he said this. Then in a meaningful, deeper vice, "In fact, this is the *only* satisfying, useful thing one can do *now*."

"The only thing?" I asked, trying to sound blank. "You mean that you have come to the conclusion that there is no other way left?"

"None whatsoever. No longer. Not the way they play their cards."

So he was answering my mute question about what had happened to his erstwhile heroic intentions, or fanciful ideas of going underground. So much for that. Was I disappointed in him? No. He was acting and speaking in character. Now I would see what he had to say about Oksana. But he would have to broach this subject himself.

As we emerged into Tverskoy Boulevard we were all at once assailed by the atmosphere of a busy thoroughfare at the rush hour. "Are you an editor of the Gos-Izdat?" I asked, referring to the state publishing house.

Whatever his answer was, it made me feel that indeed he was an editor, and perhaps more than that.

A car with a small red flag in front swung from around the corner, the frenzied hooting of its horn instantly sweeping the traffic, pedestrians and horse buggies to the edges of the sidewalks, and immediately following it, a huge black coffin of a truck. A Black Raven. I followed it with my eyes. Through the windowless black walls I saw people inside standing tightly squeezed together in total darkness, freshly torn from their families, as alone as they had never realized one could be; their eyes staring at what was coming. And among them myself? Perhaps tomorrow?

An odd torpidity seemed to have fallen over the square as the truck rumbled down the boulevard. Not that the passersby slackened their pace. They actually accelerated it, but they seemed to have shrunk into themselves, as did the street, the trees, the houses, and as did I.

I glanced at Verin. His sharp profile expressed stern concentration on something entirely his own; his eyes watched the edges of his boots crush the yellow leaves against the wet asphalt.

Suddenly angered by his smugness, I said, "You believe your work to be important. Perhaps it is. But how can it be satisfying? The fact that everyone is *forced* to serve *them* is another matter. But satisfying? All the lying, all the propaganda they will make you publish; the distortion of our history, of literature . . ."

"Oh, but they're also doing things of great cultural importance," he said. "For instance, the Academy of Science is about to publish . . ."

But I was in no mood to hear about the Academy of Science, and, nodding in the direction the Black Raven had taken, I cut him short. "While this goes on and on. They allow us, the intelligentsia, to cooperate with them only to have us run things for them, and then they'll do away with us, just like that. Leave it to fools to imagine that cooperation with them can ever help matters."

"What else can?" he asked, unruffled, actually tolerant, making me feel that I had struck a hard blow at a cushion.

"Resisting them in any way we can!" I said. Even as I spoke I knew how lame and inadequate that had sounded and was glad that a remote peal of thunder and a sudden burst of rain interrupted me.

"Oh, Olga Alexan'na, after all . . . ," he said, a trifle superior, brushing the rain from his hair. "The time for fighting was when we fought, but this time is past. Don't you see that this is the worst moment for any resistance? Now, when there is finally a promising change in Lenin's attitude? Don't you realize that his New Economic Policy is a decisive step forward?"

"What kind of step forward can there be? How can they go further without demolishing the very ground on which they stand? They will allow a few shopkeepers to sell a few sausages. . . ."

He shook his head. "It isn't only the opening of small businesses! Other important changes are taking place in different fields. For one thing, they are letting certain people out of the country. Even if these are undesirable elements, they are making them leave instead of you-know-what. Only a few so far, but it is a promising beginning just the same. Professors Berdyaev, Ivan Illine, the famous critic Julius Aikkenwald, the writer Osorguin; even if the country is losing the best minds it has, still they are letting them out."

"They are not letting me out, though," I interrupted impatiently. "Too bad I am not one of the best minds."

"Are you trying to leave?" He seemed astonished. Strangely, there was no hint of, "Ah, so you are trying to flee your country while teaching others to resist its evils." In fact I seemed to hear actual concern in his voice and this made me say somewhat less aggressively, "Yes, I have been trying to get out; I have an aunt and uncle in Harbin. Actually I came here to arrange for a passport to Manchuria so I can join them."

"And to look for Igor." There was bitter sympathy in his manner now, mixed with doubt, almost pity, as if he knew how impossible it was for me to achieve this end.

"Have you undertaken the necessary steps?"

"Have I ever! In over four months, yes! But all my efforts resulted in—well, I am now on the verge of being arrested."

"Why should they arrest you?" he asked uneasily.

"You should know why," I said, my tone sharp again.

"All I meant was, did you say anything in your questionnaire about your husband?"

"Only the literal truth: that we are separated. But I could see that the woman who was interrogating me wrote down 'divorced.'"

"Oh, then you have a good chance to leave." He nodded authoritatively. "I wish you luck. I wish with all my heart that you will join him."

But all this seemingly friendly talk could be a camouflage of the fact that he was skirting the most important issue: Oksana. And I was not going to wait any longer.

"Vladimir Vladimirovich," I said decisively, as we came out on the Arbat Square, "where is Oksana? What happened to her?"

"I hoped that it would be you who would tell me that." His voice hardened. He made a few steps, lips pressed together, silent. Then he said, "As you certainly know, she left me."

This was preposterous. "I understood from her that it was the other way around. That you left for Petrograd and refused to take her with you."

He didn't answer at once; then, icily: "I was in no position to take her. I asked her to wait for me in Irkutsk. Besides, you may know that things between us had not gone smoothly for some time and I believed a short separation might be beneficial for both of us. However, as soon as I realized that I could be kept in Petrograd indefinitely, I decided this was the time for me to act and get out of newspaper work as quickly as I could. . . ."

"This was so hard on her," I hurriedly put in. "I mean, your working for *Pravda*. Hence your misunderstandings."

He abruptly turned to me, and now it was plain I had touched the quick and made him furious. "Hard on *her*? What about me? Did she ever ask herself how I felt about it all? Do you realize what it meant to me to have to cross this bridge toward what I had in mind to do, and what a hindrance she was to me? This at a time when certain things were still feasible, and when I was living on the razor's edge?"

The bitterness, the rancor that had suddenly burst from him were genuine. "But she loved you so terribly."

Mournfully he said, "I loved her too. I miss her more than I had ever expected to. As the possibility appeared for me to be transferred to the Gos-Izdat—I had a good friend there—I wrote to her that as soon as I was settled in Moscow she would have to join me."

"You did? And what did she say?"

"She said, 'Tell me plainly that this will never happen, that you simply want to get rid of me.' The unfairness actually knocked me out. I wrote again, swallowing my pride, begging her to change her attitude, but no answer. She must have already left. And with another man. It was a blow. An insult. Perhaps you already know about all this?"

"I'm sorry, I really know so little," I stammered. He realized I had taken a step back.

There was a sudden crash of thunder overhead, and the drizzle instantly turned into a heavy rain and began to rattle like beans over the street. "Over there, quick!" Verin pointed to the roofed front porch of a building. We made a dash toward it and up the tall steps into a deep embrasure glassed on the sides, and smelling of humid stone. I was shaking the moisture off my hat, laughing as one does after running for shelter and reaching it. Verin, who was wiping his face and hair with a handkerchief, ran into the piece of cotton on his cheek, brushed it off with a grimace, and also laughed a little.

"This is my chance. I know that you never really understood me. You never made allowances for the fact that the very point of departure of my convictions was different from yours or Igor's or Lorinov's and the rest of the officers', and that I never, never changed my convictions or betrayed them—never."

The rain by now was coming down in torrents, drumming brazenly on the porch's roof. The street lamps went on, shimmering through the downpour and reflected in gathering seas below them. People down on the sidewalks were running, holding desperately to their soaked hats, crouching under umbrellas.

"It never occurred to me that we would ever meet again," he said, "and yet how often I have thought of you lately." Now that we were confronting each other in this darkish niche, separated from the street by the tall steps, Verin chose to speak to me in a new, different voice, soft and musing.

I looked at him, skeptical. "Why are you saying this? No, really! Why? Except for Oksana we have never had much in common."

"Why? Well, I tried to tell you about this when I spoke of my work with the Academy of Science, but you didn't let me finish. I was going to tell you that the Gos-Izdat had to deal with the possibility of bringing out a new edition of your great-grandfather's poetry at the request of the Academy of Science, and the head of my department, a former Socialist who had adjusted to the Communists, a certain Ivan Yeremin, mentioned to me having known the poet's grandson. I realized it was your father and regretted having known so little about him. This man,

Yeremin, considered your father to have been the greatest humanizing influence in his life. And it just occurred to me—"

"A humanizing influence? Why then did he adopt Communist terrorism?" I asked, at the same time certain that what Verin was telling me was true, for people with whom my father came in touch seldom forgot him. But Verin, knitting his brows concentratedly, went on with what he had begun:

"It now occurred to me that this man might be glad to help you." With businesslike precision he produced a small notebook and pencil from his breast pocket and scribbled something on it. "I shall try to get in touch with him tomorrow, explaining to him who you are and what your problem is. Just in case, here is where you can find him after office hours."

And so Verin wanted to help me in spite of the arrogant way I had behaved toward him. Rather forlornly I said, taking the paper from him and folding it, "Even if nothing comes of this . . . just the same, I'm touched. . . . I'm grateful."

"If nothing moves in the next two or three weeks don't hesitate to go and see him. He is a fairly rare kind of Communist. The ascetic, self-sacrificing kind." Then, sticking his head from under the porch's roof, he saw that the rain had subsided. "I'm due at a meeting at seven. I'll have to hurry."

I put out my hand to him. He kissed it and held it for a moment. A group of giggling girls was about to rush up the porch steps, but upon seeing our silhouettes redoubled their giggles and ran on.

A WEEK OR SO later, on one of my daily visits to the passport department, I was summoned to the office of the same GPU man who had been so rude with me that last time. He sat sprawling at his desk, looking more like a gloomy dignitary overburdened with work than the crude mouzhik he had appeared that first time.

"Well, Citizen Volotskoy," he began in a heavy voice, without looking at me and shuffling some papers on his desk. "Your application for a foreign passport submitted in June has hardly any supporting documents." He raised his glassy eyes to me.

"I submitted everything I had been told to at the time," I said firmly. "Identification papers for myself and Katerina Krylocka, my certificate from work at the American Relief Administration. No one told me that anything else was needed."

"And where is your son's birth certificate?"

"It should be in Tamborsk in our parish church where they keep them."

"Well, we're not going to get on the train to fetch it for you. Get that first and come again."

"Any other documents?"

"Whatever we may need later remains to be seen."

The man shoved my papers aside and rose.

"I shall get that birth certificate as soon as I can," I said brightly and turned to go, when the man said with quite an unexpected sardonic smirk:

"You could have asked Comrade Yeremin sooner to speak for you, Citizen Volotskoy. As matters stand now, your case will take some time. You might make it before winter, though."

PART
FIVE

En Route
to Manchuria

27

OH, GOD, GREAT ORPHANED GOD, deserted by us! Have pity, let me have at least a glimpse of that different world that I used to know: *Your* world, within me. Not this external one to which I am nailed, in which I have seen all that I have seen during these last three years. Have pity on such as me, blot out my memory, destroy it! For I can't live, I don't want to live, remembering all I remember and knowing all I do.

The Trans-Siberian Express train that was to take us—Bibik, Panna, and me—once again all across Siberia had left Moscow at 10:00 P.M., over an hour ago. Bibik was already asleep on the berth below mine, with Panna, as usual, curled up in the corner where his legs didn't reach. All lights had been turned off soon after we started. In pitch darkness I lay stretched on the bare boards of the third-class upper bunk, face downward, pressed into my folded coat. Oh, God, what shall I do, where shall I hide from all that I carry within myself?

The collar-hood of my coat was scratching my chin, but I hardly knew it. Someone across the aisle was snoring like a boiling-over samovar, the sound at times outdoing the rumbling of the train. Yes, I was leaving the Soviets. I was—even if still unable to grasp it—on my way to a free country where I might be reunited with Igor. Only there was no train that could carry me away, and no distance that could separate me from these last years. They would always be with me, those crowds of tattered, haggard, innocent people, driven daily through the city by ferocious-looking guards to the former Symphony Grove, where most of the executions took place; I could never erase from memory the sight of those starving peasants with bluish, transparent faces dying unattended in the street, or the scenes of massacre I had so often witnessed.

Oh, merciful God, tear all this out of my memory; for how shall I live, what shall I say to my child about this terrifying, ugly world?

The snoring coming from across the aisle, probably produced by the stumpy-looking commissar who had informed everyone in the car that he was traveling on a special mission to China, suddenly stopped; and the man began to mutter something and to make loud, mooing sounds in his sleep. On the berth beneath me, Bibik moved. I raised my head, trying to hear if he had awakened. I heard Panna's breathing, each breath ending in a little whistle. They were asleep, they were all right.

It had been different, quite different, when I boarded the train thirty months ago, leaving Siberia to join Aunt Katya in Tamborsk. I had been heading then from darkness and despair toward a gray future. All that had been in store for anyone of my kind was at best persecution, arrest, and starvation. And yet I had been taking it all in my stride, head high, my faith still burning brightly in me. So why was it that now, on my way to a free country (if such a thing still existed), to a place where I might be reunited with Igor—now when all I had been striving for was realized—that I felt as if all the horror of life had crumbled upon me, its weight crushing me, making me feel that I could no longer rise from under it?

Aunt Katya had said to me at the station, "In seven days, God willing, you will be there, already in Harbin. Tell Igor from me . . ." I tell Igor! Did she really believe I would find him, or was she trying to comfort me? ". . . that I love him, and how I shall envy him for being with you." She was saying this, her hand making quick Signs of the Cross over me, and at that very moment the train jerked and she jumped down to the platform, her small delicate hand still blessing me. Dimitri towered behind her, smart and erect in his moth-eaten, old-regime overcoat, his handsome face frozen into a strained smile. He had just been released from prison, but we all knew it was not for long. And as the train started Aunt Katya ran alongside it, forgetting how sick she was, losing her breath and waving a mitten, until she tripped and fell. I could still see Dimitri throw himself forward to help her rise.

This was the last I saw of them. The last.

Oh, Aunt Katya! With a jerk I stuck my face into my coat, pressed my forehead with all my might into the fur. Aunt Katya, *dear*, will you ever forgive me for leaving you in that abyss of sorrow? Will you ever forgive me . . . for everything . . . for the night before when I was giving Bibik a bath, and I called out crossly, "The sponge! Give me the sponge, not the soap!" I could see that moment now, when in response to my rudeness I saw unfathomable compassion in her eyes. No reproach, no resentment, but only pity and pain for me. Because she knew everything about me better than I did myself: that I was going now, in October, across five thousand miles in search of a husband from whom I had last heard in early spring, and who had been at the time and probably ever since engaged in fighting the Reds in some wild depths of Siberia.

What had made it even worse for her was that she had heard us talk, Dimitri and me, late the night before, when we thought that she was asleep. We spoke in lowered voices, of course, but when nine people live in two rooms, all of the most secret things can be heard not only by those who are appointed by the government to spy upon every word pronounced around and who are paid or promoted for this thrilling kind of activity; not only by the neighbor whom we always ran into in the corridor and whose nostrils looked like two marbles, but also by those who would rather do anything but intrude on the last crumbs of privacy between the others of the family. Since Aunt Katya wasn't asleep as we had thought she was, she couldn't have helped hearing us talk, Dimitri and myself, when we remained alone. This was in the front hall while we sat on the chest, on which Sonya's nurse used to sleep, and above which hung the portrait of Ogarin, saved from Sinniy Bor.

"They're after me again," Dimitri had said, speaking through clenched teeth. "And on top of everything else, the cattle that the government forced me to purchase have developed hoof-and-mouth disease. They're dying off, and I am accused of sabotage. They let you out for a while, you know, and then again . . . Such is their method." He was dropping his words slowly, falling silent after each phrase, as one would during a raging toothache, telling me of what his life was now. This was Dimitri, for whom it had always been impossible to give expression to his feelings. And finally he dropped his head in his hands and, in a choking voice, said in French, *"Je suis très malheureux."* Coming from him, this was the same as someone else's beating his head against the wall.

And Aunt Katya must have heard it all. In her pity for him and in her pity for me, it didn't matter to her that I had rudely torn the sponge out of her hands. Why didn't I immediately come to my senses? Why didn't I take her in my arms and implore her forgiveness for everything! Everything. Above all, for leaving her in this bottomless pit of suffering.

This last I had time to say to myself as the train whistled a signal to an oncoming train. The other one answered, and the two passed side by side, the deafening roar drowning all other sounds. Here was my chance to let go, just so as to be able to breathe afterward. And I did—I raised my head and exploded into a wild, drawn-out howl.

This was funny. For a moment I saw myself from the side: a woman lying face-down on the wooden boards of her berth, who suddenly raises her head and gives that animal wail that is stifled in the throats of millions of Russian people, silenced by iron hands and buried in darkness. After I had done it I felt better. Now I could think.

I could ask myself why it was that when I was returning to Tamborsk three years ago, I was still full of hopes, while now, when I should be looking to a new life, I was crushed by despair. Was it because I had left them—Aunt Katya, Dimitri? Or because hope didn't depend upon whether or not there was anything to be hoped for; it was simply there while still alive, not yet beaten to death. This was the way it had been with us all through these last years: hope would rise, then a blow, and it would let out a groan, fall down, and for some time lie there bruised, hardly able to breathe. But in a little while it would rally and attempt to rise again. However, if it had been crushed over and over, day after day, year in and year out, there would come the moment when it would no longer be able to recover.

"No longer . . ." This I said aloud because the train was whistling again.

But could there be faith without hope? I turned and lay on my back motionless, wondering if someone within me, a faraway self, could hear this question. Could there be faith in a higher order of things, in supreme wisdom from which you personally were forever barred? In a light that never could reach you again? For several minutes I lay there, straining my inner ear for the answer. My mind could see so clearly that this answer could not be a positive one. It could not.

But it was.

I WOKE UP in the middle of the fifth night on the train, and I opened my eyes to jet blackness, closed them again. It seemed to me lighter with my eyes closed. "Half-past three, probably," I said to myself. My waist felt sore from the bulges in the belt I wore right over my skin. I loosened it and for a few moments lay still, listening. No stirrings in the car as yet, nothing. Just the rumbling of the train. It must be making up time, now that it was close to its final destination. We were supposed to reach Chita at 4:00 A.M.

The top of the window was on a level with my upper berth. I held the blind to one side, but more blackness flying past was all I could see.

Before going to sleep I had leaned for a moment over the chasm within me into which all the jumble of my life was crashing, and said to the faceless ghost in there, "Wake me up at half-past three in the morning, hear?" And it must have heard.

Still groggy I sat up, supporting my head on my hand, swaying to the rhythm of the wheels, dimly aware of the emptiness of the snowless frozen fields through which we were tearing along toward that new "interstate," the "Buffer." The Buffer where the Reds were supposed to be just a trifle less red, diluted as they were by some drops of yellow—the Chinese railroad officials. I prodded myself into motion to find the matches and get Igor's watch out of my bag, to confirm the hour. I had impressed upon Bibik last night that he must wake up at four all by himself. I wondered if he would.

Last night after he said his prayers, kneeling in the half-darkness on the berth beneath mine, I told him how we would get up in the middle of the night: after five days in the Express, having crossed half of Russia and almost the whole of Siberia (for the third time in these two years) we would have finally come to the big city, Chita. There, I told him in promising, mysterious whispers, he, Panna, and I would get off the train when it was all dark around and see great big stars in the sky. But this was not yet where we were going, not yet! And then I told him, pushing away from myself the chilling vision of Junction 86, the border between the Soviet sphere of influence and Manchuria, that just another day and then another train would bring us to another country, Manchuria. There we would look for his father, and find him someday!

"Tell me that story again," he said breathlessly. And I knew the story he meant. I was sorry now ever to have told him that stupid, idiotically sentimental story. It was about his father, who through all these years had been fighting a dreadful foe, far away from us. One day he would see a blue-eyed little boy walk into the room. "Who is this nice boy?" he would ask sadly, because he would be thinking, "And where is *my* own son? Why must he grow up far away from me? Shall I ever see him again?" And then someone would suddenly cry: "But this *is* your little boy!"

I felt in the darkness for my bag, which hung on a hook beside me. It was swinging with the motion of the train, and it brushed my hand like something alive. I shuddered. Then I began to grope through its crowded contents: my purse on top, swollen with greasy, pulpy bills; three million rubles for the porter. . . . It would be awkward, embarrassing to tip him. I had been too young under the old regime to give tips myself and didn't know how to do it or how much. Besides, it was torture to be a beggar and tip people who despised you for being what you were—a beggar—and hated you for what you used to be—the "capitalist oppressor." If what the canary-socked youth in the opposite berth had sworn was true, and we could be allowed in a hotel (hotels were barred from us in Russia), then five million for a room. So there would be just enough left for a fourth-class ticket to Station Manchuli, and another one to Harbin.

Now my fingertips were on the thin fabric booklet, my passport. "Divorced," it said under my picture—a lie as everything was a lie nowadays. "Olga Volotskoy, age 26, divorced." Not my own fabrication this time, for I had told the passport clerk, "separated," and she had on her own initiative made short work of it. And yet what else could have been written under that faded, weary face? What husband could have stuck it out with this Olga Volotskoy, age 26? And how should I show myself to Igor if we really met?

Bitter and cruel associations from the past three years rose from every object my fingers touched in the overstuffed bag. And now Igor's watch, here it was. "I smuggled it through for you, Igor!" I wanted to have better thoughts, happy thoughts! I might be giving this watch to him soon. I saw my outstretched hand with the watch, but not his face, not him. Of course not. Because there was no truth in it, so the vision would not come into focus. And why should we meet, he and I, if all those other wives and husbands never would? All those others.

The matches were under my coat, which I used as a pillow. I struck one, another, and another—government issue, they were always damp—until finally one lighted. The cover of the watch, with Igor's crest on it, shone gold. Yes, it was 3:35 and I must not wind the watch again, because its ticking might attract attention when they searched us at Junction 86 . . . the Volotskoy crest, the crown! As the slanting bluish triangle of the flame almost singed my fingers, I blew it out.

Tomorrow I would have to stick the watch in the belt with the rest of my jewelry. The belt was stitched into many square pockets, all of them stuffed with things. Some of the pins and especially the string of pearls jabbed my flesh when I lay flat. When I stood up, my waist looked suspiciously big. But I had not much jewelry left by now. It was the letters, those tightly folded letters, written all over in the smallest script, that made the belt so bulky—letters that I was supposed to smuggle through to Harbin from people who had begged me to find their sons or husbands from whom there had been no sign of life since the outset of our fight. And I had taken the letters, promising to find out if these men were still alive.

On my last evening in Moscow, when I was dressing for the trip, adjusting this belt under my slip, Aunt Katya had stood by, holding my dress in readiness for me, watching me. "But, Nita!" she suddenly cried in horror, "it will all show through your dress!" And I had answered impatiently, "And what of it? What can I do?" I could see her now, the terror in her eyes, the emaciated face. She knew that if these letters were found on me, it would mean death. It would mean that my child would be lost somewhere in Siberia, a homeless orphan. But she said no more about it. She looked down, and the creases in her cheeks steadied into iron firmness. I knew what she was thinking. She thought that her girl was one of those heroic women who would rather take death than deny help to those already orphaned.

But of course it was nothing like that, nothing! It was just that the belt had already been fastened and the dress was on, and there was no mental strength in me to realize the danger, nor any physical strength left to make any more changes. Or to be bothered. With cruel impatience I had cried, "What of it? What can I do?" And then, ashamed of myself and in self-justification, I caught at fatalism. "Never mind! What must be, will be."

Something slipped to the floor from Bibik's berth. I leaned down to see what it was and saw that he was already sitting up. I had slept with my clothes on and now began hurriedly to fasten the hooks on my skirt. So he had awakened just when I told him to. I climbed down, knelt before him, saw his fingers weakly struggling to unbutton his pajamas. But he was only half awake, and as I hugged him he blinked his eyes with sudden recognition. He was warm, his arms and cheeks silky. I began to dress him. Soon the conductor appeared, balancing a lantern, filling the car with long straggling shadows, his booming voice shocking the car into life: "Station Chita next!"

No one was moving yet, except the youngster on the upper shelf across from mine, who had just turned in his sleep with the violence of an uncoiling spring. In Moscow on some errand, he had told us, he was now returning. Yes, Harbin was his home. Yes, indeed, he could do that—go to the USSR and back to Manchuria; why not? His brother was in the government. He had gone to visit him and was now coming back to his parents, who had a five-room apartment in Harbin.

"Honest to God they have! Why not? Ha! I'm telling you and you don't have to believe me." Harbin was nothing like Moscow, he said, Harbin was a free city. No requisitions, no arrests. The government consisted of some Chinese officials and some Russian leftovers from the old regime. All the wealth of Manchuria was in the Russo-Chinese Eastern Railway, he told us, and the whole management of the railway was in Harbin. So, since the Russian officials who had served under the czar had not been changed in Harbin, everything so far remained the same as under the old regime.

"Well, anyway, pheasants ten kopeks a pound, fish three kopeks, two cents for potatoes. Free markets, sure." One thing was certain, though: you couldn't get any work there. That you could not. "What do you expect, over fifty thousand refugees, all that's left of the White army, those who had been lucky enough to slip through in time—all that penniless riffraff are in Harbin now." Well, women could sometimes make a few dollars by giving English lessons, because everyone wants to go to America. And then he had suddenly turned to me. "You know English, maybe?"

Why on earth did he turn to me? Until that moment I had the feeling that he didn't even know I was there.

Did I know English? I nodded in answer. If the only way to earn one's living in Harbin was by giving lessons in English, then of course I knew English.

We had believed the boy about the impossibility of getting work in Harbin, but as for the price of pheasants, and five rooms for three people . . . ! We, who had learned the hard way to be done with wishful thinking, how could we accept this? In the face of our skepticism, the boy had tried logic on us.

"Don't you remember how it used to be before 1918? What's the matter with you?" But we might as well have listened to a visionary, a mystic, who was trying to persuade us that he had resided in divine habitations.

"Honest to God," he had told us about Chita, "you won't have to sit at the station till the next night, waiting for your train. This isn't the USSR for you! You can go to a hotel, any hotel. Sure! No special permits needed for it in the Buffer."

And now we were already approaching the Buffer.

BEHIND OUR hotel window the top of a bare maple was bending and swaying, lashed by a cruel north wind. Perhaps it was the oncoming of a typhoon, this wind. Last night when we were getting off the train people had said it was. We hadn't seen any stars. The passengers, huddled together, heads drawn in collars, had been a crowd of neckless shapes scurrying along the platform of the Chita station. I carried Bibik, shielding his face with the lapels of my coat, while the wind threw icy sand into our eyes, pouring it down our necks, blinding us, making it grate on our teeth.

But all that was last night. This morning, we were in a clean and spacious hotel room (so the canary-socked youth was right about hotels!).

A boiling samovar stood on the table, Bibik was across from me, clutching a glass of milk with both hands, his eyes riveted on the tossing branches behind the window.

A board with a loaf of bread lay on the checked tablecloth, white bread light and downy, the kind we hadn't seen in years. Panna was buttering a slice, the sweet half-smile of anticipation on her face showing she was not doing it for herself but for Bibik. A fire was crackling in the white porcelain stove. Its warmth radiated all over the room. I was going to make the most of all these good things in a letter to Aunt Katya: the warmth, the soft beds, tea with sugar. I was already mentally writing the letter that must reassure her about me, and yet it felt uncomfortable somehow—strange—this sudden easing of the load. "Too good for our kind," was it? Or was it that the plush sofa and armchairs and the motley rug, no matter how shabby and ugly but clean and soft, reminded one of normal life? Someone else's normal life? There also was a queer sense of void, the kind one would feel upon bursting out of a dark, ghost-haunted forest into the flatness of an unfamiliar empty field, a field where one might run into hidden traps.

For ahead of me was the ordeal of procuring these two permits: one from the Chita Soviet authorities to leave the Buffer state, another from the Chinese Mission to enter Manchuria, and right after finishing this very good breakfast I should be on my way. ("What? A permit for Manchuria? Divorced? Your papers aren't in order! Where is your divorce certificate? And whose brother is this uncle of yours in Harbin? No, you'll stay here under surveillance until we find out!") As I sat there pouring myself a second cup of tea, I was remotely conscious of that unidentified voice that would be storming at me soon. But I would know how to answer. I'd been through the mill. And if they kept me here or sent me back to Moscow, then . . . then I would . . . Well, something. There was always something.

I only wished this were some other city than Chita. Because this was the spot into which all that remained of our retreating army had poured after the "Ice March" across Lake Baikal, two-thirds of the men sick with typhus, frostbitten, maimed; most of them boys who had fought for their God and country, and who had lost everything. They were still here, they were still roaming these streets, painfully dragging their frostbitten feet, shelterless, orphaned, and unwanted.

It was noon. Our train for Station Manchuli was to leave after eleven at night. The maid who had brought the samovar, who looked like a crab, had just reappeared with broom, floor brush, and waste pail, and was working at the other end of the room, sweeping, rattling the brush, pushing the furniture around with mighty movements. Soon she was pouring conversation at us, every now and then coming toward our table and shaking out a sheet or dust rag into our faces.

"Going to Harbin? Aha!" A knowing nod. "From Moscow? Aha!" Across her bare forehead, above the prominent black eyes, two arching lines of eyebrows were drawn with burnt cork. "Going to join your husband in Harbin, eh? Lots of them girls been through here lately looking for their husbands. No news for several years. But where can they find them? Or new ones, for that matter? How many have been killed, or taken to labor camps, or executed, or died from typhus? And how many tried to escape and were caught at Junction 86, and shot or driven to the coal mines! Why, thousands of them! And whoever was lucky enough to get out of the whole business alive is sure to have found another woman for himself. So you, citizen, maybe, will be also looking for your husband when you get to Harbin?"

I reached for another slice of bread and began carefully to butter it. "My husband and I . . . we are separated." Divorced, I was going to say, but Bibik must not hear me lie. In a blank voice I said, "I am on my way to my aunt and . . . uncle. Yes, they live in Harbin."

She stopped sweeping and, as maids did in old-fashioned plays, stood leaning on the broom while holding forth on the predicament in which the hero found himself. "All the White armies, all that was left of them went through here. This here hotel was swamped with them, White officers. The carousing that went on, the drinking! My, the fun they had!"

I had just reached for the milk to pour some in my tea, and the pitcher hit the table. *"Fun?"*

"Of course, fun; why not? They had had it hard during the Ice March—that's what they called it when they crossed Lake Baikal. Sixty versts of naked ice it was, and I'll say they were a sorry sight by the time they came here. How many frozen legs and arms had been cut off in this here hospital next door alone, how many turned up their toes! And those who pulled through weren't much better off at first neither: no salary, no home, no wives . . . nothing."

"So how do you mean they had fun?" I asked in a stony voice.

"Now listen! They came to this here big city, and what do they find?" She propped the brush handle against her globelike stomach and spread her arms wide, enacting amazed rapture. "Vodka! Enough to bathe in it, costing next to nothing. Food—all you want, costs kopeks, enough for

— 276 —

everybody—for them and for Semenov's gang and for the Japanese. As for the female sex—our girls here just lost their minds! More men than you can count, and where were the wives? Cut off by the Reds. Every other guy—single. Take your pick! Of course they had fun." She took to the brush again, went through a few perfunctory sweeping motions, and then wagged her head with pitying derision. "You should've heard the wailing these girls raised when the Whites moved farther East!"

"What girls?"

"What girls, she's asking me! All sorts. Ha!"

"Why did they cry? Because the men left them or—were they also sorry the Whites were leaving?"

"Ha, the Whites! What the hell did they care for the Whites? The men was all they wanted. Man-hungry, that's what they was."

I rose swiftly. "I am off for the permits, Panna. Give me your passport, and all the rest."

The maid, so abruptly deserted by her audience, yet obviously un-abashed, began to sweep the room in earnest. Then, just as I was leaving, she called after me, pointing a short, blunt finger at my shoes. "This is the kind of high heels they are especially suspicious of."

I turned to her. "What? Who are *they*?"

"They, at Junction 86. At the border. The Red searching parties. People used to take opium across this way, used to make hollow heels and stuff them with opium. And now they know about it at the border. When they search you, they'll take off your shoes first thing. Last month they threw a woman off the train. Yeah. Took her to Junction 86 and—kaput!" She heaved a deep sigh. "Never can tell, maybe we would have been better off here in Chita if the Whites had won instead of the Reds. Maybe the peasants and workers would have had it better with the Whites. . . ."

What on earth had made her say this? Was it the urge to please me in order to get a larger tip? Was she perhaps trying to trap me into revealing my political views?

"Although," she wagged her head with a disdainful grimace, "they are all alike, all men are. All they have on their minds is to get drunk, chase women, and get the better of one another. Believe me, I know."

28

THERE WAS NOT a soul out on the platform that night. Yesterday's north wind had grown into a hurricane and its icy blasts would immediately lash back indoors anyone who ventured out, leaving him panting and shaken. It was almost two o'clock in the morning. We had been sitting here waiting for the train that was to take us across the Chinese-Soviet border to Junction 86 and then to Station Manchuli. It would be five hours late, we were told.

The floor of the fourth-class passengers' waiting room was crowded with Chinese, Mongols, Koreans, and their dilapidated luggage, on which they perched or lay. For three hours already, Panna and I had been sitting on the floor among them, taking turns trying to put Bibik to sleep. But the heavy air, the din of throaty quaking Chinese mutterings, and the unfamiliar masklike faces had frightened him and kept him awake. Panna was holding him close, speaking to him in tender gurglings, but he finally went into a convulsive screaming. Panna's rocking him was making matters worse.

Trained as a nurse during the war, I knew that only shock could stop such an attack of hysteria. Snatching the down coverlet out of my suitcase, I quickly spread it on the filthy floor and reached for him. "I'll take him now, Panna." I was going to put him on the coverlet and hold him down hard, to stop the convulsions. "I say, Panna, let me have him." But she jerked him out of my reach.

"Let me have him, Panna!" My voice lashed at her but she jumped to her feet with the obvious intention of getting away from me. My teeth clenched, I sprang up, trying to take him from her, but she wrenched him back from my hands.

"Don't you dare, I won't let you!" she shrieked, her muscles swelling, her voice drowning out Bibik's frenzied wails. "If you dare take him, I'll leave you! I'll leave you now and for good!"

The narrow slits of many eyes were watching us out of yellow rumpled faces. I was hardly aware of it.

"Then do it at once!" I snapped. She was still pressing Bibik's tossing, writhing body to herself, and I let go of him, jerked my bag open to snatch out her passport and several remaining bills. "Here! Either go back to Moscow on the next train, or *at once, at once* give him to me." I knew that I was frightful in my cruelty, but thankful for it too, as one would be thankful for a hammer to force open a stuck door behind which lay a child's deliverance from his misery. Nothing could keep me from doing what I felt I must. But nothing could stop Panna either.

"I won't go anywhere," she said, gasping for air between words as she stepped away from me. "I won't let you have him to be punished and tortured by you!"

But as he threw himself back over her shoulder, choking, his face blue, I tore him out of her arms, shoved her away brutally with my elbow and hip, and brought him down on the coverlet, holding him by the shoulders with an iron grip. Pressing my knees upon his convulsively jerking legs, I said to him in an iron voice that he dare not move, that he was to stay perfectly still; while Panna was upon me, grabbing at my shoulders, screaming something that sounded like damnation. "You are no mother, you are a monster, that's what you are! Had your father ever seen you like this . . . " The words fell meaningless on some frantically revolving disk of my mind, perhaps to be played over later.

It had been a matter of a few seconds only. Already his muscles were yielding under my fingers, his cries weakening, his eyes veiling with sleep. Gradually I began to slacken my grip, and all the while Panna was still screaming behind my back. "If this is the way you are, I've had enough of it. I don't wish ever, ever . . ." Then with some unintelligible gasps, she blindly rushed to the exit.

He was asleep. Sound asleep. I withdrew my hands from him, took a deep breath, staggered back to my feet, looked around. Where had Panna gone? Her heart! How could I subject her to such fits of fury? Was I not sorry for her? Was I not ashamed of myself? But I was not. I was not sorry for anybody—neither for her nor for myself. "There is a time for rejoicing and a time for weeping" —and this was the time for bringing one's ship into harbor. Nothing else concerned me. And these people around me, this crowd of beggars with their poverty, their squalor, the torturing struggles of their lives—I was not sorry for them either. They were simply other links in that eternal chain of human misery.

I had just fought bodily, as this mob would, shoving and screaming, and it was on this drafty, filthy floor, amid heaps of their trashy bundles that—if I never saw Igor again—there lay all that I had left: my son. But now I had to leave him alone and rush after Panna, find her. Her furies were as violent as her love: blinding. How could I tell she was not going to throw herself under a train? And did I have to be as drastic with her as I had been; was there no kinder way to get my end? Someone within me was asking this as I ran wildly from one end of the station to another, pushing my way through, unable to locate her. But I was still the same iron woman, intent on just one thing, finding her. All the rest within me would have to stay where it was, and where I couldn't see it.

"Freshening up" was one of those slang expressions born of communism and the civil war. ("To sit," for being imprisoned . . . "to take the elevator" or "be put to the wall," for being executed . . .) They "freshened us up with a few volleys," Serge Lorinov used to say; "We freshened them up with a howitzer."

And so was Panna freshening herself up out in the hurricane? I had searched all around and she was nowhere about the station, nowhere. The only place left was the platform. When I stuck my head out, the wind caught my hat, cut my breath; and as I fought with all my strength to open the door, I saw out there at the end of the deserted platform a lonely cone-shaped figure: Panna. Not another soul. She stood there hatless under the lamppost, holding to it for support. Her scarf had slipped off her head and its ends whirled and flapped above her like two imploring waving arms. But she herself stood rocklike.

I staggered toward her, holding to the wall, slipping over the icy platform, fighting the wind every inch of my way. "Panna, come back, come inside!" The wind was pushing my voice back into my throat, strangling me. "Come back, he's asleep, he's all right! I told you!" I came close now, frantically caught at the same lamppost; but she turned her back to me. I might as well not have been there. The cold was unbearable. Yes, she was committing slow suicide.

"Come back, come back inside, Panna, I *beseech* you! You'll die this way! Forgive me, forgive me for what I did, Panna!" My voice was breaking with the effort of speaking against the hurricane, against her rocklike stubbornness. But there she stood, turned into a stone pillar by her wrath at me, and her passion for my child.

I had to hurry and get back to him. Even if I had to leave her here freezing, I couldn't leave Bibik alone in the mob another minute. Moreover, if I remained here any longer, he might lose us both. I went back to him.

There she stood, motionless, holding on to the lamppost, "freshening up," until three o'clock in the morning, until the mercury eyes of an eastbound locomotive rushed at her from the wailing darkness. She joined me at the very last moment before boarding the train. Silently I lifted Bibik from the floor, put him in her arms, and took our two suitcases. Neither of us said a word.

THE RAGGED CROWD of Chinese, Russians, Mongols, and Koreans made furiously for the cars, lumped into one sticky, pushing, jostling, vociferous mass. Bibik had just awakened, and was hugging Panna's neck, his drowsy eyes darting around, curious and interested. Even at that moment of rush and struggle I could sense the tremendous current of tenderness that burst toward him from Panna, as she held him in her stiffened half-frozen hands; and now, as I fought my way across the platform, squeezing through the riotously pushing throng, the heavy suitcases knocking against my legs, the wind cutting my breath, I was clearly seeing myself in her place.

The fight was over. One was blind during a fight; one should be (or should one?). There was Panna—a lonely, childless woman, who had no rights over this boy, but to whom he was everything, her whole life. . . . Go back to Moscow, here is your ticket . . . that was what I had said. Yet there was no time to dwell on any feelings, hers or mine, regret or remorse. Squeezed in the boiling human lava, pushed and frantically pushing, I pressed my way toward the fourth-class car. Just to get inside, not to be left behind, not to lose each other—and they had to be taken by storm, those unreserved seats.

Junction 86. Tomorrow. My belt, the letters. Tomorrow: that fearful barrier that I still had to hurdle so as not to collapse into a black pit in which we would be buried alive; so that my son would not be left alone, a homeless waif amid frightful strangers, to roam the horrifying face of this earth.

THE NIGHT had been endless. So was the day, endless as the rice fields around, from which Bibik never took his eyes. It was astonishing, and a blessing, the way he never complained or asked for anything, not even a drink of water, but clung to the window standing upright for hours. This was a clear autumn day, and his gaze was lost in the distance, where the flat greenness of paddy fields was dotted with specks of yellow and navy blue—Chinese peasants in cone-shaped hats working knee-deep in the swampy soil.

We had not slept; we did not speak; we just sat there waiting and enduring it. And everyone around did just the same as we—sat there silent, enduring it all: the stench, the boredom, the discomfort, and one another, and life.

The train's rumbling kept repeating, repeating some sort of boring, senseless tale. No, I was not tired or sleepy—just in a stupor—when the sudden roar of the whistle overhead made me start. The humdrum rhythm of the wheels broke, turning into a fit of hoarse iron coughings. Lights began to flash in the blackness behind the windows; the train was jerking to a stop. But it had not stopped yet—not yet—it was still in motion when the doors at both ends of the car were flung open, and three men and two women, hatless, luggageless, darted in. At once everyone knew who they were, even before seeing soldiers appear at each end of the car, before hearing both doors being bolted. They looked neither like passengers nor like railroad officials, these beings. Not like people, but birds of prey.

The two women immediately rushed to our side of the car. One was flat-faced, pockmarked, her slits of eyes pushed up by bulging cheek-bones; the other had piercing dark eyes, shocks of henna-dyed hair hanging over a low strip of forehead, and a mouth full of gold teeth. These were beings that fed on carrion. The passengers stiffened, then shrank into their seats. But not Panna. Half-awake, she stared around, with shocked surprise, still unaware of what this was all about; that this was Junction 86.

"Get undressed, citizens!"

Against the dead hush that suddenly fell over the car, the voices of the searching party shrilled, hissed, and thundered. "Men over to that end—all women here!!" The pockmarked female was already beside me. "Starting with this here citizen." She pointed a blunt finger at my face. She was going to snatch Bibik away from me, but I swiftly handed him over to Panna.

"Get this off, citizen."

I started to slip off my jacket. Aunt Katya's face flashed before me, warning me about the belt. My jacket still hung from one shoulder. And suddenly: "Raise your arms." With a rapaciously expert movement, the woman put her cold hands under my armpits, making me shudder, went down my ribs as over the keys of an accordion, then up all around and inside my blouse, all the while breathing whiffs of boiled cabbage and stale tobacco into my face. In a fraction of a second her fingers would have been on my belt (what had I been hoping for, a miracle?)—had not her attention been distracted by the bulging inside pocket in my skirt. She caught at it. "Take off your skirt!"

I slipped my skirt down, handed it to the pockmarked woman, and stood there in my blouse and underskirt.

It was as though a whirlwind had been raised by these creatures. Some passengers were taking off their things, convulsively pulling at them, other opening their suitcases with shaking fingers; still others were already being searched as I was. Right next to me, the gold-toothed woman inspector was pulling the shoes off someone's white-stockinged feet.

The pockmarked one was still busy emptying the contents of my skirt pockets (an old sewing kit, a sandwich, a handkerchief, a scarf) and feeling with avid professional speed through the hem. As she tossed it away and was on the point of returning to my waist, I made a sharp withdrawing movement, sat down, jerked my feet, and convulsively hid them under the bench. Instantly she let go of the skirt and threw herself on her knees to make a greedy grab for my feet.

"There's nothing in my stockings," I said in a heavy and measured voice that clashed sharply with the nervousness I had just displayed. "Nothing."

In answer she gave a violent pull to one of my shoes, then the other, knocked them together and gave a fillip to each heel. In that fraction of a second when, disappointed at the sound they made, she was about to drop them to the floor, I held out my hand for them. My eyes pressing upon hers with all there was in me of determination not to be overpowered and crushed by her, I said with extra-courteous but incontrovertible finality:

"Thank you."

This thank-you fell between us like a great block of ice, glistening and slippery, at the very point when she was about to go up my legs and hips and to my waist. Unable to withstand the incongruity of whatever it was that had just taken place, confused and flustered by the overbearing politeness with which she had been dismissed by her own helpless prey, she wheeled sharply away from me. "Next one there! Take off your blouse."

I HELD Bibik in my lap. He was sound asleep. The train was rumbling on; it was night. Junction 86 was behind us. My head was drooping with exhaustion, my vertebrae were rubber, my muscles liquid, all strength gone out of me. The crab-woman had saved my life.

Panna was sitting across from me, swaying with sleepiness. People around were too tired to relax or to rejoice. From a far corner came a stifled sobbing of one of the women, whose husband had just been led away. The last moment before we had started from Junction 86, she had attempted to leave the train to run after her husband, but the guards pushed her inside; she fell. Now some women were crouching around her, crying with her.

Oh, my Lord, I was saying to myself, my heart breaking for this woman, my limbs trembling. Why is it I who am being saved again and again? Who is guarding me, who is intervening for me before You? For *me*, hard, cruel, undeserving as I am?

A few more hours and we would be in Manchuria. Panna opened her eyes and they met mine. She made an effort to wake up.

"Give him to me," she said, leaning over to take Bibik. There was gentleness in her voice now.

"No, thank you," I said. "Catch some sleep yourself." Poor, exhausted Panna.

"Tell me," again she leaned toward me, quite awake now, a spark lighting in her little hazel eyes, "is everything all right now?" She spoke as if nothing had ever happened between us, as if she had never stood freezing herself on the platform the night before in the murderous gale, to spite me, to punish me—as if she had never been hating me, damning me, and then ignoring me for twenty-four hours.

"Tell me, will there be any more searches?" Her voice was warm with eager interest.

"No, there won't, Panna. We have crossed the border."

"How afraid I was that they would discover your belt. Thank God they didn't." She crossed herself and added, "It's your father helping you again." And then, with the same gaze with which she usually looked at Bibik, the same tremulous current of tenderness and concern bursting toward me, turning the ice within me and all the unshed tears into a warm, rushing river, she said, "Poor Nita."

"We have crossed the border," I had just told her. And now, suddenly realizing what this meant, I shut my eyes and pressed Bibik close to myself.

But this could not be! It could not be true that we had crossed the border. . . .

29

THE SUDDEN URGE to rip my blue housecoat to pieces, rip off all the chinchilla trimming, and make something new out of it, something stylish—shorter skirt, lower waistline—this urge had probably been called up by the elegance of the hotel where we stopped at Station Manchuli, and perhaps by the jar of honey and the cheese.

It was late morning when we arrived at the hotel. As soon as we completed some necessary formalities at the office, I began to give Bibik a sponge bath, ecstatic over having hot running water in the room; while Panna slipped into her coat with a rather cryptic "I'll be back soon." When she reappeared, she stopped by the door, holding something behind her back.

"Guess what I bought!" Her voice tingled with mysterious excitement. I couldn't guess, but I had just exchanged my remaining forty million Soviet rubles for thirty Chinese dollars, and she had taken some of it with her.

"Look!" From behind her back she produced a package, and taking out a square of butter, put it on the table with a hearty bang. "I bought it, simply *bought* it! This . . . and this . . ." Next came out the jar of honey. "And . . . ," then a pause, a long intriguing pause, before she displayed the rest of her purchases: a piece of cheese, sugar, French rolls, tea, and milk. "I bought it all, just like that! Saw it in the window, went in and asked, 'May I have some butter?'" And now she spoke with the suave politeness with which she must have been conversing with the grocer a moment ago, reliving the delight of the decorum that she had just found out still existed in human relationships.

There was fresh snow on the street and roofs outside—the first snow, probably—and sunshine. We were some thirty miles away from the Soviet border, and our first meal had the elating flavor of freedom and truth. For this food was bought from neither thieves nor speculators, nor eaten stealthily behind locked doors. It was not the kind for which the farmer, the buyer, and the seller could be thrown into prison or a concentration camp, or be killed. Somewhere behind this honey and butter there loomed a tranquil bee garden, birds and bees whirling about in the flower-scented air, where armed men did not snatch the fruit of his toil out of the farmer's hands.

It was after this glorious lunch and after putting Bibik down for his nap that I began to rip my blue housecoat to pieces. If such a miracle was possible that you could buy anything in the stores, why couldn't it happen that I would see Igor again?

Yes, Igor could be in Harbin by now; and, if so, I might see him in a few days, three or even two! Because the train that was to take us to Harbin would be here tomorrow morning, and then some thirty hours more . . . ! Once in Harbin I would find him through Liza Molsov. Of course it was May when he wrote to me, four months ago. Still, he must be keeping in touch with Liza. Why, I could wire her from here! I had enough money left for a wire. I had memorized her address. I would say "Arriving tomorrow please notify Igor." No, no: "Notify Igor if possible."

I could see him again in two days! The glow of this revelation was dazzling. So I must never have really believed in it, not until this moment. Igor might even be meeting me at the station, and as I spun this fantastic dream I had a vision of myself alighting from the train, saw myself through his eyes—this baggy skirt, the bedraggled jacket. The only nice things I had managed to squeeze into my one suitcase at the expense of many other indispensable items were a blouse of black Chantilly and a chinchilla-trimmed blue housecoat made for my wedding and associated with most precious memories. Suddenly inspired to shorten it and turn it into a dress, I seized Panna's scissors and began to rip off the fur that trimmed the sleeves and skirt. In a few minutes long strips of chinchilla lay like a nest of snakes on the floor, the blue coat itself turning into a featherless chicken.

Panna was washing the dishes, a hidden smile still lingering on her lips. She didn't say, "Don't cut the threads, pull them out." She didn't even say, "Why spoil a good thing? You'll never put it together again— don't I know you—"

Panna was still drying the cups when there was a sudden short knock at the door. The scissors in my hand stopped. Who could that be? I was four thousand miles away from home. No one knew me here. Quickly I began to pick up the fur snakes from the floor and toss them on the foot of my bed. Perhaps someone of the hotel personnel. What did they want? My passport? They had that already. Any chance of anyone turning me back? I was moving toward the door when Panna, still full of worldliness, emitted a cordial "Come in," and the door opened.

A tall, clean-shaven man in tails stood on the threshold with a pad and pencil and some sheets of paper under his arm. "Dinner between five and eight, madame. Do you ladies wish to have a table reserved for the three of you?" And with the same movement as Panna's grocer's, he presented the menu. "Or would you like to have dinner in your room?"

The consideration, the courteousness! I took the menu. "Soupe consommé, Soupe à l'oignon," it read. "Boeuf Stroganoff, Veau Bourguignon." Oh, dear, it even rhymed!

Were we coming to dinner? And before I had time to answer, Panna said with the same queenly graciousness, "Yes, reserve a table for Madame Volotskoy. A table for three. We shall be there at six."

So there still might be such things in life as happy endings, I thought, returning to my blue housecoat with even greater destructive energy. There might even be such a thing as having a husband, seeing him again, saying to him, "I'm tired, Igor, tired of being brave, of fighting every inch of the way. Will you please lend me your shoulder, so I may have a good cry on it. About . . . everything. About life."

Oh, for the relief of indulging oneself in helpless feminine tears.

I HAD JUST sent the telegram to Liza Molsov from the post office next door and was reentering the lobby when a smart-looking young woman in a knee-length coat, hat sitting low over her eyebrows, and with crimson lips, clicked her French heels and passed me on her way to the front door. A sandy-haired young man who was sprawling in one of the armchairs quickly lowered his newspaper. Craning his neck, he followed the woman with his eyes, but the glass door had already slammed behind her, and his glance mechanically shifted to a moving and yet nonexistent object: myself. He was about to cross his long, lanky legs in worn officer's boots and resume his reading when something, apparently, prompted him to take another look at me. His manner, the forward movement of his shoulders registered sudden questioning, even worried preoccupation. Yes, yes indeed, I was just from Soviet Russia, a ghost from over there, my twelve-million-ruble government shoes—new only a month ago—already falling apart, my black stockings a heavy cotton.

All the while as I walked up the stairs and down the corridor I was aware of steps following me. Hardly had I reached my door when the same long-legged young man whom I had seen in the lobby was beside me.

"Excuse me, madame," he looked embarrassed, but there was also curiosity in his manner. "May I speak to you a moment?" I turned to him, my face a blank. A spy, I thought. It may not be true that they can't arrest us here and send us back.

"I'm sorry to trouble you, madame, but may I ask you—are you just straight from Russia?"

"I am."

"Forgive me for sounding inquisitive, but where from? Moscow?" He had fast-blinking little blue eyes, a thin face, a weak, nervously smiling mouth. "So seldom can one learn anything of what is going on there, so few people are allowed to come through, except for their own party people, that I decided to take the liberty . . . I saw you down there in the lobby and could tell at once . . ." he was blinking faster and faster, ". . . that you were from Russia. We are all so hungry for news, so may I ask you, how are things back there? I am an ex–White army officer, Captain Nevinov. I was with the staff of the Third Army until a few months ago when I fell sick. Captain Nikolay Nevinov," he repeated and clicked his heels.

I thought: a spy planted here by the border to see who is coming through from Russia. No, simply a man who is trying to pick up an acquaintance with any woman for nothing better to do, and, judging by his emaciated face and worn military breeches, a former White officer.

It was becoming embarrassing to keep him standing outside, so I asked him in. Bibik had just awakened and was sitting up in bed, and Panna was rinsing something in the washbasin. For a moment Captain Nevinov hesitated on the threshold as if taken aback by the domesticity of the scene, but then produced a strained smile, bowed to Panna, and sat down.

"When I saw you in the office, madame, I heard the manager address you as Madame Volotskoy, a name I happened to know, you see." As he said this, for some reason his face expressed anxious concern. Unable to understand what was on his mind, I stared at him blankly, waiting for him to go on. "So I thought I'd better introduce myself to you." He looked down and sighed, heavily. "I knew Colonel Igor Volotskoy of the Tamborsk Dragoons . . . any relation? I thought, perhaps, your husband . . . ?"

How did I get into this trap, I was asking myself, too perturbed to probe into the significance of that mournful sigh. So now this captain knew who I was, that I was on my way to join my husband, while my passport said otherwise. Why didn't I tell him that Igor was just a distant relative of mine, or my ex-husband, I thought aghast. But too late now.

"When was it?" I asked him tensely.

"About two years ago at the Staff of the Active Army. This was when his division joined Ataman Semenov's forces. I mean, when the Kolchak troops came under Semenov's control."

"My husband has never been with Ataman Semenov," I said sharply.

"Oh, yes, they all were. All those of the Kolchak army who survived the crossing of Lake Baikal came automatically under the command of Ataman Semenov."

Captain Nevinov seemed to have stepped upon more familiar ground; the nervous smiling and blinking became less noticeable. "You probably know that there was a succession of newly formed anti-Red governments after the fall, or rather after the tragic betrayal and death of Admiral Kolchak. So they fought—I mean, we all fought under these temporary governments to the bitter end. And I *mean* bitter."

I wanted to ask him when he had seen Igor last, where the regiment or what was left of it was now, but for some reason I didn't. Instead I said something vague about being on my way to Harbin to make my home with my relatives.

Captain Nevinov nodded slowly and resignedly. When he looked at me his light blue eyes filled with an odd sort of overdone commiseration. Recoiling from whatever this man had on his mind, my thoughts darted again down the familiar blind alley of suspiciousness, there frantically to toss between apprehension and self-reproach. What a torture, how debasing this constant necessity of deceiving so as not to be deceived. How much one would rather sometimes tell the truth and risk one's life, instead of dissimulating and feeling dehumanized. But, after all, I was no longer in the USSR. I was out in the free world again! And suddenly I heard myself declare, looking straight into the man's eyes:

"I told you that I was planning to make my home with my relatives in Harbin, but I also hope to join my husband someday later."

Captain Nevinov's little eyes opened as wide as they would go. His lids once again set in feverish motion, he cried, "How do you mean? Is he— have you heard from him recently?"

"Yes, I have," I said in an icy voice, not knowing how and why another lie came to my lips just as I had decided to speak the truth, or why this challenging coldness.

"Oh, what wonderful, wonderful news! Just to think that I was about to express my sympathy to you, madame!" I could see that he was trying hard to look happily excited. "So he has recovered! Imagine how false rumors will spread! I knew that he was badly wounded in June or July, and

I took it for granted . . . But this was three months ago and you have heard from him since! He must have fully recovered! What marvelous news—what a miracle! Now that I know this I can tell you frankly that the rumor had been . . . pretty sad."

June or July. My last news from Igor was in May, and this was the end of October.

I looked at Panna. Her bewildered eyes were darting from the man's face to mine and to his again. I saw Bibik intently watch the man. I saw Russia, Dimitri, Aunt Katya, and all those I had left there, and Junction 86 between us; I suddenly saw that for which I had waited, and at which I hadn't dared raise my eyes. *Igor!*

"Who told you?" my cold voice asked, the voice of the same hard-boiled woman who had fought with Panna at the station the other night.

"There were such reports," and he began to tell me something of which I caught only disconnected fragments. ". . . Outnumbered ten to one . . . the White army fought every inch of the way . . . constantly counterattacking . . . it was in one of these counterattacks near Spassk that Colonel Volotskoy . . . well, now that I know that he's all right I can tell you: the rumor was that he had died of wounds, posthumously awarded the Cross of St. George. But why speak of it now? Thank God for his recovery, Madame Volotskoy." And as I rose and stood before him rigid and silent, he jumped up to take leave of me with shallow, disconcerted bows. He left.

"Posthumously . . ."

The heap of chinchilla had again slipped to the floor. Many miles, it seemed to me, were between me and the bed where Bibik lay in his little sleeveless shirt, kicking the blanket with his bare legs. I picked up the chinchilla. "Life of mine," I recited silently, "have I but dreamed thee out?" And wasn't it exactly as it should be, as it had been with almost every woman I knew?

There I stood in the middle of the room, the crushing weight in my heart pushing me down, down to the floor. Panna was staring at me, pity and dread in her eyes. Dread of my future, of my grief, above all dread of Bibik's future. It was also an expectant stare, which told me that I must immediately do that for which she was waiting: I covered my face with my hands and wept.

WE CANCELED our dinner reservations that night. We were not hungry. We hardly knew what to say to each other and mostly tried to talk with Bibik, who for some reason stayed awake especially late that night. It was after ten and he had just gone to sleep, when a bellboy was at the door with the telegram from Liza for which I had been waiting, although not expecting it until morning.

I tore the envelope open with frenzied haste. I wanted quickly to read the awful words that were to kill all hope in me for good. Dimly conscious of the bellboy's expectantly lingering in the doorway, I tossed him a small coin and a nervous thank-you and closed the door.

But what did this mean? Why didn't Liza come right out with it? Was she trying to spare me? "Happy shall meet you at station. Stop. Igor temporarily away in China." Was she preparing me slowly for the blow, so as to let me reach Harbin in a comparatively calm state of mind?

In a wooden voice I read the message to Panna.

"That means the officer told you a lie," she cried. "It was all a lie!"

"Oh, but Panna! Liza doesn't want to say it in a telegram."

"And I'm telling you Igor is *alive*! He is alive! This officer didn't know a thing, I knew he did not! I could see what kind of person he was from the way he looked at me when he entered—as if I were one too many. It's all a lie!"

"But Panna! He even knew where and when! At Spassk, he said, in July. *Why* should he have told me such a dreadful thing if it wasn't true?"

"Because he was all out to start an acquaintance with you, and when he saw that you didn't like him he was hurt and wanted to hurt you back."

"Oh, Panna!" This I thought was one of her "monstrosities," however well meant this time. And yet, perhaps, I too had not entirely believed the man. Perhaps I believed nothing, neither what he had said, nor what this telegram was saying. The fog of ignorance had by now thickened in me to a density in which everything, both my anxiety and my hope, was a blur. But perhaps Panna knew the truth, Panna the pessimist, the alarmist. She must have been positive that all was well, because the warmth of life was now filling her voice and flowing into the decisive movements with which she began to remove Bibik's things from the table, and with which she rang for hot water for our tea. Perhaps I believed her and the telegram more than I thought I did, for when she filled my cup a little later, and she herself spread butter and honey on my bread, as she would for Bibik, I ate it.

30

IGOR HAD NEVER been wounded. It was a Colonel Volginsky, not Volotskoy, who was wounded in July, so the two names must have been confused. This was what Liza told me as she met us at the Harbin station.

"Who is the idiot who told you that terrible story about Igor? Igor is all right, at least there has been no bad news from Hung-Chung where the regiment was last. I'll tell you all about it in a moment, as soon as we settle down in the cab; and then you'll tell me all about yourself and Moscow."

As she led us through the churning crowd to her cab, she said that Bibik was a dear and looked like her mother's family; that I was too thin for my height, and that she didn't like the sound of Panna's cough. Tall and slender in her suit and beret of greenish tweed, she looked striking. "I'm taking you to my house; you can stay with me as long as you like," she said. "It's overcrowded, a dormitory for refugees really, but comfortable enough." Then, sharply, "Now, Nita, how are you wearing your hat? Pull it down over your eyes—that's the way they're wearing them now."

My brother Alik, even as a child, had the knack of characterizing people by just a few words that he had once heard them say. So he had always referred to Cousin Liza Molsov as Cousin "As-You-Surely-Know." This was the beginning of a sentence with which Liza had once answered my request to tell about her youth—a request that I had often made to people at the least opportune moments, its impetuosity usually causing them to respond with astonished and reluctant counter-questions. But Liza had taken it in her stride. "As you surely know," she had replied in her forceful, matter-of-fact style, and without the slightest hesitation, "in my younger days I was a dazzling beauty!"

Indeed, in her day she had been one of the great beauties of Petersburg; her rose-petal skin, cool emerald eyes, and the cruel fold of her shapely lips quite justified all the reputed attention of the predatory Don Juans of the prewar cosmopolitan "grand monde." With the years, however, her looks had already begun to acquire a sharpness and dryness that—together with her low voice and abrupt manner of speaking—gave her a witchlike sort of beauty. Still, as I was getting off the train and saw her in the throng of Chinese and Russians (the latter either sad-faced refugees or latest-fashion Harbinians), her figure clad in English tweeds stood out, statuesque and regal.

It was a clear but chilly day in October. She led us through the crowd toward a cab driven by a Chinese. As we drove on she told me that Panna would have a tiny room in the back of the house, the flat being terribly overcrowded. "I hope you won't mind being four in a room. . . . Yes, I'll tell you about Igor and the regiment in a moment. . . . Now see here, Nita! You'll have to shorten that coat of yours—it's much too long."

Squeezed three on a seat, Bibik on my lap, we drove down a broad street, the kind you would see at the outskirts of many a city in the world. Nondescript wooden houses, tall trees with a few yellow leaves clinging here and there to bare branches; a few leisurely walking, shabbily dressed pedestrians, an occasional cab rolling by. Judging by the manner in which Bibik's head moved right and left, I could tell that he was devouring it all, while all that I saw was a blurred backdrop to the visions that burst in my mind with Liza's every word. She was telling me, in her trenchant way of speaking, about the fate of the Tamborsk Dragoons, once in a while interrupting herself to point out some place we were passing.

I understood that about seventy thousand men—rather, the few who had been left of the White army—were at the moment making their way through the mountainous, wildest part of China, headed from Hung-Chung to the city of Kirin, Manchuria. The Soviets had been exerting all kinds of pressure upon the Chinese government to surrender those troops to them, but this time our allies came up to scratch and prevailed upon the Chinese to intern them in Manchuria.

"Kirin is only about ten hours away from here by train," Liza was saying, "so once they get there Igor will be able to write to you. But not until then, of course. Do you know where Hung-Chung is? No? The Maritime Provinces? Well, anyway, now that the Reds have occupied them our men have to take a roundabout route." With her narrow gloved hand she drew a downward line and then a crooked one in the air. "Down to Korea, crossing the Yalu River. Do you remember your geography at all? Well, never mind. It's wild, Hunghutze-infested country. No roads, just mountain trails. No post offices, naturally. No communication with the outside world."

"Who are the Hunghutze? I have only a vague idea," I said, to show her that I still could speak.

"What's there to be vague about? Just gangs of robbers. But our men are still armed, much better than the Hunghutze, and they have their horses. I have no doubt they'll make their way to Kirin quite safely. And knowing Igor I'm sure that, once there, he will manage to escape and join you as soon as he can. So don't give up hope."

"I'm not giving up hope," I said in a hard voice, instinctively matching her straight-from-the-shoulder manner, but my spirits sagging under the pressure of doubts.

Her fine profile under the tweed beret nodded approval. "I know you aren't. You are your mother's daughter. She was a brick. But when Igor arrives, don't meet him with those black cotton stockings on."

Panna had been coughing all through the night on the train and was now getting worse, her face burning; to any question of how she felt she responded by stubborn negative shakes of the head. The pair of Mongolian cab horses, small and iron-strong, trotted fast; buildings around were becoming taller, the pavement smoother, the traffic livelier. The passersby, well dressed or bedraggled, walked with a carefree air, chatting along the way, dropping into shops. It had been years since I had seen a free city. I wanted to enjoy the sight and feel of it, but instead I felt a tremendous void opening within and around me. It was as if another section of my life had just snapped off, severing the current in the thin electric wire that connected the broken fragments of my being.

As we reached the cathedral square of Noviy Gorod where Liza lived (unlike thousands of penniless refugees who dwelt in dingy lodgings in half-Chinese, half-Russian Modiagow), she had told me about the people who were staying with her—cousins and friends—and also about the beautiful young woman, her tenant, who had eyes of a frightened gazelle, shining auburn hair, and a grandmother in Paris who sent her a great deal of money.

"Without her I would have been destitute long ago, considering all the sick and unemployed men I've been taking care of. My flat is still crowded with them. You'll see."

It appeared that the beautiful tenant was paying Liza an exorbitant rent just for the privilege of being under her roof. "She would rather have no privacy, be the fourth in a room, but under my wing," Liza said. Then she interrupted herself to indicate a smart-looking restaurant with the sign "Des Gourmets" in gold lettering across the windows.

"One of the officers of the Kolchak convoy opened this place two months ago, and he is already on the way to bankruptcy. His hungry friends come to eat and drink, compliment him, shake his hand in gratitude, all of them jobless, taking it for granted that nowadays every-thing has to be shared. What can he do?"

There were several questions yet to be asked while I had listened to Liza. As she fell silent, I said, "Is it true that General Kostin lost his leg? Where is he now?"

"Oh, he won't give up! Became a White partisan in the employ of some Chinese anti-Communist warlord, artificial leg and all."

This sounded too exotic. A warlord!

"And his wife, Masha?"

"Oh, I heard from her recently. She is still in Kansk and soon coming here. At least it looks as if she is on the point of getting permission to leave the Soviets, although I don't know how she can manage that, living under an assumed name. She hopes to make it to America. Both her father and mother are already in San Francisco," Liza continued matter-of-factly, "and she hopes to join them there. You see, whoever can procure some money for their passage goes to America. There is no work for anybody here, men especially. None. You can't compete with the coolies."

Masha might come here! Yet she might not. I was still afraid to rejoice at any good news. Moreover, I still had a question in my mind that worried me. "Is it true that Serge Lorinov died two years ago in the Gobi Desert?"

"That's what they say. But who knows?" She shrugged. And then: "As to Igor, my premonition is that he will be here in no time. No later than Christmas, anyway. You'll see."

"NO! THEY NO LONGER roll the edges, they bind them. Just a narrow binding around the neckline and armholes."

"I still prefer a French roll, or an edging of tulle maline."

"Heavens, no! Never on a printed silk."

"Oh, but it gives such an ethereal finish. . . ."

I had just given Bibik his bath, had taken one myself, and was sitting on the edge of one of the four beds that lined Liza's former living room, unpacking my suitcases. Bibik was on the floor, looking through an American magazine. Liza's flat was spacious, filled with light, and, as she had told me, overcrowded. Through the door to the adjoining dining room I could see a Chinese boy setting the table for our lunch and the deck of a grand piano in the corner. Two girls, beautifully dressed, both about my own age, who had been carrying on the discussion about tulle maline, sat on a sofa by the window. One of them was Liza's tenant, the "frightened gazelle," the other a friend of hers, a pretty bobbed-haired blonde. The tenant really did have enormous dark eyes, but the arched eyebrows over them gave her face more of a questioning than a frightened expression. Every now and then she would turn to me smiling, as if asking my opinion on the subject of their conversation, yet at the same time a shade of condoning understanding implied that I obviously couldn't have such an opinion; although I was an intruder on her chat, she still was polite enough to include me in it by her smiles. But something had happened to my lips; they seemed paralyzed, their edges refused to curve upward.

I went on unpacking my things, trying to look absorbed in this. The belt with my jewelry and the letters lay on the bed, the urgency of all they held crying out to me. I was waiting for some opening in the young women's dialogue to ask if they knew anything about the persons to whom the letters were addressed. Finally the pretty blonde came around to ask me about my trip, and how I managed to obtain permission to leave Moscow. "We know that they don't let anyone out," she said, "and life in Soviet Russia is horrible. Isn't it?"

"Certainly too horrible even to imagine for anyone who had not experienced it," I said, "but—not all of it is awful; there is also—"

"Oh?" The gazelle's eyebrows flew up. "Is there anything—anything good? What, for instance?"

"What I mean," I said, "is that under the Bolshevik rule the morally weak in Russia turned into criminals, traitors, speculators, spies; but the stronger ones . . . became like saints—and their self-abnegation, their compassion, has deepened the tonality of life there."

Then the gazelle frowned, fluttered her long lashes, and nodded in swift dismissing acquiescence, probably thinking that females in black cotton stockings have nothing to resort to but big words. Almost at once she very wisely decided to direct the conversation into fresh channels, and began to talk about Bibik. She had a captivating way of speaking, affected perhaps, but quite her own just the same. She would hesitate between sentences, dividing them by little gasps, as if she were walking over thin ice, feeling it with her toe before trusting her foot on it, then a few running steps across, and another moment of hesitation.

"Bobby," she said, turning to Bibik. "May I call you Bobby? I once knew a nice little boy whose name was Bobby." And the look she gave her friend made me feel that Bobby was not such a little boy at all. "Bobby, won't you and your Mamma come with me to a nice little place where they have b-i-g cups of chocolate and cream puffs and éclairs? Will you come with me?"

Bibik stopped turning the pages and looked at her as much as to ask, "Why do you talk like a baby?" He had encountered all sorts of people, hundreds of people, but this was something new. And in his ignorance of what an éclair or cream puff might be, he looked to me for help. I told him to thank her.

THE SUN was streaming through the dining-room window, a Chinese boy was serving lunch, the smell of fried chicken and cucumber salad breathed into the room. About ten of us were seated at the oval table, several of Liza's relatives whom I knew slightly from Tamborsk: Liza's older cousin with a serious noble face and a black patch over one eye; a young clear-skinned but tight-lipped nephew of hers. They were pleasant to Bibik and me, offering us things, inquiring about Moscow and about our family. However, everything around me was sliding past like a movie, the middle of which I had missed and the beginning of which didn't fit together with the end. The rhythm of the train was still rumbling and beating in me, the explosions of Panna's coughing reached me from that little back room where she now lay, refusing to eat or speak; Igor with his men was riding along the edge of some cliff, skirting a mountain behind which a gang of Hunghutzes lay in wait to attack him; Serge Lorinov lay dying on the sand of the Gobi Desert. Some of the conversation in which I at first dutifully took part was becoming more and more difficult for me to follow as it drifted to local themes. When chocolate pudding appeared ("We don't usually have dessert, this is especially for your Bibik") I no longer could make head or tail of what I heard. Something about someone's third husband who was possibly a spy planted by Communists—or was it she who was a spy? Because the other day at the races . . . and where was he—or she—getting all that money for gambling anyway? . . . But once in a while there would flash a reference to something so striking that I had to stop eating and remorselessly interrupt the speaker by asking him or her to repeat what had just been said. Who? Baroness Zede's son? You mean Valery, her last son, has committed suicide? Just recently? Here in Harbin? Oh, why?

"Naturally we can't ask her, but she knows why. It's even possible that he told her the whole thing before killing himself. Oh no, it's clear that the Moscow Cheka, after condemning him to death, gave him a reprieve and had sent him to Harbin on the condition that he would report on us all."

"And he thought that once here he would be able to escape from them?"

". . . but of course they watched him day and night."

"To think he sat here with us, drinking and laughing with that horror on his mind all the time! But I'm sure that he never reported."

"Of course he never did, and when they lost patience, well, then he had to shoot himself."

They also spoke of So-and-so who was drinking himself to death, because after the five years during which he had been separated from his wife by the civil war he learned that she had married someone else. It was usually the other way around, of course; it was the husbands who married and the wives who suffered. Then the gazelle, who somehow was managing all the time to direct the conversation along these channels, her reluctant and soft voice notwithstanding, told us the story of a marvelous woman whom I was to meet one of these days, who had come recently from Omsk with her eight-year-old boy. Her husband was here and in order to join him she had fictitiously married a German prisoner of war, an old doctor who was being repatriated to Berlin. With him she had traveled to Berlin and then by herself crossed the Atlantic, to the United States, the Pacific, and China to arrive in Harbin absolutely penniless and hungry in the middle of the night. She couldn't hire a cab; she and the boy had to walk from the railroad station to the address in Modiagow given by her husband six months before.

"At the time, mind you," Liza raised her voice over the gazelle's, "he had begged her to come. She finally got there. She rang the bell, she knocked. No answer. There had been a light inside but it went out just as she rang. Finally the landlord, provoked by the noise, opened the door. When he produced that scoundrel, the woman's husband, it turned out that there was no place for her either in his room or in his bed. So she turned around and walked away blindly—"

"What about her son?"

"She took him with her, of course, but you can imagine . . ."

I had had Oksana on my mind all the while, reluctant to ask if anyone knew anything about her, afraid to hear of yet another tragic ending. So when I was astonished to hear myself say, "I had a very dear friend, Oksana Belov, do any of you know anything about her?"

No they did not, and Liza's cousin, the one with the black patch over the eye, said with a heavy sigh, "We know nothing about the fates of so many of our dearest friends who have simply vanished. Who knows: perhaps someday they will reappear. And Liza interrupted, "Now, Nita, you probably haven't had any real coffee for years, have you? I saved my best mocha for you."

I appreciated her thoughtfulness and thanked her. I drank the coffee.

How much Liza had done for us already in that single morning, at the expense of her own comfort and convenience! On top of all else she had called a doctor for Panna. He diagnosed pneumonia. So now poor Panna had that very thing for which she had been asking, when she had stood in the gale at the Chita station—but which, of course, she no longer wanted. (Was I to blame? Probably.) And Liza intended to do even more: to show me the town the next day. She said that Harbin was rapidly growing from a provincial frontier town into an international city, that some of the stores could compete with Paris. She would also take Bibik and me tomorrow to those tantalizing coffee shops of which the gazelle had already spoken, where the pastry was out of this world.

But something in me had to be put in order. Too many unmixable ingredients were churning in me, making me slightly seasick, and I had to do something about it, pour some antidote into that mixture.

So later, after supper, when all of them were lingering over wine-glasses and the conversation was growing noisier with every moment, and Panna—given some sedative—had fallen asleep, I excused myself. I put Bibik to bed, sat down beside him, and began to read to him out of his book about some sort of fox. There was a nightstand between our beds and a small lamp under a low lampshade. I read about the fox in a slow mysterious voice, my hand on his wrist. I had shut the door, and he and I were in a warm circle of our own life; and as soon as Panna was well I would find some room, no matter where, no matter what kind, and be on my own.

So was I really grateful to Liza or grossly ungrateful? All I knew was that the blend of her world and mine, for some reason, was an impossible concoction.

TWO MONTHS had elapsed since I came to Harbin, six weeks already since Panna had recovered and I had moved from Liza's. And there had been no letters from Igor as yet; only rumors. My urge to tear myself from the Liza-gazelle aura had been so intense and uncompromising that I had taken the first place I could afford—a corner in a kitchen in Modiagow (for which I was to pay three Japanese yen a week), in the flat of some Russian refugees as destitute as myself. If Panna was angry with me for having found nothing better, she also had been unhappy and lonely in Liza's back room; so sleeping under the kitchen table on top of which slept Bibik, with me on the floor beside her, was actually a welcome change.

My haunting worry was whether and when Igor would make it to

Harbin. Somehow minor problems, such as the fact that my money had all but trickled away, did not bother me in the least. The time to worry about money would come only after my very last penny had gone, not before. Unfortunately, if my confidence in God provided this enviable serenity of spirit for me, it did exactly the reverse for Panna.

One morning when the landlady was away I installed myself by her front window to wait for the postman, in the meantime teaching Bibik French words for whatever we saw before us in the street. This was still the end of November, the window was open, the sun shone on the last yellow leaves of the maple tree by the Chinese grocery across the street. "*Un arbre . . . la rue . . . le cheval . . .*" Bibik was quick to pick up words. "*. . . Un chinois . . . la poussière . . .*" I was about to start on houses when Panna came up from the kitchen: "Give me some money, I'm going to the grocery."

Her voice vibrated with an oncoming storm. Readily I snatched my purse from my skirt pocket, opened it, poured my remaining small change down on her palm. "Seventeen cents, Panna. That will be plenty for today if you buy some potatoes and milk."

"And what about tomorrow?" There was a hysterical note in her voice.

"Tomorrow, when our last cent is gone, something will happen. Perhaps I shall sell some of my remaining jewelry."

"And who is it that will sell your jewelry for you? In the meantime your child can go hungry. Is that it?"

"Oh, Panna, I told you before that such is my conviction, my faith: as long as we don't jerk things out of God's hands by worry and trust Him implicitly, He will take care of everything."

It never occurred to me to think of what this kind of dialogue might do to Panna's battered nervous system, to her heart. She took the money. She told me what she thought of me and what God must think of my crazy ideas. She slammed the door. And there she was now, crossing the street, my poor Panna who despised me.

Just as I saw the grocery door close on her, my friend the postman appeared before the window, a good-natured humorous smirk on his round Russian face. "Is this what you have been waiting for, lady?" He handed me a letter.

No, it was not what I had been waiting for. But it was a fat envelope with Japanese stamps on it, addressed to Liza and readdressed to me. I immediately recognized the handwriting of my cousin Natasha, Paul Teolin's sister.

Before I could begin to read the letter, before I could understand how my cousin could have reached me (the habit of being cut off from everybody and everything had made the Teolins' existence in Japan seem utterly unreal to me), I had to bend down and pick up something that dropped from the envelope and lay on the floor: a fifty-yen bill.

In one glance I scanned the first page: "Liza had written to us that you were with her . . . we are excited . . . hope that Igor . . . not that we can do much, but do let us know."

I had not noticed how Panna had crossed the street back to our house. I saw her only when she entered the room. In silent contempt she put two cents of change on the windowsill beside me.

"And this is for tomorrow," I said quietly, and put the fifty yen into her hand.

VERY SOON some gullible friends of my landlady, whom I had informed with rather imposing casualness of my intention to give lessons in English, brought me my first pupil, a once wealthy grocer, now a refugee preparing to emigrate to the United States. He was a huge man with a gray beard and the portly bearing of a prime minister who could not pay more than twenty-five cents for an hour's lesson (a Chinese dollar was the minimum current rate), and who during that whole twenty-five cents' worth stared at me with glazed blue-enamel eyes from which every word of mine rebounded intact.

But through him came another America-bound pupil and yet others, evidently attracted by the cheapness of my services. This meant that as I taught the first lessons of a popular English primer I desperately raced through the following ones at night to keep at least one jump ahead of my rapidly multiplying students.

There were many other things I had to do in Harbin and they were not easy: to obtain a residence certificate for Panna and myself, for which I had to get references; above all, to get a permit from the Chinese authorities for Igor to stay in Harbin, and some identification papers for him, should he suddenly appear. "You must have this permit on hand, *or else*," I had been told. Everyone knew too well what this *or else* meant. The Soviet Consulate in Harbin was a most wide-awake organization and had all sorts of ways and means of getting hold of stateless newcomers.

Christmas was near and there were rumors that our White troops were getting close to Kirin, now fighting the Hunghutzes, now peacefully negotiating with them for rice and bread, bartering their arms (which they were to surrender anyway as soon as interned), but withholding the ammunition that went with these arms. And there were rumors that snowless frosts and storms in the mountains were terrible, the men's clothing inadequate. The depth of China. There it was—a backdrop to all I did, all I thought. A winding mountain trail, the wind—Igor and his men—the former Tamborsk regiment filing through the frozen dust that whipped their faces, filled their lungs. I could see their exhausted horses, their tattered uniforms, the same in which they had left Tamborsk five years before. Five years of homelessness, of fighting, without rest, without hope . . . five years of sacrifice and heroism.

BUT IGOR did escape. Although there was the possibility that any day he could be sent to Junction 86 through a sudden change of agreement between the Chinese and the Soviets, he could also escape and appear here any time. Should he come in the middle of the night, I would awaken and run out to meet him. It would be even better should he come in the middle of the night. He wouldn't see all at once how I had changed.

But I was living in a free world. Except for Liza, who had inherited some insignificant sum of money from a relative in France, the refugees lived like paupers; however, food was so cheap it was impossible to starve. No constant fear of arrest, no Black Ravens in the street and no more crowds of half-dead people in the marketplace with their last possessions in their outstretched hands. No endless lines of prison gates. I had Bibik, I had friends—congenial or not, they were kind and helpful. Through the letters I had brought with me for unknown persons I had soon established new ties.

Sometime before Christmas, Liza let me know about a good large room that was for rent, also in Modiagow and also in a Russian family, a big room in which there were four pieces of furniture—a cot, a couch, a crib, and a table. She said I must grab the room immediately, and I did. So I now had that also. We even had a tree at Christmas, a tiny one, for which I bought a few candles; as I could not afford anything else, I decorated it with my remaining jewelry, for which there was no market in Harbin at the moment.

Indeed, compared to the past in the USSR, I was having an easy time. Only once did I give way to an onflow of desperate dejection. This was soon after New Year's Day when Liza, who still felt she was my guardian, took me to the opera *Manon*.

31

AN OLD BLOUSE of chantilly lace which I had brought with me was made in such simple lines that it could never go out of style. The opera was an occasion to wear it. For once I managed to make the wave of my hair stay high over my forehead, and as I slipped on my sealskin coat and took a last look in the mirror I was surprised that it reflected a Nita Ogarin whom I had left—for good, I had believed—on some other faraway shore.

When Liza came to fetch me, she said that she wished Igor would appear immediately and see me like this, instead of in the old rag of a sweater I usually wore. "He might turn up at any moment now, you know!"

But this was only preoperatic optimism. We knew that surveillance over escapees from Kirin had drastically increased lately, that the few handfuls of men that remained of the troops of the First Cavalry Division were already interned there. We also heard that several officers of the Kappel army had recently escaped from Kirin, one by one, but that only two of them had appeared in Harbin so far, the others evidently caught and dispatched to Junction 86. True or not, the less I knew about these rumors, the more blurred my mind was, the easier it was to go on. The opera, I hoped, would add to the blur.

As we entered the theater and were making our way through the crowded, light-flooded foyer, the appraising glances were a new surprise to me. It tickled my sense of humor to know that the pretty things I was wearing, made for my wedding, never worn, and belonging to a bygone era of the world's history and my own, were just a masquerade—a sort of curtain from behind which I, an inhabitant of another planet, was watching this part of the world twirl heedlessly around its own brittle axis.

The famous prima donna of the Maryinsky Opera and her tenor partner, both recent escapees from Soviet Russia, were to sing Manon and Des Grieux. The performance was supposed to be a gala benefit for a refugee orphanage run by the wife of our last commander in chief, Baron Dietrichs, and the theater was crowded. Many foreigners must have turned up that night, members of various consulates and representatives of all sorts of international commercial firms: English and German were heard, weaving themselves reservedly into the din of open Russian voices. In the aisle Liza introduced me first to a distinguished-looking British couple and then to a group of young Americans. The Britishers said with a smileless graciousness that they were delighted indeed to meet me—a greeting that, in keeping with the masquerade motif, I in turn tossed over with offhand savoir faire to the good-looking Americans. The orchestral tuning up was filtering promisingly through the buzzing beehive, through the glitter of lights and jewelry, through the web of interlacing glances.

We found our places in the center of the orchestra, beside a woman bursting out of sky-blue satin. Liza, who was taking pleasure in being my cicerone and who every now and then was acknowledging people's greetings by a nod and a slight curving of lips, kept furnishing me with succinct, straight-to-the-bone bits of information as to who was who. My strident blue-satin neighbor and her fat tuxedoed escort were the typical "Pristan," she said, a special breed of moneymakers (I could see that the theater was full of them) specializing in the unsteady mark, franc, or pound; importers, exporters, restaurateurs, entrepreneurs, and simply speculators. Whether dressed in the best or most atrocious taste they all had something in common: their attire, their bearing proclaimed the joys of wealth, and they were here for no other reason than to show themselves at their most glamorous and expensive. This element in them was brought into sharp relief by the sprinkling of quite another breed in the audience: the refugees from Russia, the ex-Whites immediately recognizable by their shabby clothes, the weary faces, a circumstance for which they were trying to compensate by a better-than-thou-culturally-just-the-same coolness of demeanor.

"There are the Horvats," Liza was saying, "see that box? He is the general with the white beard. A wonderful man, the head of the whole Russian-Chinese Railway zone. He has had the post since 1903. A nice old-fashioned family, the Horvats, good friends of mine. Now, those entering the other box, those are what we call the 'railroaders.' They are quite a different species, somewhat Americanized: smart, efficient, fast, have never felt either war or revolution. And there in the next box is Baroness Longden with her group. Quite a different breed again. She and her husband also go with a fast crowd, but they are the real thing, you know. She is a terrific success. Changes her lovers like a pair of gloves, but serves him right, so I don't blame her. What do I mean when I say, 'the real thing'? Oh, old St. Petersburg, the top drawer."

"The top drawer of what?"

"That's exactly it. Nothing left to support them. But how can you blame them for being fast? They have lost everything. No country, no future, no public opinion that counts. I shall see to it that you meet them. She has fire, reads a lot, sings beautifully. You'll like her."

"Oh, no, please don't, Liza!" This came too abruptly. "I mean, no, please don't have me on your mind. You are doing too much for me as it is."

"I know you are not ready yet for social life," she said condoningly, and even patted my hand. "But when Igor comes—I'm telling you that he might appear at any minute now—you'll see!"

And so what happens to the darkness that sleeps at the bottom of your heart, when it is awakened by brilliant outside lights? Does outward glitter dispel this darkness, or does it reveal it in all its density?

By the time the performance started, my spirits had dropped so low that the whole picture around me and onstage was reflected in my mind as in a soot-blackened mirror. The curtain rose on a gay tavern, where men in top hats and white jabots were drinking wine, clinking glasses and boisterously slapping one another on the shoulder. And I felt that sitting through five acts of that sort of thing was going to be torture. As to my response to the music, it filled me with a nervous impatience to have it stop before I let myself be crushed by the message that was now hiding for me in anything beautiful: Russia! Her unsurpassable art! Her composers, her poets, her geniuses. Executed as had been the poet Gumilev just a year ago; losing their minds as had Alexander Blok. Starving to death or fleeing from her in shame.

All the accumulated pain of our losses must have waited for the moment when I would go out seeking pleasure and diversion. It was then that it leaped upon me like a wild beast and began to tear me to pieces. Why was I here? Good God! What was I doing at the opera?

By the time the third act began, I was overwhelmed by such deadly weariness that I could hardly sit erect, and wouldn't have done so had it not been for Liza's regal posture, which I felt I must emulate.

In the meantime, the enchanting melody of the duet was rising on the tide of two luminous voices:

> "N'est ce plus ma main
> Qui ta main presse?
> N'est ce plus ma voix?
> Ne suis-je plus moi?"

Ne suis-je plus moi? . . . Was I also no longer I, I was asking myself. If the sense of poetry had deserted me, if I had become deaf to music, then who indeed was I?

In fact I was not I that night, but a fragment of my tortured country, and all I could hear were her screams for help within me, to which no one—neither the blue-satin woman nor the railroad executives and well-meaning foreigners, nor even the bedraggled-looking refugees, exhausted as they were with their own problems—would ever answer anymore. And I sat there wishing that Des Grieux would hurry and succumb to Manon's wiles as he was finally bound to do anyway, so I could leave and go home.

But what if I came home . . . the thought that had been hiding within me all the while shot out of obscurity and the familiar chill began to creep up my spine . . . what if I came home and Igor was there already? Neither caught by the Reds and dispatched to the coal mines, nor shot by the Hunghutze, but already sitting in our room with Panna, impatiently waiting for me to be back? Was this impossible? Didn't I know that the most unimaginable, most implausible things could happen, I was asking myself, pressing my chilly hands together to stop their trembling, seized with shattering suddenness by the feeling that Igor was near, that I was sure to see him, see him tonight! Or was it simply a dream spun by the music that I was trying to resist and reject, from whose beauty I was trying to hide, but that had, in a roundabout secret way, woven its magic web around me?

No. Igor couldn't possibly have arrived in my absence. I was trying to persuade myself in an effort to stifle the wild resurgence of hope that was still mounting in me and might collapse this very instant. My heart was hammering against my chest so violently that I stopped in front of my door, tense, reluctant to turn the knob, and stood there congealed, listening.

No stirring inside. No sound. I opened the door.

The small table lamp was burning under its lampshade of pleated wrapping paper. Panna was curled up into a pretzel on her cot, breathing peacefully, each exhalation ending in a whistling question mark.

I closed the door and for some time stood there clutching at the knob behind me. Then I came up to Bibik's crib, propped myself on the wooden railing, covered his pink toes, which stuck out from under the blanket, and for a while stood there watching him, my head in my hands.

SOMEONE'S HAND lay on my shoulder. The opera must have exhausted me more than any hard work ever had, because, used as I was by now to leaping out of bed at all hours of the night, this time I simply refused to be awakened. But the someone whose hand held my shoulder leaned close over my face and said in a whisper, "I don't believe it."

With a start I lifted myself on my elbow. It was gray in the room—the light of early dawn was seeping through the curtainless windows. Igor was kneeling by my couch.

"*Igor!* How . . . how is it possible . . ." My hand flew to my disarranged hair. "How can this be?"

He put his arms around me and was peering at me through the dusk.

"How is it possible I didn't hear you enter? I always thought . . ."

He was silent as he always was at moments of great upheavals, while I kept nervously murmuring some sort of words preposterously inadequate.

"I always thought I would hear you come, from miles away! Igor, how wonderful . . . you look . . ." It was if tremendous luminous breakers were heaving in me, crashing against my chest, deafening me and washing ashore some shapeless pieces of driftwood. "Igor! Can this be true?"

It couldn't be true that from the hell of blood, defeat, and destruction of these three years of our separation there appeared Igor looking just as he did the day we had parted. The brilliant eyes under the broad sweep of eyebrows, the tanned satiny skin were the same. He wore the same khaki shirt (only without shoulder boards), the same boots (only worn out and without spurs). If anything, his youthfulness, his vigor, the brightness of his coloring had become more striking. The odor of frost still clung to his face; his shirt, which smelled of leather and cigarettes, felt rough on my bare arms. "Igor, you look so marvelous, so young . . . while I, I'm like . . ."

He held me only closer, and all at once I cared nothing about what I was like as long as I could stay this way, my head on his shoulder, and never move again. But Panna began to stir on her cot and we both turned. She was already sitting up, staring through the blur of the room at the man who was kneeling by my couch. Then—"*Igor!*"

His name shot up like a Roman candle, exploding into a shower of stars somewhere under the ceiling. He rose and crossed toward her; they conversed in smiling, rather conventional undertones, and I darted from my couch. Hurriedly slipping into my chinchilla-less, never-finished blue housecoat, I was beseeching them in a frantic whisper not to wake Bibik. I wanted Igor to wake him up himself. At the same time another me, one who had known for so long that the meeting between Igor and Bibik was a crazy, unrealizable daydream, was shooting bewildered, unbelieving glances at me from the darkness behind.

"Bibik," I called softly, nudging him.

He opened his eyes and was looking at us. His steady gaze shifted from Igor's face to mine and back again, betraying neither surprise nor curiosity. Change, continuous change, always new faces, new places, going to bed here, being awakened there—it was all a part of his routine.

Somewhat overbrightly, Igor said, "Good morning, Bibik," then grabbed him and tossed him high and held him in his outstretched arms. "Do you know who I am?"

Dangling in his bare feet in front of Igor's chest, Bibik looked down at him unconcernedly. "No, I don't."

"Well, guess!"

"You are probably one of Mamma's pupils."

"I'm your father."

Panna stood by transfixed, eyes gleaming with tears, but Bibik shook his head. "No, I don't think you are my father." *His* father carried a sword, was covered with medals, or else just as in the story he loved so, his father, sword and all, was sitting with his head in his hands, brooding. ("And where, where, oh, where is *my* little boy? Why must I be away from him?") *His* father couldn't possibly be this grinning young man in the plain khaki shirt who, without any preamble and so uncomfortably had tossed him up when he was still half asleep.

Igor gave him a peck on the cheek, deposited him on his bed. "I'd rather not press the point for the time being," he said, trying to cover up his disappointment with a grin.

"TO THINK that instead of all this I could be on my way to Junction 86!" Igor said, interrupting his story and reaching for a second piece of toast to spread jelly on it. "Wonderful toast, Panna!"

Panna's gift of making things look festive when she was inspired to do so had expressed itself to the utmost that morning. An embroidered towel of hers ran across our rough, all-purpose table; a dainty pyramid of golden, butter-fried toast rose in the center—the slanting rays of morning sun burned on the jar of jam that our landlady, shyly wrapping the dressing gown closer around her neck, had handed to us through a crack in the door (a crack just wide enough for her arm to go through and for herself to steal a glance at Igor); the aroma of toast and coffee floated in the room.

"And then, Igor, then what? Were you locked up in Kirin? No? Not behind barbed wire? And the Chinese?" I couldn't speak coherently, or even absorb all that Igor was telling. "I still can't understand, Igor, how on earth—?"

"You know," he said, bringing his cup down on the saucer with a resolute I-give-it-up movement, "the more I think about what took place last night, the less I understand it myself. How the devil did it all happen that I am really here?" He swept the bare whitewashed walls of the room with astonished, brilliant eyes. "Simply fate! As if somebody or something quite independent of my actions or will, or what have you— Remember, Nita," he interrupted himself, "remember how you used to wonder about the word 'fate'—what it really meant?" There was a shade of happy astonishment in his voice, as if here was one of the fine threads that used to bind us together, and he was surprised and glad to have caught it unawares.

"Anyway, that whole story is like a fairy tale in which Fate rewards Ivan the Fool for his idiotic carelessness and ignorance. The typical Russian dream fulfilled."

"Igor, please, tell it all step by step so that Bibik could follow you," I pleaded, pouring him some more coffee. Although to hear the details of the ordeal that was already behind him was more than I could absorb, I still wanted him to tell his story in order to prolong this happy meal; I feared the moment when the four of us, who had lived in such different worlds and were still enveloped in them like cocoons, but were to be from now on shut together in this one room, wouldn't know what to do or say to each other. "How did you take such a risk? The danger of it!"

His hand went into his breast pocket for his cigarettes. "That was the trouble, or better say our good luck. You know, seen from aside, this whole business of an escape would make a perfect plot for a slapstick comedy; only to live it wasn't half as funny. However . . ." He took a strong drag on his cigarette, pushing himself away from the table, raised his left eyebrow with the comic expression that always came into his face when he was about to ridicule someone, most often himself, and let out a blue stream of smoke.

"Perhaps Bibik knows about Ivan the Fool. So this is going to be a story about him: about how he decided to escape from a Chinese prison camp. Want to hear it, Bibik? Fine. So there Ivan sits behind barbed wire, writing letters that don't reach his wife and family, and he decides that he can't stand it any longer. A Chinese, supposed to be an interpreter, pretends to have lost his heart for Ivan's horse. Yes, we kept our horses to the end."

He turned to me answering my question, his tone—which until now was parodying a glib raconteur of funny stories—changing to his own. "But there was nothing to feed them. Even a Chinese coolie lives on fifteen cents a day, but we were allowed four cents a day for both a man and his horse. Hungry? I'll say we were. And the *vile* stuff, *khao-liang*, we drank . . . So when this so-called interpreter began to bargain with me for Golden Brigade, offering in exchange to get me and this friend of mine, Lieutenant Bakunov, out of the camp and ship us to Harbin, I fell into the trap like a baby."

"A trap? Why was it a trap?"

"Wait, you'll see. He promised to buy two railroad tickets for us, a permit to board the train, and two Chinese coats and hats in which we could pass for Chinese. As part of the bargain, he would personally lead us out of the camp and see us settled on the train. It never occurred to us. . . ."

"You mean he was a spy?"

Panna was shifting bewildered eyes from Igor to me. "A spy, and you believed him?"

"But, Panna, Igor had no way of knowing whether or not the man was a spy," I said.

"We simply didn't choose to know," Igor said in his natural manner. "It was clear enough what he was there for." Then he returned to his sarcastic raconteur style. "So what happened next—the second scene of the comedy, I mean—is that these two brave fellows, Bakunov and I, led by the interpreter, steal silently under cover of night through the streets of Kirin past all sorts of sentries, who at some given sign by the interpreter shyly turn away. Then he sees us seated on the train, suggests that we hide our faces in our collars and keep silent all the way. Honestly," and then Igor gave a short, actually astonished laugh, "there we sat like two imbeciles, blissfully unaware of the fact that the attendants were all Communist sympathizers, and that they were rubbing their hands in anticipation of how we would be caught as soon as the train landed in Harbin, and how the Chinese would hand us over to the Reds to be dispatched straight to Junction 86."

"Oh, Igor! . . . And then what?"

"Then, as we sat there like two mummies, pretending to sleep, we suddenly heard someone stop beside us and a voice saying 'Good evening, Chinese gentlemen!' And we saw that an old white-haired conductor with a drooping mustache and sad, blue eyes—one of the old-regime type, you know—stood there beside us wagging his head with a pitying and mocking expression."

It appeared that this conductor had two sons, White volunteers also interned at Kirin, so he had realized instantly who Igor and Bakunov were and knew everything about their predicament, certainly more than they did themselves. He had good reason to believe that the Chinese officer who had put them on the train had already informed the Chinese police at the Harbin station that they were on their way and had given their full descriptions. The only possibility for them to escape was by getting off at Switch Yard Droviannoy, about eight versts from Harbin, where there were hardly any police and where the train stopped for only a few minutes. From there they could make it to Harbin on foot.

"He told us that he was not going to approach us anymore, so as not to draw attention to us. 'But *don't you miss Droviannoy*,' he said. 'We arrive there at five-fifteen in the morning. Mind you, if you miss it, it'll be Junction 86 and the *end* of you. No one has returned from there yet.'"

"Well, we were so keyed up, so tense that there could be no question of our falling asleep for the next four or five hours. Still, after three in the morning we began to feel drowsy, and we decided to have a half-hour nap, taking turns in waking each other. But heavenly intervention notwithstanding, the next thing we knew . . . !"

And now Igor's manner changed. He suddenly gave up the effort of underplaying his story and was living it all again. "The devil take it! Lights were flashing behind the windows, people getting into their coats, gathering their luggage! The train had just left Droviannoy."

"But how could you? You *both* . . . ," I faltered.

Igor frowned. "This I admit was not funny. We threw ourselves to the vestibule. Both doors were locked. We dashed to the next car and to the next. Everything locked. We tried the windows, all frozen solid. This is when I understood what it is to feel like a trapped animal. We tried to smash one of the vestibule windows, hammered on it with all our might, I with this." He took out his cigarette case and put it down on the table before him. "But it was plate glass. And then suddenly—can you believe it?—our Heavenly Messenger, the white-haired conductor, appears from nowhere, this time with a bunch of keys. 'What? You're still here?' he hisses furiously. 'Are you insane?' And he unlocks the door for us. 'Jump,' he cries. 'Bury yourselves in the snow.'"

Igor, who was until now illustrating his words with violent gesticulation, took a big breath, exhaled with an exhausted "Whe-e-ew." Then he opened the cigarette case in another deliberate gesture, Bibik watching him closely, and took a fresh cigarette.

"We jumped!"

As she sat there behind the samovar, tears in her eyes, Panna crossed herself with a tremulous, "The Lord be praised"; but Igor said, the grin returning to his face. "Too soon. Not yet."

"Go on, Igor! The train was still moving . . ."

"And we landed in a snowdrift. What? Did I what? Oh, there wasn't time to notice." He rolled up his sleeve and gave his arm a scrutinizing look. It was purple and blue and swollen. Rolling the sleeve down again, he said, "That's all. So there we lay in the snowdrift, our faces buried in the snow, afraid to move." He raised his voice to drown out my feeble mutterings about hot compresses for his arm. "But the Chinese officials were obviously not much smarter than ourselves. As the train stopped, we could see it being immediately surrounded by soldiers, who were evidently looking for us inside the train instead of in the snow outside.

"In other words, when we felt we no longer could stand the cold we decided to crawl over the snow toward the wall and climb over it. Yes, quite a high wall, frozen and slippery on top, built all around the Chinese territory of the station. And naturally, for greater comic effect we chose a spot right next to a sentry whom we failed to notice in the darkness, and who immediately shot at us, the rest of the sentries opening fire from all sides. Wait! And although while we climbed over that wall in our huge Chinese coats, one over the other's shoulders, we were sitting ducks for the sentries, the bullets, according to plot, whistled harmlessly right over our heads and past our ears!"

"Oh, Igor, Igor, how terrible," I cried through a fit of nervous laughter, and buried my face in my hands.

"Well, as you can see, they missed us, so we tumbled down into the street like ripe fruit. It was still quite dark and the street was deserted, but of all things! An empty *izvozchik* appeared from around a corner just then. We leaped into the sleigh. 'Whip her on! Faster, *faster!*' The drive was endless. Bakunov got off first, and when I finally came here and began to ring the bell and then knock, no one would open. I knocked for more than five minutes and was beginning to feel . . . well . . . awfully funny."

"Oh, forgive me! You overslept Droviannoy, and I overslept your arrival!"

"Somehow to have finally arrived and to be shut out was the worst of all."

In spite of the irony with which he said this, I felt that he was suddenly disgusted, repelled by all that he had just gone through. "I don't want to think of it all anymore," he said, his tone decisively shoving the past out of the way. "I don't want to think of all that has been, but only of everything that is here, now!" And he drew in the smoke of his cigarette with such relish, as if it were the "everything" that he had found or was going to find here any moment now.

For unrealizable dreams suddenly dropped down from their imponderable homeland, the realm of dreams, into the density of day-by-day existence have a way of suddenly tightening up, shrinking, hiding their inner fire to coagulate into a sort of time bomb, for whose explosion you wait trembling. There was too much to ask, too much untellable to tell. A physical exhaustion had obviously caught up with Igor, but he wouldn't admit it; he had slept for only one or two hours that night, but refused to lie down on my couch and take a nap. Bibik, outshadowed by his father's arrival, began first to demand that Panna read aloud to him; and as there was no place for this, he began to turn aggressive somersaults, and I had to calm him down. A north wind was whipping the bare trees outside and the landlord's family were having their morning coffee in the dining room, from where they could hear our every word.

We suddenly were like figures out of some different pictures, pasted side by side on a blank sheet of paper. Perhaps because now that Igor was here, there arose the feeling that all the others—our families—ought to be here also to rejoice with us instead of having died a cruel death; instead of languishing in Soviet slavery, separated from us, perhaps forever; that home and Russia ought to have come back with Igor for me and back with me for Igor. If not the first blooming, sparkling Russia of our youth, then the Russia of our struggle for it. Where was it all? Where was our regiment? Our cause, our dedication to it, and our sacred pledge never to give up our fight had all turned into ashes, which would forever choke every joy out of our life. And how did we know that we were the same people as when we had parted? Again a nervous chill was beginning to shake me.

"Tell me about the regiment. Who of those I know . . .?"

"Very few left. You know about Lorinov?"

"Yes. Is that for sure?"

"No. Nobody really knows what happened to that group in the Gobi Desert."

"Do you think he could still be alive?"

"Well, if he were still alive we would certainly have heard about him. And yet I haven't entirely lost hope. For one thing, Serge would never have gone south: he would have tried to make it straight east to the regiment."

This was no time for painful memories, and yet it was the moment to tell Igor about how Serge had come to say good-bye to us before he escaped.

"He came to see us at Krasnoyarsk on the day he had been released from prison," I heard myself say. "You know about it. I tried to convey some of it to you in my first letter from Tamborsk. But as I had to camouflage the whole thing, I doubt that you could understand what I was trying to tell you."

"I understood. You said 'Margarita's love,' and that they had been married. If anyone else but you had told me that Serge had married anybody, least of all Margarita, I would never have believed it."

"Yes, they were married in some little village. He told us the whole story. Such a weird story. Someday later I'll tell you." I did not want to think of that now.

Igor's face darkened again. "Yes, sometime later." Then he added, on a lighter note, "I still hope he might reappear someday. You know how it has been with so many others." And the bright, decisive way in which he asked Panna for some more coffee made it clear that the thought of Lorinov hurt him too much, and that he had closed the subject.

So I said quickly, "I told you in my letter—which you probably never received—that I am giving lessons in English to men who plan to go to the United States. Everyone wants to. There is no work here for men. But of course no one has any money for the passage. There was even a cartoon in the newspaper the other day: a beggarlike figure in tattered trousers, and the caption read: 'Had I a pair of trousers I would have gone to America!'"

"I would have also," Igor grinned. "As a matter of fact, ever since I read James Fenimore Cooper it was my childhood dream to go to America." Then, "You mean finding work here is quite hopeless?"

"Absolutely. But *you* will find something to do, Igor! We shall invent something!" And again I hurried to change the subject. "Guess who it was that helped me to receive a foreign passport. Verin."

"What?"

"Yes, he's alive, he's in Moscow. It just so happened that I ran into him once and he offered to help me to get this foreign passport. Oh, you know that I wouldn't have accepted his help if he collaborated with the Communists! He was employed in some capacity at the Gos-Izdat and he knew an important man who—"

Igor's jaw set. "If he didn't collaborate he couldn't be alive today. Anyway, to hell with him. He helped you, so good. I'm grateful and let's forget about him."

This was, of course, the wrong time to bring up the subject of Verin and so would be speaking of all our past misery in Tamborsk. What could I tell him that was pleasant, happy?

Our common past had treacherously chosen this moment of our

reunion to cry out to us that all had been in vain, in vain and lost. If only we could throw ourselves into each other's arms, send Panna and Bibik for a walk, and pour everything out to each other. But we were too tense to do so. And perhaps all at once to know everything about each other would be worse than not to know.

EVEN THOUGH most of the White refugees in Harbin had no telephones, everyone learned at once of Igor's escape, and many of our landlord's acquaintances—all sorts of bedraggled-looking and nervous individuals—began to demand to see Igor. They wanted to find out how he had managed to escape, whether he had heard of So-and-so (their brother, their son, their friend). One old woman, her discolored eyes diluted by tears, said when she came that her grandson had escaped from Kirin about three weeks ago, but there had been no word from him since. "Such a boy! Such a good boy! You have been lucky, Colonel Volotskoy, lucky!"

Panna kept the landlady's samovar boiling all afternoon for these people, presiding over our table with triumphant graciousness, answering their inquiries about our own escape from Moscow, sweeping off the crumbs they left in their wake, washing their cups. Our landlady reappeared all dressed up this time, her pretty round face touched with rouge, and with tender congratulatory smiles suggested that Igor and I rent a vacant corner from her.

The whole of this tiny room was filled by one enormous bed with bare crossboards instead of a mattress. Such good fortune was actually unbelievable. Just then a pupil of mine arrived for his lesson and Igor, all at once transfigured by the sense of purpose and an onflow of energy, declared that he was going to Noviy Gorod, to look for a straw mattress. He had just enough money left to buy one.

When I heard him come back I was still giving a lesson, while another pupil sat in the dining room waiting for his turn. Never had separation from Igor seemed so unbearable, so endless, the thought of losing him again so horrible as during those few afternoon hours. Under some pretext I once found a moment to make a dash to our new room and see what he was doing. But Panna met me in the corridor and said that she had just peeped in and saw him sound asleep. Impatience was mounting in me, and with it the realization of what had really happened. Igor—*Igor* was here!!

When the last lesson was over, I called Bibik. Together we slipped into our new room.

ONE LEG in the threadbare blue breeches and smartly fitting boot (worn out at the sole) hanging down from the bed, Igor lay blissfully asleep on his purchase, which smelled of unbleached Chinese cloth and straw.

With a rustling of straw I sat down on the edge of the new, prickly mattress. Igor opened his eyes. Raising himself on both elbows, he swept the room with a wild unrecognizing gaze; and then, staring in turn at my face and Bibik's, said slowly and quietly, as if speaking to life itself and not to us, "Can this really be?"

And life itself must have heard him and answered, for it suddenly could be and was.

As he sat up and threw his arms around Bibik and me, and gathered us both to himself, that chief something that had eluded us until now, was suddenly *here*, in this dingy little room, filling it and the world with inexpressible enchantment. In a flash we knew the measure of the other's love, which had neither diminished nor tarnished with the years. So he must have doubted my love until that moment. I must have doubted his, even if I loathed to admit this to myself.

Sensing the sudden change in us, Bibik clung to us both, in spontaneous recognition that Igor was someone his own also, while I felt that this moment—this miracle of our reunion—was also the miracle of resurrection, of transfiguration and rebirth; that it was everything in which I had always believed. And I cried, this time with a new, different kind of laughter, which was fighting a sob in my throat, "Oh, Igor! Don't break our bones! We still may be of some use to you . . . especially if you want to go to America."

And not because I wanted to go to America, but because I did not want to burst into tears at that moment, I heard myself say something I had never thought about before.

"There is always Paul's family you know, the Teolins. They will offer us a loan if we really want to go. No, no. We won't have to ask them for it, they'll offer it to us themselves. They are like that."

Suddenly excited, enthusiastic, decisive, Igor let his arms go from me and Bibik and hit the straw mattress with his clenched fist.

"Fine, then! Let's head for America!"